C / GRAUBOU

(FAIRCHILD) PORTER

(Helio) STALLION

C119 = 6 TON

To Dad
CHRISTMAS 1999
Love Jeff

SPECIAL ACTIONS
Collection

Project Editor Eric MICHELETTI

SPECIAL ACTIONS COLLECTION

Project Editor Eric MICHELETTI

© Histoire & Collections, 1998
5, avenue de la République F-75541 PARIS CEDEX 11 - FRANCE
ISBN : 2 908 182 70X

FREDERIC LERT

WINGS OF THE CIA

TRANSLATED BY JULIA FINEL

HISTOIRE & COLLECTIONS

INTRODUCTION

A short while after taking up his position Richard Helms, who directed the CIA from 1966 to 1973, asked a question which he thought
would have a simple and rapid answer :

"How many planes has the CIA got?"

Incapable of answering such a question at once, his entourage immediately launched an in-depth study.

After three long months of internal enquiries, the officer who had
been put in charge of the study could only give an incomplete answer.

He presented Helms with a map of the world on which all the different companies who collaborated with the CIA, or which belonged to
it directly, had been marked. There were several dozen, operating hundreds of aircraft!

"The picture that I'm presenting you with is only 90% accurate", reckoned the man. "The situation fluctuates so much and the web of companies is so complex, with aircraft passing from one to another under
false identities, that it would be difficult to be more precise."

This incredible situation is easily explained by the controversial history of the American intelligence agency :

The CIA is a pure product of the cold war. Its origins go back to the
National Security Act of July 1947, voted in three months after the defi-
nition of the Truman doctrine of aid "moral, financial and military to
the countries which are the victims of the communist threat."

The bugbear of a direct confrontation with the Soviet Union and the
possibilty of it unleashing a nuclear apocalypse led the United States to
give up official interventions in broad daylight. Having become the
armed limb of unofficial policy led throughout the five continents, the
CIA engaged in secret operations in all parts of the world.

Involving small groups of men or veritable armies, going from simple training in the handling of weapons to open warfare, these operations could not be carried out without support from the air, whether it was offensive or, as was most often the case, simply logistic.

By the sheer force of events the CIA had become, by the end of the sixties, the largest airline company in the world.

However it did not abandon its premier role of intelligence agency, in other words an organization responsible for collecting information and conducting analyses and evaluations in aid of the government.

The CIA used all the means at its disposal and equipped itself with the best tools possible to carry out its missions of raising information. It gave rise, at the cost of hundreds of millions of dollars, to some of the most famous names in American aeronautics, Lockheed U-2 and SR-71 Blackbird for example.

Manufactured according to the needs of the Agency, these planes brought back the known frontiers of technical knowledge and increased their range, altitude and speed to rise up over borders and violate them with impunity.

But as advanced as these performances were, the plane itself, with or without a pilot on board, was not the panacea. The CIA also threw itself headlong into research and exploitation of reconnaissance satellites, they alone were capable of being completely free of questions of territorial sovereignty.

This is how some of the most extraordinary pages in the history of aviation came to be written by an intelligence service.

CHAPTER 1

THE VERY BEGINNING

THURSDAY 3RD DECEMBER 1941, WASHINGTON

A young analyst of the Signal Intelligence Service (SIS), the organization responsible for intercepting communications for the US government, entered the office of his head of department, a sheet of paper in his hand :

"We have a strange message here, Sir."

"What is it?"

"A request for information sent to a Japanese agent on the island of Honolulu, he is asked to indicate the position of ships anchored in Pearl Harbor. I repeat, the position of anchored ships, not their movements".

"Strange indeed. Pass it on to the Navy Department."

With hindsight, this interception appears to us today as being of the utmost importance. But on the 3rd December 1941, four days before the surprise attack on Pearl Harbor, it was just one piece of information among many others in the midst of a puzzle which was beginning to take shape, yet still remained very incomplete.

For several months the Americans had been cracking codes used by the Japanese between Tokyo and Japanese embassies round the world. No less than fifty such messages were decoded every day by the SIS.

Apart from the press, these interceptions were practically the only reliable source of information concerning Japanese policy at the disposal of the US administration. For President Roosevelt, they were a tremendous advantage against the duplicity of the diplomatic game played by the Empire of the Rising Sun.

The deterioration of relations between the two countries was such that, on the 27th November 1941, all general US officers in the Pacific were warned of the possibilty of a Japanese attack in the following days. But how and where?

French Indochina would surely have been a possible risk, or the British possessions in South-East Asia. But who would have imagined that the island of Hawaii and the immense naval base of Pearl Harbor could have been a target?

The Americans were not able to spot, several days earlier, the sailing of a large combat fleet of the Japanese Navy. With the greatest discretion, six aircraft carriers and their escort were making their way towards the only base of any significance that the US had in the Pacific.

On the 6th December, a long note from Tokyo was intercepted and decoded. It was a preliminary note indicating the breaking off of diplomatic relations between Japan and the US.

"It's war" exclaimed Roosevelt when he learnt of the news. The following day, Sunday 7th December, another note was intercepted in the early hours of the morning Washington time. This time it concerned the breaking off of diplomatic relations proper which had to be presented to the US administration that same day at 13 hours, Washington time.

How curious to want to break off diplomatic relations at one o' clock on a Sunday. Why?

The answer was not long in coming.

At the same moment as the SIS analysts were sweating over the last note, 360 Japanese combat aircraft which had taken off from combat carriers were sowing death and destruction at Pearl Harbor.

Within a matter of minutes, the US Navy experienced the greatest disaster of its history. Eighteen ships sunk or seriously damaged, 200 aircraft destroyed, 2,400 sailors killed; the US left unable to participate for several months in the Pacific war which was about to start.

Chroniclers of history noted that the Japanese arrived with impunity and left without fear of attack.

The age of modern American information gathering had started with an immense failure.

Before the forties, because of its relative isolation, the US did not feel the need to have a powerful intelligence organization to know what was happening outside its borders. Intelligence gathering remained the prerogative of the old European nations out of simple necessity or tradition. For most of the time the US put themselves in the hands of their ally Great Britain, whose secret service has, to this day, an immense prestige attached to it.

Everything changed on the 7th December 1941. The surprise of Pearl

Harbor convinced the US administration that intelligence gathering services could not just limit themselves to military operations during wartime. As a consequence, the idea arose of an independent agency capable of analysing and summarizing all information useful to the government.

President Franklin D. Roosevelt appointed a New York Lawyer, William J. Donovan, to set up a centralized intelligence department. Donovan was once a fellow student with Roosevelt : the two met when they studied law at the University of Columbia, and since then Donovan never hesitated to do a little work, informally, for his old friend.

Donovan was a chubby little man with an inexhaustible curiosity and energy. With his direct approach he never failed to get involved first hand, because for him only the results counted.

William Donovan was made 'information coordinator'. Selling the idea of such a post to the American president was an appreciable success for him. It was Donovan's thinking that the coordinator would be answerable only to the President and would control a new intelligence agency responsible for collecting information on potential enemies.

This agency, the Office of Strategic Services (OSS), was created on the 13th June 1942. Donovan became the head.

The OSS was above all a military intelligence organization dependent on the general chiefs of staff. At the end of 1944, Donovan proposed to place the OSS under the direct responsibility of the president of the United States, thus making it a forerunner of the CIA. It was planned that the OSS could lead subversive operations abroad, but it would have no function whatsoever as regards internal security, which remained the prerogative of the FBI.

THE SECRET SERVICE AND AIRBORNE OPERATIONS :
BIRTH OF A PARTNERSHIP

The Autumn of 1942 was a turning point in the second world war. On the eastern front, the Germans were at a virtual standstill outside Stalingrad and were to be eventually enclosed there. In Africa, the British had retaken the offensive and the exhausted Afrika Korps retreated after ten days of fighting outside El Alamein. On the 8th November operation Torch began, this was the code name given to the landing of an Anglo-American expeditionary force in North Africa. The rationale was an allied offensive, and the next great objective was to regain a foothold on the European continent.

From the beginning of 1943, the OSS put all its weight behind the creation of special units in occupied Europe. It was, of course, a question of preparing the ground for a future invasion, by gathering information on the enemy plan of attack or sending commandos to attack selective targets.

The other objective was to create insecurity within countries occupied by the Germans, forcing them to maintain several divisions behind the front lines to 'maintain order.'

For the OSS it was therefore important to be able to place agents within the German lines and also to give material and technical support to local resistance movements. All these operations could only be carried out with the support of a specially equipped and trained air force.

British aircraft of the Royal Air Force were already operating behind enemy lines. The Lysander was the most frequently used plane, a single engine plane with a fairly limited load capacity and range. The aircraft was used at night to drop off or pick up a maximum of two agents or small quantities of material in occupied zones. The objectives that the OSS had of re-supplying vast resistance movements were a lot more ambitious. Some experiments were conducted with twin-engine B-25 Mitchell bombers, but this aircraft, which turned out to be too small, also had an insufficient range for its intended missions.

What the OSS required were four-engine aircraft with a large mission radius. In 1943, the plane answering this description was not yet available in large enough numbers to be taken away from their first task, namely bombing. Also at this time, the notion of undercover warfare was not uppermost in the minds of the allied Chiefs of Staff, who were preoccupied with the unrelenting resistance of German troops on various European fronts.

However, the course of thinking did eventually evolve. At the end of

1943 the preparations for the Normandy landings were already well under way and the planners got into line with OSS opinion; namely that a large, effective and well-equipped resistance in France could considerably upset the Germans in the great battle which was to come. The US Army Air Force (USAAF) was not yet willing to allow the special forces to use its aircraft. They had been using four squadrons of B-24 bombers for sea patrol and anti-submarine attacks from several British bases. At the end of 1943 however, the US Navy received its own patrol planes and took over responsibilty for marine missions.

What on earth could the USAAF do with all its B-24s? Having up to now been used at low altitude only, these aircraft were not equipped with high altitude systems (special sights, crew oxygen supply), which they would have needed to carry out strategic bombing missions. As well as this, the crews were not trained to fly in formation at high altitude amongst dozens of other aircraft. In their search for the U-Boote they had always flown alone, as low as possible. The OSS seized the opportunity. Negotiations were rapidly undertaken and, the following day, the special services of the army had 32 aircraft specially adapted for their needs. A godsend!

On 24th October 1943 a meeting took place between officers of the anti-submarine unit and men of the OSS who were informing them of their new mission. During the course of this meeting, the Americans chose a name for themselves, picked at random from a list of available key words : Carpetbaggers. These were the Northern Yankees who profited from the defeat of the Confederates during the American civil war, and set up in the south to make their fortune.

As newcomers to aerial secret operations, the Americans learnt their skills from the British, as they were already carrying out such operations throughout the whole of occupied Europe, from Norway to Greece, using RAF bombers withdrawn from front line operations. As a result of modifications made to British aircraft the Americans adapted their B-24 for night-time operations. The belly turret was removed and the central space kitted out for the parachuting of agents. This opening was known as Joe Hole. Joe was the pseudonym of all agents parachuted into enemy territory. For reasons of security, particularly if they were captured by the

Germans, the aircraft crew knew their passengers by this name only. As for the women, they went under the name of Jane.

To deter German opposition, on the ground as well as in the air, everything was done to render the aircraft invisible in the dead of night. The first thing was to paint it black. Matt paint was swiftly abandoned in favour of a shiny black which somewhat improved the stealthiness of the aircraft regarding radars. Special exhaust covers were installed over the engines' exhaust pipes and on the machine guns to make them less visible during firing. The major part of the defensive armament had been removed and the few machine guns which had been left in place remained solely to improve the morale of the crew.

The crew were instructed to use arms to defend themselves only in extreme circumstances, so as not to reveal the position of the aircraft. Special communication and navigation equipment had also been installed to identify dropping zones and to communicate with ground crew. The standard torch lamps which were used for giving light signals were complemented by two other more complex systems.

The first was called the S-Phone. It was, in fact, a type of rather powerful "walkie-talkie", with a range of about ten miles. The moment the operator on the ground heard the airplane, he could speak to the crew and guide the plane to the dropping zone. A more effective version of the S-Phone transmitted a signal which enabled the navigator of the plane, with the help of his radio-compass, to be guided towards the ground transmitter. From 1944, the Carpetbaggers started to use the Rebecca-Eureka system. The plane was equipped with a radar which 'lit-up' the ground in front of it. The ground crew were equipped with a device conceived to send back coded echos when it was linked up to the plane's radar, which had then simply to be guided by the echos it received.

The instruments in the cockpit were modified to improve their legibility. The essential instruments, artificial horizon, speed and course indicators, were placed directly in front of the pilot who had the difficult task of flying very close to the ground in total darkness.

"Our principal enemy is the lie of the land, not the German night fighter", the pilots used to say. It was true that the German night fighter was used to protect the environs of the Reich rather than patrol over occupied Europe.

"The crews were volunteers" recalls the ex-second in command of the unit Major Robert Fish.

"But in actual fact, when I welcomed the new crews I gave them a fairly realistic picture of what would be expected of them : that they would have to fly at night, alone, in the heart of enemy territory. That their best defence would be to fly very low beneath German radar cover. They would not have the certainty of relying on an escort of fighters. During the dropping phase they would have to fly very near the ground, in a plane both heavy and difficult to manoeuvre at barely above the stall speed, with only their skill and lucky star to help them."

"Then I left the briefing room leaving them five minutes to make up their minds. If they didn't wish to do it, they had simply to leave the room. No reference to it would be entered on their file".

Every time Fish went back into the room, none of the men had moved. As they admitted later, some pilots had indeed wanted to give up, but as no-one wanted to be the first to do so, in the end everyone stayed.

MISSIONS IN OCCUPIED FRANCE

The unit was operational from the beginning of 1944 and did not delay in undertaking operations behind enemy lines. The planes crossed the English channel at very low altitude, so as to avoid detection by German coastal radar. Approaching the French coast, they climbed to 8,000 feet to have some protection from the flak. Once this dangerous zone was passed, they flew at low altitude once again.

Navigation was carried out using the small amount of light given off by the moon. The bomber, lying face down in his plexi-glass bubble at the front of the craft, would locate the characteristic points which allowed the plane to be sited. Behind him the navigator followed the progression of his plane on his maps and informed the pilot of the path to take. The Carpetbaggers helped each other also from transmissions from radio transmitter stations placed in Great Britain. By matching up several signals it was possible for the crew to be able to estimate its position within a few miles or so.

Without a part of their defensive armament, the B-24s were used by crews reduced to eight members, instead of the usual ten : in other words without the belly turret gunner and side gunner. As for the tail gunner, who covered the rear of the plane, he remained a part of the crew but his role became essentially that of a look-out: the surprise attack of a German night fighter equipped with radar was always possible.

An aircraft was lost over England while it was carrying out a simple training flight. A single German night fighter had managed to practically infiltrate the approach zone of an American air base and got into the slipstream of a bomber without being noticed. It was only when the pilot felt the structure of the plane shake violently under German shell fire that he realised he was being attacked. Only two members of the crew managed to jump from the burning plane before it exploded on the ground.

"When we started to receive Dakotas, after the Normandy landings, the poor visibility at the rear worried us a lot" recalls one pilot.

The co-pilot spent most of the flight with his head in the astrodome, the plexiglass bubble on the top of the fuselage where he could aim at the stars for navigational purposes. From there, he could survey the skies and see if any "bandits" were approaching. With their Dakota, the Carpetbaggers could land behind German lines to drop off or pick up agents. The comings and goings of personnel between England and the continent grew considerably with the use of the well known twin engine transport plane. The planes were used on many occasions to bring battle weary crew, or resistants who had to undergo special training, back to England. To prepare for these missions the Carpetbaggers practised short landings with their planes for several weeks.

During this time, photographic reconnaissance missions allowed a list of potential sites for secret landings in France to be drawn up. The first mission took place on the 6th July 1944. Colonel Clifford Heflin was at the controls of the aircraft which took off from an English airfield in the middle of the night, its destination was Nantua , in the centre of France, near the Swiss border. A crew of five was on board along with eleven passengers and over 3,000 lbs of material.

After crossing the whole of France diagonally, the aircraft approached the designated landing zone.

"We were waiting for the agreed radio signal and you could have cut the atmosphere in the plane with a knife", recalls Heflin. Less than six miles before the planned zone, the signal came at last. Then we immediately saw four shining beacons which marked out our "airport." In fact it was merely a narrow strip of land at the top of a hill.

An identification code was exchanged by radio and the aircraft landed perfectly.

"As soon as it had landed, the plane was guided to one side to be camouflaged" continued Heflin, "some local resistance men arrived and put small trees into holes which had been dug in advance. Within a few minutes the plane had disappeared inside an artificial wood!"

For two whole days, the crew of the Dakota played host to the resistants, as they travelled across the region taking note of the position of their settlements. Forty-eight hours after its arrival, the Dakota took off for England again at night. It brought back a half a dozen battle weary allied aviators who had been hidden by the resistance, as well as a couple of Frenchmen leaving for England to undergo training.

OPERATIONS THROUGHOUT EUROPE

Resupplied with arms and ammunition at night by the Carpetbaggers, the resistance was an effective means of helping allied troops who landed in Normandy. In the days following the landings multiple delay tactics forced German troops into the theatre of operation, allowing the weak allied bridgehead to consolidate. In the following weeks, the Carpetbaggers profited from the mastery of the skies obtained by the allies to organize drops on a massive scale during daylight. Bringing together more than 150 bombers of the 8th Air Force 'loaned' for the occasion, three operations to resupply the maquis took place at the end of the summer.

Parallel to that, resistance operations were also developing on the southern European front. From December 1942, Donovan, who had reached the grade of General, had received authorization to deliver men and equipment as far as North Africa, in order to help resistance movements operating in the south of Europe. After a very slow beginning the allies went as far as to organize a 'Balkan Air terminal service' in 1944, in order to rationalize the logistic effort between an Italy recaptured by the allies and Yugoslavia still fighting against the German army.

With the liberation of France and the war which was continuing to approach Germany, the Carpetbaggers were also involved in drop missions in the heart of the Reich.

The idea of General Donovan was to constitute an espionage network behind German lines as quickly as possible. He named a young lieutenant 'Head of Secret Service on the European front', with his principal mission being to set up teams of agents in Germany.

This lieutenant was no other than William Casey, a promising young man as it turned out, when he finished his career he was Director of the CIA.

Casey set about selecting his spies. Evidently an American would have deceived no-one at the Gestapo headquarters in Berlin. He decided therefore to choose anti-nazi prisoners of war. Casey violated international conventions which forbade such a use of prisoners of war, he was totally aware of this but for him and Donovan only the result mattered.

Very great care was taken concerning the 'cover' of these agents. The OSS made sure that they read recently obtained German newspapers which had been carefully filed in England, so they were up to date of the situation in their own country. A large quantity of false papers were made and the OSS also supplied them with German made clothes. Once they had been parachuted into Germany the chief difficulty for the agents was to 'bring out' as much information as possible. The radio system 'Joan-Eleanor' was thus conceived. The agent had in his possession a radio which transmitted only vertically upwards with a very narrow transmission cone, which meant that detection on the ground was very difficult. An agent reported one day that while he was transmitting from the steeple of a church a goniometrical detection vehicle, listening for any secret transmissions, passed just at his feet. He was not detected.

These transmissions were received by an aircraft flying more than 30,000 feet high. At this height the cone was considerably wider, reaching a diameter of nearly sixty-two miles. It was therefore easy for a pilot to fly within this circle to collect and record coded messages. For these missions the Carpetbaggers used Mosquitos of the RAF.

The Mosquito was an exceptional aircraft without equal. It was a thoroughbred twin-engine fighter, powerful but also very light because of its wooden construction. It reached high altitudes effortlessly which protected it from German fighters. At normal altitudes, because of its speed, it proved a difficult prey to catch.

"I had a rather interesting experience one night", recalls a Mosquito pilot. "Having finished my mission above Germany, I was heading west to return home. But the moment I crossed over into allied territory, above France, I didn't link up with the signal which would have identified me as "friend" on allied radar screens. The radars had seen me arrive and had identified me as hostile. By listening to our radio frequencies I heard that they were starting to get rather excited down below about this non-identified aircraft coming direct from Germany. They consequently gave the go-ahead for their fighters to take off. I could hear the ground controllers briefing the fighters on my position. They were terribly frustrated : "The target is getting away from you, he's very fast, he's getting away!"

I then called them to offer my reassurance:

"Call your dogs off, I'm a 'friend' returning to England...!"

THE INVADER ENTERS THE SCENE

In February 1945, the OSS only had two agents operating in Berlin. The following month, Casey was using thirty units. In April the figure reached sixty for the whole of Germany. In order to have such an impressive result Casey had to battle hard to equip the Carpetbaggers with planes allowing agents to be dropped within the heart of Germany. He eventually managed to obtain some A-26 Invaders, one of the best planes of the second world war. The Invader was such an exceptional aircraft that its use in secret American operations lasted nearly a quarter of a century. As much as the Mosquito was tailor made for high altitudes, the Invader had its place in low altitude penetration missions in hostile territory. Conceived in 1942 by the firm Douglas, the Invader was a twin-engine bomber. It was light, fast and manoeuverable, which gave the Carpetbaggers operating above the Third Reich a certain degree of immunity against German night fighters. The first crews completed their training in April 1945, before being immediately engaged in operations. Like all aircraft engaged in nighttime missions, the OSS Invader had an all-over black camouflage. This sometimes aroused the curiosity of other pilots.

In 1945, Ross White was a pilot of an A-26.

"That plane was a real delight", he recalls, "it was as fast and as pleasant to fly as a fighter while at the same time capable of carrying a considerable bomb load. Moreover it did not accelerate like a bomber as such, but more like a fighter"...

Flying at more than 280mph at cruising speed, it was twice as fast as the heavy B-24s which were the usual setting for the Carpetbaggers.

"One night I had to pick up two agents from one of our advanced bases in the east of France" continues White. "I then had to drop them in the north of Germany, near Kiel. This advanced base sheltered a unit of night fighters and when I landed, my totally black plane immediately attracted the attention of all the pilots present. They asked me where I was going and what I was doing, questions to which of course I could not reply."

"We have a mission tonight. If you want we can escort you," the night fighter pilots offered.

"Thanks, but I'll manage alone."

The pilots insisted, "With our P-61 Black Widows equipped with a radar you have no choice, you will not be able to escape us", they replied laughing. The rapid P-61, another twin-engine, came into service at the end of the war and specialised in night fighting. But the Invader, minus all its bomber equipment was yet more rapid.

"I told them they would never manage to keep up with me. They laughed disbelievingly. Of course they did not know that my plane contained no equipment or devices needed for bombing missions."

The A-26 took off straight into the black night, a P-61 on his tail. Several hours later, the Invader came back and landed on the same airfield, its mission accomplished. Its pilot leapt from the plane and headed casually for the mess. There he found the dismayed P-61 crews. To have every chance on their side they had decided to fly two of their aircraft : one in front of the A-26 and another behind. In spite of that, they had not been able to follow the A-26 which rapidly shook them off. They were astounded at the speed of the bomber which approached 370mph on a level course.

The Invader however did have its faults. The narrowness of the fuselage meant that no manhole could be installed for parachuting agents, as existed on the B-24. The agents had to lie down in the bomb bay on an exit hatch. Nearing the target the pilot opened the bomb bay and, at the necessary moment, he gave a brief warning and pressed the release button which opened the hatch. The agents were therefore dropped like bombs, at very low altitude, barely high enough for their parachute to open. The procedure was very frightening and an unenviable task for the OSS agents. But this technique, which proved to be very useful for drops behind German lines, was used again several years later in Asia.

THE OSS : VICTIM OF THE NEW FOUND PEACE

The OSS survived several weeks after the end of the war before being dissolved in 1946. Without doubt this disbanding was rather hasty, because very soon the cold war between the west and the Soviet Union began, relaunching the need for a powerful and effective intelligence organization. Anticipating the head-on collision between the two sides which never materialized, the confrontation with the Soviet empire was carried out underground. Once again, the Americans left for battle remarkably ill-prepared.

From the Autumn of 1944, Donovan had campaigned for the setting up of an intelligence organization capable of functioning during peacetime. His idea, unchanged since he had been named coordinator of Intelligence in 1941, was to create a governmental agency coming directly under the presidency. This agency would be responsible for gathering all necessary information for the executive, in order for it to prepare and conduct its policy. Donovan came up against the scepticism of Roosevelt, but also of the FBI, and other intelligence agencies jealous of their prerogatives. A leak to the American press concerning his project was organized doubtless with the aim of destabilizing it. Donovan suspected the all-powerful director of the FBI, Edgar Hoover, of being the origin of the leak. Several newspapers were talking of the danger that such an organization could represent and they named it 'super Gestapo'.

On the death of Roosevelt, on the 12th April 1945, Vice-President Harry Truman became the thirty-third president of the United States. Truman welcomed Donovan's project no more favourably than his predecessor had. Worse, he viewed unfavourably the excessive increase in strength of the OSS during the war and indeed suspected Donovan of wanting to establish his own secret service. Moreover, the FBI did not escape criticism from Truman. Even though he wished to reduce FBI operations, he never envisaged purely and simply to put an end to operations of the federal bureau. The OSS was in a bad situation. Created as a 'war-time' secret service organization it had no support within the White House, nor in Congress, to ensure its survival once the war was finished. Donovan had already said goodbye to the OSS but he continued to actively campaign the President by praising the work done during the war and pushing for the creation of a central intelligence organization during peacetime.

But it was all in vain.

In September 1945, Truman signed the dismantling of the OSS whose sections were split up. The OSS had 12,000 people working for it. Donovan was thanked for the work he had done during the war.

THE CIA, OFFSPRING OF THE COLD WAR

Truman saw nothing but difficulties with the possibilty of engaging his country in espionage operations against the old ally, the USSR.

Soviet penetration in the United States, which was updated in the immediate aftermath of the war, forced the Americans to re-think their position. In 1947, the Cold War began and communism and the USSR were both designated as enemies to beat. Fifteen months after becoming President of the United States, Harry Truman finally allowed himself to be convinced by the facts, and with little enthusiasm, recognized the use of an effective intelligence agency active other than on US soil.

On the 26th July 1947, the National Security Act was voted by congress. It created a department of Defence grouping together all the departments of the Navy, Army and Air Force, which were at that time autonomous. The National Security Act made the creation of a Central Intelligence Agency (CIA) official, and it was set up in Washington in the old OSS building.

The status and administrative procedures of this new agency were specified by Congress several months later, through the Central Intelligence Agency Act (CIAA). The CIA was exempted from revealing the functions, names, people, titles, salaries or indeed the number of people employed in its organization.

Its role was defined as follows : to coordinate the intelligence activities of the different government ministries and organizations in the interests of national security. But, in a deliberately vague wording, it was added further on in the text that the work of the CIA could also include "other interventions affecting information and national security, that the National Security Council could direct." As a legal expert of the time suggested, it was an open door for secret operations which were to be widely talked about over the next fifty years : "If the President of the United States, whose responsibility for foreign affairs is written in the constitution, gives the agency the appropriate instructions and if congress releases funds to carry them out, the agency therefore has the lawful capacity to lead secret operations."

Fortified with all manner of legal and lawful blessings, the new agency could start to live and prosper. It was indeed the moment, for at the end of 1947 the State Department sounded alarm bells by informing President Truman that Soviet secret service operations would possibly torpedo US foreign policy abroad. It had become vital to act, and use whatever subversive methods necessary, similar to those the Soviets were using. The new agency was therefore authorized to mount secret operations in Europe to counter Soviet influence. In June 1948, President Truman made a clear reference to psychological warfare and paramilitary operations as being part of the attributes of the CIA. A department was specially created to take care of secret operations, the Directorate of Plans.

At the same time, responding to the worry of giving a legal basis to something which seemed to want to escape any kind of control, a presidential directive sought to define precisely what a secret operation could be :

"Any operation supported or directly led by the US whether by means of support of friendly governments or opposition to enemy governments, and it being specific that it shall be prepared and carried out in such a way that the responsibility of the US government will not be known to non-authorized persons and in the event of discovery, the US government would be able, in all plausibility, to deny any such responsibilty."

A vast range of possible actions was then named: propaganda, economic warfare, direct preventive action such as sabotage, anti-sabotage, demolition, subversion against hostile states, assistance to secret resistance movements, guerilla and liberation groups, support for local anti-communist movements in countries in danger in the free world...

The range was large, indeed practically without limit. Only a large scale classic war could escape the prerogatives of the CIA, which was to operate for several decades.

ATTEMPTS IN EUROPE

In 1947, Europe was a bubbling cauldron in which the CIA did not delay in playing its part. In the war of the old allies, the CIA had to be the secret weapon of Truman and American diplomacy.

The American Intelligence agency started by playing its hand in Italy where a general election was planned. Fearing the success of the local communists who were generously supported by Moscow, the CIA intervened in the electoral campaign by financing the Christian Democratic Party to the tune of several million dollars. They won the election.

This initial success enabled the CIA to justify its worth. The existence of a power-house of intelligence was from then on part of the calculations of American diplomacy. When all standard means of action were exhausted, the CIA then became the last resort.

Not far from Italy, Greece also presented the risk of going over to the Soviet camp at the end of the war. The power in place had been confronted with a solid communist guerilla war since 1944. American technical and financial aid started to reach Greece from 1947, complementing the assistance already given by a British military mission. At the request of Truman, the US Congress had voted for aid of 400 million dollars to help Greece, as well as for Turkey, to escape the communist grip.

This was very difficult for the government in Athens until 1948. But after the guerillas were refused the use of Yugoslav territory as a withdrawal zone, the Greek army gained the advantage. By 1950 the civil war was practically finished. The role played by the CIA had been relatively minor, but it nonetheless deserves to be mentioned : the Greek conflict witnessed for the first time the use, albeit very briefly, of the B-26 which had already proved their worth in the hands of the OSS. Some C-47s also participated in parachuting agents in guerilla held territory.

One of the keys of the settlement of the Greek civil war was therefore found in Belgrade. By stopping the Greek communist guerilla from finding refuge in his territory, Marshal Tito, the strong man of post-war Yugoslavia, had thus hastened victory for the troops of Athens. His pro-western stance owed nothing to chance. In the summer of 1948 the break between Tito's Yugoslavia and Stalin's Russia gave an inkling of the existence of a breach in the eastern bloc that up until that point had been seen as monolithic and unshakeable. Links had been strengthened during the German occupation between US agents of the OSS and Yugoslav partisans. When these partisans, led by Josip Broz, known as Tito, took power at the end of the war, the Americans had no difficulty in establishing a discreet dialogue with their old comrades in arms. Tito, who wanted to distance himself from Moscow, feared that daylight deliveries of American weapons would give Stalin an excuse to initiate military intervention in his country. Truman therefore gave his agreement so that the CIA could carry out secret deliveries. After which, feeling reasonably strong against the Soviets, Tito openly accepted US economic and military aid which represented more than a thousand million dollars throughout the following decade.

After Greece and Yugoslavia, Albania was the first real theatre of operation in which the CIA had the relative freedom to develop its strategy through paramilitary operations. For its first intervention in the Balkans, the organization wanted to prove that it was possible to push back communism which seemed to be triumphant everywhere. To win in Albania would also mean depriving the Soviets of an outlet on the Adriatic, opposite Italy.

OPERATION VALUABLE IN ALBANIA

Operation Valuable was launched with its objective as the creation of an internal opposition and the overthrow of the dictator Enver Hojda. Valuable was carried out in cooperation with Great Britain who considered the Balkans as part of their zone of influence. The idea to overthrow Hojda came, in fact, from London. Seeking a financial and logistical aid, the British had suggested to the Americans the idea of a joint operation. The CIA jumped at the chance, Albania was going to be a wonderful opportunity to experiment.

Anti-communist partisans were infiltrated into the country. The British controlled infiltration by sea whereas infiltration by air was under the responsibility of the Americans. Wheelus Field, the US Air Force base in Libya, served as the logistical hub.

From 1950, Albanian resistance units were trained by the CIA on Greek territory. Seven Polish pilots, who had flown with the RAF during the war, were engaged by the CIA to lead parachuting missions.

Unfortunately, one of the people in charge of the operation was a certain Kim Philby, a mole working for the Soviets. As British liaison officer for the CIA from 1949 to 1951, Philby had access to all the files relating to Anglo-American cooperation. Operation Valuable was of course part of this.

Invariably, attempts at infiltration in Albania by air or sea resulted in failure.

In July 1951, three four-man groups were parachuted in by the CIA.

A first group was eliminated as soon as it landed. Hojda's secret police were waiting on the ground for a second group, but they managed to escape. Followed for several days by several hundred men, the four men were finally trapped in a house where they had sought refuge. The house was surrounded, set alight, and the four men were burnt alive. The fate of the third group was a little better, two men were taken prisoner while the other two managed to escape.

This failure was one of many and was a serious blow to the small Albanian community who were fighting against communist power.

The CIA nonetheless carried on with VALUABLE until mid-1953, the point at which any additional operations seemed to be fruitless. Albanian society was under such tight control by Hojda's secret police that any hope of a popular uprising would be forever out of the question. Kim Philby had worked well and Hojda exulted in showing his prisoners in public.

Gaining in both assurance and ambition, the CIA wanted to be able to act directly in the Soviet zone of influence. An initial alliance was made with the American ministry of defence which had resources that the CIA did not. The men of the secret service met with hostility from the ministry who did not want their officers to have a hand in secret operations. This element of resistance was rapidly quashed however and in August 1948 it was officially established that the secret war had to backed up by armed forces. They could provide training zones, specialists, technical advisers, even ships or planes. The army on the other hand was forbidden to form special units, leaving responsibility for that to a special department of the CIA, the Office of Policy Coordination (OPC). Under this rather innocuous sounding name there was in fact an organization having control over all paramilitary secret operations.

In January 1950, Truman requested his departments to organize a vast think-tank on the state of the world and particularly on the confrontation of the two blocs at the origin of the Cold War.

A report resulting from this think-tank, with the code name NSC 68, suggested reinforcing military means to put into a policy of containment which had been defined in 1947. But according to the authors of the report the doctrine of containment should not stop at a uniquely defensive posture for the United States. It should give itself the means to fight in the rival camp, with the objective of reducing the power and influence of the Kremlin. From that moment on it was an open door for secret actions to develop behind the iron curtain. This new course of events occurred too late to be of any effective help to the nationalists of the Baltic countries who had been fighting against the Soviet invasion since the end of the war.

The CIA proceeded to parachute several agents, especially in Lithuania, to maintain contact with anti-communist resistance, but the results were disappointing. The resistance which had been powerful immediately after the war yielded after several years of struggle under the weight of assaults by the Red Army and the Soviet secret police, the NKVD. Poland would be a more promising field of conflict.

AT THE HEART OF THE COMMUNIST EMPIRE

In 1949, the CIA made contact with a secret anti-communist organization called 'Liberty and Independence'. When abbreviated, the Polish name of this organization became WIN. The Americans saw this as a good omen.

In the first weeks of 1950 the CIA started to parachute weapons, radio transmitters, and gold pieces to the Polish organization. These operations above Poland were in all probability carried out by flying over the Baltic sea at low altitude, from German bases at night. The B-26 was the aircraft best adapted to these missions. In return WIN provided spectacular assessments of anti-communist operations to the CIA which had no publicity in the national press. Reading these reports, an official enthusiast of the CIA remarked one day that the only thing the Poles lacked were anti-tank weapons to chase the Soviets out of the country.

This wonderful picture came crashing down however the day the CIA realised that the WIN organization was nothing more than an invention of the Polish secret service, who, in 1952, even allowed themselves the luxury of revealing over the radio that they had been financed by the CIA to the tune of one million dollars!

Other anti-communist resistance movements of Eastern Europe may have seemed authentic but they were always infiltrated to a greater or lesser extent by the secret police from their beginning. The existence of movements which could have eluded the communist powers were revealed to them by the master spy Kim Philby, who had so easily turned operation Valuable in Albania into a failure.

To fight against the USSR meant supporting the Ukranian resistance in its fight against Moscow. Until 1949, a veritable army, several tens of thousands of men strong, fought against the central power of Moscow. From 1949 onwards this army took on a secret dimension. It was at that point that CIA aid appeared.

Operations began with the parachuting of two liaison agents who took off from Germany and crossed the whole of central Europe to reach their destination. Other teams also left from Greece. At the beginning of the fifties, parachute drops into Soviet territory followed a rather slow rhythm. The constant presence of Soviet moles in western secret service organizations and even in Russian emigrant organizations, from where the majority of agents working for the CIA originated, without doubt scuppered a good number of these missions.

Soviet fighter aviation and the aviation of Eastern bloc countries whose airspace was used rendered these parachute missions extremely dangerous. Flights could only be undertaken at night, flying very close to the ground to avoid detection by radar. These precautions were not always enough: intercepted by two Hungarian fighters, an aircraft of the CIA had a lucky escape purely because he was able to disappear in the clouds.

In the mid-fifties the constant intensification of aerial surveillance apparatus meant it was more and more difficult and dangerous for the CIA to fly over the Soviet Union and its satellites.

Some severe blows had been brought by the Soviets to the Ukranian resistance movement which did not have a great operational value in the eyes of the CIA. Aid to its members was also blocked.

Despairing of being able to strike at the Soviets on the European continent, the CIA brought its efforts towards Asia. Stirred up by an unprecedented wave of decolonization, communism threatened to destabilize entire areas of the continent. In Asia, the CIA had found a field of action that was vast indeed.

CHAPTER 2

THE FIRST INTERVENTIONS IN ASIA

For almost thirty years, from the end of the Second World War until the fall of Saigon in April 1975, Asia was a theatre of operations favoured by the CIA. The Second World War had seriously harmed the brief stability gained from colonization. With the East/West conflicts the "Complicated Orient" was turned into an area of confrontation where the emergence of nationalism and the struggles of influence between the super powers combined into a fatal maelstrom.

With the United States not wanting to be officially implicated, the intelligence services dominated the scene. The operations were, at this stage, clandestine or at least 'anonymous'. In no circumstances were the operations to be traced back to Washington, even when they were carried out in broad daylight. That way at least appearances where kept up.

Distances and the insufficient road network with its renowned insecurity all led to the aeroplane then the helicopter becoming essential tools for CIA operations. The Agency alternately used the services of civilian airlines, the armed forces or its own aircraft of which the fleet was ever expanding.

The majority of pilots who flew in the Far East were civilians and sometimes recently demobilized military pilots. They went to Asia to start a new life and to earn good money. They knew how to fly and they also knew not to ask too many questions! It was of no importance whether the client was an American official, a drug trafficker, the CIA or one of its many assumed names, the most important thing was to fly.

One company offered them this chance: the CAT, which stood for Chinese Air Transport. The CAT had been founded by a born leader, Claire Lee Chennault, a pilot and an adventurer of high calibre. Chennault had started his career as a pilot in the US Army. He was an unorthodox officer and professed very innovative ideas on air combat, maybe too original as he soon found himself in a very awkward position with his hierarchy. The latter thought it wiser to station this troublemaker some place where he would not bother anybody.

Thus Chennault became the leader of the acrobatic patrol of the US Army. He was a talented pilot and, during an air show, the special envoy of the Chinese Generalissimo Tchang Kai-Chek noticed him. The Commander in Chief of the Nationalist Chinese Force was looking at that time for a leader for his embryonic air force. Chennault accepted the position. Released back into civilian life in 1937, he went to China where, surrounded by a few American mercenary pilots, he tried his best to organize an operational air force.

However the group was still too diverse.

The situation changed when the American authorities really started to worry about the expansionist intentions of the Japanese who had set off to conquer Manchuria. Washington decided to support Tchang Kai-Chek and Chennault by unofficially providing pilots and aeroplanes. Chennaults' unit took shape and became an air force in its own right, adopting the name of the Flying Tigers after one of the pilots had the idea of painting shark jaws on the aircraft.

The Flying Tigers won 297 confirmed victories for the loss of four American pilots killed in action.

TEAMING UP WITH THE CHINESE NATIONALISTS

At the end of the Second World War Chennault went back to the United States to, as he thought, a peaceful retirement. However Louisiana, his birth place, was nothing compared to the Far East and he soon became bored. Leaving behind his wife and children Chennault returned to China. The country was in ruin. The united front that had helped the communists, led by Mao Zedong, and Tchang Kai-Chek's nationalists to fight side by side against the invading Japanese, had fallen to pieces. The two factions were engaged in a ruthless struggle for the control of the country.

With money from the Chinese nationalists, Chennault, who had become very good friends with Tchang Kai-Chek, created the CAT in 1946. The airline company started up with about fifteen C-46 Commandos and four C-47 Dakotas obtained from the US Army Air Force surplus. These were completed with a fleet of light aircraft used for liaison flights. When the CAT started its operations it was to the benefit of the nationalist forces, delivering food, medication, even cash for the banks in besieged towns. Some passengers tried to find room amongst the cargo, which occasionally even consisted of live animals ! Very quickly the

CAT gained the reputation of being able to transport anything that was physically possible of fitting in aeroplanes.

"Passengers and animals often found themselves side by side in the aircraft without either being too bothered", said Stuart Dew, one of CATs first pilots. "The movement of cows in the cabin was continually modifying the planes stability, but you soon got used to it...." He goes on "One day a curious cow even put her head into the cockpit. Its nostrils were only a foot away from my nose. She was chewing her hay as if everything was quite normal. She looked around and then returned to the back, apparently quite satisfied. My co-pilot was killing himself laughing and I was flabbergasted!"

Mercenaries, adventurers, oddballs of the aeronautical community, some of the pilots even had the experience of air combat with the Flying Tigers. These men would have followed Chennault to hell and back, which actually nearly happened a few times.

Anticipating the rapid advance of the communists, two pilots were taken to Weishien, a small Chinese town, to recuperate company records. But the communist advance had been under estimated and the town was soon surrounded. The two trapped pilots called for help by radio, stating that they had managed to find refuge in a school yard where a light aircraft could try to rescue them. Chennault wasn't in China at the time so the vice-director of the CAT, Whiting Willauer, took charge of the rescue operation from the terrain in Tsingtao, 85 miles away from Weishien. But what started out as a simple return flight rapidly became a strange and exciting game of musical chairs where the chairs were replaced with aeroplanes!

At Tsingtao, Willauer and Richard Kruske, one of the most talented pilots of the company, bent over a map.

Underlining the name of Weishien with a lead pencil Willauer gave Kruske some brief explanations :

"Burridge and Plank are stuck in a school yard. You take a Stinson and you get them out of there for me in two rotations before the communists make them into spring rolls."

The Stinson was a small two seater plane renowned for its capacity to do short take offs and landings. Even so the idea of landing in a school yard in the middle of a town made Kruske pull a face.

"How big is your school yard?"

"You'll have to take the measurements when you get there. Now go!"

Kruske got into the Stinson and set off for Weishien. Seen from above the school yard looked extremely small. Kruske spotted his two friends who were waving frantically. After flying over once to examine the area Kruske attempted to land. With just one person aboard, the aeroplane was sufficiently light and he landed with no problem.

"Pleased to see you Kruske" said Plank when the aeroplane finally stopped. "Burridge will be your first passenger. Try not to wreck the plane and come back quickly to get me."

With Kruske and Burridge aboard the Stinson set off again, jolting towards the end of the yard in order to have the maximum room possible for take off. In a cloud of dust Kruske opened the throttle and launched the plane. He nearly made it but being overloaded it caught the yard wall and then fell heavily to the ground. Kruske and Burridge miraculously climbed out unscathed from the wreck. Now three pilots had to be rescued. The next day another pilot tried to land, but he broke the propeller on landing. Then there were four !

A new propeller was parachuted to the four Americans who succeeded in mending the second aircraft. Kruske and Burridge climbed aboard and this time succeeded in taking off. However the situation in the school yard was back to square one with two pilots needing to be rescued. Two other light planes landed in the yard, turning it more and more into an airfield as the days went by!

The first plane, a Piper Cub, succeeded in picking up a pilot. Unfortunately the second one wasn't so successful and finished its flight against the yard wall that always got in the way of the take offs. That meant that there were two wrecked planes and still two pilots to rescue. At Tsingtao, Willauer was pulling his hair out by the handful.

The Piper Cub returned to land at the school but broke its propeller on landing. Once again a new propeller was parachuted in by a C-47. On his way over, the pilot of the C-47 bombarded the communist troops that were encircling the town with empty beer cans. When they fell they made a whistling noise that made the soldiers dive into their shelters.

Once the Cub was repaired one of the trapped pilots got aboard with the pilot of the plane. For the first time considerable progress had been made : there was only one pilot left to rescue at Weishien.

Gathered around the map, Willauer, Kruske and the others followed, with concern, the military situation at Weishien.

"The communists are gaining ground", confirmed Kruske who had flown over the town several times. "We have to do everything possible to get our guy out of there tomorrow, other wise it'll be too late." Willauer agreed.

On his initiative, a few planes were used that very night to go and drop several light bombs on the communist positions. The next morning a last attempt was successfully carried out which allowed the last American in Weishien to leave the town. A few hours later the communists swept away the last pockets of resistance of the nationalist troops.

SCENES OF EXODUS

In June 1948 the CAT transported thousands of tons of provisions every month to the troops of Tchang Kai-Chek's Kuomintang, although this was not sufficient to help change the outcome of the war. In 1949, under the pressure of the communist troops, Tchang Kao-Chek and his army left the continent to establish themselves on the island of Taiwan with the protection of the US Navy VIIth Fleet, Chennault and the CAT followed them. The scenes of panic and the fratricidal confrontations which marked the exodus was a bloody rehearsal of what was to happen again, 26 years later, in Vietnam.

"We were overloaded with refugees, others were still arriving, hanging onto the doors of the aircraft, frantically trying to get on board", tells Ed Morton who piloted a C-47. "We had to hit them to make them let go so that we could take off."

Some tried giving dollars, others jewellery or gold. During the last few days the panic spread to the military of whom some even tried to force themselves aboard.

"One night when we were evacuating refugees we saw a small group of soldiers approaching the front of the plane. In their haste they forgot about the propellers and walked straight into them. They were wearing helmets and I will never forget the horrible noise of the propellers striking the helmets and decapitating the poor guys."

The war was lost and this cost CAT a lot. Several dozen aircraft that were in the British colony of Hong Kong were the object of a grotesque legal battle with the local authorities. As London had legally recognized the existence of the Chinese Communist government, Hong Kong's court of justice declared that the aircraft should be returned to them. When after two years of procedures this decision was finally annulled, the aircraft that had been abandoned were of no further use to CAT. Chennault's company was failing. The pilots had seen their wages cut in half and they had been strongly advised to look for work elsewhere. Anxious to keep his company afloat and to help the nationalist cause Chennault asked Washington for assistance.

Help arrived but from the CIA. The agency had been a faithful customer for two years. CIA agents had often slid between two Chinese VIPs and the chicken cages, the crew had learnt not to ask them questions. This collaboration had enabled the CIA to realise the importance of using the services of a 'cooperative' civilian airline.

When Tchang Kai-Chek started to lose ground against the communists the nature of the cargoes rapidly changed. More and more frequently the animals were replaced with boxes of ammunition for the besieged garrisons or the retreating troops. Risk and the unexpected became routine for the pilots of CAT. The CIA financed the operations by putting fresh money into the company's accounts. In exchange they used whatever aircraft they needed. During the summer of 1950 Chennault once more pestered Washington for some funding, the CIA then decided to take the plunge. Through a screen company based in Delaware, the Airdale Cooperation, it took over CAT which also changed its name : the initials stayed the same but its corporate name became Civil Air Transport. CAT ended up being integrated into a group of societies owned by the CIA and controlled by a holding, the Pacific Corporation.

Owning CAT opened new horizons for the CIA. An airline company was above all an excellent cover for their foreign agents. Who, apart from air crew, could travel without causing suspicion?

The CAT crew were also familiar with unusual and clandestine operations and most of them had been in combat. Their knowledge of the Far East was perfect.

For the CIA, who were thinking about developing para-military undercover operations in that region, CAT was their best asset.

A civilian company had numerous advantages compared to the services that the military transport aircraft could offer : there was no need to report to the government, borders were easier to cross and a lot of bureaucracy problems were easier to deal with. In short, the rules and regulations that were made to bend were easier done so with a private company than with a government service.

Once installed in Taiwan CAT went through a short period of uncertainty before multiplying its activities due to an aggressive commercial policy. Obviously there was no mention of who the real owner was and CAT carried on like any other airline, looking for any commercial opportunities. Regular passenger services were set up between Taiwan, Japan, Bangkok and also Hong Kong. The company also did a lot of freight transport, a few of its aircraft were even used in Japan to spread the clouds so as to obtain rain. Certain charters took CAT aeroplanes to Europe and Africa. The shorts and tee-shirts that had been worn by the crew during the 'Chinese years' were thrown out and replaced with uniforms more suitable to the image of a classical airline company.

OPERATION PAPER IN BURMA

While most of Tchang Kai-Chek's army retreated to the island of Taiwan part of the nationalist forces penetrated into the east of Burma to escape the advancing communists. As they entered the country the CIA regrouped and reorganized the combatants.

From this assembly of defeated soldiers the CIA wanted to make a coherent force that was capable, to begin with, of setting up a cordon sanitaire against communism on the southern Border of China. In the long term the US Agency's ambition was to re-conquer China. The secrecy around this operation was such that even the American ambassador in Rangoon, the capital of Burma, was not informed of its existence. It was in all sincerity that he denied the involvement of the United States in the troubles that were caused by the presence of this illegal army in the east of the country. Within a few weeks more than 1,500 fighters of the Kuomintang were installed in the province of Shan. The Burmese Army who were already weakened by the presence of other guerrilla groups in the country, mainly Karens and communists, were unable to find the resources necessary to stop their arrival.

The Burmese Army reported having seen on numerous occasions aeroplanes without any national markings. These were in fact CAT aircraft dropping supplies to the stragglers that continued to pour into Burma. This was known to CAT as Operation Paper. A base camp, supplied by CAT aircraft, had been set up on the Chinese border.

In the same way it was soon to be established that the commander in chief of these troops, the General Li, would, on the same aircraft, make return trips between Burma and Taiwan via the airfields that were available in Taiwan.

After a few months the CIA, who by then were at the head of an army of more than 4,000 men, decided to spring an offensive against the Chinese province of Yunnan.

This was the first military offensive to be carried out by the CIA.

In April 1951 two armies, each consisting of two thousand men, penetrated into Chinese territory. CIA advisers trained the soldiers of the Kuomintang while CAT aircraft regularly dropped in fresh supplies.

This wasn't enough to ensure the success of the nationalist offensive. It was a total failure. It took less than one week for the troops of the Chinese peoples army to drive back the invaders who suffered heavy losses of which some were men from the CIA.

However this did not dissuade the Americans and they doubled their efforts.

An old airfield dating back to the Second World War was secretly restored to working order in Burma. The transport aircraft of CAT carried out direct return trips from Taiwan to Burma and no longer did parachute drops. An airlift was set up to carry several thousands soldiers from the nationalist island to Burma as well as hundreds of tons of arms : individual weapons, mortars, heavy machine guns...The troops stationed in Burma received so much material that they were able to recruit and equip 8,000 peasants who lived in the surrounding mountains. According to Rangoon, the Americans had organized a regular shuttle service that twice a week flew from Taiwan to the secrets airbases in Burma. Within a few months the numbers of the Kuomingtang in Burma had tripled, reaching a total of 12,000 men. For the Burmese authorities the situation was becoming more and more unbearable as the days passed by. The Kuomingtang troops were forming a state within a state, raising taxes and controlling the opium market in the zones which they occupied. According to these same sources the opium was often loaded aboard CAT aeroplanes who then flew it to Thailand or Taiwan. Once during a diplomatic reception in Rangoon the Ambassador of the United States once again denied that the United States were involved in the conflict.

The Chief of Staff of the Burmese Army answered coldly :

"Mr. Ambassador, you bore me. If I were you I would shut up..."

In 1952, a supposedly 'final' offensive was sprung against the Chinese. Twelve thousand men trained by the CIA and backed by CAT aircraft penetrated a few hundred miles into the Yunnan. But the peoples uprising and the rallying of the peasants that the Kuomingtang troops thought they could start never happened. After several weeks of combat the Chinese Army once again pushed out the invaders.

Not being able to succeed in China, Kuomintangs troops then chose to spread their area of influence into Burma itself.

The situation was intolerable for the Burmese authorities who indirectly accused the CIA and constantly asked the United States to put pressure on Taiwan to repatriate its troops. Numerous requests to the United Nations finally resulted in the signing of an agreement involving the retreat of 2,000 Kuomintang fighters.

These men were supposed to go to Thailand where CAT aeroplanes were waiting for them to take them back to Taiwan. It was a parody of a retreat. The evacuations, mainly concerned the older fighters and the civilians, while the best troops stayed put. Exasperated the Burmese government launched a large-scale offensive against one of the Kuomintang camps, which resulted in a few thousand soldiers fleeing to Thailand. From there the CAT aircraft took them to Taiwan. However there were still several thousand present in Burma, who had strong bases from which they carried on dealing in the opium market. In 1960 Burma chose to secretly join forces with communist China to deal, once and for all, with the Kuomintang problem. Three divisions of the Chinese People Popular Army and several thousand Burmese soldiers simultaneously launched an assault on the Kuomintangs main base which was defended by 10,000 men. On the 26th of January 1961, after several weeks of bitter fighting the last defences were overwhelmed.

When the Burmese entered the defeated base, which had a runway capable of receptioning big cargo aircraft, they got a surprise or rather a slight surprise..., they discovered several tons of ammunitions carefully packed in cases stamped with the American flag. The United States denied any involvement in supplying these compromising cases. Taiwan Officially explained that these ammunitions had been obtained by way of a private association, the "Free China Relief Association" who had also been responsible in getting them to Burma by way of private aircraft.

After this defeat many Kuomintang soldiers made their way to Thailand by their own means. The CAT then organized their repatriation to Taiwan. But once again these retreats were nothing but a screen, as at the same time, nearly six thousand fighters crossed the Mekong and entered into the north-west of Laos, as always under CIA guidance.

These men didn't have to wait long before participating in operations led by the CIA in that country.

THE KOREAN WAR

While the guerrilla war developed along the southern border of China, a war of a completely different severity broke out in the Korean Peninsular in 1950. The end of the Second World War had left Korea divided into occupied zones, as in Germany. The Soviets in the north and the Americans in the south had each organized a government in their respective zones. Unlike what had happened in Germany however the two super powers had quickly left the peninsular, leaving the Koreans to sort their problems out for themselves.

The invasion of the south of Korea by the communist troops took the Americans completely by surprise. Although the start of the hostilities in the small hours of the 25th of June 1950 were not a direct threat for the United States, they were extremely embarrassed to note that once again their intelligence services had been flagrantly incompetent. A few months before the attack on North Korea, the CIA had presented President Truman with an exhaustive study on the possible attacks that the Soviet Union could carry out in the world. Korea was only in fifth place far behind Europe and the Middle East.

The "land of the morning calm" appeared at the same time too close to the American bases in Japan and too far from the Soviet bases to be of any interest to Stalin. Apparently nobody at Langley had considered the possibility that the North Korean dictator Kim Il Sung would himself instigate a conflict.

After a few hours hesitation the Americans convinced themselves that the North Koreans had started the invasion to fight over the Korean Peninsular. When Truman was told the facts his reaction was direct and frank :

"We must stop these sons of b... one way or another."

The Korean War had the effect of dramatically increasing the number of clandestine missions carried out by the CIA. The OPC (Office of Policy Coordination), who were in charge of these operations watched its personnel increase tenfold going from 300 to nearly 3,000 people. Counting the 'foreigners under contract' this figure more than doubled from 1950 to 1952. In the same space of time the OPCs budget was multiplied by 17.

Early in 1951 when the front line stabilized, the OPC carried out several guerrilla operations behind the North Korean lines.

Between April and December 1951, 44 teams of Koreans infiltrated behind the enemy lines to disrupt the North Koreans lines of communication with China.

Jack Smith, the OPCs boss, kept Truman regularly informed of the progress of the operations being undertaken there. The number of agents steadily increased : in the beginning of 1952 there were nearly 1,500 operating in the North. The reports sent to Seoul, the South Korean capital, were excellent. One of them gave details of the whole of the Korean and Chinese Units present at the front.

It was only with the arrival of John Hart, the new CIA Head of Station in Seoul, that the less glorious truth came to light. Of the 200 American agents in Seoul, none spoke fluent Korean. This meant that the agents in North Korea were under the management of the Korean personnel which soon aroused Hart's suspicions. These started off an internal inquest that lasted three months. At the end of this period of time all the Korean personnel of the Agency took the polygraph test, otherwise known as the lie detector. The result was awful for the CIA who realised that most of the 'exceptional' reports they had been getting were in fact false, some were complete inventions made up by the enemy.

What had been happening in the North was completely dumbfounding : the CIA agents had regularly visited the « reception centres » held by the North Koreans or Chinese. They were interrogated about what was happening in South Korea after which they received false information as to what was going on in the North to send back to Seoul, which they did conscientiously. It goes without saying that the document which had been received describing in detail all the communist forces was false.

"We'll start back at square one", declared Hart during a stormy meeting of the CIA at Seoul. "The selection of personnel, the network, we change everything and we start again."

Smith, in Langley, gave his support. Trusting in Hart's organizing qualities he chose to give him a free hand. Hart had managed to detect the fiasco on arriving in Seoul, he'd know what to do to make sure that it wouldn't happen again.

During the following weeks the station at Seoul recruited new agents, real people from the North who had fled the communist advance. They spoke with the right accent and they had a certain knowledge of the zone were they would be operating. They were put through the lie detector when recruited, this was followed by training on how to use a transmitter and finally they were parachuted into communist territory. Despite their training no agent seemed to be able to succeed in their mission for longer than a few days.

All were presumed to have been captured or executed. At least the station at Seoul was no longer the victim of the false information widely diffused by the North Koreans.

The CIA regularly used the means of aircraft that the US Air Force held at their disposition. A young officer, Flight Lieutenant Henry Aderholt, was put in charge of organizing the unit responsible for special operations. Aderholt arrived in Korea on the first of August 1950, less than six weeks after the start of the North Korean offensive. He commanded Detachment 2 of the 21st Transport Squadron. Aderholt set up HQ at Taegu, at the North end of the pocket of Pusan where all the allied troops were regrouped, with their back to the sea, encircled by the North Koreans. His unit, consisting of aeroplanes and their crews, were based one hours flight away in Japan, the other side of the Strait of Korea. Sometimes their missions were such that they never touched down on Korean soil. They came from Japan, made their airdrops then turned round and went back to Japan. On other occasions they stopped over in Korea and slept in their aeroplanes between two flights. The aircraft of Detachment 2 mainly made night flights, sharing their time between the transport of ammunitions and airdrops of spies behind enemy lines. On the 15th of September 1950, the allies landed at Inchon, not far from Seoul, behind the North Korean troops. This excellent manoeuvre thought up and carried out by General McArthur enabled a total inversion in the progression of the war. The South Korean capital was rapidly retaken and Aderholt then based his operations from there. He continued the special missions and adventured into Chinese territory. Aderholt worked for both the Military Governor and the CIA, for which he carried out clandestine drops, in the same way that the Carpetbaggers had worked for the OSS during the Second World War.

"With our Dakotas we made flights of six or seven hours that often took us to the Yalu river, which marked the border with China, sometimes even further..." explained Aderholt. "The missions with the CIA were very special because they took us nearly always in very unusual places, outside the combat zones. When we flew for the Military Governor, it was totally different... ."

The operations were set up in the most simple way possible. Aderholt always took pleasure in applying the basic principle in that a unit responsible for special operations should produce the bare minimum of paper work, so as to totally devote themselves to the task in hand.

"Our 'clients' would arrive at the unit and ask us if we had an aircraft available for a mission."

To go where?

Into Chinese territory.

When?

Tonight.

It could be done...

"We'd get an aeroplane ready and, at the pre-arranged time, they would arrive, get in the plane, and we'd be off. Nobody was notified. The business was done and that was that. Only a minimal trace was left of the missions carried out. The unit's books just show the aeroplanes number, the time it took off and the time it came back. Sometimes the pilots name. Nothing else..."

One of the units routine missions consisted in re-supplying a guerrilla training camp that the Americans had installed on an island near the West coast of the peninsular.

An aeroplane landed every day on the beach when the tide was out, unloaded its cargo and took off again before the tide turned.

When he left Korea, Aderholt joined the ranks of the CIA. It was the start of a long career at the heart of the intelligence agency. One of his assignments took him to Japan.

Less than ten years after the end of the Second World War, the defeated empire rose from the ashes in account of the Korean War. To provide for their war efforts the Americans had restored the industrial power of their old enemy. Their closeness to the theatre of operations made it an ideal depot. The CIA's transport unit who were stationed there used the B-26s at their disposition to experiment different methods of infiltration and exfiltration of its agents. One of the most original ones consisted of towing a light aircraft, in this case a DHC Beaver, by a B-26. The action range of the light aircraft was increased accordingly and therefore it could be used for missions that penetrated far into enemy territory. The idea was experimented but it doesn't seem to have been used in an operation. Again trying to gain action range, but also discreetly, another idea was to suspend a Piper Cub under a balloon. The whole thing would have been sent, during the night, over the enemy lines. When it had arrived near its objective, for example an agent to be picked up, the Piper would then unhook from the balloon, land and make its own way back to base. It seems as though this project never got past the good idea stage...

For the CAT the war in Korea provided the opportunity to do some extremely good business. Leaving practically all of the special operations to the military aircraft, the company belonging to the CIA committed the maximum of its capacity to the operations resupplying allied troops present at the Korean theatre of operations. These operations benefited from international financing which allowed the CAT to recuperate a healthy bank balance.

In the space of two years the company made more than 15,000 flights, on average twenty per day. The CAT assured fairly regular flights between Korea, Japan, Okinawa, Guam, Manila and many other ports in the Pacific. The company gained notoriety but, surprisingly, even with its reputation of working in war zones, its links with the CIA were unknown to most people. At the end of the Korean War the CAT had developed tremendously and only had a very distant connection with the company that Chennault had created not even seven years earlier.

With the number of aeroplanes used and the profits that it made the CAT could easily claim first place in the Far East.

The CIA couldn't believe it's luck : the airline company that it had bought to cover up its clandestine activities actually made money, a lot of money !

This didn't stop when the armistice was signed in Korea. Neil Hansen was one of the first pilots recruited by the CIA after the war. His first assignment was to pilot a DC-6 between Japan and Korea to deliver 'Stars and Stripes', the American Army magazine, to the forces stationed at the peninsular.

The CIA's company even delivered newspapers!

This was only one side of the work. Not long after the Korean conflict

49

had ended in 1954, the CAT joined forces with the French Air Force in the Indochina conflict. On a par with their French military colleagues the CAT crews paid the price of blood in the line of enemy fire. If piloting for the CIA had sometimes seemed like child's play this illusion didn't last long with the geopolitical changes in Asia in the second half of the century...

THE COMMITMENT IN INDOCHINA

Alongside the Korean conflict another war was taking place further south on the Asian continent. France was fighting in Indochina, vainly trying to save its colonial empire from slipping through its fingers. In May 1953 General Navarre had been appointed Commander in Chief of the French Expeditionary force in the Far East. In their fight against communism the United States financed two thirds of a war in which the metropolis became less and less interested as the days went by.

Like every Commander in Chief, Navarre soon presented a plan of action for the following months.

The "Navarre Plan" foresaw the investing of the Dien Bien Phu 'basi' and its development into an 'airland' base.

"Whilst blocking the road to Laos you will fix and then destroy the enemy" Navarre had said with meaning to General Cogny, who was in command of the land forces of Tonkin.

The principal idea was to protect Laos by placing an obstacle in the way of the Vietminh divisions causing them to stop in their tracks. With the Vietminh attacks on Dien Bien Phu broken it would have been easy to negotiate a peaceful settlement from a position of strength.

This strategy of a fortified camp, with a landing strip in the centre allowing air supply, had already been successfully tried out at Na San.

In 1953, after a first attack, the Vietminh hadn't managed to capture the airland base Na San. They withdrew to see to the wounded and to prepare a second offensive of a larger scale. The French, sensing the danger, carefully withdrew from Na San leaving the adversaries without the chance of winning a victory. Ironically Na San had been evacuated to provide Dien Bien Phu with a garrison. The only things that the new

Commander in Chief wanted to remember about Na San were Giaps first broken attack and the successful evacuation.

When Navarre went to Paris to present his plan to the government, he found that he had a weighty opponent in General Corniglion-Molinier. Minister but also former pilot, Corniglion had landed in 1946 in the Dien Bien Phu basin which he knew very well. He gave a detailed description to his colleagues in the government who listened to him with amusement and astonishment :

"Dien Bien Phu ? Imagine an airfield that is spread out on the Champs de Mars with the enemy over on the Chaillot hill..."

"From a pilots point of view", replied Navarre, who didn't try to hide the fact that the going could be tough.

Nearly a year later, when the fight was definitely lost, Corniglion-Molinier offered to jump at Dien Bien Phu to show his solidarity for the garrison.

"What are you wanting to do, let the Vietminh take a member of the government as prisoner?" replied the Prime Minister at that time, Joseph Laniel, in amazement.

The gesture wouldn't have lacked gallantry...

At the beginning of Autumn 1953, General Nicot, who commanded the Transport Command of the Expeditionary Force in Indochina, received the order to round up his fleet of freighter planes. The Air force had always been against the setting up of a base at Dien Bien Phu as it hadn't felt capable of regularly resupplying it. Without realising that he was only repeating what Corniglion-Molinier had said before, Nicot, who had also experienced Na San, spoke his mind :

"The Transport command is not capable of assuring permanent resupplying of Dien Bien Phu. It's not possible to cheat with the numbers and potential of the aeroplanes." he added directing his remarks to Navarre.

The latter acted as though he hadn't heard : he'd listened to all this pilot talk before....

The 20th of November marked the beginning of Operation Castor, the paratroopers taking hold of the Dien Bien Phu 'basin'. An operation that went according to plan with hardly a shot fired. Once on the ground the men started to dig shelters and get the old landing strip into working order. As soon as that was open a never ending flow of man and material arrived. A few thousand round trips were made to the entrenched camp that dug itself in a bit more each day. Nearly 200 miles of jungle separated Dien Bien Phu and the Tonkin Delta which the French Army controlled. The links could only be made by air and each round trip took about 3 to 4 hours. The fact that the basin was surrounded by hills, some as high as 5,900 feet, meant that access to the landing strip was something of a delicate matter.

When there were bad weather conditions the aeroplanes were spaced out to avoid the risk of collision. Without even taking into consideration the eventuality of an enemy intervention, right from the start the resupplying of Dien Bien Phu was a nightmare for the men of the Transport Command and Logistics.

The aircraft that carried most of the burden was the C-47 Dakota, of which the transport capacities were insufficient. These aircraft were supported by several C-119 Packet which the Air Force had started to receive in May 1953. Like the Dakota, these aircraft came directly from the USAF who were letting go of their stocks on account of the end of the Korean War. The first aircraft arrived the 6th of May 1953 and were put into working order by twelve civilian flying personnel from the CAT and eighteen USAF people. This staff stayed in Indochina until the first flying personnel were trained for the new aeroplane. The American decorations that were too loud, especially the large paintings of pin-ups on the side of the fuselages, were obliterated and the French national markings were painted on in their place. The Packet (called as such by the French after a confusion with another aircraft, the C-82) was much appreciated for its charge load capacity. Its large rear doors allowed the dropping in one go of charges weighing six tons. Unlike the Dakota that could only take 2.5 tons on board and which had to be dropped in several bundles.

THE FIRST CANON SHOTS AT DIEN BIEN PHU

In January 1954 fifteen Packets, representing a loading capacity of a few hundred tons, was available to resupply French camps. But due to lack of time only twelve French crew had been trained for this aircraft. It was even more noticeable that there was an insufficiency as the same crew had to assure the Dakota missions as well! When in fact the combats had already started at Dien Bien Phu on the 31st of January. The first Vietminh 75mm canon shots sounded that day in the 'basin'. The Anti Aircraft Artillery (AAA) also made its first apparition. The crews had the unpleasant surprise of finding out that the enemy had several batteries of 37mm at their disposition, very lethal at medium altitude.

To compensate for this shortage of pilots France, with the authorization of the American authorities, once again called upon the services of the Cat 'volunteers'. This decision had not been an easy one to take due to the sometimes turbulent relations that existed between the American company and the French authorities.

The CAT was not unknown to the French Intelligence Service who had a pretty good idea about its links with the CIA . Wasn't the CAT's lawyer none other than General Donavan, the former OSS boss ?

The public relations service of the company, set up in Bangkok, was also well known as serving as a screen for American intelligence.

Operating from Taiwan over continental China the CAT aircraft made frequent stop overs in Tonkin. The French authorities always kept an eye on what the company which it had been said didn't hesitate to send aeroplanes to land secretly in Vietminh territory. At the end of the Second World War the Americans had effectively decided to give their support to Ho Chi Minh and the Vietminh cause against the French 'colonial' interests.

French fighters had intervened a couple of times against C-46 and C-47 registered in nationalist China. One aircraft caught in the act of clandestine parachute dropping over Tonkin had even been shot down.

The logical consequence of this situation had been that the permanent authorization to fly over the Indochinese territory was refused to the CAT when requested it.

However a Dakota from the CAT was detached on a permanent basis to Saigon from the beginning of 1951. It operated mainly for the benefit of the STEM (Special Technical and Economical Mission), an American government agency also known to be financed by the CIA. The Dakota droned across Indochina, flying over, on its way, all the French Military sites that were of any interest....

The Korean War brought the Americans to a new way of thinking. Having realized the dangers of a communist victory in South-East Asia the Americans turned about face, dropping Ho Chi Minh to fight alongside the French in the combat against the Vietminh.

They financed the war effort, armed the French Expeditionary force, but they still weren't ready to intervene directly with military troops or crew, things that would be seen as a provocation in the eyes of the Chinese or Soviets.

OPERATION SQUAW II

On the 9th of March, the fighting having already started one month earlier at Dien Bien Phu, the first contingent of American pilots from the CAT arrived at Hanoi with their aircraft.

It was Operation Squaw II. (Operation Squaw I also carried out by the CAT had involved an unique flight to resupply a French post at Laos).

The CIA had taken advantage of the situation to fill the aeroplanes with intelligence agents and material destined for the network that they were building up in Tonkin. The American pilots created a sensation when they got down from their aircraft. Was it the refrigerators that they brought with them or the Hawaiian shirts that they wore that left the mocking French pilots looking on in wonder?

The operations started at once. From the 12th of March 1954 each French pilot took an American pilot with him to initiate him in the work at Dien Bien Phu and to familiarize him with flight procedures. As from the following day the Vietminh lanced its offensive against the entrenched camp. The AAA gave all it had got against the aeroplanes that were trying to land or simply dropping supplies. This was an unfortunate coincidence for the American crews who had to face extremely violent combat without having had time to get into the feel of war. At the end of the missions on the 13th of March the men from the CAT refused to continue their work due to the intense AAA. The company gave them the choice : either they flew or they were given the hand-shake.

The flights started up again the following day...

The respite didn't last long. Regularly surrounded by AAA explosions, notably from the formidable 37mm canons, the American pilots stopped work once again on the 27th of March. For the already overloaded French crews this was hard. The resupplying of the entrenched camp had to take place whatever happened so they were obliged to take it upon themselves to carry out the missions that the American pilots had abandoned.

One figure detached itself from the little group of CAT pilots : James McGovern, alias McGoon, also known as 'earthquake'. McGoon was a veteran of the Flying Tigers, with whom he had won nine air victories against the Japanese. At the end of the war he had followed Chennault when he created the CAT. During a resupplying mission to the Chinese Nationalists, he was forced to land his C-46, due to a shortage of fuel, in a river bed which, luckily, was as dry as his aeroplane.

McGoon, his co-pilot and the radio operator, who were both Chinese, were made prisoner by a communist patrol and taken into captivity. After several weeks of imprisonment McGoon was mysteriously released by his jailers, without any other form of trial.

"They got fed up of his bad temper and they couldn't feed him any-more" tells one of his comrades.

It was true that McGoon weighed around 23 stone. His build and his Herculean force had allowed him to help his two Chinese crew members escape whilst he was prisoner. McGoon had simply prised open the bars of the cell; the Chinese had been able to slip outside but McGoon had been held back because of his waist size...

Legend or truth there were always stories to be heard about McGoon. It was always said that he took off horizontally because his stomach didn't allow him to pull the wheel back all the way...

One thing was sure and that was with his eloquent service record nobody could accuse him of being a coward. McGovern had been chosen by his colleagues to represent them to the French authorities. He duly went to General Dechaux who commanded the aviation at Dien Bien Phu :

"General", he said, "the AAA over Dien Bien Phu is worse than any we have known over China or Korea. We would never have carried out this type of mission without being escorted by fighters."

American civilians and 'volunteers', the Cat pilots could not be blamed for not wanting to sacrifice themselves in a war that didn't directly concern them.

Dechaux relayed their remarks to General Cogny. He in turn promised increased fighter protection for transport missions. The American pilots took to the air again two days later. They demanded however to be allowed to make the drops at medium altitude, between 8,200 and 9,800 feet, with delay drop parachutes so as to escape the light anti aircraft fire. As from the 5th of April, due to the intense AAA activity, all parachute missions that were carried out during the day were preceded by bomber command intervention. Conforming with the agreement taken by General Cogny, the C-119 were also escorted by fighters. When bad weather did not allow this protection, the drops were cancelled. To make up for lost time the C-119 flew at night with lights out and flash-suppressers on the motor exhaust exits.

"The AAA impressed us even more at night", admitted McGovern. "We could see all the trails climbing towards us. This permanent danger that materialized in front of our eyes played havoc with our nerves."

The Americans also complained about the French fighters, accusing them of staying out of altitude and not going down to attack the AAA with all the ardour necessary. However in the space of a few days several fighters were shot down by the Vietminh AAA which they had tried to attack.

However the American crews did show kindness : some didn't hesitate to add to the resupply bundles they dropped, cigarettes that they had paid for themselves. As for McGovern he took advantage, while flying to Dien Bien Phu, to read his mail. He took great pleasure in throwing his unpaid bills over board, above the Vietminh territories. When he heard that Colonel Castries, who commanded the garrison, had been made General, he added a bottle of champagne to the bundle that held the new generals stars as well as other decorations for the men at the garrison.

But Castries never received his stars. It's possible that the bundle fell into Vietminh hands who could then have raised their glasses to their next victory. Only a few hours after the start of the Vietminh attack on the 31st of January, all aeroplanes were denied access to the runway, which was being covered by enemy fire. For a few more nights the medical aircraft risked landing so as to evacuate the wounded.

But very quickly they had to give up and no other landing was attempted. The only links the garrison had with the outside world were the parachutes and the radio. Obviously the drop zones were getting smaller alongside the progression of the Vietminh. In one flyover the aeroplanes were only managing to drop a small part of their cargo to the entrenched camp. This meant that they had to increase the flyovers, with the risk of being hit by AAA. On ground the collecting of the bundles sometimes took on an air of a deadly game.

Another consequence of having to make several drops was that the air space above the basin was congested with aircraft who couldn't get rid of their cargoes. The Packets, that carried out about thirty missions per day, were allowed two slots of 90 minutes each every twenty-four hours.

Every day that went by brought back its load of damaged aircraft, some more than others. The pilots of the CAT had their fair share. During the night of the 23rd and 24th of April, the American crews were on stand by. They dropped most of their 117 tons of supply into the basin that night and took great risks. One aeroplane received a direct hit in the wing from a 37mm. He somehow managed to get back to base. One pilot had his oxygen bottle pierced by a .50 bullet that missed his head by only a few inches. The chief of the American pilots Paul Holden wasn't as lucky : a shell that exploded near his aeroplane riddled him with fragments and he had his left arm torn off. He was the first wounded American. The co-pilot flew the plane home.

The following evening the Americans, once again, refused to fly.

"It's surpassed anything we ever encountered in the Ruhr or in Korea" they said.

"We flew with flak jackets on" remembers one of them. "To protect myself even more I used to sit on the thickest books I could find and make myself very small in the seat."

To make sure that there was a minimum of precision when dropping, the pilots had to follow precise trajectories which the Vietminh artillery soon worked out.

"We flew straight towards hell» one of the crew said, summing the situation up."

The Dakota crews were assigned to the C-119 to replace the CAT crews. Due to the desperate situation of the soldiers on the ground, the latter accepted to resume their places in the fleet as from the 30th of April.

The weather conditions that prevailed over the basin hindered the work of the pilots. There were days when bombers and fighters flew round in circles unable to intervene as cloud cover was too thick. The Dakotas had to sometimes head back to base without being able to drop their cargo. Even when the drops were not being picked up as much by the worn out soldiers, the missions still carried on. It was hoped that this would mislead the enemy about the real strength of the last defenders.

The 5th of May the CAT crews volunteered to carry out drops at low altitude over an isolated company strong point. The next day, even with a reinforced presence of fighters, McGoverns plane was hit by the AAA.

"A direct 37mm hit" announced the pilot over the radio.

Kusak, the pilot in a C-119 which was flying slightly behind, spotted the damage as McGovern's aircraft went into a slow left-hand curve.

"Your left wing looks pretty badly hit and your motor is losing as much oil as it can", declared Kusak over the radio.

McGovern's aircraft was in fact very badly damaged : the leading edge of the left wing had had several feet ripped off, and the left motors propeller, which had stopped working, spun in thin air. A very impressive trail of oil evaporated behind the aeroplane, spraying Kusaks aircraft as it went by. The Vietminh AAA fiercely attacked the wounded plane. A second direct hit severely damaged the right hand side back girder. The aeroplane veered to the right, only just missing the one behind. It was getting increasingly harder to control.

"Jump", shouted Kusak into the radio. "Jump!"

McGovern was not a marathon runner. The idea of having to carry his 23 stone in the Vietnamese jungle so as to save one's skin didn't really appeal to him. Hiking was not his greatest passion. This jovial exhuberant person, who always wore light weight moccasins, would say to anybody who wanted to hear that he would never jump from an aeroplane.

"Tell me the best bearing for Haiphong", he asked Kusak. Then went on :

"I'm going to carry on for as long as possible..."

The aeroplane, flying with one motor and leaving behind it a trail of thick smoke, skimmed the relief inexorably losing height.

"Do you think you're going to make it?" asked Kasak.

"Piece of cake!" answered McGovern.

A few seconds later the aeroplane was only a few feet above the ground. On seeing the end of his days approaching McGovern said tersely :

"This time I've had it son..."

The plane hit the summit of the hill with its left wing, toppled to the ground and exploded in an immense burst of flames. McGovern and his Franco-American crew hardly had time to suffer.

Ironically, only a few miles from there was an old landing strip on which they could have attempted a crash landing. It would only have taken a few seconds. The tragedy deeply shocked the other American pilots. On the same day two other aeroplanes were been badly damaged by the AAA. Once again the CAT pilots decided that they wouldn't fly the next day.

The day in question turned out to be the day on which the last entrenched defenders at Dien Bien Phu surrendered. It was the 7th of May 1954.

The CAT pilots had carried out a total of 684 sorties over Dien Bien Phu. The record being held by a certain Judkins, with 64 sorties above entrenched camps. Then came Kusak with 59 flights.

The Eisenhower administration was so impressed by the results obtained by the CAT at Dien Bien Phu that it thought about creating another 'stateless' unit equipped with jets.

The idea was to set up an International Volunteer Air Group (IVAG) which would be placed, in the context of the Indochina War, under either French or an Asian country's supervision. The IVAG would be equipped with F-86 Sabre and maybe even B-29 heavy bombers which had so often been missed during the battles of the fighters in the entrenched camps.

The French in Indochina could have been the first to take advantage of the IVAG, but the American ambitions went even further : that was to have a striking force at hand, whenever needed in the area, to support American policy.

The signature on the 21st of July 1954 of the Geneva treaties, which put an end to the Indochina War (at least for the French), stopped the preparation in its tracks. Deep down the American administration was still attracted to the idea of having a strong air group without any direct attachments to the United States government.

During the weeks that followed the end of the war, the CAT experienced a strong renewal of their activities. In preparation of the separation of the country that was taking place they helped transfer several tens of thousands of Catholics, who chose to run away from the communist regime, to the south.

Chennault followed the company's operations with interest even though he was extremely ill. In 1958 he returned to the United States to die after suffering from lung cancer. Until the last moment he kept up his interest in China.

RAIDS OVER COMMUNIST CHINA

Throughout the 1950's the CIA was very active, even though the operations from Taiwan were overshadowed by the Korean and Indochina wars.

In 1950 more than 600 CIA employees were present on the island of Taiwan. Most were employed by fictitious occidental societies such as Western Enterprises and Western International Company which served as cover ups. The CIA worked at supporting the anti-communist networks that were present in continental China, all the time keeping up its intelligence and propaganda operations.

Chennault who had never come to terms with communist victory, had without respite, asked Washington to re-form a group of Flying Tigers, but without success. He fell back onto the only instrument there was to fight against the Peking power, the CAT.

To begin with the CAT were to be involved in the operations of delivering arms to General Ma Pu-Fang, a Muslim leader from North-West China. Ma Pu-Fang claimed that he had 50,000 soldiers available immediately and four times as much in reserve.

But even before the CAT could organize anything to be sent, Ma Pu-Fang was defeated by the communists. The only role the CAT played was limited to evacuating the General and his war treasures, 1.5 million dollars in gold ingots. As soon as Ma Pu-Fang was evacuated from China he went on a pilgrimage to Mecca.

At the end of 1950 the Chinese nationalists claimed that there was a strong anti-Communist guerrilla army of nearly a million men on the continent.

The United States were a little more cautious in their estimations : according to them only 600,000 to 650,000 could be counted, only half being considered as loyal to the Taiwan government.

The Chinese communists admitted the existence of this rebellion and regularly carried out operations against these 'bandits' in the south of the empire.

In June 1950, Peking announced that in just over a year it had arrested 20,000 American agents. At the same time more than one million soldiers from the People Popular Army were mobilized to fight against the different guerrillas who were against the central power of Peking.

The CAT were committed without any restraint to the CIA operations. These missions, which sometimes took the aircraft deep into Chinese territory, could last anything from twelve to fifteen hours. The aircraft either left from the American base, Clark, in the Philippines or from terrains in Taiwan. But wherever they left from the basic principal and the key to survival was the same for the crews that flew at night : they had to fly low over the sea so as not to be detected by radar and to miss the Chinese fighters that patrolled above the Formosa Strait.

The Taiwanese Air Force also participated in these clandestine operations over the continent, mainly using the four engined aircraft PB4Y Privateer from the Naval patrols. However the Taiwanese were soon short of aeroplanes. They could not provide both Naval patrols and penetrations over the continent at the same time.

So the CIA, once again, carried out all the clandestine missions itself. Soon three B-17 were in service in the cover up companies. In 1953 up to thirty flights per month were organized, mainly to drop tracts. Precise accounts state that, up until then, 300 million tracts had been dropped. There were still not enough B-17s and as well as that they were not adapted to the more delicate penetration missions.

The CIA turned its attention to an aeroplane they knew well, the B-26 Invader. During the first few weeks of 1954 a series of tests were carried out, and without any surprise the aircraft was entirely satisfactory. A dozen Invaders were then based in Taiwan. The Americans controlled the use of them but the crew and ground staff were provided by the Taiwanese.

Certain aeroplanes wore nationalist emblems. All were painted black and could only be identified by the serial number written on the fin in very small numbers. Because of their camouflage and the clandestine nature of use, the B-26 were nick-named the Blackbirds by their crew.

The bomb bays had been modified so as to be able to transport all kinds of cargo as well as explosives. They could be anything from prospectuses to forged money and ration cards. The CIA tried to saturate certain areas with forged items in an attempt to destabilize the economy and heighten the discontent towards the Communists. Occasionally the B-26 were also used to infiltrate agents, using the techniques that were perfected by the Carpetbaggers during the Second World War.

The B-26 missions were mainly directed towards the coastal regions, between Canton and Shanghai, very occasionally inland. Most of the flights were carried out on nights when there was a full moon so as to take advantage of reasonable visibility. Thick cloud cover meant that the mission was quite simply cancelled. The B-26 flew fast and low, very low : less than 160 feet off the ground.

Even with good moonlight the exercise was extremely perilous. On the 5th of November 1957 a B-26 and its Chinese crew were lost over the continent. With out even realising it, during the flight, the pilot had gradually been losing height until he finally hit the ground. But the aeroplane came in at such a small angle that, after the initial shock it bounced and the pilot was able to retake control for a few minutes. However the damage was such that the B-26 finished by crashing. Two members of the crew were killed in the crash and the three that escaped were captured. After less than a year in prison they were released and repatriated to Macao.

Another mission could have ended badly : in July 1958 the International Fair at Guangzhou had just been opened by Mao Zedong, a B-26 was send to drop tracts to ridicule the communists. The B-26 with its four man crew took off from Xin Zu, stopped over at Taiwan to finish its loading, then crossed the Formosa Strait and carried on over the continent.

The crew was made up of three people : the pilot and two navigators. Sat in the Plexiglas nose of the aeroplane the first navigator took care of the sight navigation using natural pin points. The second navigator sat behind the pilot and took care of the electronic-radio help with the navigation.

As in many previous missions the entry over Chinese territory was made at Macao. Normally there was only slight, if any, AAA as the communists did not possess the means to accurately detect a plane at low altitude. To the crews greatest surprise that night was an exception. The aeroplane was targeted on several occasions throughout the mission.

The reason was only found out after their return to base : a fault in the electrical circuit had meant that the lighting on top of the fin hadn't been extinguished...!

OPERATION TROPIC IN MANCHURIA

Another programme had gone on at the beginning of the fifties in the direction of Manchuria. It involved another independent Tchang Kai-

Chek anti-communist faction.

The operation, which consisted of infiltrating teams of instructors, was code named Tropic by the CAT pilots who took part. C-47 Dakotas, stripped of all markings, left from Japan to carry out night missions. The programme did not last long : the 29th of November 1952 a C-47, with its CAT crew and two other Americans from the CIA (young men in their twenties) aboard, had to land on Chinese territory. The capture of the Americans put an immediate stop to the Tropic programme.

In 1957 the Burmese Prime Minister, U Nu, offered to arbitrate to renew the links between the Americans and the Chinese. The latter offered to release the CIA agents : all that was asked of the United States was to authorize journalists to go to China to investigate Mao's 'New China'. The director of the CIA at that moment in time, Allen Dulles, refused the offer. The tragic outcome of this inflexibility was that the men from the CIA were liberated much later, after spending over twenty years in Chinese prisons.

CHAPTER 3

FIRST ENGAGEMENTS IN
LATIN AMERICA

EISENHOWER, THE HEAD OF SECRET OPERATIONS

The election of Dwight D. Eisenhower to the White House in 1952 marked a turning point in the history of the still young CIA. His predecessor, Harry Truman had come to the Presidency as a total novice in the subject of intelligence operations. This was absolutely not the case with Eisenhower. As commander in chief of allied forces in Europe during the second world war, he understood perfectly the importance of intelligence, especially the interception of enemy communications, or SIGINT, and image intelligence, or IMINT.

His experience as commander in chief was not always entirely beneficial. Having kept a very flattering memory of the work accomplished by the OSS behind enemy lines during the war, Eisenhower made secret operations the major tool of his foreign policy. More and more means were put at his disposal, eventually ending up with secret fleets of aircraft. Inevitably, as these operations for the most part illegal grew in their excessiveness, they lost their secrecy.

Latin America was a first choice as a theatre of operation. Many aircraft operated in the region throughout the fifties and sixties to satisfy the needs of the CIA. Infiltration, aerial reconnaissance, liaison flights discreet as they were rapid, the range of missions was very wide in a region of the world where the lack of any kind of infrastructure rendered the plane indispensable. Of course, none of these planes displayed the real nature of its work, nor the identity of its true owner.

Officially, they all belonged to different mining or oil companies which employed them for the transport of senior staff, the supply of opencast workings or geological surveys. At the will of the CIA, these planes never ceased to change official owner, or to disappear suddenly from one country only to appear in another, with new colours and under a new identity. In other cases, the presence of these planes in Latin America was purely theoretical. Panama, with its reputation of obligingly giving itself over to unscrupulous shipowners, extended this 'know-how' to the world of aviation.

If the civil aviation registers were to be believed, in the early sixties, a

Panamanian company was the official owner of several Douglas A-26 Invaders and Curtiss C-46 Commandos as well as a four-engine Douglas C-54. In fact, these aircraft never touched Panamanian soil ; they flew in the far east.

Another practice was that civil Panamanian registration numbers were 'reserved' by local civil servants who were not averse to receiving a few extra dollars. The CIA thus made use of a pool of legal registration numbers which it could dip into at any time in order to ensure the legal cover of an aircraft anywhere in the world.

OPERATION SUCCESS IN GUATAMALA 1954

While the Korean war was going through its last hours, the American administration found the time to be closely interested in the situation in Guatamala. Jacobo Arbenz, the new President of this central American country, profoundly irritated his powerful neighbour to the north.

Arbenz had been democratically elected with more than 50% of the vote in November 1950. His efforts to reform agriculture and the economy of his country resulted in an increase of his popularity among the farmers. But was he justified in negotiating with the communist opposition in his country, in open defiance of the United States?

In 1953, Jacobo Arbenz worsened his case by expropriating at the same time as compensating, the multinational United Fruit Company, which was the first landowner of the country. One year later he committed a subsequent offence when he bought arms from Czechoslovakia. It concerned 2,000 tons of armaments from Skoda factories which were practically of no use. The Czechs had swindled the Guatamalans by selling them anti-tank guns and heavy artillery mounted on railway track, in a country where tanks were as rare as railway lines. The rest of the cargo was made up of barely usable light weapons, recuperated from the battlefields of the second world war.

After having dismissed the idea of sinking the freighter in the port of Puerto Barrios where it was due to unload its cargo, the CIA eventually mounted an attack against a train which was transporting the cargo to the interior of the country. But the sabotage of the railway line failed and resulted in the death of a CIA agent.

This did not prevent the CIA from accusing Arbenz of arming the unionists of the country, not only to be able to fight, if need be, against his own army, but also to attempt an invasion of his neighbour, El Salvador.

To crown it all, alarmist reports coming to the attention of the CIA in Guatamala city spoke of communists preparing to take power in the country. This was more than enough for a wind of hysteria, carefully fostered by the lobbyists of the United Fruit Company, to begin blowing throughout the higher realms of Washington. Arbenz's case was rapidly and closely examined and then his fate was sealed: the obstacle had to be removed.

The CIA reflected on the means of carrying it out in the most discreet way possible.

"There is no question of an intervention directly from the United States." Eisenhower had made it clear that he did not want to attract hostility from the other countries in the region. The idea of using the opponents of the regime supported by the CIA came to mind. The favourable outcome of the coup d'etat initiated by the CIA in Iran several weeks earlier persuaded Eisenhower that this type of classic plan could also work in Guatamala. So operation Success was launched. Eisenhower closely followed the preparations at every stage throughout the first part of 1954.

The 'protégé' of the CIA was Carlos Castillo Armas, a colonel in the Guatamalan army. In 1950 a first failed coup d'etat against the predecessor of Arbenz had left him seriously injured. According to legend, he was left for dead but miraculously recovered just before his funeral! Thrown in prison, he carried out a second exploit by digging an escape tunnel with his bare hands. "I shall return!" he made it known to the President. Then he fled the country.

Castillo Armas was the perfect man for the CIA. The agency rapidly gave enough arms and money to equip his 'National Liberation Movement'. A small group of combatants from all over Latin America were also recruited.

The CIA had also planned a small aerial component. Secret airstrips had been built in Honduras and Nicaragua.A dozen planes including the fighter-bombers P-47 Thunderbolt and P-51 Mustang for the use of Armas were based there. The majority of pilots were ex-CAT.

"If a pilot were to be captured, the Guatamalans would be confronted with somebody speaking...Chinese!" noted an officer taking part in the operation.

However, intoxicated by his new resources, Castillo Armas prepared his conquest for power rather half-heartedly.

Pushed on by his 'sponsors', he launched his offensive from Honduras. At the head of 150 men, with little training or motivation, Castillo Armas penetrated Guatamala, leading a small column of trucks, on the 18th June 1954. P-47s and P-51s provided aerial cover, without encountering opposition from the Guatamalan air force.

Castillo Armas drove eight miles towards the interior of the country then set up in a church where he ceremoniously launched an appeal asking President Arbenz to step down. Believing that they had fulfilled their mission, the revolutionary and his men established themselves as best they could in their church and waited for a response...

"Incredible!"

Nervously skimming through the reports that were reaching him on the inactivity of Castillo Armas, the CIA Unit Head in Guatamala could not hide his anger. The affair was turning into a farce!

Armas had been given as much money as he wanted and he sets himself up in a church until Arbenz chooses to give up his power...

In order to save Operation Success the CIA tried hard to make Arbenz believe that Armas had a veritable army ready to fight against him. To create this illusion the Agency undertook a vast campaign of disinformation relying on a small fleet of aircraft and on powerful radio transmissions from the Caribbean. The planes carried out several missions where they dropped leaflets.

Three days after Castillo Armas had set up in the church, P-47s were flying, repeatedly over the capital Guatamala city.

President Arbenz was so overawed by this that he ordered a black-out in the principal towns and cities in the country. At the same time the CIA broadcast an interview with a pilot who had deserted, over the

'Voice of Liberation', its secret radio.

Once again, Arbenz was troubled by this.

Fearing more desertions, he ordered his air force to stay on the ground! Nonetheless the CIA was not yet the victor. The rebel air force was also becoming weaker; an aircraft was lost when its pilot, uncertain of his position and short of fuel, landed on its belly in Mexican territory. The pilot in question was American and Operation Success could have been finished from that moment, but the CIA managed to have him discreetly released by the Mexican authorities and everything carried on as before.

In the following days, two other aircraft were badly damaged by light-arms fire. The Americans feared that the "Liberation Air Force" would die out completely through lack of planes.

The rebels could only count on four planes, at the most, being available at any one time. The supply of ammunition and particularly bombs, was also very chaotic : because of a shortage of explosive bombs, the pilots dropped anything that was available: smoke grenades, leaflets, and even empty bottles of Coca-Cola which made, according to them, a noise which resembled the sound of a bomb when they hit the ground.

One day Eisenhower asked Dulles, the director of the CIA, what he thought the chances of Castillo Armas' success were if he didn't have any more planes :

"Zero" replied Dulles without hesitating.

"And if we provided him with some more planes?"

"20%."

Eisenhower, who had a clear and precise idea of the importance of aerial support, authorized the CIA to make up the numbers of the rebel air force, and that it be done rapidly. Two P-51 Mustang from the Honduran Air Force were placed at the disposal of the CIA and aerial raids became the principal activity of the rebels. The new planes were then engaged in bombing civilian targets, which had enormous repercussions.

Very shortly afterwards, a CIA pilot commanding a P-51 attacked and sank a British frieghter suspected of transporting fuel to Guatamala. The attack took place on the orders of Tacho Somoza, the Nicaraguan President who was harbouring aerial CIA operations in his territory.

Somoza feared that the fuel transported would enable the Guatamalans to launch offensives against his country. He therefore asked the person responsible for the region if planes could take-off to attack the ship. The CIA man sought instructions from his senior and the response was a very definite no.

Somoza was furious. He insisted long and hard that the CIA give in to his demand and a plane took off carrying two 550lbs bombs. It had no difficulty in finding the frieghter in question and placing one of its bombs against the hull. The ship sank in deep water, the attack resulted in no casualties whatsoever. It came to light later that the ship was transporting cotton.

The British protested, as they had protested against the attitude of the Americans when Guatamala had called upon the UN to expose the role of the United States.

This did not trouble Eisenhower, who pursued operations in Guatamala with a persistence that was soon to be rewarded. To calm the British, the CIA accepted to pay the sum of 1.5 million dollars to compensate for the loss of the ship.

On the 27th June, less than ten days after the beginning of the operation, Colonel Carlos Diaz, head of Guatamalan armed forces, met with the American ambassador to give him a dramatic account of the bombings conducted by the rebel air force. Diaz was in a state of shock and his account was somewhat exaggerated. The extent of the destruction was in reality significant however.

Diaz suspected that the rebel colonel could not have obtained such a fire power without the active support of the United States. When he shared these suspicions with the American ambassador the latter took offence and threatened to put an end to the discussion. Diaz retracted and better still he asked the Americans to intervene to obtain a cease-fire ;

"Put an end to the communist threat in your country and we will help you to obtain a cessation of fighting." The United States fixed its conditions through the voice of its ambassador.

Diaz chose to turn against President Arbenz and, after some tortuous negotiations, accepted the accession of Castillo Armas to the Presidency.

The active role played by the CIA throughout the operation was an open secret. And although there were no casualties amongst the ranks of the revolutionaries, for the civilians, subject to aerial bombardments, it was a different story. This waste of human life discredited the United States in the eyes of Guatamala and Latin America for a long time.

Without becoming preoccupied with its medium and long term negative effects, the success of Operation Success was celebrated by the CIA. From then on the agency felt authorized to intensify its efforts against the spread of communism in Latin America. Washington was jubilant, Eisenhower could scarcely hide his joy and satisfaction in private. The atmosphere was one of having dealt a severe blow to communism.

The satisfaction was short-lived.

A CERTAIN FIDEL CASTRO

On the 1st January 1959, after a rather dull New Year's eve where coffee rather than champagne was drunk, Fulgencio Batista, leader of Cuba, left his house in Havana. Surrounded by his family and several close collaborators, the dictator arrived at the airport of the Cuban capital and disappeared into a military aircraft. At 2.40am precisely the plane took off for Miami. It was the end of the Batistan dictatorship. The era of Castro was about to begin.

Against all expectations the young Fidel Castro had managed to fight back against Batista for two years. His guerilla army, initially billeted in the Sierra Maestra mountains, had gradually spread throughout the country, thereby reducing the extent of the authority of the Batistan government. Eight days after the planned departure of Batista, the revolutionary Castro arrived victoriously in Havana.

The Americans were dismayed at this news; a gang of uncontrollable youths, most in their twenties, had taken over power in a country that the Americans considered part of their 'back-yard'. For the American government, it was a question of an inadmissible attack on the security of the United States. However, it was not that clear-cut ; ex-president Batista no longer had a good name in Cuban society and the arrival of Castro was in fact viewed with some relief in Washington. The CIA itself experienced some difficulties in determining the personality and the intentions of the new master of Cuba.

Giving evidence before a senatorial commission, the director of the CIA, Allen Dulles, gave a surprising analysis of Castro :

"He is not working for the communists, furthermore he has no fondness for them."

The director continued : "Castro benefits from very wide popular support and an American intervention would be, for the moment, counter-productive"...

Less than a month later Dulles started to be more reasonable. More and more reports noted a communist penetration in the machinery of the Cuban government.

This did not, however, prevent Fidel Castro from visiting the United States in April 1959 and meeting vice-president Nixon. This semi-official visit was a triumphant success. Castro signed autographs and kissed children and the crowds that came to see the revolutionary grew in number with each day that passed.

Castro proclaimed that he was not a communist. Few believed him, or wanted to believe him, even if some American politicians preferred to see a nationalist rather than a communist in this young lawyer from a rich family.

This way of seeing things did not last. Under the pressure of events, and facing an American opposition without concessions, the Castro regime became more radical. At the same time the communists confirmed their implantation in all key posts of power in Havana. With nationalization and agricultural improvements, Castro developed his programme of reforms to be in alignment with Moscow.

With Castro, the CIA had found a good bone to chew on the very doorstep of the United States. Because they hadn't seen Castro coming, or because they didn't know how to stop him, the CIA, from November 1959, engaged in the struggle against the new leader of Cuba, with its objective being to chase him from power. It's a struggle which lasts to this day.

OPERATION PLUTO

In February 1960, the United States issued an embargo on all weapons to Cuba. Several days later a French freighter, 'La Coubre', which was transporting ammunition from Belgium, exploded mysteriously in the port of Havana. This was the climax in a series of skirmishes between Cubans and Americans. Castro showed his irritation by seizing, in a single strike, all American property on the island, this amounted to nearly a thousand million dollars.

During the last few months of 1960 the CIA started to prepare a vast military operation to overthrow Fidel Castro and Che Guevara. The code name was Operation Pluto.

A direct intervention on Cuban territory was definitely not a novelty for the Americans. After the island was released from Spanish control at the end of the 19th century, the Americans gave themselves the right of direct intervention in the domestic affairs of the island.Several landings of Marines took place throughout the first part of the 20th century, until the Platt amendment, which officially authorized the American government to interfere in Cuban affairs, was repealed by the Roosevelt administration in 1934.

In 1960, there was no question of legal intervention in broad daylight.Nonetheless Eisenhower authorized the use of American soldiers to train anti-Castro troops in Guatamala (Miami and Panama considered too indiscreet). But he was absolutely against any use of American armed forces directly in combat, to the detriment of his vice-president Richard Nixon who wished to have a victorious military adventure involving the American armed forces against the public enemy number one of the moment. A success would have reflected on him. He was at that time a Presidential candidate in the forthcoming elections.

The CIA also supported an anti-Castro guerrilla army in Cuba with rather limited manpower. Initially, the Americans wanted to reinforce this guerrilla army so it could depose the leader itself. But by the autumn of 1960, the strengthening of the position of Castro, the reinforcements of his army and the arrival of heavy armaments from Eastern Europe rendered this situation null and void. Without adding that Castro enjoyed real prestige in his country which rendered the idea of any popular uprising illusive.

The CIA pledged itself therefore to an 'anonymous' operation and was prepared to be generous with the resources. Involving several hundred combatants, with the consequent air and naval power, Operation Pluto was beginning to resemble a veritable war operation. Originally it was estimated to cost 13 million dollars, but the final cost was more than 100 million. This excessiveness was yet more amplified by the electoral campaign between Nixon and Kennedy, during which both men took an anti-Castro stance. (It is worthy of note that a short time before, in September 1960, Castro was in America for a short trip during which he met, in a Harlem hotel, the Soviet number one Nikita Kruschev who was on an official visit to the United States...)

In November 1960, Allen Dulles met the newly elected President John F. Kennedy to inform him of the operations in progress. Dulles was accompanied by Richard Bissel assistant director of operations. Bissel was in fact responsible for all secret operations. He was also the power behind Dulles' throne. He was the man whose name never appeared but who nonetheless held the real power, who enabled operations decided at the highest level to be translated into action. His power was enormous.

Bissel was also very well known for being very persuasive when it was necessary to sell an idea or a project. This persuasive force was used with a great deal of talent when he had to present Operation Pluto to Kennedy.

"Mr. President, if we have your agreement, we are going to land several hundred anti-Castro combatants on the south coast of Cuba. They will secure a bridgehead which will enable them to proclaim a provisional government. The popular uprising will then enable them to march on Havana and put an end to Castro."

The proclamation of a provisional government solidly anchored on Cuban soil was essential to give a semblance of legitimacy to the movement. If need be it would even provide a pretext for the United States to carry out a direct intervention.

The plan was subject to the restrictions of political considerations and it underwent several re-arrangements throughout the weeks.

SOME UNWELCOME CHANGES

As a result of political pressure the CIA changed from day-time to night operations, as it was believed that the dark would help to conceal their activities. The CIA objected that a landing carried out secretly would not have the desired psychological effect of sweeping along the crowds behind the anti-Castro troops. On the contrary, Kennedy had insisted that American participation be as invisible as possible, and that the landing operations bear as little resemblance as possible to those that were seen during the second world war. Of course Kennedy's viewpoint won the day. The CIA had to make an effort to ensure that all operations kept a slightly 'amateur' aspect, so that it was conceivable that it could have been carried out by anti-Castro troops operating alone. As we will see, this part of the bargain was fulfilled beyond all expectations.

After several reversals of policy, la Bahia de Cochinos, the Bay of Pigs, near the village of Giron, was chosen as a landing zone. Two distinct beaches, about twenty-five miles apart, were retained to receive the anti-Castro brigade which were deployed in two distinct forces.

The Bay of Pigs had been chosen by Castro for the construction of a sort of holiday village with several dozen chalets. These chalets were in the process of being built and the area was still empty of people. Next to the beach there was an airfield with an airstrip nearly a mile long which offered excellent logistical possibilities.

Aerial reconnaissance photos taken at very high altitude had confirmed that the zone would be difficult to reach from inland as it was surrounded by marshes. There were only two roads which crossed these marshy areas and the nature of the terrain would stop any vehicles from leaving the road to seek shelter in the surrounding vegetation. It was therefore an ideal area for preventing any Castro counter-attack and facilitating the consolidation of a bridgehead.

Kennedy insisted on a very specific point : there must never be, at any time, any question of any direct American intervention. The CIA had to do everything to form and train the anti-Castro brigade and then direct it on to the landing beaches, for the rest it would have to manage on its own.

This notion was not always very clear in the minds of the anti-Castro brigade who were sometimes carried away with the idea that the Americans would always be behind them, to take the lead if things did not go as planned.

There was a certain amount of opposition to the plan such as it was, not only within the CIA, but also the armed forces. Several superior officers involved in the preparation of the operation felt that the amphibious part could not succeed without a lot more planning. The anti-Castro movement had expanded to be a strong brigade of 1,300 men. Was it enough to hold off Castro forces ten times that number?

General Shoup, commander in chief of the Marines commented : "If this type of operation can succeed with this type of soldier and this type of training, then the existence of the US Marines is a complete waste of time. We may as well be on leave three months out of every four."

Other critics concentrated on the logistical aspect of the operation : it was planned that ships of the brigade would unload their cargo (provisions, ammunition, means of support) onto beaches which had absolutely no infrastructure.

"Even with no adversary it would be difficult" predicted the Marines. "With any fighting on the beaches it would be, quite simply, impossible."

The CIA swept away these arguments. "Enough pessimism! In any case the Cubans will not react. They will be completely disorganized by preventive air-strikes. There will be no opposition on the beaches"...

Besides, the CIA was counting on a massive popular acceptance of their stance. Not everyone was quite as confident. Even if the landing was successful, some saw themselves engaged in endless street fighting against the Castro troops.

"I had grave doubts about the operation" said John Kennedy afterwards, while acknowledging the fact that he had been astounded by both the scale and audacity of the operation. If the operation had been a success maybe its official code name would have gone down in history. But writers and historians preferred to retain the rather ridiculous name of the Bay of Pigs for what was the greatest fiasco in the history of the CIA.

As one commentator later said, it was 'the perfect failure'.

A LIBERATION AIR FORCE

In order to support ground troops and to neutralize Cuban aircraft, the CIA created, almost out of nothing, a "Liberation Air Force". Harry Aderholt, a veteran of special operations in Korea was in charge of the task.

The principal worry of the CIA was to conceal its role in the operation. In order to do this, the CIA started by creating or buying different companies with the responsibility of overseeing the different phases. Southern Air Transport was in charge of logistics. This company, which was in a fairly bad financial state, was bought by the CIA for the moderate sum of 307,506 dollars. It possessed only one aircraft, a C-46 Commando.

The Double Check Corporation took charge of recruiting American pilots, whereas Cuban exiles were engaged by the Caribbean Marine Aero Corporation. As for Zenith Technical Enterprises Inc., it had the responsibilty of technical support.

In order to relieve the United States of any responsibility whatsoever, it was essential that the CIA give credit to the rumour of an internal revolution. It was also important that the media believed that the aircraft which were to open the attack on Castro troops had taken off from Cuba itself. In order to create this illusion two departure bases were chosen by Aderholt outside the United States. Both were in Central America; one in Guatamala with the code name Rayo base which was used principally for training, whereas the main one was in Nicaragua, at Puerto Cabenzas, code name Happy Valley.

"Provided the price was right, the Nicaraguan leaders were not particular concerning American activity in their country" noted Aderholt. Tachito Somoza, brother of the strong man of the country, was an enthusiastic aviator. He had learnt to fly in the United States, and in 1956, became the Commander in Chief of the Nicaraguan Air Force. He occupied himself modernizing structures and material, with the ambition of making it the most powerful in Central America. Having served as a rear base during operation Success against Guatamala, Nicaragua was thanked by the United States with several of the P-47s which had been used in the Coup d'Etat.

Somoza was very keen to renew this type of operation, which was very fruitful for him, as the CIA explained to President Kennedy. They came to an agreement with Somoza that several of their planes would be left at the end of hostilities.

Nicaragua however had a serious handicap, its distance from the theatre of operation.

"It was a 1,300 mile, six-hour return flight over the sea. We were not exactly pleased with this arrangement" recalls Captain Farias, an old member of the Somozist air force and a Cuban exile.

Forty or so Cuban pilots exiled in the United States were selected by the CIA throughout 1960. The selection was carried out in anonymous offices in Miami, rented for the occasion by the CIA. Like Farias, they were all sincere opponents of the Castro regime. "Who would risk their life for $200 a month without having strong convictions"? they said.

The CIA interrogated them concerning their piloting experience. Several had served in the Cuban Air Force or Navy. Others came from the civilian sector, from local cargo companies or the national airline Cubana Airlines. Eduardo Ferrer was one of them. "We were asked questions for four days, for ten hours a day. Our past history, political convictions, our experience as a pilot, even our sexual habits; everything!" he said.

Several days passed, then Ferrer and 45 other pilots were called to a new address in Miami, in fact it was the headquarters of Cuban exiles.

The men came one evening to the indicated address. There they exchanged all their personal belongings for fatigue dress and a name badge, on which their pseudonym was written. Ferrer and the others had plunged into the world of secrecy.

Several minutes were required to ask regulation administrative questions, then the men were regrouped and piled into a lorry which immediately set off on its way.

"The journey lasted an eternity" recalls Ferrer. "I later learnt that we had simply been driven to the airport at Opa-Locka, a journey that should have lasted no more than forty minutes. But the level of secrecy was such that the lorry made a great number of detours. We eventually arrived after a drive of three hours!"

Opa-Locka airfield was bathed in semi-darkness. The pilots embarked in a four-engine C-54 where the windows had been made opaque. No nationality mark was visible. The crew spoke with a strong European accent. The mystery deepened.

When the doors opened again after a flight of seven hours, the Cuban pilots were astounded to discover that they had arrived in Guatamala. After a long and difficult journey by road, they were set up next to anti-Castro troops who were also training in Guatamala. The installations were very improvised, whereas the airstrip, their very reason for being there, wasn't even finished. Their training was delayed as a result. The situation improved in September, the airstrip was at last completed and the pilots were rehoused in more acceptable barracks. Morale improved greatly when training was able to begin.

FIRST MISSIONS OVER CUBA

The pilots had to be trained with C-46 and C-54 transport planes, often very different from those which they had flown in previously. They carried out practice flights around the airfield and sometimes parachute drops.

"Our aircraft bore no markings, but they were all in excellent mechanical condition", remembers Ferrer. "We realised very soon after that the planes had most probably come from China, as we discovered Chinese writing on certain places!" Proof that the cleaning of the aircraft, following secret operations in Asia, had not been carried out with the necessary rigour. The 'Liberation Air Force' had five C-46s and seven C-54s at Happy Valley.

The training followed its natural course, with the usual bevy of incidents and accidents. Following a particularly hard landing, a C-46 collapsed onto its belly. The landing gear was destoyed and the Cuban trainee pilot, suffering from crushed vertebrae, was repatriated to the United States to be operated on. Several days later, a four-engine C-54 damaged the tip of its wing. The plane finished its flight and landed on a deserted beach. Considered irreparable, it was abandoned where it had landed.

At the beginning of October 1960, the aircraft based in Guatamala took part in their first missions above Cuba, in preparation for operation Pluto. It involved resupplying by air anti-Castro underground forces set up in the Escambray mountains in the centre of the island. A C-54 carried out the first mission.

Instead of finding a guerrilla welcome committee, the plane was welcomed by heavy firing. The number four engine was destroyed, there were several hits in the fuselage and the wings and the C-54 just made it to the Mexican coast where it crash-landed.

After this disastrous beginning, Operation Pluto was very nearly terminated. The Cuban crews had received very precise orders from the CIA :

"In the event of any problem, you must not, under any circumstances, seek refuge in Guatanamo, you will be immediately handed over to Cuban authorities." (When the Americans had given back Cuba to Spain, they had the pleasure in keeping a large military base on the east coast of the island. Isolated from the rest of the island by a double cordon of barbed wire and mines, nobody really knew who was being protected from who. Guantanamo is still today an American enclave in Cuban territory.) If you land in hostile territory, you must set fire to your aircraft by firing at the tank. If you have to land at sea, choose an area where the depth is sufficient for the aircraft to be irretrievable. If it happens at night, choose an area away from any light source etc..."

The Cuban pilots had difficulty in accepting these orders uncomplainingly : "These guys are completely crazy. To ask us to look out for the darkest places to carry out a sea landing is tantamount to suicide!"... Nonetheless because of the immense presige that the CIA had, the pilots put their trust in them.

The day after the first failed mission, Eduardo Ferrer took off with another C-54 for another parachute drop over Cuba. He was carrying around five tons of supplies for the guerrillas. Determined to carry out his mission as effectively as possible, Ferrer set off for Cuba and a return journey of more than 1,300 miles.

"After an ordinary flight, we were able to see the island around midnight. We descended very low over the water to avoid being detected by possible radars, then we headed for our DZ (drop zone) in the interior of the country."

Arriving above the DZ, Ferrer and his co-pilot looked intently for the agreed reconnaissance sign, seven light markers arranged in an L shape formation. Nothing was visible. "We did a 360° turn, then a second, there was still nothing visible. When we started to circle for the third time, fire beacons were lit up. There were five, not seven, and they were not really arranged in the shape of an L." Ferrer decided nonetheless to drop the supplies.

Returning to Happy Valley, he informed the CIA officer of the progress of the mission. The American took careful note of everything that the Cuban said. Just when the pilot was about to leave he said : "One detail Ferrer, you do understand that as far as your comrades are concerned, this mission has been a complete success".

Compared to what was to follow, perhaps this mission could indeed be considered a success. Between the months of November 1960 and March 1961, Ferrer completed eleven parachute missions during which he only really saw his DZ just twice. Every time however, he dropped his load and relied solely on the accuracy of his navigation, and always hoped that there was someone on the ground to pick it up.

A total of 68 flights were organized to resupply the anti-Castro guerrillas. Few were real successes. The aircraft were very often hit by ground fire. They therefore were re-routed towards Jamaica or the Cayman islands. Conversely, the guerrillas complained of the risks that they had to take to reach the drop zones, with, in the majority of cases, the disappointment of not receiving anything.

On one occasion it happened that, as a result of an order from Miami, and with the sole aim of filling up the empty space in the aircraft, 100lb bags of rice and beans were dropped as well as the usual ammunition and supplies.

Apart from its incongruity (rice and beans were available in Cuba without having to be dropped from the sky), these drops led to a furious radio communication from the local guerrilla chief :

"Is everything all right? Those dam bags you dropped almost killed my men. And you expect us to carry such a weight to our camp?"

Evidently these supply missions were a failure and the Cuban pilots were only too aware of that.

At the end of 1960, their morale was at its lowest ebb. Missions were carried out only rarely, pilots were becoming frustrated and indeed began to doubt the justification of their activities.

Worse, the Cuban pilots were conspicuously segregated from the American instructors, who for example, had reserved access to the bar on the air base. Several pilots went on a symbolic strike, whereas thirteen others chose to abandon their collaboration with the American services. They were authorized to return to the United States but kept a low profile for several weeks, until Operation Pluto was completely finished.

THE B-26 ARRIVES

Pluto necessitated a very offensive use of anti-Castro aviation; combat aircraft came therefore to be added to cargo planes which operated from secret CIA bases.

A twin-engine was required not only for autonomy but also for flight safety. The B-26 Invader answered the needs of the CIA and was also widely available in American stocks. Apart from its recognized offensive capacities, its range, with extra fuel tanks carried under the wings, enabled it to remain nearly two hours above Cuba leaving from Nicaragua.

A lucky coincidence was the fact that the Cuban air force also used this type of plane, which it had inherited from Batista. By disguising its aircraft with Cuban colours, it was easier for the CIA to make the fact of an internal uprising believable. Twenty, possibly even thirty, were released from US Air Force stocks. Intermountain Aviation, another CIA cover, took charge of the operation and of the reconditioning of the planes.

All that remained was to train Cuban pilots with their new aircraft and familiarize them with their new missions.

The CIA made a courtesy visit to General George Doster who was in command of the Air National Guard of Alabama. The Alabama ANG had the peculiarity of having been the last regular American unit to have flown the B-26. Its pilots possessed therefore a valuable experience with twin-engine propeller aircraft that the CIA was keen to profit from.

84

In the American system, the Air National Guard is in fact a reserve force made up of civilians who regularly undergo periods of training. Because of this very particular experience, certain pilots had already had the opportunity of working for the CIA elsewhere. Doster's men and the CIA knew each other, Doster was welcoming and the CIA stressed the importance of the mission they would be involved in :

"General, we need your help. It concerns a mission of the utmost importance for the security of the United States.

"You have my support. What can I do for you?" asked Doster.

The CIA wanted above all to know the number of pilots and technicians with a good knowledge of the B-26 and who would be available for a mission of a few weeks. After making the general swear to secrecy the men of the CIA admitted the objective of the operation :

"To overthrow Castro"...

"About time! I will try and find you all the men you need."

General Doster was delighted and made a first class recruiter.

Several days were all he needed to bring together 80 pilots and mechanics of all specialities. The majority came from Alabama, but not all. Doster unearthed some of his old contacts from Arkansas and other states in the South.

In spite of very strict orders concerning secrecy, a rumour spread very quickly through the Alabama guard that something unusual was about to happen. Some specialists disappeared from one day to the next.

"Change of posting", came Doster's enigmatic reply.

An initial briefing took place in the National Guard buildings at Birmingham airport.

A civilian introduced himself to a group of twenty or so voluntary pilots. He remained vague but explained that the mission consisted of supporting national pilots during a combat mission, somewhere in the south. It was training only, there was no question of a direct intervention. All the pilots present were sure that the man had come from the CIA, and that Cuba was the country concerned.

"If you accept, you will receive a new identity. You'll be paid $2,800 a month."

A pilot stood up at the back of the room, "If anything happens to me, will my wife be taken care of?"

"She will receive $550 every month for the rest of her life. I think these are acceptable conditions."

They were indeed excellent conditions and all the pilots present chose to play a part in the adventure.

Once the selection had been completed, the American pilots followed the identical and tortuous path that, several months earlier, had led Cuban pilots to Guatamala.

At Rayo base and Happy Valley, the thin silhouettes of the B-26s were alongside the larger C-46 and C-54 cargo planes. Nearly three hundred men, 150 Cubans and as many Americans were employed in the secret air force. The training of the Cubans on the light bomber commenced. It was a new experience for the American instructors. The Cubans were in a good frame of mind, their morale had improved when they had started flying with the B-26. Working with them however was not always very easy :

"Their aeronautical experience was often quite limited", explained an instructor, "they did not always have the same notion of discipline as us."

One question however was uppermost in the minds of the Cubans : the B-26 had no self-protection. The defensive armament, in fact a top turret equipped with two 12.7mm machine guns, had been removed to lighten the plane and allow it to carry more fuel.

The American instructors explained there would be no need of defensive weapons, as Cuban aircraft would be destroyed on the ground within the first few minutes of the operation.

The Americans also ambiguously referred to the existence of a protective 'umbrella' over the anti-Castro force. A US Navy aircraft carrier would be present within the zone throughout the duration of the whole operation. The Cubans readily believed in a US fighter intervention in the event of a serious problem. In the mind of the American commander in Chief the situation was very clear however, any direct intervention was prohibited.

The idea of having the B-26s protected by 'anonymous' jets was raised then swiftly put to one side : a rapid reaction combat plane was simply too sophisticated to be seen to be part of a rebel force. The American signature would have been there for all to see.

The question of the protection of the B-26 was rapidly resolved, it was sufficient to destroy all Cuban aviation on the ground and the problem would be solved.

The CIA would have to be certain not to delay the launch of the operation as Castro was about to receive several MiGs from the USSR. The pilots were being trained in Czechoslovakia.

CASTRO IS ALERTED

Before the invasion of the island, the B-26 was used to test the Cuban defences and drop leaflets appealing for the population to rise up.

"The missions could last up to eight or nine hours" remembers a pilot. "Cuban defences had to be tested, and it was necessary to identify the location of anti-aircraft batteries. On the way we flew over villages and dropped leaflets."

In other instances, the action of the planes was closely coordinated with the presence of American ships with electronic listening equipment present in international waters. A B-26 penetrated Cuban airspace, set in motion the anti-aircraft defence systems while the Americans, listening to the radio frequencies, noted the reactions and procedures of the Cubans. These missions were a complete success and enabled accurate information to be collected.

On the other hand, they only served to reinforce Castro's certainty that an operation was being prepared against him. In fact, the Cuban leader was in danger of collapsing under the weight of all the signs and indications: if his agents present in Guatamala, near the training camps, or in Miami, in the heart of the Cuban community were not enough, then it would have been enough to read the press. The Guatamalan dailies initially, and then the American press, were echoing the growing agitation within the anti-Castro force. On the 27th January 1961, Time magazine published a photo of a CIA plane at the base in Guatamala. The existence of training camps was mentioned. Everyone knew the American government wanted to fight. The real questions were where, when and how.

Castro did not anticipate a popular uprising against him. His prestige was immense within the heart of the population and the first reforms undertaken gave him a great popularity. Justifiably, he feared the establishment by force of a bridgehead on Cuban territory and the proclamation of a provisional government which would have given a semblance of legality to a direct intervention by the United States.

Despite his insight, he was nonetheless mistaken on one point : never for a single moment did he imagine that the invasion froces would only number 1,300 men. In his most pessimistic estimation, he thought he would have to fight against 10,000 men. At the very best, he thought the landing would involve 3,000 men.

The Cuban government increased official preventive measures against any American aggression. It seemed that the whole of Latin America was aware of what was brewing : pro-American heads of state of the region went as far as to warn the United States against any ill-considered operation.

Kennedy was also anxious, but for different reasons. He had asked for several last-minute adjustments, but he nonetheless gave the green light for the launch of the operation, the landing would take place on Monday 17th April at dawn.

Foreseeing, with every passing day, the vastness of the operation that was being prepared, the doubts of the American President grew. But faced with the quiet reassurance of the CIA Directors, he could not bring himself to abandon it. However, wanting to make concrete his internal doubts, he imposed serious restrictions on the use of the air force.

He insisted in particular that the air strikes involved the responsibility of the United States as little as possible. That translated into fewer raids with fewer planes. Two missions of fifteen or so planes each were originally planned for the day before the landing (D-1) and D day itself. They were replaced by a single mission of six aircraft on D-2, the 15th April. Despite these cutbacks, Kennedy still found the air raids too 'noisy' vis a vis the international community. The ideal situation in his eyes would have been to get rid of the pro-Castro air threat without flying a single plane.

This change was a gross error which carried within it the seeds of a painful defeat. Through wanting to adjust the military operations to fit in with the political obligations of the moment, Operation Pluto lost, little by little, its coherence. In a surprising turnabout, the raid on D-2 served more to substantiate the idea of a revolt within the Castro forces rather than to eradicate the Cuban air force.

If there had only been a single aircraft involved, the responsibility of the Americans would have been the same. But with only six B-26s retained, the 'right hook' that should have knocked out Castro within the first minutes of the fight singularly lacked power.

Not only was Fidel Castro able to save part of his air force, but he also benefited from a generous 48 hour warning before the main attack. The aces were in his hand and he knew how to use them with consummate artistry.

The planners of the CIA had however seen the danger and had several times warned against restrictions in the use of the forces.

"The operation will have to be abandoned if political restrictions do not enable us to have the necessary means to obtain an adequate aerial support" they wrote in a memorandum. A memorandum which went, of course, unheeded.

A further snub, the raid on D-2 should have coincided with a diversion landing in the east of the island. This did not take place, the 170 Cubans who were to carry it out preferred to cancel it; Castro patrols had been spotted on the selected beaches.

As surprising as it may seem, the assailants were not informed by the CIA, because of the cult of secrecy, that their landing was in fact an important diversion operation. They had simply been told that they were to land in order to support the guerrilla army already present in the area. They had judged that such a mission was not worth their sacrifice.

THE B-26S ATTACK CUBA : OPERATION PUMA

Happy Valley, Saturday 15th April 1961. 0200 hours.

In the dead of night there was feverish activity on the secret base. Mechanics and armourers were busying themselves around the B-26s. This time it's certain, the attack is set for today.

Three missions of two planes each were planned. Gustavo Ponzoa, the ex-pilot of a national Cuban air company had to be the leader of one of them. He did not take off. They had the use of sixteen planes but they had to fight with only six aircraft.

Walking in the darkness several steps behind him, his navigator confirmed the pilot's fears with a grunt. The subject had been discussed at great length in the previous hours.

The men who were leaving to fight did not understand the CIA decision to reduce intentionally their attack force by engaging only a third of the planes available.

Would they be able to neutralize Castro's air force with this reduced strength? Some had serious doubts.

All night long the pilots were assembled for a detailed briefing around an immense map of Cuba which practically covered the entire wall in one of their barrack huts. The "big shots" from the CIA came from Langley, they detailed the objectives which had to be attacked :

"The recapture of Cuba will commence with your planes. In the very early morning you will attack three Cuban military airports: Campo Libertad the airport at Havana, San Antonio de Los Banos thirty miles south west of the capital and Antonio Maceo airport at Santiago de Cuba, at the eastern end of the island."

When he learnt that he was to lead the raid on Santiago de Cuba, Ponzoa could not help bursting with laughter; he knew the airport like the back of his hand as he had been based there for almost twelve years.

Despite that, Ponzoa and the other pilots studied the objective very carefully. The Americans had brought some extraordinary photos with them taken at high altitude by U-2 reconnaissance planes. Military craft positioned on the apron, the AAA sites, the trenches surrounding the parking could all be seen very clearly. And there at the edge of a civilian car park, buried fuel tanks were detectable which would also be an objective for him and his aircraft.

Images floated through Ponzoa's mind as he made his way slowly towards his plane. The temperature was mild and the cloudless sky seemed like an extraordinary heavenly canopy.

"My country will soon be free" he thought.

He reached his B-26 number 929. The weapon fitters were checking the security systems on the weapons : two 550lb explosive bombs and eight 275lb fragmentation bombs were suspended in the bomb bay. In addition, the twin-engine transported eight rockets under the wings. The eight nose machine guns were supplied with 2,080 rounds. Accompanied by the chief mechanic, Ponzoa carried out a rapid pre-flight check of the plane, a torch in his hand. Everything seemed to be in order. It was time to get on board.

Ponzoa climbed into the cockpit, this rather acrobatic exercise seemed a little peculiar in the near darkness which reigned over the apron. Left foot, right hand, right foot... the pilot and his navigator scaled the fuselage using footholds which enabled them to reach the top of the wing. From there they slid into the cockpit through the windscreen. The threatening silhouette of the two Pratt and Whitney engines were at the same height as the pilot. In the half-light the propellers were turned...once then twice. The mechanics checked that the oil had not accumulated at the bottom of the cylinders of the large radial engines.

The chief mechanic raised his thumb indicating that everything was in order. Ponzoa replied:

"Ready to start the left engine?"

"Ready!"

Fuel pump on High, mixture on full-rich. Contact! The engine spluttered, snorting like bolting horses that had suddenly been freed. The oil pressure rose correctly, everything was fine. Ponzoa went through the same sequence for the right engine. It was 0220 hours.

Last check over the engine parameters, oil temperature, temperature of the cylinder heads, everything seemed OK. After several minutes of warming up, the heavily laden aircraft started to move towards the runway. As well as bombs and rockets, all the planes carried extra tanks under their wings which would enable them to fly for more than seven hours. Loaded with fuel, the planes weighed almost 19 tons, the maximum for a B-26 at take-off. It was too much to be able to fly on a single engine in case of difficulties...

To take off at night with such a heavily laden B-26 is not an easy exercise. For the Cuban crews it was, however, a relief. The waiting and the uncertainty were over. It was their moment to act, the outcome of their country was in their hands. The opportunity had arisen and they were not going to let it pass.

At 0230 hours, with the roaring of the 2,000hp R-2800 engines, the first B-26s left the runway at Happy Valley. The die was cast!

SATURDAY 15TH APRIL, D-2

After several minutes flying, cruising height was reached. In his aircraft Gustav Ponzoa adjusted the throttle to select an economic cruising speed. The minutes passed, the patrols formed up, the radios remained silent. After three hours of flying the horizon was beginning to lighten, the sign that dawn was not far off. Ponzoa was vaguely able to make out the profile of the Cuban coast in the far distance. But before reaching it, they had to pass via Jamaica in the West Indies.

Only a brief glance was necessary to cover the whole island from Kingston on the right and Montego bay on the left. Santiago de Cuba was at least 100 miles to the north east.

Ponzoa left his comfortable altitude and let his plane descend to be only a few feet above the waves. It was unlikely that Castro had any radars covering the approach to the island, but the CIA had decided not to run any risks. The last 60 miles were therefore crossed at great speed and practically at sea level, under the radar detection zone.

Radio silence was still being strictly maintained. It was now fully daylight.

Ponzoa concentrated on piloting his plane ; one careless error and it would hit the surface of the sea, disintegrate and their amazing adventure would be over.

More or less at the same moment, another B-26 was preparing to land at Miami airport. The aircraft was not announced and a plume of smoke, which seemed to be coming from its right engine, trailed behind it. The airport emergency services were alerted and as soon as it had stopped, the plane was surrounded by different security vehicles.

The aircraft was a source of intrigue. Clearly visible on the fin was a Cuban flag next to the figures 933 and the letters FAR, standing for Fuerza Aerea Revolucionaria. The number 933 was repeated at the fore of the fuselage, while a Castro roundel adorned the rear. For all the Americans present, there was absolutely no doubt : this was a Castro craft!

The pilot made a sign to show he was unarmed. Under the surveillance of the airport police he unfastened his equipment and jumped to the ground.

"My name is Mario Zuniga and I want political asylum in the United States." Zuniga repeated his story to the press gathered at the scene, a pilot of Fidel Castro, he had fled Cuba on board his plane. On the way he had attacked the air base from where he had taken off, San Antonio de Los Banos, in an attempt to destroy several aircraft on the ground.

"I was hit by flak in the right engine during the attack" he explained. "I never thought I would get this far." The bullet holes on the right engine were there for all to see. The American authorities announced that the name of the pilot would be kept secret so that his family in Cuba would not suffer any reprisals. Some photos were taken by the reporters present. Even though Zuniga was hiding his face with his hands, his family and friends would recognize him on pictures which would appear in the newspapers the following day.

Everyone was asking themselves the same question ; why would Zuniga tell such an escape story when he had already been in the United States for several months?

The journalists thought they had a remarkable story. But they soon were surprised by several details which did not seem to correspond to the account which they had just heard: one of them noticed that the weapons on board the aircraft had not been used, the protective covers were still in place, conflicting with what the pilot had just said. Also, it was not clear why the name of the pilot was held secret. Castro would have known which pilot had left Cuba that very morning with a B-26 coded 933!

With a little reflection, the whole affair seemed like a set-up. Indeed if the aircraft was a real B-26, everything else was false in this adventure which had been set up by the CIA in order to give substance to the theory of an internal uprising in Cuba.

Based, along with the other aircraft, in Nicaragua, the B-26 piloted by Zuniga had taken off from Happy Valley in the night, its destination being Miami. A little earlier a CIA crew had removed the right engine cover to riddle it with bullets, to make it appear they had been hit with flak. The covers were then put back in place. Zuniga had himself added the finishing touches when he arrived in sight of Miami, by firing the contents of his automatic pistol at the right engine.

Spurred on by Fidel Castro's vehement protests, the press had, in the following hours had the time to devote itself to a simple game of 'spot the difference' on the aircraft and the cover. Rapidly the CIA set up fell to pieces. The agency had, in particular, made a significant mistake : Zuniga's B-26 (and all those in Operation Pluto) was a B-26B, the ground attack version of the B-26, equipped with eight 12.7mm machine guns in the nose. However, the Cuban Air Force only had B-26C in flying condition and these were equipped with a plexiglass nose to permit the installation of a bomber-navigator.

"We were aware of this mistake" a CIA member admitted later. "But at that time, we did not know with certainty the version used by the Cubans."

An agent working for the Americans had indeed taken several photos on Cuban bases, to allow the decoration to be copied. But the resulting pictures were of bad quality and did not enable a decision to be made concerning the version used. After having officially asked for poitical asylum, Mario Zuniga rejoined Happy Valley in Nicaragua to carry on the fight alongside his comrades. The CIA had sixteen B-26 at their disposal, the majority were heavily armed with eight 12.7mm machine guns in the nose. Like the 933 that had landed at Miami, all the aircraft had received the markings of the Cuban air force, so as to spread confusion among the pro-Castro troops. On some planes, the registration numbers painted on the fuselages corresponded to numbers that were in actual use in Cuba.

A second B-26 false deserter, whose arrival at Opa-Locka airport was not subject to media scrutiny, was also used that same day to substantiate the idea of an internal revolution.

The most surprising thing happened several hours after this clumsy scenario : a real Cuban pilot landed in Florida to ask for political asylum!

Ponzoa was now a mere fifteen or so miles from the coast and Santiago de Cuba.

The Cuban pilot got ready to experience the longest minutes of his life as a pilot. The moment is forever engraved on his memory :

"Several minutes before reaching the coast, we flew over a ship, most likely belonging to the Cuban coast guard; we had been seen! The ship started to exchange light signals with the airport control tower, a small distance from the shore. It was too late for them, together with my wing man I literally flew the plane just above the waves. In a few more seconds we were going to be able to fire our first shots."

The engines were pushed to the maximum. The external loads were armed, the bomb bay doors opened. The two planes hopped over the strip of vegetation which marked out the shore and then gained a little height to discover their target.

"Herrera then positioned himself on my left to machine gun the anti-aircraft defences. I started my first run by dropping my two 550lb bombs on buried fuel tanks." It was a direct hit! The tanks exploded and threw a thick column of flames and smoke into the sky. A DC-3 nearby was blown away by the explosion. Ponzoa saw from the corner of his eye a wing of a plane fly through the air like a feather, as if in slow motion. How strange, thought Ponzoa, that DC-3 was one of the planes that I flew when I was based here.

On the ground the effect of surprise had been total, but the flak had been very rapid. The two assailants finished their first strafing pursued by the first heavy machine gun fire from the anti-aircraft defence.

Staying very low, Ponzoa and Herrera carried out a 180° turn and prepared for a second attack.

"During the second passage, I attacked the anti-aircraft positions and Herrera dropped fragmentation bombs on hangars and B-26s on the ground. It was difficult to appreciate the effect of these attacks because of the thick smoke which was starting to cover everything"... The anti-aircraft fire was beginning to react with great vigour. The two aircraft which had gone a long way from the coast to regroup and start on a third passage were followed by tracers. There was complete chaos on the ground. Ponzoa still had his fragmentation bombs, rockets and several hundred rounds of ammunition in the machine guns. He returned to fire against the aircraft present on the parking. When everything was on fire, he shot his last rounds of ammunition at a hangar which had remained intact. The building exploded in a riot of flames.

"We were terribly excited," remembers Ponzoa. "My wingman and I talked over the radio all the time to find out where we were, to coordinate our attacks. The codes had been forgotten, we called each other by our first names..."

A fourth, then a fifth attack left nothing on the ground except smoking ruins. The Castro B-26s exploded on the ground. The control tower was destroyed by rocket fire.

The attack lasted nearly twenty-five minutes, an incredibly long time in the middle of all this hell. The two attacks had exhausted all their ammunition, bombs, rockets and machine guns. They themselves had also been hit. Ponzoa and his wingman had felt several impacts in the airframe of their plane. Luckily the engines and controls were intact.

The way back was to be at very low altitude. After one hour's flying, estimating they were sufficiently far from Cuba to no longer risk being caught by fighters, the two aircraft took a bit of height and started a mutual inspection. Ponzoa examined his wingman's plane :

"You have several impacts at the rear of the fuselage and one landing gear is hanging half open. The engines and wings seem intact. There is also a trail of hydraulic fluid on the fuselage".

"Received. The plane is vibrating a little but all indications are that the engines are OK. We should make it."

The two planes reached their base at Nicaragua without incident. If the attack was a success for Ponzoa and Herrera, the results were rather mixed for the other crews.

AND FIRST LOSSES

During the attack against San Antonio de Los Banos and Campo Libertad, two assailants' B-26s were heavily damaged. Unable to return to their base of departure, they were forced to re-route. One landed at

Key West, on US Navy territory, the other turned towards British terrain in the Cayman Islands. A third plane was shot down by anti-aircraft fire and was destroyed in the sea near the Cuban coast. Its crew was reported missing.

The most important thing was that the overall objective of these raids had not been fulfilled. It was imperative to destroy Cuban aircraft on the ground so that they could not intervene in the landing planned for two days later. The six planes engaged in the raids had done a fairly good job but, because of a lack of numbers, they were not able to do any more.

While the assailants were on their long way home to their base, Castro was already calculating the strength of the force at his disposal; a major part of his combat aircraft had escaped the bombings. The CIA estimated that the Cuban Air Force had a dozen or so combat aircraft : six B-26, four T-33 and two or three Sea Fury. These estimations revealed themselves to be fairly accurate. The debriefing of the crews as well as photos brought back after the raids by U2 reconnaissance planes were positive : only five aircraft could be considered totally destroyed, including a T-33. The Cuban leader still had one or two Sea Furys, a powerful propeller fighter of British origin, two B-26s and two T-33s. Derived from one of the very first jet fighter models, the T-33 was originally an aircraft used for training. For the Americans who only used it as such, and for liaison purposes, it did not constitute a great threat. However, the Cuban T-33 had been equipped with 20mm cannons, which gave them appreciable offensive capacities. This important detail had escaped the CIA.

A second raid would have rapidly destroyed these survivng planes. But this second raid never came.

The Cuban victims of the bombing were buried the following day, during national funerals, attended by Fidel Castro.

The strong man of Cuba did not of course miss the opportunity to condemn the role played by the United States :

"The United States supplied the planes, the bombs and trained the mercenaries." He shouted at the large crowd who wanted revenge. "The yankees tried to deceive the whole world, but the whole world knows that behind all this is the CIA."

Castro then commented on the false-defection of a Cuban craft at Miami airport :

"Even Hollywood wouldn't want such a lousy script!"

Castro was at that time certain of the landings to come. He mobilized the 200,000 men of his popular militia and took great care to protect the planes he had left. The pilots remained permanently with their aircraft, they took turns to sit in the cockpit, ready to take off in case of any surprise attack.

Castro was ready to counter-attack. During this time the Americans kept a low profile and hid their involvement as much as possible.

To prevent any connection being made between the CIA and the operation in process, the director Allen Dulles kept up his work schedule that had been planned well in advance, he spent the weekend in Puerto Rico at a conference.

A short time before his departure, Robert Amory, assistant director of intelligence, exchanged several words with him. Amory was not supposed to know about the operation.

"Mr. Director, I am on duty Sunday and I'm not sure if you are aware, but I know a little of what's about to happen. What should I do if there's a problem with Cuba?"

Dulles paused. He stared at Amory and said simply "That is nothing to do with you."

Then he left for Puerto Rico. Amory said later that when he arrived at his office on the morning of Sunday 16th April, he saw several cables from Uruguay and Nigeria.

"I dealt with that for several hours, then I decided I'd had enough. I went home thinking 'Let them go to hell...'"

SUNDAY 16TH APRIL, D-1

As for President Kennedy, he was spending his weekend in his Glen Ora residence in Virginia. Like Dulles he had decided to follow a normal programme of activities so as not to alert the press.

After hesitating up to the last minute, he gave the go-ahead around midday for landing operations to begin the following day, Monday 17th

April. The ships had certainly been on their way for some 48 hours, but it was still possible to turn them back from their final destination and to abort the mission right up until the moment when the first men landed.

Kennedy decided to go forward with Operation Zapata, code name for the landings on the Cuban coast, which would indeed take place at dawn the following day. This question was settled but another problem arose; should he authorize a second air raid to knock out Cuban aircraft completely? For the people in charge of the operation the answer was yes. For the American administration, with a newly elected President at its head, nothing was certain. In the afternoon, Adlai Stevenson, United States ambassador to the UN, called Kennedy. All the weight of international condemnation fell on his shoulders.

"Mr. President" he said, "You must not launch any more air raids against Cuba, otherwise it will be clear for the whole world that the United States are solely responsible for the whole operation. There could be problems with the UN."

Even though he was aware of the risk that it represented for the expeditionary corps, Kennedy came into line with Stevenson's view. He ordered that no new air raid must be launched until the landing forces had taken possession of the runway situated near the beach. Once this objective had been reached, as many planes as necessary could be sent and the illusion that it was an internal Cuban conflict could be maintained. For the moment, it was out of the question to send a second raid from Nicaragua.

This decision had the effect of a cold shower on the men of the CIA. Without any anti-aircraft protection, the ships transporting the anti-Castro brigade ran the risk of experiencing a difficult time if Castro still had combat aircraft that were able to fly!

That same evening, Richard Bissel, accompanied by General Cabell, the assistant of Allen Dulles, met the Secretary of State Dean Rusk. He pleaded the case for a second series of raids.

"It's essential for the success of the operation" he explained. "If no more raids are launched, we run the risk of seeing Castro carry out aerial counter-attacks against the landing operations."

Rusk listened carefully to the arguments, then he called Kennedy at

Glen Ora. He explained Bissel's position, before concluding of his own opposition to any new raid.

Once again, the President fell in with the opinion of his secretary of state. On the Nicaraguan base of Happy Valley that Sunday evening they were preparing to send off the second wave of bombers which were to arrive at Cuba by dawn, just in time for the landings. The sea rescue plane, an ancient Catalina, had already taken off to position itself off Cuba. It would be there to try and pick up pilots who were forced to parachute into the sea in the case of any problem.

The message cancelling the raid arrived at the HQ of the air base amid a feeling of general disbelief.

What on earth was going on in Washington? It was as if they were banging their heads against a brick wall. In the game of poker that was being played, they were handing Castro a handful of trump cards.

The American in charge jumped into his jeep and raced towards the hardstand where the engines of the B-26s were already warming up. With one gesture of the hand he made a sign to the pilots to turn everything off.

Then he went to see Ponzoa who was supervising the refuelling of his plane.

"The raid is cancelled. We're going to have to wait 48 hours, the time for the landing beaches to be secured, before we can intervene again."

Ponzoa replied with a tirade of swearwords.

"How could they do such a thing?" Appalled, the Cuban pilots gathered under the wing of a plane. They all thought that it was a monstrous and unforgiveable tactical error. Some mentioned the possibility of taking over the airbase, eliminating the American guards and of launching the raid themselves.

"Unfortunately, things like that only happen in John Wayne films" one of them said.

As soon as they learnt news of the cancellation, different participants from the US Air Force or the US navy, which were bringing logistic aid to the assailants, could not hide their anger either. At 4 o'clock on Monday morning, when the landings were due to begin at any moment, General Cabell intervened. He went directly to find Dean Rusk, and woke him up. The American Navy had a sizeable fleet near Cuba, including the aircraft carrier Essex.

Cabell pleaded for a plan of direct intervention by the Essex.

"Couldn't the Essex at least be a support along with the fighters when the boats near the coast carry out the landings?" he asked.

Once again Rusk called Glen Ora. He woke the President and passed the receiver to Cabell.

"Explain yourself to the President." Kennedy listened carefully to Cabell then he asked to speak to Rusk. A brief conversation followed.

"It's no." Rusk said simply as he hang up.

MONDAY 17TH APRIL : FIASCO FOR ZAPATA

Thirteen hundred anti-Castro combatants on five landing boats were nearing the Cuban coast. Like the rest of the material for the operation, the boats had also been supplied by the CIA. They were small, wheezy cargo boats that were far from ideal for military operations, all the more so a landing. To bring heavy equipment to the beaches, the US Navy brought in one of its own landing ships, the San Marcos.

Unobtrusively in the night, several miles from the Cuban beaches, the San Marcos rejoined the invasion flotilla. Several landing barges loaded with heavy material came out of the hold along with lorries, jeeps and several tanks. Its mission accomplished, the San Marcos turned round and went back into the dark night as unobtrusively as it had arrived. With all this equipment ready, it was now the Cubans turn to play.

They were alone at that time, perhaps more so than they could ever have imagined.

When the landings began, more than forty-eight hours had passed since the first air raids against the air bases. The effect of surprise had long since gone.

From the beginning, Operation Zapata was a fiasco.

The invasion flotilla came into contact with an uncharted reef bank. In fact, the reef had indeed been seen on aerial photos taken during reconnaissance missions, but by an incredible mistake they were interpreted as being seaweed!

The invaders also had bad luck; when the reconnaissance elements of the assault forces reached the shore to mark out the beaches, they came face to face with a militia patrol. Contrary to what the intelligence services had predicted, the zone was not as deserted as all that. In the anticipation of the landings that he felt certain were coming, Castro had sent small detachments of a hundred or so men that could set off 'alarms' on every beach which was considered to be at risk. He had even accorded special attention to the bay of pigs that he knew well because he used to go fishing there. The area seemed to him to be particularly favourable for a landing and he had ordered an infantry battalion to be in position in the proximity. As a result of Cuban indolence, the battalion was not yet in position when the landings took place.

The militia unit present however fulfilled its role. Contrary to the hopes of the CIA, the militia showed no sympathy for the invasion force and rapidly gave the alarm by radio; Castro was immediately informed of the landing. The heavy units, with armoured vehicles and artillery, which were more than sixty miles from the zone, were immediately put into action.

From that moment on, deprived of the effect of surprise and of having superior material, the fate of the expeditionary force was sealed. From first light, Castro launched all available planes, in fact six aircraft against the ships of the brigade. Still occupied unloading soldiers and material when they should have been retreating to the sea before sunrise, they were sitting ducks. Opposed to any new raid against Cuban air bases, Kennedy however accepted the use of B-26s in the early hours of 17th April to support landing operations.

It was once again a bad idea; devoid of all means of self-protection, and in any case very badly designed for air to air combat against fighters, the B-26 rapidly found itself confronted by Castro fighters prowling above the beaches.

THE PLOT THICKENS

The B-26s took off from Happy Valley a little before 4 o'clock Monday morning, they reached the combat zone approximately three hours later. It was now daylight and the spectacle that greeted the pilot's eyes was catastrophic.

"One of our ships had already been sunk in the bay" recalls Captain Matias Farias who piloted a B-26 code 935. Like all other B-26s, Farias' had false Cuban identification markings, still with the idea of substantiating the notion of an internal revolt.

"A short time after our arrival, two Cuban fighters attacked another ship with a rocket. It started to burn immediately. We could see the crew trying to escape on the inflatable rafts. The fighters returned and started to machine gun the people in the water." To crown it all, the ship sank with all the radio equipment in its hold, that was necessary for communication between the brigade and the United States as well as fuel needed for refuelling the B-26s leaving from the air field near the beach. Castro had seen the situation clearly when he personally gave the orders to his pilots :

"Don't concern yourself for the moment with fighting on the ground. Priority must be given to attacking ships to stop them from unloading heavy material..."

After the loss of the Rio Escondido, the men of the brigade deployed on the ground were almost completely cut off from the rest of the world. No further communication was possible with the aircraft which were coming to offer aerial support.

Faced with this dramatic situation, Farias tried to engage combat with the Cuban fighters, the Sea Fury. Confused by the false Cuban identification markings of the the B-26s, the Castro forces did not respond to Farias' firing. The situation was yet more muddled for the Castro forces because at least one 'real' Cuban B-26 that had survived the raids of the 15th April was also participating in the combats. Farias could hear Castro's pilots trying to communicate with him over the radio.

"B-26, number 935, are you receiving me ..? 935 are you receiving me?"

Farias was careful not to reply. Short of fuel, the Castro fighter turned back to rejoin their base. Farias then tried to follow one to shoot it down, but the Sea Fury was more rapid and seemed out of reach of the twin-engines' machine guns. However the pilot of the fighter plane, because he was not being careful, committed the error of banking to the right which immediately put it in the range of fire of the B-26.

"Little by little I caught the Sea Fury up, then I opened fire at less than 400 yards" explained Farias.

"I was able to see the tracer bullets hit the plane. It therefore reduced its speed and started to lower its landing gear."

Farias thought the destruction of the Sea Fury would be easy but suddenly he was surrounded by tracer bullets.

"Evidently he had led me to a terrain where he had alerted the anti-aircraft personnel of my presence!"

Farias turned back and returned to the beach to offer support to the ground fighting. It was after ten in the morning when the pilot realised that he had stayed too long, more than three hours, above Cuba. The remaining fuel was not sufficient to get him back to Happy Valley in Nicaragua.

His navigator gave him a rapid analysis of the situation :

"We have two possibilities, either we land at Miami, or we attempt a landing on an airstrip that is under the control of our men, next to the beach. We can refuel there and take off again for Nicaragua."

"I prefer the Miami option, but we'll have to fly over the whole of Cuba to get there. With Castro fighters on the prowl and flak all around, I'd rather not attempt it", replied Farias anxiously.

"So let's land on the terrain near the beach, but quickly, before the fighters come back."

At that very moment a Sea Fury re-appeared. It gave off rapid fire in the direction of the B-26 and then disappeared as quickly as it had appeared. Evidently the ruse of false markings had ceased to be effective. A fire started in the plane, but it remained under control.

The coup de grace was given by a T-33, which gave a short deadly burst of fire on the crippled B-26. The navigator was killed instantly and the right engine burst into flames. Farias, who was making his final approach, tried to make a crash landing. The B-26 was on fire, barely under control and the T-33 came back to give the final blow. With no power available in the engines, Farias had no choice other than to bring the plane down. With a terrible violence, the crash ejected the pilot from his cabin. Seriously injured and burned Farias was immediately picked up by men from the brigade who had witnessed the entire scene. He was evacuated two days later, by air, to Nicaragua. As for the wreck of his plane, it was inspected by Fidel Castro in person after the combat, and for that reason, was photographed many times.

Four other B-26s were lost the same day because of Cuban fighters. Operation Pluto was taking a very bad turn for the worse.

The good news was that the pro-Castro forces had lost their B-26s, victims of firing from the ships. Two Sea Fury were also struck down by ground fire. But Castro had kept his two T-33 intact, planes which had caused havoc in the ranks of CIA aviators.

A little earlier in the day, five Curtiss C-46 Commandos and one C-54 Skymaster had brought 177 parachutists who were to jump to the north east of the beaches. The mission of these men was to neutralize the access routes which would enable Castro forces to counter-attack. Approaching the island, the planes flew over the aircraft carrier Essex and its escort of destroyers. The sight of these US Navy warships so near Cuba had inspired the enthusiasm of the combatants in the planes.

Not for one second did they imagine that the ships were mere extras, and were not going to support them actively.

Several minutes later, the C-46 flew over the ships of the anti-Castro brigade who were preparing to reach land.

In each plane, the parachutists got up and prepared themselves for the jump. The green light was given by the pilots and the combatants threw themselves into the air. In less than fifteen seconds, 177 men were floating to the ground, carefully scanning the land beneath them in the early morning light to make out their landing zone. The six cargo planes then started on their trip back to base. It was then that the worries started. In the lead C-46, Captain Ferrer, one of the first pilots selected by the CIA, had a little extra mission to fulfil; he had to use the return flight to fly over the terrain near the beach and confirm that it was usable. Ferrer circled twice above the terrain, everything seemed in good order. He had just started to head south when his co-pilot warned him that a plane was approaching :

"A B-26! Without doubt one of ours, Castro's must have been reduced to ashes by now!"

"Wait", shouted the co-pilot suddenly. "It's a Castro plane, it has a plexiglass nose." Ferrer was terrified. At that moment he could see the B-26 open fire on them. The C-46 was disarmed, and much slower than the B-26.

Without thinking he positioned his aircraft in front of the B-26 which was approaching at great speed. It then stopped its attack and dived under the C-46 to avoid a collision.

Ferrer used this respite of several seconds to head in the direction of the ships of the brigade. He thought, rightly, that the soldiers aboard the boats would fire on the B-26.

From the corner of his eye he had the time to see another C-46 pursued by a Sea Fury. The twin-engine transport plane had no chance of escape. The aircraft caught fire and crashed into the ground. The scene lasted no longer than two minutes.

Making the most of the heavy cloud cover, Ferrer was able to flee Cuba without any other problems.

He was tired out when he arrived at Happy Valley. On his last legs and suffering from nervous exhaustion, he went to collapse on his makeshift bed as soon as his plane was parked. His day had only just begun.

Two hours later a man from the CIA came to wake him up. Keeping quiet about the loss of two boats from the invasion flotilla, the man from the CIA explained to Ferrer that he was needed for a flight to resupply fighters on the landing beaches.

"They are loading your plane now. It is vital that the combatants on the beaches have ammunition. You will land on the terrain that you flew over this morning. You will leave the engines running while your plane is unloaded and possibly embark several casualties. At the most, you will stay twenty minutes on the ground."

"And what if there are Castro fighters in the zone?"

Then you'll come back. In any case a B-26 will escort you to Cuba."

With nearly ten tons of supplies on board, the C-46 was only just able to drag itself off the runway at Happy Valley around mid-afternoon. The B-26 took off behind him. Tired of being without defences, Ferrer had taken two automatic rifles with him. If the need arose, his crew could always fire through the windows.

A short time after take-off, the pilot of the B-26 called him over the radio :

"My machine guns are jammed and I have some problems with the central tank."

"Go back" replied Ferrer.

"No question. I'm not leaving you alone."

"I'm telling you to go back. In any case with jammed machine guns you'll be of no help..."

The B-26 went back, leaving the C-46 alone on its way to Cuba.

Ferrer was in view of the Cuban coast when the radio came back to life : a B-26 pilot was calling for help. Ferrer came onto the frequency giving his code name.

"Do not approach the coast" warned the pilot of the B-26, the pro-Castro forces are there with two T-33 and a Sea Fury. One of ours has already been shot down and I have been badly hit by firing from the beach.

The C-46 went back therefore without being able to rid itself of its load. The pilot of the B-26 explained that his life was saved thanks to the unexpected arrival of two American jets from the Essex. Their presence alone was enough to dissuade the Castro pilot from continuing with his attack.

His plane had been badly hit, the left engine was destroyed, the navigation equipment out of use. Numerous impacts were visible on the wings. Ferrer offered to guide the B-26 pilot back to Happy Valley.

"I don't think I'll make it, my plane is losing altitude and speed all the time. I'm going to have to land on the sea..."

After two hours flying from Cuba, the pilot of the B-26 contacted Ferrer over the radio once again :

"The situation is not looking good. I'm only three hundred feet or so above the water and the plane is still losing height. I think I'll be taking a bath..."

"God bless you" replied Ferrer. "I hope that everything goes as well as expected. We'll come back and pick you up with the Catalina first thing tomorrow morning." The following morning, Ferrer returned to the zone with a B-26, the less rapid Catalina followed behind. After several hours of searching, neither of the two planes could find any trace of the plane or its crew.

The need for ammunition being exacerbated, another resupply mission by air was therefore planned at the end of the day. The ammunition had, this time, to be directly parachuted on to positions occupied by the brigade. Four C-54 and two C-46 were used for this mission. The flight passed off without any problems and once the parachute drops were carried out all the planes were able to return to Nicaragua.

The drop was, unfortunately, not done with the desired accuracy and many packages and pallets fell in the marshy areas where, at nightfall, they were practically all lost. These parachute drops had in fact little effect on the ground fighters.

Even using the eleven transport aircraft which remained available, it was a delusion to think it was possible to resupply the 1,300 men on the beaches, more than 600 miles from the logistical base in Nicaragua. All the more so with the threat of Castro planes marauding continuously above the beaches.

TUESDAY 18th APRIL, D+1

Whereas the American spokesmen made strenuous efforts to explain that the US had nothing to do with the combats which put one Cuban against another, the situation continued to deteriorate for the anti-Castro forces. Of the two sites chosen for a landing, one had already been reduced to silence.

The other, larger bridgehead had been attacked by a dozen or so Cuban tanks.

The loss of four B-26s the day before had brought Kennedy back to reconsider his initial decision. He therefore gave his agreement for the Cuban air bases to be attacked again.

In the night of the 17th and 18th of April, three B-26s were prepared to attack the airfield at San Antonio de Los Banos, near Havana, where the T-33s were thought, rightly, to be based. With a delay of a few days, the priority targets were eventually identified by political authority.

But wasn't it already too late?

The B-26s took off, but two or three aircraft made a U turn on the way because of mechanical problems. The leader of the mission flew on alone and continued on to Cuba where he arrived in the middle of the night. It was totally dark and the ground was hidden by low cloud and fog. The Cuban pilot could not find his objective and returned towards Nicaragua without firing a single shot.

In the meantime, following the premature return of the two B-26s, a second mission was launched against Cuba, but on reaching the island the pilots experienced the same difficulties reaching their targets.

In the hope of making the Castro forces reveal their positions, a pilot even fired off some rockets blindly into the black night, in vain. The Cuban Air Force, whose effectiveness had been systematically underestimated by the CIA, thus had an extra day to harass the last combatants of the brigade.

At Happy Valley, the pilots were demoralized and exhausted. Some even refused to fight. Finding crews to carry out support fire missions was becoming more and more difficult. For one reason or another, the Cubans refused to take off and risk their lives.

Cancelling the previous instructions, Richard Bissel authorized American pilots to fulfil combat missions.

At 1400 hours, 18th April, six B-26 took off for Cuba. At the controls two Americans and four Cubans including Gustavo Ponzoa who showed faultless courage.

Reaching the skies above Cuba, they spotted a long column of vehicles heading for the front, including tanks. Believing them to be Castro planes, the soldiers waved happily to them.

What a mistake!

The B-26s went into a dive and dropped their external loads. They returned and used heavy machine gun fire on the fleeing soldiers. More than 600 men were put out of combat and thirty vehicles, including seven tanks, were destroyed. The bridgehead had gained a brief respite.

The problem of supply was nonetheless still very serious, the surviving ships were not able to bring the ammunition on the beaches and it was decided to organize a new parachuting mission. Three C-54s were engaged this time. For fear of being intercepted by the T-33s, it was decided that the planes should approach Cuba at just above sea level. On reaching the beach they would climb to 900 feet, drop their loads quickly on to the airstrip and dive very low again towards Nicaragua.

To reduce the possibility of being intercepted, the planes reached their destination objective just after sunset.

They went one by one to the DZ. The first plane came by surprise and met with no opposition. The situation was not so easy for the following two aircraft which had to deal with fully alerted anti-aircraft fire. In spite of this, the planes left the danger zone more or less intact and all managed to reach Nicaragua.

Apart from the load of the first plane which fell a little short, partly in the sea, the other pallets fell into the right hands. But once again it was too little, too late.

The situation on the ground was so serious that another operation was organized that very night, with, once again, American crews. Five B-26s took part, four of which were piloted by Americans. The Intelligence Officer announced to them that their area of operation was to be the zone around the beach. All visible vehicles, especially the tanks, must be destroyed.

The B-26s were, as usual, equipped with extra tanks attached under the wings. The novelty was however that this time they were carrying napalm for the first time.

Take-off was planned for the middle of the night for an arrival at the zone at sunrise. The pilots had a few hours to snatch a little sleep.

At three in the morning the planes took off and after an uneventful flight, arrived in sight of the island. By a stroke of luck a cloud of dust indicating the presence of a column of vehicles was visible on the horizon.

"There is our target for the napalm," announced the flight leader over the radio. But before he had the time to position himself for the attack, his wing was hit.

"I've been hit! My plane is on fire!"

"What hit you?"

No response. The B-26 fell towards the sea at more than 300mph and disintegrated in an immense ball of fire. The drama lasted no more than a few seconds.

No time to feel pity for him. Death was on the prowl in the form of a solitary T-33 which had managed to approach the B-26 unnoticed.

The leader spotted the T-33 when he was just about to be subjected to the same fate. The American pilot instinctively engaged his plane in a tight turn which positioned it in front of the T-33. The jet had no other solution other than to break off combat to avoid a collision. The B-26 took advantage of this and made his escape.

At Happy Valley it was becoming clear that the day had been catastrophic; two American crews, four people in all had been killed on board their B-26. The first had been shot down by a T-33, the second was hit by anti-aircraft fire and had crashed into the sea. All the other planes had been hit.

STRONG IMPLICATIONS

In Washington, in the control room of the CIA from where operations were being closely monitored, the first two days of the invasion seemed nightmarishly slow. News trickled in slowly, the important communication equipment having been lost in the destruction of Rio Escondido. As for Kennedy, even though news of the catastrophic landing had started to arrive in fragments and even though the United States was at the centre of the media storm that was beginning to brew throughout the world, he stoically carried on following the normal course of his obligations.

On the evening of the 18th April he slipped out of a reception given inside the White House and took refuge, still wearing his dinner jacket, in an isolated room to follow a crisis meeting with his advisers. Richard Bissel used the occasion to argue in favour of a salvage operation. The assistant director of operations remained convinced that Operation Pluto could still succeed.

"Mr. President, we can still save face if the jets from the Essex intervene and destroy Castro's last planes."

"It is out of the question that the United States be directly implicated, Bissel" "But Mr. President, we are already implicated up to our necks!"

Kennedy eventually decided on a compromise. Six planes from the Essex, including one whose US markings had been removed, were authorized to fly over the landing beaches.

But these flights were to be dissuasive, the American pilots were under strict orders not to intervene directly in the confrontation and above all not to engage in combat against Cuban planes. This intervention, as belated as it was naive, would of course change nothing of the situation of the ground troops, which was becoming more desperate by the hour.

The pilots of the US Navy endured with difficulty the fact of having to be mere spectators to the agony of the Cubans that they were supporting. Some pilots, seeing their allies being beaten to the ground and without being able to intervene, could hardly hold back their tears. Tears of anger and frustration.

Engaged in one of these 'show' flights on board an A-4D Skyhawk, a Navy pilot spotted a Cuban T-33. Within a few seconds, he managed to position himself behind it. He held its fate in his hands as he could have shot it down at any second. But on board the Essex, the situation was being followed on the radar screens and the air controller understood what was happening when he saw that the echoes of the two planes were very close to each other :

"Hold your fire, do not fire" shouted the controller into the microphone. "Do not fire, the rules of engagement do not allow it!"

On another occasion, an American pilot saw a B-26 which was being cut to pieces by a Castro Sea Fury. The right engine of the bomber was on fire and the fighter was coming in for the kill.

"I have a Sea Fury which is killing a B-26" he said to the controller. "I'm asking for permission to open fire."

"Stand by, I'm requesting authority."

The answer came after several seconds.

"Negative. I repeat negative, do not open fire."

Deeply appalled by this, the American took his plane to within several yards of the Sea Fury, they were practically wing to wing.

"We stayed in that position for several moments, maybe even as long as a minute" recalled the pilot when he had returned from his mission. The Cuban was looking at me and I was looking at him. Then the guy must have had enough and he left in the direction of Cuba."

The Skyhawk then approached the B-26. The pilot gave him a large smile and gave him the thumbs up, indicating that everything was OK. The US Navy had at least managed to save one aircraft without firing a single shot. This bravery remained nonetheless exceptional, and mostly the Navy had to put up with simply watching the agony of the brigade without being able to intervene.

WEDNESDAY 19th APRIL, D+2

The last combatants on the beach called for help, in vain. The ammunition was exhausted, the majority of the supply of ammunition was not offloaded from the ships in time. No popular uprising materialized to relieve pressure on the bridgehead. Castro had taken precautions : from the first signs of the bombing he put several thousand of his opponents under preventive arrest.

Demoralized and exhausted by three solid days of combat against 20,000 of Castro's men, the men of the brigade were starting to give up. The airfield was now under direct fire from the Cubans, thereby preventing its use as an advanced base for the B-26s.

In a last ditch effort, the Americans thought they could make drops of ammunition onto the beaches at night from C-130 Hercules, heavy four-engine tactical transport planes. They spoke also of reinforcing the anti-Castro aviation by some extra B-26s and even some T-33s. Neither one of these last minute plans were put into operation, due to lack of time and pilots. Would they have reversed the course of events? Probably not.

On the beaches the game was already over. The last combatants of the brigade were giving themselves up to the Cuban regulars. Several hundred attempted to flee into the marshes which surrounded the combat zone. They were rapidly recaptured.

Several dozen men, with more luck, managed to escape by the sea. They were rescued by US Navy ships which were cruising off the coast.

The final toll of the operation was very distressing: out of the 1,300 men who had landed, approximately a hundred were killed in combat and 1,100 were taken prisoner. A handful, 26 to be precise, managed to escape by sea and were picked up. Seven B-26s were shot down and their crews killed. Five others were destroyed during various crash landings. Added to this were several transport craft, C-46 and C-54, lost during parachuting operations before and during the landings.

The anti-Castro air force led a last mission with one of its C-46s. A mission which is symbolic of the failure of Operation Pluto. The twin-engine took off at first light with 15 million leaflets on board calling the Cubans to rise up and revolt against Castro. The plane took off, and above the West Indies threw its cargo into the sea. There was no longer any question of an uprising in Cuba. Thursday 20th April was a victorious day for Fidel Castro. With a large quantity of captured documents in front of him, the great leader improvised a very long one-man show on Cuban TV.

Before his compatriots congregated together in front of the few TV sets that existed in the country, he detailed smugly the events which had shaken the island during the previous days.

He took a malicious pleasure in being ironical about all the mistakes of the CIA, on the inadequacies of its intelligence work. He read out certain CIA documents quoting the "bad maintenance of Cuban aircraft," machines "in flying but not fighting condition." He revealed that CIA bombers were deceived by false aircraft at the airport of Campo Libertad.

Sometimes threatening, sometimes amused by his own jokes, serious when he spoke about Cuban deaths, caustic when he mentioned the incompetence of the CIA, Castro held his public enthralled for more than four hours.

When the programme was finished one thing was certain, the Cubans were for once far better informed than the Americans on the incredible fiasco which had just taken place several dozen miles off the coast of Florida.

The adventure of the bay of pigs caused a real stir in the United States. President Kennedy had the style to take the whole responsibility of the affair on his shoulders.

"I am here to prove that the old adage which says that victory has a thousand fathers and defeat is an orphan, is a lie", he declared during a press conference.

In private, he shared his wish to be able to take the CIA, cut it up into a thousand pieces and throw it to the four winds. He recognized also that his inexperience in dealing with intelligence services had meant that he was not critical enough of Bissel and Dulles.

"If this was the British government", he said a few days later to Richard Bissel, "I would have to resign and you, a senior government official, would remain. But this is not the case."

To spare the two CIA men the humiliation of an immediate resignation, several months passed before it was carried out.

After the failure of the invasion, Nicaragua recuperated all the surviving B-26s. They were in varying condition and none had a legal existence. Four aircraft, those which had the best potential, were convoyed to the airport of Las Mercedes, near Managua, and integrated into the Nicaraguan Air Force. American technicians, on a mission of military cooperation helping to maintain planes of the Nicaraguan Air Force, saw these planes arrive.

"It is out of the question that we have anything to do with these planes", they said. "Anyway nobody knows where they have come from, all the identification numbers have been removed. Let the Nicaraguans deal with it!"

However after several obscure negotiations, the US authorities reviewed their decision a little later on and footed the bill for these planes to be put into operation. Everyone in the United States tried to forget as quickly as possible the terrible humiliation of the bay of pigs. Other worries were soon to haunt the minds of the American administration : all eyes were turning at that time towards Asia, where a new wrestling match against the communists was beginning.

Very quickly the CIA found itself once again in the front line.

CHAPTER 4

ASIA : THE SITUATION DETERIORATES

INDONESIA 1958 : OPERATION HAIK TURNS INTO A FIASCO

The existence of this operation, which was brutally interrupted and ended in failure, was never admitted by the CIA. But once again American implication in this affair was an open secret.

Operation Haik came under the usual pattern of operations during the cold war.

Since its independence in 1950, Indonesia, which is made up of more than 13,000 islands divided into six archipelagos, had to face up to a rebellion of numerous groups who contested the central authority of Java. The military was moreover unhappy with the reduction of their funds and also with the obvious weakness of the government concerning the communists. All the necessary conditions were coming together to deteriorate a situation that was already very unstable.

In 1956, the military commanders of several isolated areas, notably Sumatra and the Celebes islands, had fashioned veritable mini-empires for themselves, with an economic power that had escaped the notice of the central government. At the end of the year, two colonels announced that they had taken control of the centre and north of Sumatra.

In February of the following year, the rebels in Sumatra sent an ultimatum to Djakarta asking President Ahmed Sukarno to give up power. At the same time they formed a revolutionary government which the rebels in Celebes joined.

Because they thought Sukarno would become pro-communist, the United States supported the cause of the rebel colonels wholeheartedly. Forgetting rather too quickly that it was Sukarno himself who had outlawed the Indonesian communist party, after an attempted coup d'etat.

But Sukarno, who had launched the idea of a third force, the 'nonaligned', independent of the super powers of the moment, was no longer held in favour by Washington.

Nine months later, Eisenhower authorized the CIA to conduct Operation Haik, with the overthrow of Sukarno as its declared objective. Eisenhower thought that it would be a repeat performance of Operation Success, which four years earlier had evicted the Guatamalan president Jacobo Arbenz for similar reasons.

The CIA started by supplying arms to the rebel colonels. One very imaginative strategy of the agency was to make and broadcast a pornographic film, using a double of Sukarno, in order to discredit him. The film did not have, outside Washington, the success they were counting on. They returned to more traditional methods and started planning a campaign of military intervention.

A REBEL AIR FORCE CREATED OUT OF NOTHING

Some camps had already been set up in the Philippines for training rebel leaders. Benefiting from an impressive logistics bought in by the US Army, several thousands of guerillas were trained before being sent to fight in different areas of the country. But up until then no American had been directly implicated in the combats. This situation changed during the first days of 1958 when it was decided to provide aerial support directly to the rebels.

The CIA selected three rapid B-26 bombers among the dozens of aircraft which were ending their days on the apron of the Clark US air base in the Philippines. The planes were rapidly brought up to flying condition. They were each equipped with 12.7mm machine guns, six in the nose and the same number in the wings. The old American markings were removed and replaced by a uniform black paint which covered over all distinctive signs. It was also necessary to remove the serial numbers on several parts of the plane so that its real identity could not be discovered. In March the same year, three F-51D Mustang from the Philippines air force joined the B-26s. Just as for the twin-engines, the fighters had all identifying marks and signs carefully removed. They were subsequently entirely painted in black. At the same time, the CIA started to bring together the crews, which originally were to be Indonesian. But few men with the necessary experience were recruited and the only Indonesians who participated in the operation were co-pilots or radio operators. For this reason, the CIA had to resign itself to using half a dozen American pilots. All of them were ex-CAT who had played a part in operations since Taiwan. To complete the numbers, several pilots of eastern European origin were also recruited, the majority were Polish who had flown with the RAF during the war, along with a few Hungarians. Several of these men had also participated in CIA operations in Greece.

On the 21st March 1958 President Sukarno ordered his aircraft to attack the rebel transmitter stations at Padang, capital of Sumatra, and at Bukittingi on the same island. B-25s escorted by Mustangs did the work. These attacks pushed the CIA into using its own aircraft and on the 12th April, three B-26 took off from Clark, destination Celebes islands, where an old terrain dating from the second world war had been updated. Two or three hundred people, Americans as well as Philippino and Taiwanese, responsible for the maintenance and operation of the aircraft followed in CIA trucks. It was the concept of the International Volunteer Air Group, conceived during the war in Indochina, which was being developed. Meanwhile the Americans experienced their first alert when, on the 23rd March, a US Navy plane on a reconnaissance mission was intercepted by an Indonesian aircraft Even though the plane was hit, it nonetheless managed to reach a friendly base and the matter was not pursued.

The first mission of the B-26s was accomplished the morning of the 13th April when a single aircraft took off from its base at Mapengat to attack, with machine gun fire, the airport at Makassar, at the southern end of the island. On the 17th April, another B-26 attacked the refinery at Balikpapan on the eastern coast of Borneo. The plane, which managed to sink a small oil tanker, also destroyed several oil tanks and damaged a C-47 belonging to Royal Dutch Shell on the ground. Several other attacks were launched during the following weeks mostly on Celebes or the small surrounding islands. No attack was ever made against Sumatra. Instead of constituting a threat to governmental troops, all these actions gave a lift to the morale of the rebels. The lack of drive among the rebels was a malaise well known by the CIA and the presence of American advisers was not enough to overcome this problem. The Americans willingly told the story of the rebel unit who was expecting a parachute drop of weapons. The men had been informed of the planes' arrival. This however did not stop them from clearing off when the CIA plane was heard approaching the drop zone. On the 18th April, the day after the successful raid against Royal Dutch Shell, the government launched an air/land operation against the rebels in Sumatra. The operation, which combined dropping parachutists and an amphibious assault, was crowned a success. It made the rebels flee in the direction of Celebes. During this time the CIA was preparing three other Invaders in the Philippines. These planes were equipped with machine guns in the nose, but not in the wings. They had been given a metallic finish, only the engine pods had been painted in black.

The setbacks suffered by their proteges pushed the CIA into intensifying their aid. The Mustangs which were prepared in the Philippines were sent to Celebes at the end of April. They were destroyed several days later on the aerodrome of Manado when the governmental aviation launched a raid of three B-25s escorted by two Mustangs. Three extra Mustangs were therefore borrowed from the Philippine air force, with their identification markings removed, ready to be sent to the rebels. At the same time, three B-26 were given to the rebels whereas six others, from a stock at Clark, were prepared.

The CIA did not know that all these preparations were rapidly going to be rendered null and void.

ONE MISSION TOO MANY

18th May 1958, a B-26 piloted by the American Allen Pope took off from a rebel base for a bombing mission.

The briefing given by the CIA person responsible for the mission was particularly succinct:

"Our information is that a convoy of several government ships will take troops in the direction of the island of Morutai to the north of the Molucca island archipelago."

"Where is the convoy now?"

"It has just left the island of Ambon. It should still be reasonably near to its port of departure. Have a good flight!"

The plane was fuelled up, bombs positioned and machine guns loaded.

On reaching Ambon, Pope chose to briefly machine gun the aerodrome that he found. Then he headed towards the convoy that was still in view. Even though he was flying at very low altitude, in order not to be detected, the CIA pilot was in fact spotted by soldiers on the ships. When he started firing he was welcomed by a deluge of fire coming from weapons of all calibres.

"We're taking hits from all sides", announced the radio operator over the intercom. The comment was superfluous.

Pope had felt the aircraft vibrate dangerously as a result of the impact. He felt he was losing control. The plane had been badly hit even before it had been able to launch its first attack against the boats and return to base. Before he had finished the manoeuvre the radio came back to life :

"A fighter at 4 o'clock!"

"This is it! Prepare to jump, I'll take the plane up while there's still time..."

The government P-51 only needed a single firing run to finish off the B-26 which crashed into the sea. Meanwhile Pope and his radio operator had succeeded in jumping from the plane. For Pope, the CIA, President Eisenhower and the United States their worries were only just beginning!

Pope broke his leg landing on a reef. He was nevertheless picked up along with his radio operator by ships which had come to attack. Ironically, he saw the attack on Morotai and the governmental victory which had been his mission to prevent.

The capture of Pope was a source of much embarrassment in Washington. With their hands on their hearts, US officials had denied several times since the beginning of the rebellion that their country was in any way involved in the fighting that rocked Indonesia.

The United States was playing with fire, which could lead to a third world war as President Sukarno had warned. He also brandished the threat of an intervention of Chinese 'volunteers' to fight the rebels.

During a press conference, President Eisenhower was there in person to show good faith:

"Our policy aims at maintaining strict neutrality" he declared. On the other hand any rebellion has its soldiers of fortune, attracted by the lure of gain or adventure...

This did not explain how the rebels had been able to equip themselves, practically from one day to the next, with a considerable air force, whereas the Indonesian air force had remained loyal to President Sukarno.

Three weeks after this announcement, Pope was shot down in his B-26. For nine days, the Indonesians kept the capture of the pilot quiet. When it was publicly announced, the ambassador of the US in Djakarta promptly relayed the information which had been given to him by Washington :

"The captured pilot is merely a simple American citizen who has chosen to fight as a mercenary alongside the rebels."

The CIA hoped that Pope had no compromising documents on him at the time of his capture.

"Pope is an old hand, he will know how to manage," they affirmed.

This hope was rapidly demolished. When they captured Pope, the Indonesians had also found USAF and Civil Air Transport identity cards, and his contract for Operation Haik along with two or three other documents of lesser importance. His links with the US Air Force and more seriously with the CAT generally recognized as being linked with the CIA, were thus formally established.

Pope had indeed kept on his person documents proving his links with CAT and in so doing had broken one of the most basic rules of operation of the CIA. Four years earlier, he was among the American pilots engaged in the resupply operation of Dien Bien Phu. Before that he had also participated in the Korean war where he had 55 night missions to his credit. After several years spent in the CAT he became a captain, lived in Saigon and earned a very comfortable living. It was there that the CIA approached him offering him combat missions on board a B-26. He accepted without hesitating.

CIA procedures were very strict : to be certain that no compromising document was carried on them, the crews had to undress completely under the surveillance of a CIA man before every departure on a mission. It was at this point that the interests of the agency and the pilots that it used diverged greatly. If the CIA fervently wished that no formal link could be established between itself and the crews, the latter were seeking above all to prevent themselves from being executed in case of capture. A stateless mercenary with no value can be executed, but not a man on a mission for the US government whose liberation can be subject to negotiation. Following the example of the other pilots no doubt, Pope had hidden several official documents in his plane before he left on a mission. Just in case...

ALLEN POPE, A VALUABLE PRISONER

Sukarno had the Americans at his mercy. He played the Pope card with a consummate skill against the American administration which was tangled up in a web of lies. Washington allowed itself to be manipulated pathetically and in the days following the capture of the American pilot, Operation Haik was abruptly called to a halt. The United States even went as far as to lift the embargo that they had put on Indonesia. From the month of August 1958 the Americans started to deliver a million dollars worth of armaments to the Indonesian government, the same government thet they had been fighting against several weeks earlier. From that moment on, the fate of the rebels was sealed. They gambled on a single aerial victory.

At the cessation of hostilities, the Indonesian government announced it had destroyed a total of three B-26s, five P-51s, a C-47 and a Catalina seaplane. These figures were, most probably, a little exaggerated because only three P-51s had been delivered by the Americans. The three others which had been borrowed from the Philippines did not in fact ever leave that country; they were returned to their owner from the month of July 1958. It is also highly likely that at their departure from Celebes, the CIA men destroyed the B-26s which were not in condition to make the return flight to the Philippines. With the end of the combat, the Invaders, which were prepared at the Clark airbase to be handed over to the guerillas, concealed their original marks. These planes were subsequently used by the USAF in Vietnam.

But the adventure did not end there for the captured pilot. Pope was presented in front of an Indonesian military court where he was tried for being a mercenary. The military judges studied the personal notes and flight logs found on Pope to give some dimension to their act of accusation :

"You have carried out six bombing missions for the rebels. You have killed 23 Indonesians including 6 civilians."

Pope recognized having carried out only one bombing mission, the one during which he was shot down.

"The other flights were only reconnaissance missions" he explained.

"You are paid $10,000 to assassinate innocent people."

"Your honour, my contract was $200 for each completed flight."

"In that case, what was your real motivation?"

"Your honour, I have been fighting against communism since the age of 22. I fought first in Korea, then in Indochina..."

Pope pleaded not guilty, which did not stop him from being condemned to death. Even though Indonesia had never executed a condemned prisoner both Washington and CIA HQ were deeply concerned about the possibility.

While he rotted in prison, the CIA did not remain inactive and a team was trained in the Philippines to prepare his escape. It was planned that the Fulton system would be used, a system which had just been perfected.

The Fulton system had been conceived to enable a person on the ground to be picked up by a plane in flight. It was ingenious yet fairly delicate to put into practice and required the person on the ground to be very courageous or foolhardy! It's inventor, the engineer Robert Fulton, presented the operation of his special system to the special forces of the army :

"You are on the ground, with no possibility of being picked up by orthodox means. You are therefore dropped a rescue kit which consists of a harness, a cable, a balloon and a bottle of gas to inflate it. You attach the harness to the balloon by means of this long cable. The balloon is then inflated with the helium. The balloon rises up and the cable becomes taut. A specially equipped plane comes in front of the cable and hooks it up. The cable is then pulled up into the plane with you at the other end..."

Well!

The special forces were fairly dubious. "That's a strange kind of lift" commented one officer.

"I'd rather go by foot than try that type of exercise" said another.

The Fulton system was nonetheless declared operational.

As far as the Pope operation was concerned the idea was to get a harness to him inside the prison using friendly locals. A team would then come at night outside the prison, inflate the balloon and position it near the surrounding wall. Once in position, the nylon cable would be thrown over the wall so that Pope could grab it and attach it to his harness. Then he would simply have to wait for the plane to fly over.

This plan was of a breathtaking naivety. It supposed firstly that the balloon could be manipulated in all impunity near the prison. It counted on the CIA, thanks to friends inside, being able to get Pope out into the prison courtyard in the middle of the night. If that were the case, couldn't he be made to escape using a more conventional method?

The plan was finally abandoned in 1961, after the pilot having the best knowledge of the Fulton system was killed in an operation over Laos. Perhaps the abandonment was the best thing for Pope whose sentence meanwhile had been reduced to life imprisonment. He finally left prison after four years, the election of Kennedy as President had brought about a warming of US-Indonesian relations which Pope benefited from; he was freed in 1962. Washington continued to pay for forgiveness : 37,000 tons of rice and four C-130 Hercules cargo planes, at the time the most modern transport plane of the US Air Force, were given to Indonesia. Ray Cline, head of the CIA station in Taiwan, and therefore one of the men responsible for Operation Haik, summed up the fiasco;

"The problem with clandestine operations is that a single piece of information which reveals CIA participation makes the United States change its attitude either to an abandonment of the whole operation or to an operation of open warfare."

TIBET : COMBAT ON CHINA'S DOORSTEP

Following the defeat of the nationalist troops of Tchang Kai Chek in 1949, the communist army of Mao Zedong attacked Tibet, a Kingdom lost in the mountains. Several weeks of a more or less even fight was enough to establish Chinese supreme rule. The Tibetans, by nature a peace loving people, would have doubtless resigned themselves to their fate but for the excessive iron rule of the Chinese which pushed them to a rebellion.

Alone however, they could do very little. After several years of desperate fighting, the leaders of the resistance, notably the immediate entourage of the Dalai Lama, made contact with Washington.

For Washington, the Tibetan affair was an excellent opportunity to fight against the Chinese on their very doorstep, while at the same time supporting a very clear-cut cause. But in order to avoid any risk of direct confrontation with Peking, the Eisenhower administration chose the secret operation option which was entrusted to the CIA. The Tibetan resistance support operation ST Circus was rapidly launched, (ST signified Tibet in CIA classification). The strong point of ST Circus concerned the setting up of a resupply operation by air, this was ST Barnum.

The CIA had no doubts concerning its capabilities to lead this new operation : with CAT, which was soon to transform into Air America, it had use of a remarkable transport tool in the region.

Throughout 1957, a first group of six Tibetans managed to leave their country secretly to join a CIA training camp. These six combatants learnt how to use modern weapons, to lay demolition charges, to prepare drop zones ; they were also trained in the use of radio transmitters and were initiated in the use of coded messages.

With their return to Tibet in mind, which had to be made by air, they also received parachute training. Each one of them carried out three jumps from a B-17 that the CAT had inherited from the Air Force several years previously.

After several months of intensive preparation, they were at last ready to return home and train the core of a new resistance movement.

One night in October 1957, the anonymous B-17 took off from the runway at Kermitola, an emergency airfield used by the Strategic Air Command, near Dacca, now capital of Bangladesh. Covered with an all-over black paint, the old bomber of the Second World War was without any identification markings.

In the best tradition of the CIA, a crew made up solely of Eastern European took its place in the cockpit : in case of any problems, Washington could thus deny absolutely any participation in the adventure. At the rear, two Tibetans were, in a manner of speaking, settled in the noisy, ice cold cabin. The hour of return to their country had at last arrived.

After a flight of a little more than two hours, the aircraft flew over the first foothills of the Himalayas. Through the windows in the plane, the pensive Tibetans could pick out the narrow gorges in the pale moonlight, gorges which, four months earlier and with great difficulty they had crossed by foot in the other direction.

In the cockpit, there was no time for daydreaming :

"The most difficult part of the operation was the navigating", explained the operation ST Barnum pilots unanimously. "We had to fly over unknown territory for several hours, cross over the highest mountains in the world and find drop zones no more than several hundred square yards in size, all that without any exterior assistance."

The region was quite obviously devoid of any radio-electric navigation beacon. The few maps available were not always reliable. The most accurate of them showed vast expanses of white, signifying that no precise information was available on that particular area. A further oddity was that the maps were not always the same. The trace of rivers and mountain crests differed from one edition to another...

Navigation could only be done by sight, which meant the CIA could only launch missions five days before or after a full moon. In spite of these drawbacks, the first team was parachuted without any problems. The two men touched the ground near the Bhramapoutre river, south of the capital Lhassa. Their material, notably a powerful radio transmitter, was picked up without any difficulty. So as not to lose trace of it during the drop, one of the Tibetans attached himself with a several hundred yard long rope to the package which had been supplied with its own parachute. Once on the ground, it was a simple matter of following the rope to pick up the material. This was then hidden in the area and the two men started their journey to Lhassa, to make contact with local resistance leaders.

A second team of three agents was to be parachuted in the east of the country on the following day. But a thick layer of cloud forced the CIA to postpone the mission until the next full moon, in the month of November.

When this finally took place, a catastrophe was only just avoided : the three men landed not far from a group of rebels who confused them with Chinese parachutists. It was only after an exchange of heavy firing that the mistake was revealed. Fortunately, no-one was hit!

Once the two teams were in place, information on the forces present, Chinese as well as Tibetan, started to flood in. The Tibetans requested parachute drops of weapons, ammunition and communication devices, indicating in their radio messages the possible drop zones. It was at this time that the use of radios meant the first simultaneous offensives could be coordinated between different fronts of the resistance in Tibet. Incidentally, the first clothes made from parachute silk also started to appear among the local population...

Authorized by the Eisenhower administration to move up a gear, the CIA therefore took stock of its aircraft potential. The B-17 alone was not going to be enough to ensure all missions. As for the C-46 and C-47 in service in the CAT, they did not have the necessary range to carry out non-stop return journeys in the direction of Tibet. The CIA turned once again to the Air Force to obtain the material that it lacked.

The 322nd Troop Carrier Squadron was a transport unit used to special missions : it had within it a small team of agents of the CIA whose role was liaison between the military authorities and their HQ. The 322nd supplied the CIA with a C-118, a military version of the Douglas DC-6, it was the job of the agency to find the crew, pilots, flight engineers, navigators, air dispatchers...

Even though it was a relatively recent plane with a good reputation, the DC-6/C-118 was not much appreciated by the different participants in operation ST Barnum. It seemed, above all, very badly adapted to the missions to which it had been entrusted :

"The C-118, more than anything else, lacked power" recognized the crews.

When fully loaded, its four 2,000hp Pratt and Whitney R-2,800 engines did not allow it to take enough altitude to cross over the contours of the lan : the pilots were forced to zigzag between the highest summits in the Himalayas, which put a significant burden on the range of the plane.

The CIA specialists prepared the navigation of the plane depending on the supplies requested. The photographs taken at very high altitude by agency U-2 aircraft were carefully studied to find routes through the hills and mountains away from sensitive Chinese zones.

Last-minute adjustments were also made according to the weather which was expected en route. Every mission was then presented to Richard Helms : the man who was to become the head of the CIA under Johnson and Nixon was at that time the number two in the secret operations division.

The other major fault with the C-118 was the fact that during flight the cargo door was impossible to open, therefore commencing drops was a problem.

"The door had to be lifted before the flight", explained the air dispatchers. "This meant the cabin lost pressure. At the altitudes we were flying at, we had to use oxygen bottles permanently, which was very uncomfortable. As well as that, the narrow width of the door stopped us from dropping all the load in a single passage. The loads had to be divided up and we had to fly over the drop zones several times before everything had been jettisoned, this went against the most basic safety rules..."

In 1959, a new phase of operation ST Barnum was started. The year had begun successfully for the CIA, which had helped the Dalai Lama and his entourage to flee to India, under the very nose of the Chinese. The small group that surrounded the Tibetan spiritual leader had managed to escape unobtrusively from Lhassa, occupied by the Chinese. A CIA trained radio operator was part of this group, which meant supplies could be dropped at regular intervals while the small column was on the move.

Resistance against Chinese troops took a new turn when the CIA was authorized, in May of the same year, to train several hundred Tibetan combatants in one go.

This training was carried out at Camp Hale, in the mountains of Colorado. The site was chosen for its seclusion and because it resembled the rocky terrain and harsh climate of Tibet. The men had left their country overland, before being put under the responsibility of the CIA and flown to the United States.

Detachment 2, 1045th Operational Evaluation and Training Group of the US Air Force was responsible for the transport of the 700 Tibetan resistants.

A seemingly inoffensive unit, Detachment 2 had in fact been put at the disposal of the CIA for its secret operations in the Far East. At its head was Major Harry Aderholt, the officer of the US Air Force who was to be the link in all CIA operations in the region throughout the following years. At the close of the Korean war, during which he had organized a transport group for all special operations, Aderholt had seen his collaboration with the CIA intensify. Sometimes in civilian clothes, sometimes in the uniform of the Air Force, Aderholt was present wherever the intelligence agency mounted an operation of any scale. Before participating, in 1961, in Operation Pluto against Castro, at the end of the fifties Aderholt found himself on the base of Kadena in Japan, where he directed Detachment 2.

While the first group of combatants were just beginning their training at Camp Hale in August 1959, the CIA was already considering a means of infiltrating these men into Tibet once their training was finished. The best way was obviously by air; but 700 men and the hundreds of tons of equipment and supplies which would be necessary to sustain their combat meant that a simple C-118 would not be enough.

The Air Force once again came to the rescue and agreed to put several of its new Lockheed C-130A Hercules at the disposal of the CIA.

Equipped with four turbines with a unit power of 3,750hp, the Hercules offered a superior margin of manoeuvre compared with the venerable DC-6. It flew higher and further, while at the same time transporting a heavier load. However, the particular geography of Tibet nonetheless led the C-130A to operate to the limit of its potential : to reach the most distant drop zones, the crews had to carry more fuel (40,000pds), the payload was reduced to the strict minimum, a little less than 26,000 pds.

This limitation forced the planners of the CIA to multiply the number of supply flights, which was not always feasible if the operation was not to be delayed. Aderholt, who had taken command of the operation, quickly found a way of remedying this problem :

"The constructor informed us that maximum mass at take off of the first version of the C-130 was 124,000 pds. But I soon learnt from Lockheed that this figure was in fact dictated by the resistance of the landing gear on the ground when it was taxiing: during a phase of turning, the weight was transferred on the main landing gear from one side or the other of the plane and could lead to the tolerance level being exceeded."

Aderholt bypassed this limitation by loading the planes to the maximum with cargo, then making them taxi to the threshold of the runway with very little fuel in the tanks. The tanks were filled at the last minute, once the taxiing had been completed and the plane was aligned on the runway, ready for take off.

Thanks to this strategem the maximum mass at take off passed to 135,000pds, the absolute limit fixed by the constructor.

The CIA gained a payload of five tons per plane.

The loads were divided up into packs of about 90pds, so as to be easily separated and put on to the beasts of burden by the recuperation teams.

Usually based in Kadena in Japan, the C-130s were transported by Air Force crews to Takhli in Thailand, sixty miles or so north of Bangkok. On this base, which was to become a hub of Air America and CIA operations over the following years, civilian crews took over from Air Force crews, and all the identification markings of the planes were removed so as to render them 'anonymous'.

It was not unknown for the resupply missions to be regrouped:up to three planes could leave the same evening, at intervals of several minutes. The Hercules took off from Takhli, crossed Burma and a part of India to finally reach Tibet and the zones within reach of anti-Chinese resistance. Burma had protested against these flights over its territory, but what could it do? Not in the least impressed by the recriminations from Rangoon, the CIA continued its operations.

On reaching the area of the zone, the C-130 made a rapid descent and positioned itself barely a few hundred feet above the ground. A powerful bell and a red light came on in the hold indicating that the plane was approaching the drop zone. The plane was depressurised, the rear ramp lowered to enable entire palettes to be dropped quickly, while the Tibetans checked their equipment for the last time.

Even though the plane was flying near the ground, the altitude was high enough above sea level for the air dispatchers to have to work wearing oxygen masks.

Arriving above the drop zone, with its fire beacons arranged in a cross or T shape, the pilot gave a last signal to the air dispatchers who were busy in the hold: the red light had turned to green, indicating that the moment to completely unsling the palettes had arrived. A second later the pilot put the nose of the plane up and the palettes tumbled out of the gaping hole in the hold under the force of their own weight. The parachutists then followed them in the moonlit night.

In the following minute, the ramp was raised, sealing the hold hermetically. The plane was repressurised and set off in a south easterly direction, towards Thailand.

The first missions with the C-130 started in 1959. At that time it was simply a matter of sending provisions. From the month of November, the first recruits trained at Camp Hale took part in the operations. Ten to twelve Tibetans were parachuted during the course of each ST Barnum mission.

Forty or so missions had already taken place when, on the 1st of May 1960, several thousand miles to the west, a U-2 of the CIA was shot down during an espionnage mission in the heart of Soviet territory. The outcry this incident provoked pushed the Americans to hastily interrupt other secret aerial operations which involved flights over non-authorized countries. ST Barnum was evidently in this category and the resupply of the Tibetans by air stopped from one day to the next.

With the exception of two or three isolated flights, the resupplying was sometimes carried out overland, but with an altogether different level of efficiency.

Ceding territory before the Chinese army, the centre of gravity of the Tibetan resistance movement repositioned itself towards the west, to eventually establish itself, at the end of 1960, approximately 120 miles north east of the Nepalese capital Katmandu, far removed from the direct zone of influence of the Chinese in Tibet. Katmandu as a result became a hub of CIA activity in the region, the agency even creating its own air company, Air Nepal, to satisfy its logistic needs. Air Nepal supplied the link between Bangkok and Katmandu, while a fleet of light aircraft used the Nepalese capital as a base.

The new installations of the Tibetan guerilla took on the appearance of a permanent camp. This situation would last until the seventies. At that time the political rapprochement between China and the United States dealt a fatal blow to the Tibetan resistance movement, the last vestiges of its structure would succumb to a large Chinese offensive.

It seemed that the aid given to the Tibetan resistance movement had been one way - among others - of harassing the Chinese communists. When this necessity disappeared at the beginning of the seventies, because of Asian 'realpolitik', the Tibetan resistance movement lost its raison d'être in the eyes of the American administration.

Independently of the fate of the Tibetans, whose complete passing under Chinese law had only been delayed a few years, ST Circus and ST Barnum had been good operations for the CIA. By arming the Tibetans and by controlling their operations, the agency was able to put its hand on a quantity of Chinese documents recuperated by chance from the fighting. Paradoxically, it was during the fighting in Tibet that Langley learnt the most concerning the functioning of the Chinese army, its organization, its inadequacies and its internal difficulties sprung out of the Cultural Revolution...

LAOS 1961, OPERATION MILL POND

At the end of the fifties, Aderholt was also concerned in the Laotian theatre of operation, which was to become of critical importance throughout the years. The CIA was there to support a man of extraordinary personality, Lieutenant-Colonel Vang Pao, the charismatic leader of the Hmong people. The kingdom of Laos was part of the colonial empire of France in the far east. Becoming independent in 1949, it remained under French influence until the signing of agreements in Geneva in 1954, which put an end to the war in Indochina. At that time, the disengagement of Paris from the region was almost totally accomplished.

The Geneva accords stipulated that Laos remain neutral and that all foreign armies stationed there leave. These good intentions rapidly collided with each other with the test of time. The north-east of Laos was under Pathet Lao communist control, and actively supported by the new North Vietnamese government. At Vientiane, the capital, the struggle for power involved different factions of the army, each one supporting their favourite : Prince Phouma represented the neutralist party whereas General Nosavan led the Royalist party. In the north-east of the country the Pathet Lao communists opposed the Hmong guerillas of Lieutenant-Colonel Vang Pao.

When the Americans started to replace the French during the mid-fifties, the situation was already very confusing. It nonetheless freed several major policy directions : the Pathet Lao received significant aid from North Vietnam and the USSR, whereas the royalists and the Hmong were supported by the Americans. The risk of a confrontation between the super powers was real indeed.

To avoid this stumbling block, the Americans contemplated in 1961, creating an air force capable of backing the Hmong and the troops of General Novasan, but without displaying any direct links with the United States.

The CIA was responsible for setting up this aerial unit capable of leading offensive actions. Aderholt was at the head of the operation baptised Mill Pond.

It is worthy of note that this was to be the last wide-ranging para-military operation, using combat planes, organized by the CIA. In July 1961, the responsibility for such projects was handed over definitively to the Department of Defence.

Only a few hours were needed by Aderholt's crew to evaluate what material was needed; the majority of planes would be B-26 Invaders.

Between October 1960 and April 1961 no less than forty-five of these aircraft were taken out of US Air Force stocks to be put at the disposal of projects classed 'secret'. The majority of these planes came from Davis Monthan, an open air storage base where the US Air Force stored thousands of machines that it no longer needed. Laos was not the only destination for these craft, a good number of which were also used against Castro during Operation Pluto. The CIA kept several Invaders in the United Staes for training purposes. The Mill Pond pilots had to be on secondment from the US Air Force. One of these pilots, Captain Ronald Allaire, explained the conditions under which the operation was launched :

"I was offered a mission of the highest importance for the United States. A very black picture was painted : difficult conditions, high risk, no legal cover; I was detached to the US Air Force and if I got caught my country would not admit to knowing me!"

There was everything to satisfy the adventurous impulses of young pilots and following the example of several other foolhardy individuals, Allaire volunteered. He went first of all to the Pentagon to undergo a series of tests. From there he went to the Eglin base to receive training to pilot a B-26B.

For Allaire it was a mere formality as he had already piloted an RB-26, the reconnaissance version of the B-26.

"After only two transitional flights, linked up with several firing and bombing exercises, I signed the paper the following day which meant I had officially left the US Air Force!"

In the company of several other pilots, Allaire, soon after, got on board a PanAm plane heading for Bangkok. On their arrival, the pilots were employed by Bangkok Contract Air Service. This was a cover activity organized by the CIA, as the Americans were only staying a few hours in Bangkok. Very rapidly, they found themselves on board a C-130 Hercules flying to Takhli air base in the north of Thailand.

Takhli sheltered a unit of T-6s of the Royal Thailand air force, planes capable of providing light support fire. But this large base served as the hub of American aerial activity in the region. Deployment exercises were regularly organized there and the presence of American planes was nothing exceptional.

Shortly before the beginning of operation Mill Pond, one of these exercises had just taken place, enabling the positioning of large quantities of material without arousing suspicion. It remained to bring the planes, which for the moment were still in Japan where they had arrived by boat. As for the other CIA operations, the planes had been carefully gone over with a fine toothcomb to remove any identification marks likely to establish a link with the American government. The old US Air Force markings had, of course, been taken off and replaced by black paint.

Several days after their arrival, the pilots took a plane back to Kadena air base in Japan to pick up the B-26s.

THE FIRST SURPRISES

Approximately fifteen B-26s were brought back from Thailand by escort flight which was carried out in absolute radio silence. This was of course a blatant violation of the law of the air as the aircraft were flying with no identification markings.

As incredible as it may seem, it became clear at that time that several of the eighteen pilots engaged in the operation had never piloted a B-26 Invader; there was a confusion between the B-26 Invader and the B-26 Marauder. The Douglas Invader was known during the second world war under the name of A-26 (A for Attack), whereas at the same period the B-26 Marauder was in existence, a twin-engine medium bomber, constructed by the Martin company. At the end of the war, the A-26 Invader was re-named the B-26 Invader because of the withdrawal of the 'A' category, and also the last B-26 Marauders, from US stocks. It was always a possibility that this toing and froing would cause confusion several years after the end of the second world war. During the Vietnam war, the Invader was known under its original name of A-26.

All these administrative complications, as well as the lack of combat experience of practically all the pilots engaged in the operation, led the CIA to organize a firing zone in the Gulf of Siam, so that the pilots could train with their new aircraft.

At the same time, efforts to end the Loatian crisis diplomatically were failing. With each one supporting its local champion, the two superpowers were preparing for battle. In the month of April 1961, the Marines prepared some plans of action with the idea of an intervention from the US. As for a direct intervention by the B-26s, it seemed to be more and more imminent.

One evening, the pilots were informed that the game was to be played the following day. Four objectives were to be hit at the same time in the Jarres plain. Sixteen planes in all were engaged in the attacks. At the same time, three 'anonymous' C-130 Hercules were to transport troops. The B-26s were armed with bombs and canisters of napalm in anticipation of flights the following morning and, after a final briefing, the pilots went to bed. While they were sleeping, the wave of a massive scale fiasco was following its inevitable course on the other side of the world; it was the Bay of Pigs operation in Cuba.

Its resounding failure had the effect of a cold shower on the American planners. They preferred to cancel all other offensive actions in progress, notably in Laos.

They were justified in this, as the planned operation could very easily have resulted in failure. The relatively inexperienced American pilots, who perhaps did not all have a combative spirit, would have come up against positions which were heavily defended by anti-aircraft fire. Heavy losses were forecast.

No offensive mission was eventually launched. Instead, the B-26s were used to carry out reconnaissance missions. The stocks of aircraft were even enriched after several days by the addition of RB-26s, the reconnaissance version of the twin-engine bomber.

Also, a jet plane (an RT-33) devoid of all markings carried out several reconnaissance missions from the Thai base of Udorn.

Ronald Allaire, who had experience of reconnaissance flying and of the RB-26, was in charge of the first missions. These flights were also used to train the other pilots for their new task.

The first flights only attracted a little firing recalls Allaire. "All that changed after a few days when the enemy started spraying us with heavier calibre fire."

A photographic reconnaissance mission almost cut short the young pilot's life :

"It was the very beginning of May, and Aderholt had asked me to bring back photos of Route 8, which was later known as the Ho Chi Minh trail. We took off and went in an easterly direction, to cross into Laos at Nakhon Phanom."

The R-26 descended to an altitude of between 60 and 300 feet above the ground in order to carry out its mission.

The first part of the flight passed off uneventfully : the area was clearly seen, the pilot activated the camera sporadically when sections of the route became visible amongst the vegetation, or when there were clearings.

"We followed the route to North Vietnam, without noticing anything in particular. We turned and followed the route back. Because we still had a lot of film available, I switched the cameras on. We flew over a fairly large village where nothing out of the ordinary was visible; no lorries, no military equipment... only a few people around."

The plane had almost left the village when the pilot heard a deafening explosion behind, swiftly followed by another. Their plane jumped. "We'd been hit!"

"To get some good shots we had gone up to 450 feet where we became a perfect target. We immediately went into a dive to a very low altitude and escaped the firing."

A brief glance over his shoulder and Allaire immediately measured the extent of the damage : a direct hit from a 37mm had practically destroyed the flaps. The steering control had lost a lot of power but Allaire believed he could still control his plane by using the power of the engines.

"I put more power through the engines, the plane started to climb and we returned directly to Takhli without hesitating!"

LAOS NOT WORTH A WAR

Some time after, Kennedy and Khrushchev decided on a common accord that Laos was not worth a third world war. A ceasefire was signed in May 1961 and the independence of the country was reaffirmed during an international conference which took place in Geneva.

Reconnaissance missions were therefore interrupted but training continued on the Takhli base. Every single hour of flying time was carefully recorded by the pilots, who were taking great care to mask the exact nature of their work. No reference was made to the B-26 nor to Thailand. Officially all pilots were stationed at Andrew's base, more than

140

6,000 miles away, and were serving within a reserve unit. That way appearances were kept up and secrecy guaranteed, theoretically at least.

The saga of surprises concerning Laos was not yet over. A serious discussion took place at the American embassy in Bangkok when the American ambassador learnt one day, to his great surprise, of the existence of armed B-26s in Thailand. Despite the obligation that was made to different American agencies in the country to keep him informed of their activities, nobody had considered informing him of the spying operation in progress. The same day, the ambassador ordered Major Aderholt for the planes to leave before sunset. The planes in fact left the country progressively over the next few days.

It was not however the end of the story; the Americans only accorded a very limited trust to the North Vietnamese, suspected of strengthening their position in Laos a little more every day. Two RB-26s and one RT-33 returned to Takhli to take over reconnaissance missions over Laos from the end of 1961. The RB-26s were piloted by Air America crews, the airline company of the CIA, within the framework of Operation Black Watch. Once again, Aderholt was guaranteed control of the operation.

The planes flew only when required to by operational demands. This did not prevent them from being subject to ever more present and incisive anti-aircraft fire.

These aircraft were subsequently completed and progressively replaced by jets of the US Air Force based near Bangkok. In the spring of 1962, the RB-26s went to Vietnam to participate in the first assistance operations led by the US Air Force. A new war was being born in the Indochinese peninsular.

BUTTERFLIES FROM LAOS

When the war gained intensity in Vietnam in 1965, the position of Laos became more important than ever. All Vietnamese logistic effort going south passed through Laos, via the famous Ho Chi Minh trail, at certain points resembling more a motorway than a mule track. In these circumstances, Vang Pao and his Hmong fighters were essential to the Americans. Even though they were very close geographically, the two theatres of operation presented a surprising contrast.

Whereas the Vietnam war was widely covered by several thousand journalists, what was going on in Laos remained shrouded in secrecy. In Vietnam, the Americans took it on themselves to fight the essential combats. In Laos the dubious honour of fighting and dying went to the Hmongs. The American presence was limited to a strange collection of CIA agents and soldiers, pilots and technical advisers, all in civilian clothing. The most sensitive American aid came in fact from the air: combat planes taking off from Thailand or Vietnam penetrated Laos to attack communist targets there. To better direct and coordinate, a small group of FAC (Forward Air Control) were engaged alongside the forces of Vang Pao. Detached from the US Air Force, this handful of men were acting secretly in the country. There was no question of uniforms for them.

The FAC operated from light aircraft piloted by men of the CIA. The crews were completed by a third man, a Hmong interpreter who could communicate with the ground troops.

The roles were clearly divided; the man from the CIA, usually an Air America pilot, piloted the plane. The NCO of the US Air Force noted the targets and was in charge of the jets, whereas the interpreter ensured coordination with ground troops. The crews were nick-named "Butterfly" and flew aboard a Pilatus Porter, a craft with very short take-off and landing which greatly pleased the Air America pilots.

For Richard Secord, who directed the operation for the CIA, this three-man system, which could have so easily been a cacophony, in fact functioned rather well.

"When the Butterfly reached the fighting area, the aerial controller took his erasable pen and drew a plan of the terrain on the window of the plane. The interpreter who was in radio contact with the ground positions of friendly and enemy forces on the diagram. The controller was thus able to give all the necessary indications to the fighter-bombers of the US Air Force who were arriving at the scene…"

Because they were civilians, the pilots were not authorized to use armed planes. They were not even meant to fire smoke rockets to mark out targets. This forced them to guide the planes solely by using natural reference points existing on the ground. This led to communications such as :

"The enemy is 400 yards to the east of the bend in the river, near the copse, which joins the...etc"

This method often lacked accuracy, which could have dramatic consequences in the case of close quarter combat between the factions.

Not a great deal of time was required for the rules decreed in Washington to be forgotten in the depths of Laos. The Pilatus Porter was equipped with an exit door to enable small cargo loads to be dropped during flight. The American crews had the idea of dropping 100lb bombs through the opening. Some even went as far as dropping clusters of hand grenades. The surprise effect against the troops on the ground was devastating.

The very nature of their new mission placed the Butterflies in direct contact with the fighting. One of the pilots remembers a day of madness, during which a fortified Hmong camp took a severe hammering from the communist troops.

"We spent the day going backwards and forwards, we took several dozen gallons of fuel with a hand pump on the ground, then took off to guide the fighters, then came back to land and take some more fuel and so on. We hadn't enough time to pump enough fuel for a full tank, nor to guide in one go all the planes which were circling above the camp before going on to attack."

It must be said that, on that day, the bad weather over Vietnam had made a number of aircraft available, they were taken to Laos, instead of being able to attack their initial objectives.

"It was incredible! There was wave after wave. They came from Thailand, South Vietnam, the tankers waited for them at such an altitude as to enable them to make the return trip to the north of Laos. All that to defend a small camp! The assailants must have been the most surprised, they were on the receiving end of several dozen tons of bombs."

Another example of what the Butterfly could carry out is illustrated by the battle of the Lima 36 site. Because of its proximity to North Vietnam, this site was used by the Americans to launch helicopter operations to rescue pilots who had been shot down. But Lima 36 also very much interested the North Vietnamese for whom it represented a key resupply point in the middle of the Jarres plain, of major interest and a source of confrontation between Vang Pao and the communists.

After having changed its owner several times, Lima 36 eventually came back in the hands of Vang Pao, when on the morning of the 6th January 1967, almost 800 enemy soldiers launched a huge attack. From the very first hours of the fighting all means of retreat was cut off by the attackers, and one of the two CIA advisers present was killed. The second American requested urgent air support over the radio.

"The weather did not make it easy," remembers the Butterfly pilot who was in the zone that day. "The thick cloud layer hid the surrounding peaks."

Several American jets attempted to penetrate the layer of cloud to deliver their armaments, without success.

After several attempts however, an F-105 pilot found an opening in the sea of cloud and managed to fly over the combat zone at great speed. But because he was flying too low he could not drop the bombs on the assailants as he risked being hit by the resulting explosion. Its spectacular and daring run, however, dampened the ardour of the assailants. Several minutes later, some Skyraider appeared in the zone. A strike aircraft motorized by an enormous propeller driven Wright 2,500hp engine, the Skyraider was better adapted than fast jets to this type of mission. Its manoeuvrability allowed it to move around at ground level and in a small air space, yet it also fired with great accuracy.

Under the direction of the Butterfly, the Skyraiders started to spray the assailants with 20mm rocket and gun fire. Severely weakened, they gave up the attack in the night and would begin their withdrawal the following morning at dawn.

But it was already too late for them. Their withdrawal route, which passed by a small canyon, less than a mile from the place of attack, had been spotted by the Butterflies.

"It was a very woody area which meant that ground movements could not be easily detected", remembers one of the men. "It did not stop the air force who systematically treated the zone with rockets and 500lb bombs."

At the end of the day the little wooded canyon looked more like the moon. According to the men of the CIA, the communists had lost more than 250 men in the attack, whereas the friendly losses amounted to no more than nine, including the CIA adviser. Despite the excellence of their work, the story of the Butterfly stopped at the end of 1966, after a General in the US Air Force realised the huge incongruity of what had happened in Laos : the most sophisticated jets in the world were led into battle by simple NCOs in planes piloted by civilians. From a military point of view this was a distressing situation and had to stop, as indeed it did.

At the beginning of 1967, a special training programme was set up in the United States so that pilots of the Air Force could replace the Butterflies. But the change was a minor one for the CIA. The secret war in Laos was still its war, and wherever the pilots had come from, they still worked under CIA authority and with no uniform. The US Air Force was soon to acknowledge these basic truths.

THE STEVE CANYON PROGRAMME

The CIA managed to resist with a certain degree of success the will of some American generals who wished for only one thing: to be able to intervene openly using their large battalions in Laos, as they had started to do in Vietnam. The US Air Force's FAC eventually replaced the Butterflies, the only concession to conventional warfare desired by senior level military staff.

Still the representativeness of these military pilots was very limited. The war in Laos remained above all a CIA affair and they determined the means of engagement. Theoretically, the pilots of the US Air Force flying to Laos were dependent on the 56th Special Operation Wing based at Nakhon Phanom in Thailand. In practice, they were placed on the terrain under the direct command of the CIA men who were in charge of ground operations.

The influence of the air force was above all lessened by the particular development of operations in Laos. The war led by the Americans there was considered as a secret operation, no uniform was allowed to be worn. Even prior to treading on Laotian soil, the pilots of the air force had swapped their dark blue uniform for a civilian outfit based on jeans and a T shirt. Well beyond a simple change of clothes, this immersion in a secret operation, far removed from traditional military hierarchy, led to radical changes in the mens' behaviour. They very rapidly formed a separate clan. They were, above all, pilots but also adventurers in a kind of fringe group. Some even remembered vaguely that they were part of the air force.

The pilots carried out one-year tours of duty in Vietnam. After six months, the US Air Force offered them the possibility of changing the theatre of operation to rejoin what was known discreetly as 'the other war'. Nobody knew too much about this other war. It was said that it was very bloody, without knowing precisely how and where it was unfolding. When superior officers spoke about it they mentioned the "Steve Canyon programme." The name was not chosen at random.

Steve Canyon was a very popular comic strip hero in the United States. He was the prototype of the aviator-adventurer, a sort of John Wayne, whose horse was replaced by a plane and the Colt by a .45 Automatic. John Wayne defended the widow and the orphan, Steve Canyon defended democracy and the West. He travelled the world accepting any mission, provided it was perilous, exciting and... politically correct as we would say today. In 1950, his creator put a stop to his adventurous life; to face up to a 'danger from the north', he volunteered to fight in the ranks of the Air force in the far east.

The evocation of Steve Canyon made the young pilots smile, but it also created a profound curiosity.

The officer who welcomed the newly arrived pilots to Vietnam mentioned the name in front of them but remained enigmatic concerning the exact contents of the programme. Without doubt he would have been hard pushed to add any details.

"Start by doing your six months of FAC. If you are still interested in adventure after the first six months come back and see me and we'll talk about Steve Canyon."

After six months the majority of pilots had no desire to change things as the Vietnam war and its routine suited them very well. In the south of the country, long periods of inactivity or slow activity were interspersed with short intensive operations. Harshly prepared for combat, the FAC were

146

sometimes surprised to fly only 15 days per month. The majority did not complain; the less time they spent in the air, the less risk they had of being shot. If they could have night missions or high-altitude missions, out of range of light-arms fire, or even in low-risk zones, it increased their chances of returning to the US in one piece after their tour of duty.

THE RULES OF ENGAGEMENT

This dull situation however did not suit everyone. For those who were nick-named "shooters", each day spent away from the war was a day lost. Whereas they only asked to do battle with the enemy, Vietnam for them often came down to pointless drinking sessions ending either in the arms of the military police or those of a bar girl. The choice was always the same. And when, happily for them, the hour of battle arrived, the incredibly restricting rules of combat had the result of discouraging even the most motivated among them.

With the development of the war, these rules, which codified the action of the pilots on the terrain, had become ever more complex. This was the mistake of the powers that be in Washington, who wrote these rules with political considerations in mind. Considerations which did not take into account the reality of the terrain.

The novice pilot spent his first two days in Vietnam learning these famous rules by heart. He then had to take an exam every month to prove that they had been perfectly assimilated.

"The rules were not only very complex, but also terribly frustrating for everyone", explained the pilots. "We often had the feeling of fighting with our hands tied behind our backs."

Some of the more grotesque examples were legion; a fighter pilot could not, for example, attack a North Vietnamese MiG if it was on the ground. To be attacked, the MiG had to be flying, clearly identified and showing hostile intentions.

"What sort of MiG doesn't show hostile intentions in Vietnam?" quipped the pilots.

In certain areas, enemy logistical lorries could avoid being attacked simply by leaving the road and lining up on the verges; only the roadway was considered to be a war zone. American politicians decided also that the pagodas could not be attacked. The Vietcong rapidly stored ammunition, mortars and anti-aircraft batteries there.

To contravene these rules of engagement could mean a court martial. The level of frustration among the pilots was consequently very high among the pilots of the FAC, especially the shooters.

Terry Murphy was one of these pilots for whom the Steve Canyon programme had become a kind of last hope.

"The weight of conflict in Vietnam was stifling", he recalls, "along with the hierarchy and the rules of engagement, and a whole population of parasites in the background who were singing their own praises while we were fighting... I had to get out!"

Rumours were circulating about the Steve Canyon programme which remained shrouded in mystery. The name of the CIA appeared more than once.

"Nobody really knew where it took place", Murphy continues, "or what the job consisted of. One thing seemed certain, it was outside Vietnam, far from all this absurdity, and it involved a lot of flying."

When Murphy made it known to his superior that he wanted to rejoin the programme, the officer dissuaded him from doing so by repeating the terrible rumours that were circulating :

"The losses are very heavy over there Murphy. You'll have a one in two chance of coming home in a body bag."

"Maybe it is risky, but at least I'll escape all the military administration, the hierarchy who are having a great time. That's what counts." concluded Murphy.

Just as a light always attracts insects, the appeal for the Shooters was just as irresistible. The pilots who flew for the Steve Canyon programme were nick-named Ravens. This name, which was in fact taken from their radio code, fitted them like a glove. A mysterious, highly intelligent, cunning bird, with excellent flying abilities, the raven captured the essence of qualities which were demanded of the pilots.

On choosing to join the Ravens, the pilot saw his status change immediately.

"Even when I was waiting for the plane to join the Ravens outside

Vietnam, I could detect a change in attitude of the superior officers," explained another pilot. "The kind of respect they showed us made us really think that the Raven played a very special part within the military microcosm."

After leaving Vietnam, the pilots were transferred to the American base of Udorn, in Thailand. They were welcomed by a US Air Force colonel who gave them the following speech :

"While you are away, all the administrative queries relating to you will be taken care of here. Apart from that, even though I am officially your commander I don't know where you are going and I don't want to know. Good luck...!"

The Ravens quickly realised that Udorn was nothing more than a stepping stone. Before taking the plane for their final and still secret destination, they realised that the American base was just a passage between their old military life and their new life as a secret pilot. The new Raven gave back his uniform and his military ID card. In exchange, he was given a series of vaccinations and a hand gun.

To the curious pilots who insisted on knowing their final destination, the answer was always the same:

"Listen guys, we don't know anything here, we are serving as a front. You'll see soon enough where you are going..."

After 24 hours spent at Udorn, the Ravens boarded an Air America plane. The CIA pilots were willing to give information to the newcomer : "You're going to Vientiane, guys. You've landed Laos!"

On arrival at the Laotian capital, the pilots passed through the bureau of the air attaché at the American embassy which gave them a local driving licence as well as a US AID (Agency for International Development) ID card, an American governmental aid organization for underdeveloped countries. Officially, the Ravens were foresters working for AID. This unconvincing cover didn't fool anyone, and certainly not the Chinese agents who systematically photographed all the Americans arriving at Vientiane with a telephoto lens. It was above all a question of conserving appearances in an officially neutral city, where the embassies of the United States, China, North Vietnam and USSR were cheek by jowl, even though the war was raging several miles away.

After a riotous night spent in Vientiane, the pilot was put under a CIA officer. A Cessna O-1, similar to the plane he was to use during his missions, led him eventually to his final destination, in the north of the country. Serious business was about to begin.

Seen from the air, Laos was a beautiful sight. Craggy, rugged mountains emerging from a carpet of green through which the rivers meandered slowly. From a distance, several villages perched at the top of hills appeared, a single goat's track linking them to the valley below. Sitting on the rear seat of the Cessna, the new Raven was more and more puzzled. Nothing he saw tallied with the apocalyptic desciptions that he had heard about 'the other war'. It was only a question of time however. For if very large areas of Laos seemed to have been spared by the war, the fighting was raging furiously in other parts of the country.

A SECRET TOWN

The Cessna was heading for Long Tien, the nerve centre of the secret war led by the CIA in Laos. Long Tien (code 'Sky'), was a real town that had grown secretly, without ever appearing on official maps. With more than 40,000 inhabitants it had become the second city in the country, after the capital Vientiane.

The town was positioned in a valley enclosed on three sides by mountains. The hard-surface landing strip went along the centre of the valley, bordered at one end by traditional Hmong dwellings and at the other by a number of pre-fabricated buildings.

In the eyes of the newly arrived visitor, Long Tien offered an incredible contrast. The natural setting and the Hmong village itself seemed to have come right out of the past. Children played naked in the streets where a whole farmyard of animals seemed to circulate freely. There were no vehicles in Long Tien.

This age-old sight was brutally contrasted by a high-tech background of CIA activity : Long Tien was also a labyrinth of pre-fab buildings, and a forest of telecommunication aerials shared space with a continual traffic of helicopters and planes. The base was equipped with radio-navigation beacons and a system allowing planes to land in all weathers.

"There were more aerials than trees at Long Tien", wrote one of the first jounalists to cast an indiscreet eye in the Holy of Holies, at the beginning of the seventies.

"There was incessant activity", recalls Craig Dunn an old Raven. "At the end of the afternoon, before nightfall, there was a constant flurry of helicopters and planes returning from missions. In the middle of all that, were strange-looking men from the CIA, Air America pilots in eccentric uniforms, Hmong guerillas, ten-year old kids armed to the teeth...It was like a pirate's den in the Caribbean."

Nothing satisfied the newcomers better than these extravagant goings on that they discovered at Long Tien; it corresponded so well with the idea that they had of the Steve Canyon programme. They had already forgotten Vietnam and its catalogue of stupidities.

The pre-eminence of the CIA on the ground did not pass without a certain gnashing of teeth and the odd clash between the different administrations. The US Air Force felt particularly frustrated at having to "lend" pilots and planes, for a programme over which it had no control. This gave rise to some bitter exchanges between Ravens and the Air Force authorites present in the Laotian capital.

The American air attaché present in Vientiane drafted new rules of engagement that he had transmitted to the Ravens by a superior officer. The man was welcomed rather coolly at the Long Tien base. The Ravens had not left Vietnam and its host of rules and regulations simply to see a new set imposed on them in Laos :

"You can get lost" the pilots told him. "We'll drop our bombs where we want, wherever it will help our men on the ground."

"You work for the US Air Force and your job is to carry out what the Air Force tells you to", replied the emissary who was starting to see red.

"The Air Force pays us and that's all", replied the Ravens. "We fly first and foremost for Vang Pao and the CIA"

It was precisely that which irritated the Air Force, but also the other services which felt obliged to accede to the demands of the CIA without being able to ask any questions. For reasons as diverse as they were secret, the CIA took its officers from the Navy, Marines, Army or the Air Force. The agency used these men to lead its own operations, without costing it a penny as the officers continued to be paid by their service of origin. Not only did this service pay people who were working for another governmental organization, but it also had to justify every one of its expenses, which of course was not the case for the CIA.

"Our role was to sustain the war" explained Dunn. In return the CIA fully supported the activity of the Ravens.

"We could always ask anything of the CIA explained another pilot." "They would always do their utmost to satisfy us. The logistics which passed by Air America was also under their jurisdiction. We were in fact very autonomous vis a vis the Air Force; the freedom of action was unbelievable compared with Vietnam."

In the eyes of the senior officers of the US Air Force, the Ravens were nothing more than a band of pirates. Several attempts had been made to gain back the pilots from the Steve Canyon programme. Every time the Air Force tried to integrate new men fresh out of military academy, the newcomers were rapidly snapped up by the Ravens' system. According to an officer from HQ, they were becoming 'Mexican bandits'.

One young officer, Larry Sanborn, was selected in that way to lead the Ravens. A brilliant pilot, and a paragon officer of the US Air Force, Sanborn had, it was said, a personality which was the antithesis of the dissident minority who inhabited LongTien. Sanborn was conscientiously informed about Long Tien and the 'Mexican bandits' that he was going to have to get back into line. He was the best asset the US Air Force had to get this band of renegades under control. On his arrival at Long Tien, during a casual conversation over a beer, he asked the several pilots present to describe their mission to him.

"We kick butts and take names" said one of them.

The others all agreed and laughed loudly. Only a short time was needed for Sanborn to fully realise the extraordinary work accomplished daily by the Ravens. It was not unusual for them to have 18 hour days. More commonly, pilots were in their planes every day for ten to twelve hours, seven days a week for the whole six months of their assignment and all that in a high-risk environment. The days when they were not fired at were exceptions.

"My principal worry was that the pilots were wasting away because they were simply flying too much." explains Sanborn. "From time to time, I sent one or two out of the country on forced leave so they did not, literally, kill themselves on the job."

The Ravens presented an inverse problem compared with the majority of American fighters present in south-east Asia; they had to be held back from fighting too much, rather than pushed to fight.

This said a lot for the personality of Vang Pao and the Hmongs for whom the Ravens had a profound respect.

Following the example of all those who had gone before, Sanborn took up the cause for the Ravens and came to serve as a benevolent intermediary between the men of Long Tien and the strategists who had wished to impose their will from Vientiane, Saigon or Washington.

MAKE THE ENEMY SHOW ITSELF

The work of an advanced aerial controller was thankless indeed. They did not benefit from the aura of glory which surrounded the fighter and fighter-bomber pilots. Very rapidly however, the FAC operating in Laos earned the reputation of doing work as dangerous, difficult and essential as their colleagues who had the chance of piloting infinitely more sophisticated aircraft. This reputation was justified; an average 90% of Ravens were hit by the enemy at least once during their six month presence in the theatre of operation. Two thirds of them found themselves, at some time or another, on the ground with an aircraft damaged or destroyed by enemy fire.

Along with the other FAC, the work of the Ravens was to fly very slowly and very close to the ground, to be able to make the most of tactical situations, sight targets and guide the ground attack jets.

"A good FAC, who indicated the target for the jet pilot, had to be able to put himself in his position" explains Craig Dunn. But at the same time, he had to accept to fly in a combat zone at the controls of an aircraft barely worthy of an amateur air club."

Until the beginning of the seventies, the Ravens flew Cessna O-1s, a light two-seater built for the US Army at the very beginning of the fifties. Removed of all its armour and auto-sealing tanks, the plane had a maximum speed of less than 120mph, and much less than that when it was carrying several rockets under its wing to mark out targets. Slow and without any protection, without the skill of its pilot and the small-ness of its silhouette, the FAC was an easy prey and losses amongst the Ravens were very heavy.

Confronted with the FAC, the enemy often faced a dilemma. He could chose to hold his fire so as not to reveal his position, or give in to temp-tation and fire at the tiny plane which represented such an easy target. Knowing that roughly a third of Ravens were killed or injured in ope-ration, they were forced to recognize that the enemy often gave in to temptation... These terrible statistics, totally out of proportion to what would have been seen and tolerated in 'regular' units of the US Air For-ce, meant that recruitment of new Ravens was a high priority. The num-bers involved however were extremely small because even during the heaviest periods of combat, there were never more than twenty or so Ravens in the whole of Laos, half of which were allocated to LongTien base. No doubt the fearsome reputation and the aura of mystery whi-ch surrounded the Ravens made it appear that their numbers were much greater. The work of the FAC was so effective that it enabled the forces of Vang Pao to effectively stop the advance of enemy forces, Pathet Lao and North Vietnamese, from the beginning of 1969.

But the price paid in blood by the Hmongs was enormous, whereas for the American strategists the war in Laos had above all been a pre-text to fight the North Vietnamese on a secondary theatre of operation. For Washington, the object of all these preoccupations remained the Vietnamese conflict and the multiple diplomatic efforts at the begin-ning of the seventies, resulting in a disengagement, were proof of it.

The most important thing in these efforts, the Paris accords signed on the 27th June 1973, put an official end to American military invol-vement in the region. These accords had been ratified between the Ame-ricans and the North Vietnamese. The South Vietnamese and the Lao-tians had not been invited to the negotiating table.

A short paragraph of several lines included in the peace accords sea-led the future of Laos, without the authorities of the country taking part in the discussions.

154

North Vietnam and the United States both undertook to respect the neutrality of Laos. Giving in to strong American pressure, the government of Laos eventually accepted the terms of the treaty. Believing sincerely, or pretending to believe, in the North Vietnamese promise of neutrality, the Americans withdrew their aerial support from their Laotian allies and the CIA dismantled its organization.

The accord signed in Paris was the last in a long series of accords, and just like the previous ones, was openly violated by communist signatories. It mattered little to the Americans, such was their desire to finish with their military engagement in South-East Asia that it dominated any other consideration.

A SHAMEFUL END

Conversely, the Ravens learnt with shame and amazement the conditions of the American disengagement. The cease-fire was planned for the 22nd February 1973 at midday and the American pilots fought right up until the last minute. In anticipation of any reaction of objections from the pilots, the US Air Force threatened to court martial any pilot who did not respect the time of the cease-fire.

As the fatal hour approached, the combat on the ground continued but the Air Force jets gradually deserted the skies of Laos.

Jack Shaw was one of the last Ravens to fly. While he was in the skies over the town of Paksong, he could clearly see that friendly troops fighting on the ground were finding the situation very difficult. Shaw implored the US Air Force to send strike aircraft to the area. In vain.

In the rear seat of his Cessna was an officer of the CIA. He also was not able to reconcile himself to the planned desertion of the allies and he fired M-79 grenades and his M-16 on to the communist troops. A rather pathetic intervention which did not even have a pacifying effect.

At ten minutes to midday, Shaw turned back to join his base.

"I felt pitiful, we were well aware of the fact that as soon as we had turned our backs, the North Vietnamese would not respect the peace accords and would make short work of our comrades on the ground." And that is exactly what happened. Paksong fell at 12.30, barely thirty minutes after the official cease-fire. In the following days, the Vietnamese and the Pathet Lao launched a vast offensive, thus openly violating the cease-fire.

A handful of Ravens stayed on for several weeks in position at Vientiane, without the possibility of intervening in the conflict. Along with the great frustration felt at not being able to participate in the fighting, there existed an intense boredom. They were meant to symbolize American vigilance and be ready, if the need arose, to fly if the enemy did not respect the peace accords. As we have seen, the accords were finished before they had really begun. But as the American administration was tangled up in the Watergate affair it had other preoccupations. The fighting multiplied in Laos, without Washington being greatly worried. In September 1973, the last Ravens left the country definitively. They went in the opposite direction along the path which had led them, several months earlier, to the heart of what had been the most secret war of the CIA. At Udorn, in Thailand, they retrieved their uniform, military ID card and their personal effects.

Then they got on board a military transport craft which took them back, across the Pacific, to the west coast of the United States.

CHAPTER 5

AIR AMERICA

THE AIRLINE OF THE CIA

In 1959, after Chennault had returned to the US and died of lung cancer, CAT international operations were reorganized under the name of Air America. This new company was placed under the control of the Pacific Corporation, a holding company secretly owned by the CIA and based in the state of Delaware. At the height of its activity the Pacific Corporation employed more than 20,000 people.

CAT operations involved in the Taiwanese domestic market existed under the name of CAT, whereas all maintenance activites were regrouped within the Air Asia company, also under the control of the Pacific Corporation.

Even though the Pacific Corporation controlled several other companies over the years, none other knew as much notoriety as Air America.

With the development of wars in south east Asia and the ever increasing involvement of the United States, Air America had grown in importance to become the jewel in the aerial empire of the CIA. An empire that not even the US intelligence service knew completely.

By the number of planes that it put into operation, 167 in total at the height of its operations, from Boeing 727s to Cessna two-seaters, not forgetting dozens of helicopters, Air America was sometimes thought of as being the largest airline company in the world. It was perhaps exaggerated, but the sheer paradox of an airline company belonging to the secret service at the same time as being at the top of the world league table would have been delectable. At the end of the sixties, Air America manpower reached 5,600 people.

Without the links with the CIA being openly admitted, many rumours circulated concerning Air America. How could it be otherwise for an airline company which seemed to prosper only in areas of bad fortune and destruction?

The boastful company slogan did nothing to calm the questions : "Anything, Anytime, Anywhere, professionally." This commercial argument was an open door for questions to be asked. Its pilots were described as being men who craved adventure, yet they were remarkably untalkative with journalists. Very few certainties were known about the company.

This did not stop excellent business deals from being made in Laos. The excellent financial health came from near exclusive contracts which linked Air America to American governmental agencies working in Laos, notably AID (Agency for International Development). The only activity of AID, which used Air America craft to resupply the civilian population, victims of the war, assured the company a revenue of several million dollars per year. The raison d'etre of the company nonetheless remained the support of the secret war led by the CIA within the country. The American intelligence agency had no scruples whatsoever in grafting its own activities onto those of AID which served as a decoy, as well as being lucrative.

The loads were mixed up within the planes and even in the vocabulary; rice destined for the people was often found next to 'hard rice', a company slang word for ammunition.

The CIA found itself faced with a new problem; instead of costing money here was a cover operation bringing in money, a lot of money. Although this money did not reimburse the CIA for the investments undertaken to set up and launch the initial activities of the airline company.

A debate had taken place within the CIA before this period of prosperity to decide whether the agency should continue to pour money into the airline companies. When the pilots and planes were engaged in the operation, the CIA could console itself with the fact that it received a good service, in spite of the cost. But during periods of inactivity, the companies were still horribly expensive in terms of fixed expenses, salaries and the regular maintenance of planes, for a non-existent profit.

"Carry on", the CIA top brass eventually decided. They were aware of the enormous advantages that the ownership of airline companies available "anytime, anywhere", could bring about for the least declarable types of operations.

That is how in Laos the inverse question came to be posed ; what could be done with an airline company that was earning so much money?

The phenomenon was unusual enough for certain highly placed personnel at Langley to start to worry;

The money thus earned by the CIA could easily escape any control and be used for, among other things, secret operations unknown to any political power. A solution conforming to requirements of administrative logic would have necessitated that the money be given to the US Treasury. This idea was quickly quashed. In the country of the free market, it was almost a sacrilege for a company with a capitalist infrastructure to hand over hard earned money. But the real problem was more underhand, in receiving several million dollars from nowhere, the Treasury could have legitimately posed questions on its origins and thereby initiated an enquiry, with the inevitable complications that would have resulted.

But not a great deal was necessary for the US agency to find a simple solution that satisfied everybody : Air America could keep hold of its profits if it was responsible for reinvesting in its operations and the growth of its activities.

The HQ at Langley held minimal control over the airline company. The two parts worked in close collaboration, but according to client-supplier relations. The reality of power held by the CIA remained unknown to the majority, even within the heart of the airline company.

Air America was not the only company held by the CIA. Langley kept a ruling hand over a veritable network of dozens of companies throughout the world.

Obviously, the majority of pilots did not know the true identity of the owner of these companies. Some of them would come across an article in the press many years later quite by chance, informing them who had been their real employer.

The air activities of the CIA were not limited to the companies whose capital it controlled. The American agency also had numerous shareholdings in different foreign companies, such as Air Ethiopia, Air Jordan and even Iran Air. Without being linked by formal agreements, these companies proved themselves to be very cooperative when required and always kept aircraft available at any moment for the American agency.

If the CIA took a share in companies of countries considered 'high risk', it was as much to avoid the controlling hand of the communists as to have a very worthy information gathering instrument.

"When you are curious about a region or a country, two things interest you", said the businessman Orvis Nelson. "Information and a means of transportation. The latter can allow you to get the information out, to move men, to control movements, that is what an airline company is used for."

Orvis Nelson knew what he was talking about. While denying working with the CIA, he had, during the course of his career, participated in the creation of no less than sixteen airline companies throughout the world. There were even air companies which fully and assiduously cooperated with the CIA without having capitalist links with the US secret service.

Continental airlines was the best example. Interested in the ripe Laotian market, the L.A. company complained bitterly to the American federal authorities that Air America, this real-false private enterprise, had the largest share of the cake without any other competition being possible.

Concerned at the idea that Continental could bring about legal action against this monopoly, a process which could have shown the real link with Air America, the CIA permitted Continental to create a subsidiary in 1965, Continental Air Services, for its operations in Laos. Continental Air Services reached its rhythm of activity within the space of a few months. From 1966, the US company put a fleet of 21 planes into operation from Thailand, including twelve C-46 and C-47s. Continental Air Services could thus work practically on an equal footing with Air America under AID contracts.

This explosion of aerial activity owed nothing to chance : Continental was content with taking over, for the tidy sum of 4.2 million dollars, a company already very active in the region : Bird Air.

William Bird was an entrepreneur whose company was based in Seattle, Washington. He was a specialist in the construction and repair of airfields and had carried out the major part of his business in the Pacific area after the war. In 1959, he had gone to Laos to take part in a bid for the construction of a new airport runway in the capital, then he realised the profit that could be made in the country working from different American agencies existent in the country.

Bird soon learnt that the majority of aerial transport contracts went, without any bids ever being launched, to Air America. A visit to Washington and some influential senators allowed him to remedy this situation, respecting little the most elementary rules of free competition. The competition was finally opened and Bird rapidly won the first contract for the air company that he had just created : Bird Air.

Bird Air very soon operated on the tracks of Air America, transporting bags of rice as well as secret agents to the most unlikely areas. And like Air America, Bird Air carried out the majority of its business with AID contracts.

After having begun its activities with a single aircraft, Bird Air had become a major company in the region when Continental offered to take it over.

At the same time Air America had more than 150 planes and 8,000 employees. To put things into perspective, Flying Tigers was the largest transport company working for the US when Air America was born. Flying Tigers had a mere 28 planes and 2,000 employees.

If they vehemently denied any direct link with the US intelligence agency, the directors of Continental Air Services showed themselves to be patriotic by authorizing the CIA to use them as a cover company when circumstances allowed it. In other areas, notably in Latin America, PanAm also collaborated with the CIA by offering 'covers' to its agents.

It must be recognized that in this there was nothing exceptional, the majority of secret service organizations throughout the world had occasion, to a greater or lesser extent, to a voluntary or enforced collaboration with national airline companies.

A COCKTAIL OF DOLLARS AND ADVENTURE

Marked by a certain disenchantment, for many young pilots who had just finished their operational tour in Vietnam, disillusionment was at its peak. Money was still the strongest motivation, along with a genuine pleasure in flying.

Air America possessed a strong smell of money which had the power to retain their attention. "Air America is a company where you can easi-

163

ly make money", they recognized. "And yet we are not just mercenaries. We wouldn't fly for the communists even if they offered us $10,000 a month..."

To fly for Air America was nonetheless a little like flying for the star-spangled banner, flying for something that was right. The CIA pilots were definitely not mercenaries, if the bitterness vis a vis American engagement in the region was widespread among the pilots, a number of them continued to think that the survival of the free world depended on their sacrifice. The vast majority of them acknowleged that "it was easier to save the world for $4,000 a month than for $1,000..."

But not everyone went along with this reasoning. Air America offered to certain individuals a heady cocktail of adventure and risk, easily comparable to the Steve Canyon programme which occupied the pilots of the Air Force, a cocktail which would have been impossible to find elsewhere in civilian life. The CIA company offered an out of the ordinary existence, far from the burden of paying the mortgage and the everyday routine of the sales representative or factory worker... For some the freedom was priceless.

For others, it gave the possibility of changing their lives, escaping from past mistakes or re-living a youthful adventure, or of finding something that they had never experienced before.

"I used to say to my friends that the company could have had me for a lot less, even for nothing at all", explains Garry White, helicopter pilot. "I liked the risk, and the challenges which I faced everyday as a pilot. They were without doubt the most interesting years of my life."

This spirit of adventure made Air America, which was after all only a regional airline company, a force of energy and dynamism. The salaries were good, the pilots motivated, the hierarchy very flexible, and activity incessant. This was a dream to many, but a dream that a well-aimed bullet could instantly transform into a nightmare.

There was never a shortage of volunteers. By working hard a pilot could earn up to $5,000 per month, to which savings made on tax and travel could be added. This situation sometimes created tensions and jealousies with their old colleagues, the military pilots. The Air America pilots sometimes behaved ostentatiously, displaying their 'visible signs of wealth', bracelets, watches and gold chains. "All this gold will allow us to save our skin the day we are shot down..." they explained.

One day, one young pilot of the US Air Force called an Air America base in Laos to say that he was maybe going to have an emergency. The hydraulic system of the aircraft was showing signs of weakness. It would be necessary for Air America to get ready to pick him up if he had to eject.

"Negative for the emergency", replied the duty pilot, himself an ex Air Force pilot. "We can't take care of you for the moment, we are too busy."

"What do you mean? What are you doing?"

"What do you think we're doing, we're counting our money..."

For those pilots who came back and landed next to a plane covered with bulletholes, this money was well-earned. The dozens of deaths of crew-members that the company experienced was confirmation of that.

Air America, and CAT before it, had no difficulty in recruiting its pilots from the ranks of the US Air Force during the first years of its existence. The pilots could earn two or three times more by following a civilian career and the change did not go unrewarded.

But with the ever increasing American engagement in south east Asia, recruiting pilots from the US Air Force was soon not enough to satisfy requirements and the company began hiring from the civilian sector. It's principal worry was to find people a little out of the ordinary, people who were up to the work that was expected of them.

Art Wilson, a fighter with a strong personality, was the prototype itself of the Air America pilot. Wilson was a legendary figure known throughout the world of flying in the far-east under the nickname of "flip-flops".

He had begun his career as a pilot at the controls of C-46 Comman-dos which were resupplying the Chinese flying over the Himalayas. One day, he was shown a Dakota by a young pilot who asked him how many hours he had spent flying the plane.

"About 4,000" replied Wilson.

The young pilot could not hide his astonishment. "I would have thought you'd have done more than that!"

"That's right, son. I have flown 4,000 hours in this Dakota."

In 1966 when he was able to count more than 25,000 flying hours, the company realised that he did not have a valid American pilot's licence. Wilson could only show a Chinese licence, a rather vague document with no value in the eyes of the American authorities.

Wilson was sent to the United States to earn a licence worthy of the name. On his arrival at a pilots' school in Louisiana, he explained to the instructor the reason for his presence : "I would like a commercial pilots licence."

"Let's start at the beginning", said the instructor. "First you have to obtain a private pilots' licence and then climb the ladder."

"No I'm not interested in that. In fact what I want is to fly one of those". He pointed to a Dakota clearly visible on the hardstand.

"My dear man, you'll have to start with something a little smaller!" The instructor gave Wilson a condescending smile that he really didn't like. The pilot with 25,000 flying hours under his belt was losing patience.

"Son, I've had more flying hours than you've had hot dinners..."

Wilson was born in China. He could speak and write the language fluently and enjoyed living like a Chinese. The company hierarchy was prepared to look the other way concerning his rather particular culinary requirements. But it was less prepared to do so with his taste for flip-flops which he wore constantly.

One day a CIA instructor came to Vientiane to conduct a jungle survival course for the pilots. While he was giving his exposé, the man could not take his eyes off Wilson's 'shoes'. Not able to help it, he finally spoke directly to Wilson :

"If you are shot down, how much time would you need to escape from the jungle with those things on your feet", he asked.

"Let me think about that son...the last time I needed two weeks. The time before that took me a little longer, let's say about six weeks..."

After that the instructor didn't ask Wilson any more questions.

Nonetheless among the top brass, the flip-flops continued to irritate. When the company insisted on him flying with normal shoes, Wilson got hold of a pair of regulation jungle boots, which he wore to walk to his plane. Once in the cockpit, he couldn't wait to take them off and put his flip-flops back on. He turned to his co-pilot and, if he was a young man lacking in a little confidence, Wilson told him to sit on his hands and touch absolutely nothing until they reached their destination :

166

"I don't want to die, son."

Legend or reality, it was also said that he had a home-made survival kit for use in case he was shot down; it contained a sandwich, a can of beer and a spare pair of flip-flops.

AN ATMOSPHERE OF INSECURITY

If the CIA had only from time to time kept launching isolated secret operations, the demand for aircraft would not have been what it was. It was the fact of conducting a real secret war in Laos that enabled Air America and, to a lesser extent other CIA companies, to develop enormously.

Aerial CIA operations in Laos were of two types. We have previously mentioned how the agency used its pilots, or the pilots of the Air Force placed under its responsibilty, in offensive or guidance operations, in order to carry out its war.

Alongside this, a considerable number of missions requiring more of a logistic effort were assured by a great variety of transport aircraft. That was the role of Air America. In the majority of cases, it was simply a question of coasting between the different towns and villages to transport supplies. A basic task which any airline company could have carried out. With the difference being that very often, Air America aircraft had to fly in a combat zone. Air America did not fire bullets, but it received more than its fair share.

"Not a day went by without one of our craft coming back with a hole in its fuselage", as Ron Zappa, a C-123 pilot, summed up.

"Being fired at was part of everyday life. I certainly took more risks in Laos with Air America than in the three wars where I was a fighter pilot", recalled another pilot who had served in the second world war and the Korean and Vietnam wars.

"In a classic war situation, the danger was there when you arrived at the target or in enemy territory. In Laos, danger was present everywhere. Between taking off and landing, you just weren't safe."

The pilots knew with certainty that when they flew to such and such a place that they were going to fly over communist Pathet Lao anti-aircraft installations. They therefore made detours, and hoped that new positions had not been created, or that AAA sites had not changed position.

Zappa continues : "The great difference with a classic situation, is that in a "normal" war the army would not have sent us under such conditions : knowing that anti-aircraft was in existence, combat aircraft would have accompanied us to attack the installation. In Laos, we had to do it alone."

The war in Laos was a war without any front. The situation was fairly similar to Vietnam, but even so in Vietnam the pilots were able to rely on a minimum of protection around the bases and airports. Take-offs and landings, moments of great vulnerability for the planes, were relatively secure. It was not the case in Laos.

The runways were carved out in the vegetation and the pilots could never be sure if a communist was waiting for him, on the edge of the runway, hidden in the foliage, to empty his magazine on his aircraft before rapidly disappearing.

Sometimes, for want of anything better to do, the Vang Pao combatants shot at passing planes.

Something like that happened one day with an Air America liaison plane. The aircraft, with a dozen or so passengers on board, flew over a fortified position held by the Hmongs, where it had just taken off from a nearby runway. A soldier saw a rapidly climbing plane coming towards him. The soldier could not take his eyes off the white belly of the craft which was now flying slowly, accompanied by the humming of its turbine. He lifted his M1 rifle to his shoulder, he aimed carefully and fired a single bullet. It was a game.

The bullet passed through the fuselage of the plane and directly into the pilot's heart. He was killed instantly. The plane crashed into the mountains, killing all its occupants. The last victim of the story was the soldier himself, who was immediately executed by Vang Pao.

The conduct of a secret war on a terrain as difficult as Laos required a very large range of aircraft. It was necessary to carry out in the air all the different missions that were undertaken on the ground by tactical vehicles.

STOL planes (Short Take off and Landing), capable of operating from very basic terrain and small sized runways, played a leading role. The Helio Courier was the first plane of this type used by the CIA in Laos. Fifteen or so models of this aircraft built in the United States were bought in 1957 and they rapidly became a favourite of the pilots.

The Courier could land within fifty feet on unprepared or ill-maintained terrain, provided there were no rocks in the middle. Very rapidly the available terrain in Laos was classed into two categories; there were Helio terrains capable of receiving a STOL craft, and there were the rest.

"A terrain classified as 'Helio' was an open door to the most unbelievable runways", recalls a pilot. "Some were like goats trails cut out of the side of the mountain or on the crest of hills. From the sky, they were nothing but narrow tracks, like a crooked pencil line."

The runways were rarely horizontal, it was not uncommon that they followed the contours of very steep slopes. Inclines of thirty or forty degrees were not impossible and the difference in height between the two ends of the runway was more than several yards. But landing on an uphill slope did have its advantages.

For the Courier pilots, the gravitational pull which pulled the plane back down towards the bottom of the slope was the most efficient braking system when it was a matter of landing on the side of a hill : a pilot used to this exercise could stop his plane within several dozen metres without using his brakes!

But there was worse than that :

"The Courier also enabled us to negotiate curved runways thanks to its slow landing speed", remembers an old Air America pilot. "Not only did we land on mountain paths but as well as that we had to cope with bends..."

The large propeller of the Courier enabled a minimum speed of forty miles an hour. If there was a slight head wind, this speed was further reduced.

"A head wind of twenty miles an hour reduced our ground speed to twenty five miles an hour. This meant an athletic passenger could get out of the cabin, hold on to the wheel of the landing gear and jump on to the ground without the plane having to land."

Dozens of Helio Courier and Super Courier flew in Laos either under Air America colours or without any other markings apart from the legal registration number. Nonetheless the Courier was not unanimously accepted by the pilots. Everyone recognized the qualities of STOL craft, but some found that the way it handled in flight was not always very safe :

"It was a tricky little plane, the controls were badly balanced", protested some of the pilots.

"The tail of the plane was too light and it was a nose landing if you were too heavy on the brakes! The little beast did us many favours though..."

The PC-6 Turbo Porter was the noble successor of the Helio Courier. The aircraft was conceived by the Swiss constructor Pilatus under tight security in the heart of the Alps. The plane was later constructed under licence by the American company Fairchild.

William Bird imported into the region the first models of the Porter, propelled by piston engines rapidly followed by Turbo Porter, equipped with turbines.

Created for the Alps, the PC-6 Turbo Porter was also at home in the Laotian countryside. A 550hp turbine ensured excellent altitude and warm weather performance. The PC-6 could transport a dozen people in its cargo compartment and could reach 180mph.

"This plane was a solid all-weather aircraft, to which an enormous triple propeller and indestructible landing gear with huge wheels had been added", said Eric Shilling chief engineer of STOL craft for the Bird Air company. It was not designed for great speed, but with the power of its turbines you could easily make fun of the laws of aerodynamics...the plane could wrench itself away from any kind of terrain within several dozen yards."

Pilots recalled that even with a strong wind, the aircraft could land almost vertically :

"A guy did that one day during a very windy day at Long Tien. He positioned himself in front of the tower, facing the wind. With flaps down and brakes on, he opened the throttle progressively. With just enough power to compensate for the wind, the plane started to lift itself up. Then it went up just in front of the tower. Inside the guys were fascinated..."

As well as its motorization, the Pilatus had a flight handling capacity virtually without equal, much better than the Courier that it was gradually replacing.

STOL pilots spent their time ferrying between different terrains held by the CIA and its allies. The short distances within the country meant more missions could be accomplished in one day; the flights lasted, as a general rule, less than an hour and it was not unusual for a pilot to carry out twenty missions in one day.

"We were at the disposal of our client, the CIA. We were asked to transport the wounded, bags of rice, weapons, VIPs, soldiers...if it would go in the plane we loaded it and took off. Between two runs we took fuel to a terrain, then we left. Site Lima 5, Long Tien, Vientiane, return to Long Tien, then parachute drop onto Lima 12. A run to Lima 32 to pick somebody up, then a parachute drop of rice to a patrol, and so on until nightfall. And the following day, at dawn it started all over again..."

Without even taking into consideration enemy fire, the Bird air planes were wearing out at such a fast rate that the company asked the Swiss constructor to help them find out why. Pilatus sent his chief pilot over to try and understand the problem.

The Swiss man got into a Porter and in the company of Eric Shilling, carried out a normal days work. After seven and a half hours flying, the plane and its crew had endured sixteen take-offs and landings on various size goats tracks.

"There is no problem with your planes", said the Swiss expert to William Bird, "No problem either with the pilots or the maintenance. The trouble is, that out of sixteen take-offs, only two took place on terrain that the plane had been designed for. The other runways were so short, steep or rotten that it was simply a matter of time before an accident happened."

At the peak of its activity, Bird bought a plane every two months, simply to replace the worn out ones. Taking all models together, Bird Air lost 24 planes in Laos, only two of which were to enemy fire.

RICE AND PIGS

Certain Porters had been specially fitted out to carry out air drops. The rear cabin had the bench seats removed and two hatches had been fitted into the floor. It was possible to put a load of up to 620 pounds on each one of the hatches and the loadmaster who was in charge of the loading positioned himself at the side of the pilot or at the end of the plane. The opening and closing of the doors was controlled by a simple lever.

Dropping loads during flight was mainly carried out using bags of rice destined for civilians. There was a real art involved; the drop had to be undertaken at a height of between six hundred and nine hundred feet, so that the bags would lose all the horizontal speed from the plane, but without hitting the ground too hard. A vertical speed which was too fast would make the bag explode with the impact, which meant a mass of villagers coming out to pick up the rice.

The pigs which roamed freely in the tiny villages also expected the planes. Showing proof of their reputation for being extremely intelligent animals, they had understood that food fell from the sky and that you mustn't dash forward too early or you'd have a bag land on your head, but not too late either otherwise the humans would push you out of the way. With their round eyes fixed on the approaching plane, they waited along with everybody else for the drop to begin.

Sometimes pigs were themselves dropped from planes, suspended under a parachute. When the parachute didn't open, the pig hit the ground with a loud explosion. For the villagers it was the sign that pig rissoles would be on the menu that night. On other occasions, the box in which they were parachuted broke when it hit the ground and the pigs would run free, having unwittingly escaped their miserable fate, pursued by the villagers.

For liaison or light transport missions, Air America used a wide collection of more classic light aircraft such as Cessna, or De Havilland Beaver, a variation of the 'flying truck', solid and reliable.

The other great part of the action of Air America concerned heavy logistic transport by cargo planes.

The mad war that Laos was experiencing knew a brief respite in 1962 with the signing of a peace accord. Under the terms of this accord, all foreign armies present in Laos had to leave the country.

The North Vietnamese present alongside the local communists were however wary of evacuating the country. They were stationed in regions under the control of the Pathet Lao, forbidden to the International Control Commission.

For their part the Americans had replaced the 600 soldiers in uniform who were working in the country by as many technical advisers wearing civilian clothes, working under the auspices of governmental agencies such as AID. As for the genuinely indispensable soldiers, they were housed in Thailand and crossed the frontier evey day to go to work in Laos. They left the country at the end of the day on board Air America aircraft which ensured daily liaisons with both planes and helicopters. One way or another, everyone managed to live with the 1962 accord.

Another consequence of the signature of the accords : the US Air Force was banned from the zone and the responsibility for transport operations fell entirely on the shoulders of Air America. Commercially speaking, it was a real financial godsend because the company of the CIA took over financial control of all logistic flights on behalf of the AID agencies for development. Laos was in such a poor economic state and the operations with AID represented a revenue of several million dollars a year.

Air America put more aircraft into operation, whereas resupply of the civil population programmes became ever more complex.

In 1966, Air America transported 6,000 tons of freight and 16,000 passengers. The pilots left every day to work their shift like simple workmen, with the difference that the majority of flights were carried out over combat zones or hostile territory. During the run the CIA would resupply the troops under its control.

One village chief was so fascinated by the parachute drops that one day he asked if he could go in a plane to see where the rice came from. Air America invited him to take part in a parachute drop on his own village. The man went to Vientiane from where the plane in question was due to leave.

He climbed in the plane and, at the invitation of the pilots, observed the take-off from the cockpit. His wonder was complete.

"Why are there so many watches", he asked looking at all the instruments.

When the parachute drops began he went down into the cargo bay and watched all the work in progress. When he was told that at last they were to drop over his village, his curiosity grew ever stronger. He moved towards the rear ramp, lost his balance and fell onto his village among the bags of rice!

Several days later, an envoy from the village in question appeared in the premises of Air America at Vientiane. "Thanks for the rice", he said. Then he added, without emotion, "Our chief has broken his head."

A WORKHORSE NAMED PROVIDER

Air America was still using several of its indestructible C-46 Commando and C-47 Dakota which had made the CAT so happy ten years previously. It even had a small fleet of Dornier 28, a light twin-engine of German construction, half-way between an observation plane and a light cargo plane.

But in Laos, the workhorse of the company was the Fairchild C-123 Provider. This large, bulky, inelegant plane was propelled by two R-2,800 Pratt and Whitney piston engines, with a power of 2,500 hp. Three hundred of these aircraft, the first model of which had flown for the first time in 1949, were built. Following this, about 180 of them were transformed into C-123K by the addition of two small jet engines under the wings, so as to improve its performance at take off. The C-123 could carry about five tons of cargo and compared with the C-46 and the C-47 which it replaced, it presented the enormous advantage of being equipped with a rear loading ramp enabling the rapid loading and unloading of entire pallets.

Because it actively supported the secret army of the CIA throughout the country, Air America did not content itself with transporting rice. Between the sacks of food, it was also carrying ammunition, weapons, in fact everything which would help in the fight against the communists.

"These loads had become so common that they held nothing secret for us anymore", admitted the pilots. Evidently, the company which highlighted its role in humanitarian operations was anxious to keep this side of its activity hidden.

Day or night, often at low altitude over hilly terrain, parachute drops with the Provider were never relaxing. Heavily laden, the plane did not possess quite enough reserves of power to reassure the pilots.

The situation improved when the Americans put delayed opening parachutes into operation. Normally, in order to have very accurate drops, the plane had to fly fairly low, roughly six to nine hundred feet above the ground. Therefore the load under the parachute scarcely had time to drift before touching the ground. Piloting the Provider at this height during the day was not easy. At night the exercise became extremely perilous. The delayed opening parachute limited any problems associated with drift and enabled drops to be carried out at a higher altitude. The principle of its operation was relatively simple : the load was dropped normally, but the parachute remained folded during the major part of the drop which reached speeds of up to 100mph. A sixty-yard rope was hooked under the load, which was supplied with an electrical contact at its end. By touching the ground a fraction of a second before the load the contact sent an electrical signal which immediately opened the parachute. The load was slowed down therefore in the very last few feet of the drop. This system gave the crews a larger margin of safety and also the loads were dropped with greater accuracy.

On certain occasions, the C-123 were offered to supply North American T-28 support-fire planes with ammunition, the latter operated by men of Vang Pao.

They sometimes used sections of road as an advanced base and Air America planes had the responsibility of bringing in all the necessary logistics required for the conduct of operations.

In 1962, the Air America pilots knew the T-28 well enough to pilot the planes themselves. When the US Air Force had to leave the country, the Americans had compensated for this departure by supplying the forces of Vang Pao with several of these planes. The T-28 was a large two-seater single engine used in the US for training and which incidentally showed interesting support-fire capacities. More or less at the same time, the French Air Force was using it in an offensive role in

Algeria. But as the training of Laotian pilots was not yet completed, some American pilots were employed in the interval to put these planes into operation. The T-28 were based at Udorn, in Thailand, at least sixty miles from the border with Laos.

Some American civilian pilots therefore were operating from Thailand for combat missions in Laos! Any journalist who got wind of the affair would have been a serious contender for the Pulitzer Prize. Luckily for the American government, the secret was very well kept and nothing concerning the operation, which lasted several months, filtered out. To have achieved this result, no detail was overlooked : the Air America pilots, who were no more than half a dozen, had strict instructions to leave their barracks with their flight helmets on and visors lowered so as not to be recognized. They were even asked to wear their flight gloves so the colour of their skin could not be made out. Nothing could be done however to conceal their American build, which was rather different from the average Laotian.

TOY MONEY AND HOT SOUP

Soft rice, hard rice and many other things besides : Air America aircraft really did transport everything.

"We were asked one day to drop a large quantity of counterfeit money over the sectors held by the communists", recalls an old member of the company. "It was to be carried out after a night parachuting mission and the sum involved was several million dollars. The idea being to torpedo the local economy by artificially creating millionaires. I don't know if it worked or not, but I imagine that down below there were a good few people that ate pretty well for a few days...!"

A lot less pleasant was the task of having to drop canisters of napalm. Doubtless the only example of this in the history of airline companies! The idea came in fact from an officer of the CIA who had found nothing better for "cleaning certain areas infected with communists", as he put it. The napalm was made by hand by two or three Laotians, by mixing petrol with washing powder. The resulting concoction was a sort of highly inflammable gel, a 'hot soup' as it was called. The mixture was prepared in fifty gallon standard containers on which two incendiary devices were attached to ensure it would set alight.

"The canisters were mounted two at a time on pallets which were thrown from the plane via the rear ramp", explains the developer of the system. "A parachute cable removed the pins from the grenades as they went past. After a few seconds, they gave off an intense heat which made the canister melt and set the 'soup' on fire. When it hit the ground, the canister burst open and projected the burning napalm over several hundred square yards."

An aircraft such as the DHC Caribou could carry seven pallets, in other words fourteen canisters. The destructive power of such a load was all the more phenomenal as it was put into operation by simple cargo planes. The technique, which was perfect for releasing soldiers solidly entrenched on the ground, was used several times in different points in Laos. The only handicap in its operation was the great vulnerability of the 'bomber', which constituted an easy target at the moment the pallets were dropped. To obtain better results, the plane had to fly very low, less than 300 feet above the ground, and in a straight line. At the desired moment, the pilot put the nose of the craft up, as if he was dropping normal pallets, and then gravity did the rest : the deadly load that nothing could hold back slipped out of the aircraft by itself. There was nothing official in these procedures. The man from the CIA met the pilots to negotiate the dropping of his special cocktail with them directly. Some pilots refused, others accepted the napalm missions.

When the American ambassador in Laos got wind of the affair, he immediately opposed his veto to such practices. But from his office at Vientiane, could His Excellency really control all aspects of the secret war that was going on throughout his country...? If the use of the 'infernal soup' was stopped in certain areas, it continued in others up until the last minutes of the conflict.

HELICOPTER PILOTS

There were pilots who dropped rice or ammunition, sometimes even both at once, with C-46, C-123 and other Caribou aircraft. There were those which landed on the hillsides with their Courier helicopter and Pilatus Turbo Porter.

But Air America was also an incredible collection of helicopter pilots which really formed a separate entity within the company. The helicopter was a relatively recent and revolutionary machine, a fact which was reflected in the personality of its pilots. These were as a general rule younger than their fixed wing pilot colleagues and they liked to show off.

The majority of pilots who were engaged by Air America in the second half of the sixties had only just finished their tour of duty in Vietnam. At twenty-five years old, thirty maximum, they had already amassed a solid and trying combat experience.

"The rotor has turned their brains mushy", said the fixed wing pilots. This mockery in fact hid a certain amount of resentment. The aircraft pilots were above all vexed to see that this frail and strange machine, that was still considered by some to be a gadget, had gained such a considerable military importance in the Vietnam war only a few years earlier.

"Those old blockheads didn't like us because we stole work from them with our machines", recognized certain helicopter pilots. "We had just got out of Vietnam where it had been sheer hell. Most of the old guys had not seen combat since the end of the Second World War, and they wanted to teach us our job...!"

It was certainly not a coincidence that a lot of ex-pilots from the Marines were to be found at Air America. There was doubtless enough of similarity between these gung-ho types and the men of the CIA.

The helicopters of Air America took part in numerous operations transporting soldiers or evacuating troops depending on the successes or setbacks of the army of Vang Pao.

The company of the CIA was a large user of Bell Huey, a machine which rapidly became symbolic of the conflict in Vietnam. But alongside these turbine-powered helicopters, Laos was also the test ground of the venerable Sikorsky H-34.

In March 1961, the US Air Force had transferred the ownership of sixteen of these machines to the CIA. Replaced in Vietnam by the Huey, the H-34 was found in fairly large numbers in Laos, where their simplicity and solidity were enjoying great success.

The H-34 was the most successful representative of the first generation of helicopters powered by piston engines. Motorized by a 1500 hp Wright Cyclone, the H-34 could carry about fifteen people in the hold, in normal conditions at any rate. In Laos, where the effects of altitude combined with those of the heat and reduced engine performance, it was a completely different story. The pilots studied complicated calculations in order to try to reconcile the necessity of the fuel carried (synonymous with the autonomy of the helicopter), with the transport of a useful load.

Apart from simple supply missions, Air America helicopters were used relentlessly during rescue missions for downed pilots. For the American pilots who had to emergency land in flat countryside, notably the Ravens, the orders were simple 0:

"Stay back from the wreck, but not too far. Drink a little water and wait for the Air America chopper..."

The advice was valid in a friendly as well as a combat zone.

To honour their reputation, the helicopter pilots took incredible risks. The capacity of their machines to take blows very often made the difference between the success or failure of the rescue mission.

TOP SECRET MISSIONS IN THAILAND

Four complete Air America C-123 crews, each comprised of a pilot, a co-pilot, a flight engineer and two loadmasters, were engaged in an operation far more secret than anything they could have known in Laos.

The CIA had approached each one of the men individually to offer them the opportunity of participating in top-secret resupply missions. Only a small number of senior staff of the company were aware of these operations which were carried out under the leadership of the CIA.

The planes used were Lockheed C-130 Hercules based at Takhli in Thailand. Takhli, code name 'Pepper Grinder', was without doubt the most sensitive in the whole of south-east Asia. It served not only as a departure base for secret resupply missions, but also it sheltered the most up to date and secret spy planes of the American air force, the U-2 and SR-71 Blackbird. In part guarded by CIA men in civilian clothes, Takhli could in fact be considered as a mixed CIA/Air Force base.

The C-130 at Takhli came from a special unit of the US Air Force based at Okinawa, but following the usual practice, any identifying mark had been removed. The process was simple when only the exterior of the plane was taken into account. A lick of paint and several stickers and the identity of the plane could be changed. But the process of 'camouflage' meant that every item in the interior also had to be considered, and all the serial numbers were either disguised or removed. Maintenance operations, usually based on a regular supply of spare parts, became a difficult task.

The Air America crews had just spent in turn periods of eight to ten days on the base at Takhli. During this lapse of time, the demand for secrecy meant that they had to live in complete isolation in the zone which had been reserved for them on the base.

The flights were sufficiently time-consuming and the distractions interesting enough for them not to suffer too much. Besides, Takhli benefited from a good deal of attention from American logistics experts for life to be judged very pleasant by the personnel that were based there.

Under cover of darkness, the C-130 piloted by men of the CIA flew practically every night for their secret parachute drop missions. Burma, India, China... the destinations differed from one night to the next. All shared however a high degree of confidentiality ; every night an American aircraft and its crew flew in the air space of a third world country to drop arms and ammunitions. How simple...

Some missions took crews above North Vietnam and the Ho-Chi-Minh trail. It was therefore a question of resupplying recce teams that had infiltrated North Vietnamese held territory.

CUTTING THE HO-CHI-MINH TRAIL

The Ho-Chi-Minh trail was used by the communists to sustain the combat in South Vietnam. It started in North Vietnam, headed to Laos to bypass the buffer zone which separated the two Vietnams, followed its course to Cambodia before reaching South Vietnam where soldiers, arms and ammunitions flowed in.

The equation was simple for the Americans engaged in Vietnam : to dry up the flow of armaments and combatants that was pouring into the south it was absolutely necessary to cut the Ho-Chi-Minh trail. To attack its many ramifications where it crossed the south would have been a pointless and futile exercise. To bring any kind of definitive blocking, the trail would have to be attacked at the highest point possible, in other words : Laos.

That is where the simplicity ended. Because under the word «trail» hid a far more complex truth. The Ho-Chi-Minh trail, whose construction had begun in 1959, regrouped a sprawling network of several dozen roads and routes which snaked throughout Laos, in some areas it was three or four vehicles wide. Along with that there were several navigable rivers. A workforce estimated at more than 75,000 people was used permanently to maintain and upkeep the trail, repair the damage caused by the American bombing, construct new routes, camouflage installations which had to remain invisible from the sky...

From 1965, under the code name Yankee Team, the US Air Force started to launch reconnaissance missions above the supposed Ho-Chi-Minh trail zone. These planes were welcomed by anti-aircraft fire which led the US Air Force to have them escorted by fighter aircraft. That was how the first American bombs were dropped on the Ho-Chi-Minh trail in Laotian territory. The results of the missions were fairly hopeless : in a report sent to Washington, the US Ambassador in Laos noted in 1965 :

"The Ho-Chi-Minh trail has recently been used by the North Vietnamese to infiltrate one of their regular divisions in the south. The reconnaissance flights undertaken up to now have not enabled any obvious indications of the existence of a route to be identified..."

When the Ho-Chi-Minh trail reached its maximum potential at the beginning of the seventies, it was estimated that around two thousand anti-aircraft positions, from simple heavy machine guns to cannons guided by radar, protected it against aerial attacks. In spite of all American efforts to stop it, the flow of supplies continued uninterrupted, representing more than 10,000 tons per week. Very soon the CIA, which was very present in Laos, had the responsibility for surveying the Ho-Chi-Minh trail and several operations were launched.

The first thing to do was to infiltrate reconnaissance crews capable of observing the movements and to be aware of any activity, indeed to guide aerial attacks. Air America was in charge of the infiltration of these mixed teams made up of Hmong combatants and special forces of the US Army.

Even though commando units a dozen men strong had occasionally been used, most of the time small teams of two or three men were used equipped simply with a radio to give a report.

Infiltration was carried out most often by helicopter, men were dropped several miles from the main roads which they then had to get to under their own steam. For the Air America pilots, that was the easiest part of the mission. As one of them explained "it became very difficult when the men had to be picked up once their mission was over."

The commandos dressed like the communist troops that they were to spy on. Their favourite weapon was the AK-47, the famous Kalashnikov.

"After several days or even several weeks of the mission, if we had not agreed in advance of a precise rendez-vous point, the crew contacted us by radio. We started off to go and look for them. Despite the existence of signals and codes, we were never totally sure of coming across the right people."

After two weeks outside in the wild, had the crew been killed and its codes captured? Those men in the clearing, dressed like North Vietnamese regulars and waving at the helicopter, who were they really? Friends or enemies?

The pilots were always very cautious but that was not always enough. On one occasion a helicopter fell into a classic trap that everyone suspected. The helicopter had come to pick up a patrol that had been absent several weeks, it was welcomed by heavy firing as soon as it landed. The engineer on board was immediately wounded in the chest. Dragging their injured comrade behind them, the pilots only just managed to evacuate the aircraft before it exploded. Their bad luck ended there.

Another Air America plane which was manoeuvring in the area arrived rapidly on the scene and managed to pick up the three men before they were captured by the communists.

If the need arose, Air America was also responsible for resupplying these crews during their time in enemy territory, the majority of the time at night. At a time when flying with Night Vision Goggles had not yet become commonplace, this demanded exceptional piloting skills.

"The greatest danger came without contest from the hilly terrain and the weather, each as tempestuous as the other in Laos", explained one veteran. "In fact we knew two sorts of clouds : those made only of water vapour and those which had to be avoided at all costs, the ones made of water vapour and rocks. The tops of the mountains shrouded in clouds were our obsessive fear when we flew at night."

For reasons of discretion, radio contact between the teams on the ground and craft which supplied them were non-existent. A pilot describes the procedure employed :

"We used our navigational skills to find the rendez-vous point as accurately as possible, in spite of the absence of radio-navigational aids. Then we waited until the guys on the ground showed their presence with their torches or strobe lights. They were never large parachute drops, as we were supplying men who travelled by foot, carrying everything on their backs."

Faced with the difficulties that this type of mission raised, the CIA wanted to equip several aircraft with very accurate navigational equipment enabling the crew to fly at night, close to the ground and without any external aid. One plane lent itself particularly well to the missions envisaged and the expected developments : the unbeatable Douglas B-26 Invader.

All Invaders used by the CIA until the beginning of the sixties were standard planes in military configurations. Several aircraft were subsequently modified in order to fulfil special mission requirements. The B-26 'On Mark' were in this category.

Two B-26 only were brought up to 'On Mark' standard, (On Mark was the name of the company which carried out the transformation), in 1963. These changes had not been made with a specific operation in mind, rather to put specially equipped aircraft at the Agency's disposal, in case of need.

The B-26 On Mark were equipped with more powerful engines which enabled the maximum take-off weight to be increased. The landing gear had been replaced by that of the more solid four-engine DC-6. This aircraft, which had practically been transformed into a rapid cargo plane, presented a profoundly modified shape. The rear end of the fuselage had been widened whereas some rollers had been installed on the floor : small pallets could thus be loaded and dropped in flight by an opening made in the floor. A loadmaster at the rear of the plane directed the manoeuvre. If the need arose, the pallets could be replaced by seats and the B-26 would be transformed into a passenger plane. The cockpit had also been modified; access was gained by an opening in the rear of the fuselage and members of the crew, pilot, co-pilot and navigator had to crawl under the spar of the wing to reach their seats. It is certain that an evacuation in mid-flight would have posed certain problems...

Once their airframe was modified, the two planes (figures remain ambiguous, varying sources state from one to six B-26 On Mark) were fitted with complex electronic equipment. This consisted of navigational aids (VOR, ILS, LORAN), VHF and UHF radios as well as an IFF identification system enabling the identification of a plane as "friend or foe", by means of a coded electronic signal. Electronic war systems were also installed later.

One of these planes was used in 1965 to train two Cuban pilots, veterans of Operation Pluto, with operations on China from Taiwan in mind. Training was however interrupted before being finished.

At the beginning of 1966, both aircraft received terrain following radars. Similar to those which were to equip the F-111A of the US Air Force, these highly perfected radars were still at the time only prototypes which were practically built 'by hand' by technicians from Texas Instruments. This installation enabled the planes to fly with no visibility or outside help at less than 300ft from the ground.

It was exactly what Air America needed to carry out its night missions over the Ho-Chi-Minh trail. One of the two planes ended up in Thailand at Udorn, where the majority of supply flights left from. After several conclusive test flights the plane was used many times above the trail, at the rate of one or two flights a week.

Because of the many modifications which had altered its line, the

B-26 On Mark was not an easy plane to pilot and only those pilots already having a good knowledge of the 'classic' B-26 were authorized to take command. The performance of the plane had deteriorated slightly compared with the original and its use in parachute drop missions induced a flight handling capability which could have surprised a pilot with limited experience. The minimum speed of the plane remained rather high, very low altitude flying, a very average front visibility for the pilot, the narrow width of the drop zones, many factors came together to increase the difficulty of drop missions.

The "On Mark" were used for more than one year in Laos. At the end of March 1968, the ownership of a plane was transferred to the Overseas Aermarine Company Inc. based in Seattle. On the 30th April 1968, this company informed the American Civil Aviation Authority that the plane had been destroyed and scrapped, without any additional details. In fact, it seems that at that date the plane was still flying in Laos.

After the Laotian episode, rumours spoke of the possible connections between On Mark and operations from West Germany and Taiwan.

The last On Mark was finally scrapped in the United States in 1971. It was then, in all probability, the last surviving Invader of the CIA.

The B-26 On Mark was not the only aircraft to receive terrain following radar to carry out secret infiltration missions. The CIA used several DHC-6 Twin Otters, a light, twin-engine aircraft with short take-off and landing capabilities perfectly suited to Loatian operations. One of these aircraft subsequently received a radar similar to the one that equipped the F-111, the most sophisticated strike aircraft in the US Air Force's arsenal at that time. This Twin Otter was to be used in particular to carry out a very daring raid deep inside North Vietnam: it involved dropping a commando team near an SA-2 anti-aircraft missile site. The attack, which was to have used a light mortar, was finally cancelled.

SOME BAD SMELLS...

The surveillance of the Ho-Chi-Minh trail was also the business of electronics engineers. Some technicians had the idea of positioning acoustic or seismic sensors near presumed enemy routes thereby detecting the movement of vehicles or combatants by either vibrations on the ground or any sound emitted. These sensors were dropped in by aircraft of the US Navy or US Air Force and stuck themselves in the ground as a result of a free fall drop. Only the aerial, which enabled them to transmit the information, was above ground. Others fell from parachutes and became hooked up in branches of trees. The Americans hoped to detect the roads which, because of the camouflage, remained invisible at night or in daylight. Once corroborating clues and indications had been gathered on the presence of enemy troops, fighter-bombers would be sent to the zones where the movements had been detected.

In theory, the idea was perfect. In reality, things were a little less simple. A dozen Air America aircraft had been specially equipped with communication equipment to receive and relay information transmitted by these sensors. For the pilot the task was uninteresting in the extreme. It involved circling at altitude inside a sensor transmission cone, for several hours. From March 1969, these aircraft were replaced by the QU-22A, planes without pilots obtained by modifying Beech Bonanza tourism aircraft. The five QU-22A operated from the Thai base of Nakhon Phanom. They were then replaced by QU-22B which offered certain improvements.

The programme cost a fortune and was an obvious failure, in the sense that the traffic on the Ho-Chi-Minh trail was not affected overmuch. It was stopped definitively in June 1970. It is necessary to understand that the sensors did not always reach the ground intact. They could smash against rocks or be damaged on impact against hard ground. Those which planted themselves correctly in the ground could end up being discovered and destroyed. One other deficiency of the seismic sensors was they were not able to distinguish between wild animals and the passage of soldiers. How many raids were launched after the alert had been sounded because of wild animals.

In the same style, where hi-tech systems were being developed along with a fierce will to win, the Americans dreamt up the idea of detecting communist troops by their smell. A system loaded on board a helicopter and supplied with very great powers of discrimination allowed the detection from the sky of the presence of urine or faecal matter on the ground. A fascinating idea, which gave rise to a rather interesting fiasco on the ground. Apparently, not one of the designers of the system had imagined that the detector would indicate, without distinction, all the odours given off by animals or humans, civilians (women, children, the elderly...) and combatants.

The fact remains that the most reliable intelligence from the Ho Chi Minh trail was as a result of the eavesdropping devices placed secretly on North Vietnamese telephone lines.

The teams infiltrated by the Americans were therefore regularly used to position listening devices on the military telephone network running along logisitc routes. The intercepted signals were emitted towards the sky where planes, circling several miles away, picked them up and were able to relay them to analyzing ground stations. The communists, who soon became aware of this strategem, carried out regular examinations of their lines in order to detect the presence of any pirate installations.

In 1971, it was the CIA's ambition not only to listen in on telephone lines around the Ho Chi Minh trail, but also within Vietnamese territory. To be able to infiltrate and exfiltrate a team in total discretion, the intelligence agency on this occasion chose to use an aircraft that seemed very promising, a Hugues 500, nicknamed 'The Quiet One'. Initially developed by laboratories of the US Army, 'The Quiet One' was the result of a project aiming to render the helicopter as silent as possible. Various technical devices had enabled the sound level of the aircraft to be reduced considerably, which then could be used to carry out discreet missions in enemy territory. The CIA perfected the helicopter by equipping it with a very accurate navigation system, a FLIR system and infra-red spotlights. Combined with the use of night vision goggles the spotlights, which lit up the terrain with a light invisible to the naked eye, enabled the helicopter to fly just above the ground at night.

After several weeks of preparation, a mission was finally launched in December 1972 with Air America pilots at the controls of the helicopter.

After an uneventful flight over the North Vietnamese countryside, two commandos were dropped off near an important telephone pylon that was to be tapped. Several minutes of trouble-free work allowed the two technicians to position their eavesdropping device on the pylon. Both men then got back in the helicopter which took them back into friendly territory. The mission was one of the most successful of the whole of the Vietnam war. Without doubt it enabled the Americans to gather information concerning the political intentions of the communists, at the same time as peace negotiations between Washington and Hanoi were taking place.

THE ROCK

Laos was not only used by the communists to bring war to South Vietnam via the Ho-Chi-Minh trail; the Americans also knew how to use the geographical position of this unfortunate little country to bring war to the heart of North Vietnam.

Several navigational aid installations had been set up in Laos by the US Air Force, as guidance for combat craft leaving to bomb Hanoi, less than 200 miles away.

These installations, radio electric beacons emitting waves on which the planes contacted each other, enabled more accurate navigation and consequently more precise bombing.

One of the key installations was a mere 30 miles from the border with North Vietnam, at the top of a mountain nicknamed by the Americans 'The Rock'. The official code was Site Lima 85. The rock was a natural fortress which seemed impregnable, within a zone traditionally under the control of the communists. A sheer vertical drop of several hundred feet protected one face whereas several bunkers prevented approaches on the other.

Lima Site 85 was directly accessible by helicopter, even though a short runway 300 yards long had been cleared a little lower down in the valley. Air America STOL craft could land there to bring in three tons of supplies a week needed for the installation to function. At the height of its activity, the Rock had approximately three hundred combatants guarding it, along with a handful of American technicians who operated the highly sophisticated equipment.

The US Air Force had started in 1966 by installing a simple TACAN beacon as a navigational aid. The following year, the installation was perfected and more than 150 tons of electronic equipment and pre-fabricated buildings were brought to the summit of the mountain. The new installations were to facilitate the precision bombing in all weathers above North Vietnam. The contingent of Laotians and Thai mercenaries in charge of guarding Site Lima 85 had been increased. Everyone knew that it was insufficient to defend the site in the event of a massive Vietnamese attack, but in case of a big problem, they relied above all on the strength of the US Air Force.

Even if they did not yet know its exact role, the communists had a perfect idea of the importance the rock seemed to have in the eyes of the Americans.

Despite being under their very noses, the site seemed inpenetrable, except by launching a full-scale helicopter attack, which was not within their possibilities. They did not get discouraged and started to plan an attack. Several weeks before it was launched, a surprising aerial encounter gave Air America one of the most extraordinary episodes of its history :

On the 12th January 1968, two planes from the North Vietnamese air force came in sight of the rock. The spectacle this offered to its defenders was absolutely incredible : both aircraft were Antonov 2, enormous biplanes of Soviet construction with the appearance of prehistoric monsters. The Antonov 2 (An2) had begun its career just after the war, in 1947, as a supply plane, both civilian and military. As beautiful as a lorry with propellers could be, the An2, which had the dubious honour of being the largest single engine biplane in the world, was the aerial workhorse in socialist countries. The North Vietnamese had decided to make it a ground attack aircraft, which, for use in broad daylight, amounted to nothing but recklessness.

So, in this concerto of pistons from their reciprocate engine, the An2 dived onto the rock at the fabulous speed of 120mph, while their crews gave bursts of fire with their Kalashnikovs and threw mortar shells through open windows.

The attack was surreal. But so was the reaction of the crew of an Air America Huey helicopter who witnessed the scene. The helicopter had been sent on a reconnaissance mission to evaluate the advance of communist troops who were slowly approaching the rock, opening in front of them a logistic route.

Seeing the An2s attack Site 85, the co-pilot said :

"We can go faster than those things..."

"So let's go", replied the pilot in the intercom.

Sitting behind, the engineer grabbed his personal weapon, a Uzi submachine gun that never left his side. A large smile spread across his face.

"Charge...!" he shouted into the wind of the rotors.

The helicopter rapidly came up close to the first An2 and the engineer emptied his Uzi on the cockpit of the plane, killing its crew outright. Crippled, the An2 slipped away and crashed onto the ground. As for the second An2, it crashed into the mountain, a victim of ground fire.

Thus the CIA achieved a major first: an aerial victory in a plane made from a helicopter!

As a souvenir of this exploit, a section of the fuselage bearing the number 665 was recovered from the wreck of an Antonov and brought back to the CIA company premises at Long Tien.

This unprecedented victory had no consequence on the future of the site. Having decided to remove the section, the North Vietnamese and their Laotian allies assembled a sizeable assault force whose progression was closely followed by the Americans.

When the assailants arrived at the foot of the mountain, the defenders were entrenched and were ready to confront the shock of a frontal assault. But the surprise came from the cliff which seemed impassable. In the night of the 10th and 11th of March 1968, a North Vietnamese commando succeeded in scaling it by skirting its defences. All night long the battle raged on the rock.

From the first hours of daylight, Air America helicopters were present in great number on the site to evacuate the survivors, Americans, Laotians and Thai. Alone on board their aircraft, and without benefitting from any protection, the Air America pilots threw their planes into the blazing fire to try and haul out the last defenders.

Several heavy rescue helicopters belonging to the US Air Force were circling a good distance from there, without being able to intervene in the melee ; the loss of one of these aircraft in Laotian territory could have had very grave political consequences. As a result, the weight of the evacuations rested firmly on the shoulders of the Air America pilots who took considerable risks right up to the last minutes. Along with several dozen Hmong and Thai combattants, four American technicians were saved. A dozen of them were killed in the attack.

The total number of casualties on the rock remains a secret.

In the days following the capture of the site by the communists, the whole zone was destroyed by bombs of the US Air Force. The Americans were extremely anxious to leave nothing intact in the hands of the North Vietnamese, but it was already too late. In spite of very heavy losses, they had not only succeeded in putting Site Lima 85 out of action, but also in swiping a quantity of information and codes of great value.

THE END OF A SECRET

The good fortune in combat, which had been favourable for Vang Pao during the rainy season of 1968, turned as soon as the dry season arrived. The combined forces of the North Vietnamese and the Pathet-Lao represented at that time more than 100,000 combatants, supported by several tens of thousands of coolies working on the logistics and the opening of the major axes of advance. Faced with this cascade, the CIA made more and more use of Thai mercenaries who did not always show a very combative spirit. As for the Vang Pao, it was reduced to enrolling children as young as thirteen and fourteen to compensate for the losses of its army. The communist offensive launched at the end of 1969 appeared so threatening in the eyes of Washington that, after a number of procrastinations, B-52 raids were authorized from 17th February 1970.

At more or less the same time, the existence of the secret base at Long Tien was revealed to the entire world. The revelation did not come from Washington, where the American politicians 'in the know', were still wondering if it was necessary to inform the public about the secret war, and Long Tien. With the aid of the American ambassador at Vientiane, a group of journalists present in Laos had chartered an Air America plane to visit the village of Sam Thong, a symbol of the social work carried out by AID. Sam Thong had a 200 bed hospital and a medical training centre where more than a thousand Hmong nurses and medical specialists had been trained. All that was indeed very impressive from a people who had only just discovered Western civilization, but three of the journalists taking part in the press voyage decided that there was perhaps something of more interest to see in the zone. Long Tien, whose very name brought to mind the CIA, was only a few miles from there and the three journalists rapidly slipped away from the group of officials. A walk of an hour or so was all they needed to reach the most secret town in Laos.

Among them was a freelance journalist from the New York Times who had the nerve to penetrate the interior of the base in order to observe, for more than two hours, the incessant aerial activity.

The three journalists were eventually spotted and sent back by force to Vientiane. But the harm had already been done.

Accounts appeared in the American press. They spoke about planes landing every minute, hardstands full of observation planes, combat planes and heavy helicopters. The journalists who had been able to wander about in Long Tien had seen a number of windowless low buildings spiked with aerials. They had met young men, with short hair dressed in civilian clothing but carrying automatic weapons over their shoulders. Their nationality was all but obvious...

The reports that appeared about Long Tien cracked the shell of secrecy that still surrounded American operations in Laos. There was even discussion in the press of the battle of Site Lima 85.

1971, RED ALERT

At the beginning of 1971, the situation deteriorated yet more in the territories held by the Hmong. The flow of refugees increased daily, whereas the North Vietnamese seemed to be everywhere. Rumours spoke of North Vietnamese tanks circulating in the mountains. More than 100,000 people were fleeing before the progress of an enemy receiving a steady flow of arms and ammunition from North Vietnam. Within the space of a year, the number of anti-aircraft weapons protecting its logistic routes and its axes of advance had tripled.

Air America, which was the centre of the agitation had the bitter experience of this new situation. Its planes and helicopters relayed continuously to evacuate civilians and redeploy the last troops still in fighting condition.

Faced with the communist advance, Sam Thong and its hospital were abandoned and the secret base of Long Tien prepared to receive an assault.

Thus panic took hold of the secret town. The defenders evaporated into thin air. The capture of the town seemed inevitable, a question of hours it was said.

Air America therefore threw itself into a last minute airlift. An aircraft took off or landed every two minutes. The planes touched down, moved on to the end of the runway and manoeuvred to take off again. With engines running, the rear ramp was lowered and the people that had amassed near the runways rushed towards the plane. Once it was full, the ramp was raised and the plane took off again without waiting, while yet another aircraft was preparing to land.

Fearing that the communists would arrive and destroy the runway before they had the chance to board a plane, several hundred people fled into the mountains by foot, in the direction of Vientiane.

To enable them to survive during their exodus, Air America followed their progress from the air and parachute dropped sacks of rice at regular intervals.

At Long Tien, the CIA had started to burn secret documents. A fine layer of black ash began to cover the famous windowless buildings which had so intrigued the first journalists to have entered the secret town.

Meanwhile, CIA aircraft were bringing in reinforcements to ensure the defence of the town. Some Thai mercenary troops (whose number was to reach 17,000 in Laos alone at the end of the war), and some Hmong combatants were dropped off by Air America helicopters on the hills surrounding Long Tien. There they remained, waiting for the attack. It never came.

The communists remained at a distance, content with bombing the defenders and the runway which continued to receive Air America planes.

Under enemy artillery fire, the planes of the CIA still carried on ensuring the resupply of the defenders. The planes only remained on the ground for several seconds, scarcely the time necessary to throw its cargo off.

The helicopters were responsible for the evacuation of the wounded.

After eleven days of uninterrupted bombing, the communist troops withdrew, choosing not to sieze Long Tien. Perhaps they feared that it would be too much for them, or that once inside they would be the perfect target for the B-52s of the US Air Force.

The surprise having passed, the Hmongs and the CIA set themselves up once again at Long Tien and the war got back on its 'normal' course.

THE SARAVANE MASSACRE

For the Americans still present in Laos, the priority was the surveillance of the Ho-Chi-Minh trail and to stop it being used.

In September 1972, Operation Black Lion IV was launched, with the aim of blocking an important nodal point of the trail. This operation rapidly became known under the name of Saravane, the name of the town where the majority of combats were concentrated.

Saravane was in fact the first objective of the 3,500 Laotian soldiers who were engaged in the combat.

It was planned initially that the US Air Force would supply several heavy helicopters for the transport of troops. But the intensity of the fighting right from the very first hours of the operation meant that the plan was abandoned for fear of losing a crew which, officially, should never have been in Laos.

To compensate for this, Air America used all available resources and it alone supported the weight of fighting.

On the first day, one of its helicopters was shot down and a CIA man and two Laotians were killed. Another craft from the company arrived to pick up the survivors and also suffered from heavy firing. The co-pilot was seriously injured.

The news spread like wildfire among the Air America pilots : Operation Saravane was a massacre.

After this violent beginning, tension was such between the officers of the CIA and the Air America pilots that fists flew during one particularly stormy briefing.

When the argument had finished, a man from Langley, who was particularly exasperated by the position of the pilots who refused planned missions, addressed them very sharply :

"You are paid enough to get killed." His remark cost him several teeth.

To supply ground troops, planes and helicopters had to fly over 100 miles of enemy territory. That was however the most dangerous part of the mission. The combat zone was saturated with anti-aircraft installations. The communists and 12.7mm and 37mm weapons forming a lethal cocktail.

An Air America DHC-7 Caribou was thus shot down while it was heading for a parachute drop of supplies. Several days after the launch of the operation a C-123 Provider was hit by a long burst of 12.7mm fire just after it had dropped its load of pallets. The starboard engine caught fire almost immediately and the pilots, who were experiencing great difficulties in keeping their plane under control, asked for help over the radio.

"Head for Pakse and parachute over in that direction", replied the controller. "The area is free of bandits and I'll try and find some helicopters to pick you up..."

When the C-123 crew were evacuating the plane by parachute, two Air America helicopters were already en route to pick them up.

Pilot and co-pilot landed together in a clearing, whereas the others, having jumped from the plane a little earlier, had landed some distance away.

Barely several minutes later, the first helicopter arrived on the scene and picked up the two air dispatchers. Several seconds later, the second helicopter was heard and headed towards the two pilots. Up to then, everything was fine. But when taking off from the clearing where it had landed, the second helicopter touched a tree and seriously damaged one of its rotor blades. After a flight of several minutes the Huey pilot turned to his passengers and apologized :

"Sorry guys, but I'm going to have to land, it's vibrating too much for my taste... the other chopper will pick us up."

Both helicopters landed in a field and the passengers from the damaged machine ran to the other one. It was better not to hang around in this area where communist soldiers could appear at any time...

But the adventure was not over. Less than fifteen minutes after take-off, the pilot manoeuvred the aircraft into a descent.

"What's happening?" asked the pilots behind in unison.

"You won't believe this... we're out of gas! We're going to have to land."

This was the third emergency landing for the C-123 crew in one day! The risk of being hit was so great that Air America helicopter crews flew systematically in groups of five, the fifth aircraft always flying empty, in order to pick up crew immediately whose aircraft had been shot down ; if the need arose.

"We brought ammunition and left with wounded", recalls one helicopter pilot. The ammunition was thrown out even before the aircraft had completely landed. When the helicopter had scarcely touched the ground, those wounded who were able to walk hurried to get on board. We were surrounded by enemy artillery explosions. Judging by the amount of dust created, we knew that it was rocket, mortar or classic artillery fire..."

In the best of cases, the explosions were far off. But they were from time to time sufficiently close for the helicopter to be covered in dust. Sometimes the stretcher bearers were so shaken up by the explosions, they would drop their load and hurry towards the helicopter.

Because of a lack of sufficiently accurate firing, the enemy chose to saturate a zone with all available artillery when it heard the helicopters arriving. The pilots varied their landing zones every day, but it still strongly resembled Russian roulette...

The opposition was so strong that the planned 3,500 men could not be landed. The operation was to last more than two weeks, leaving the pilots exhausted.

THE END OF THE STORY

All that was in vain, for the signing of Peace agreements in Paris in January 1973 established a communist takeover in the country. The

Laotian coalition government born out of these agreements therefore wanted Air America to leave the country as quickly as possible. Not in any hurry to comply with this, The CIA nonetheless greatly reduced the number of aircraft in Laos.

Forty or so pilots and many aircraft left the country to withdraw to Udorn, on the other side of the border with Thailand. A major part of these planes and helicopters that were repatriated in the same way were simply given to the Thai government, in recognition of services rendered.

The majority of the 350 terrains of all types which had been developed for the needs of Air America throughout Laos were also abandoned. In only a few months the 'runways' resembled nothing more than pathways overgrown with plants.

However, operations did not entirely come to an end. Several dozen pilots continued to fly over the country and were fired at by the Pathet Lao or the North Vietnamese. In the year 1973 alone, Air America counted eight deadly crashes and fifty or so wounded.

There was an increase in losses at the very moment when the war was coming to an end. Between 1970 and 1973, the company counted "only" 17 deaths during combat. This added to the reduction of numbers, and the number of available pilots started to disappear at a dangerous rate.

This resulted in a conflict of sorts with the management of the company and the CIA. Represented by their union, Air America pilots were insistent on the fact that enough crews had to be available round the clock to carry out medical evacuations throughout the country. They threatened their management with a strike if the problem was not resolved. The CIA on strike!

On the eve of the planned 'social movement' the CIA reacted swiftly. Some formal demands were sent to all the crews : they were expected to show up the following morning on the terrain failing which they would be placed under arrest. For the pilots at Vientiane, even the threat of prison seemed a possibility.

The strike movement was quickly stifled. Sickened by this attitude, certain pilots resigned from the company on their return to the United States. Others profited from their return to the mother country to meet their elected representatives and lodge complaints. Feiry and ardent, they declared themselves ready to fight together against the infringements of workers' rights which had multiplied in the company. But when they realised who was hiding behind Air America, there was not a single Senator who wanted to confront the problem and get his hands dirty.

At that time the war in Laos was nearing its end.

In June 1974, Air America left the country definitively and at the same time they decided to stop their activities from Thailand.

In fifteen years of more or less secret war, the United States had dropped more bombs over Laos than during the second world war. And all for nothing, because a coalition neutralist government, which Eisenhower had wanted to prevent, had been formed.

In the meantime, the Laotian communists were considerably reinforced and several tens of thousands of Laotians had perished in the absurd conflict. American losses were estimated at around a thousand men.

LAST MISSION

There remained however one last scene to play before the curtain fell definitively on CIA aerial operations in Laos.

In March 1975, when South Vietnam was preparing itself to fall like a ripe fruit under the attacks from the north, the Pathet-Lao launched its final offensive against the forces of Vang Pao, the last obstacle to its complete control of power. The absence of any aerial support, the exhaustion of its army, the lack of sufficient supplies, everything pointed to an inevitable Vang Pao defeat.

After two months of desperate fighting, the Hmong chief was ready to give himself up at Long Tien, surrounded by the remains of his army.

The CIA liaison officer who remained near him managed to convince him that he would be more useful to his people alive and in exile, rather than dead at Long Tien.

It remained for the CIA to organize his evacuation.

The operation was given to Harry Aderholt, then General of the US Air Force and the last General on duty in south east Asia. As we know, Aderholt was very close to the CIA and very knowledgeable about delicate missions.

198

To the evacuation of Vang Pao, it would soon be necessary to add the evacuation of as many Hmongs as possible before Long Tien fell into the hands of the communists. It was therefore a mini airlift that Aderholt had to organize.

For obvious reasons of political neutrality, the craft and crew of USAF could not be engaged in this operation. With the support of the CIA, Aderholt started to assemble a small aerial fleet in Thailand.

A C-130 Hercules was the central figure. The plane had been found without difficulty, but to find a crew capable of operating it was altogether more complicated. All the American pilots who could have been engaged for the mission appeared to have already returned to the United States.

After meticulous research, fortune smiled on Aderholt : A C-130 pilot had his departure from Thailand delayed and, it seemed, remained available in the country. At the very moment when the general of the USAF identified the name, the pilot in question, Matt Hoff, was driving with his wife to Bangkok airport. Two seats were reserved in his name for the next flight to the US.

"It was incredible", recalls Aderholt, "this guy that we needed so much was at Bangkok airport queuing with his wife at the check-in desk. The son of a ... was going home when we needed him so much."

In front of the check-in desk, Hoff was daydreaming. He saw himself sipping an ice cold whisky 30,000 feet above the China sea, on his way home, when an officer approached him.

"Matt Hoff, General Aderholt would like to speak to you..."

"Pardon?"

"I think you'd better come with me to the telephone."

Aderholt knew how to be very persuasive. Hoff had no desire to extend his stay in the zone, even less to carry out one last, perilous mission. However the two men rapidly came to the subject of big money.

"Name your price" said Aderholt.

"5,000 dollars."

Aderholt managed to form his little aerial fleet in record time. Apart form the C-130 piloted by Hoff, the operation involved a Pilatus Porter, a helicopter and a C-46 Commando. Practically all the pilots were ex Air America.

When the transport craft landed at Long Tien, the crush was indescribable. The planes were besieged by Hmongs for whom they represented the only hope of salvation. Six rotations were organized heading for Thai territory. Each time there were so many passengers that they had to travel standing up, packed tightly one against the other.

At the same time, Vang Pao and two of his bodyguards were discreetly evacuated from Long Tien on board a helicopter. The three men were taken to a rendez-vous point where the Pilatus Porter was waiting for them. Then it took off for Thailand. Several hours later, Long Tien was overcome by communist troops.

Laotian resistance was finished and the country was swallowed up by communism and Vietnamese colonization.

CHAPTER 6

VIETNAM

GETTING CAUGHT UP IN THE SYSTEM

After the withdrawal of the French from the country, the increasing commitment of the Americans was first and foremost borne by the special forces. Several hundred green berets were sent to the newly created South Vietnam to replace the French army in its role of technical adviser. Washington had an immense fear of this geostrategic void. Since its creation, South Vietnam had to stand up to the Vietcong guerilla whose offensive spirit was such that it was never seriously threatened by the work of the regular forces of the south. In this context, the progress of the Vietcong could be none other than swift and spectacular. And that is indeed what it was.

From the moment when the United States chose to erect their South Vietnamese protege as a symbolic victim of communist imperialism, a clear way was given for its defence.

From the first months of his short presidency, Kennedy flirted with the idea of sending regular American troops to fight against the Vietcong on several occasions. After a series of hesitations, this possibility was ruled out every time, the President chose to rely on the know-how of the US special forces. It was for that reason that the number of secret actions undertaken in Vietnam increased regularly throughout 1961.

From less than 700 American advisers present in Vietnam at the time of Kennedy's election, the figure reached more than 12,000 men by mid-1962. Marines, Navy, Air Force and Army, each service present in the field had its own detachments, which included secret teams.

After the assassination of Kennedy in Dallas on November the 22nd 1963, the arrival of President Johnson to the White House speeded up this movement yet more : 15,000 men in 1963, 22,000 the following year. The American forces in Vietnam could no longer reasonably be designated under the name group, as had been the case up to then.

A specific command was created for the Vietnamese theatre of operation, the Military Assistance Command Vietnam (MACV).

Everything was ready for the American contingent to discover the joy of doing a 'tour' of duty in the Mekong delta.

Since the end of the fifties, the CIA had been very present in Vietnam. The American intelligence agency had led its own operations on two fronts : whereas the 'urban CIA' shamelessly infiltrated the whole of the South Vietnamese political microcosm, giving its dollars generously to almost all politicians in the country, the 'rural CIA' multiplied its paramilitary operations in South as well as North Viatnam.

The special forces of the CIA, Studies and Observations Group (SOG), hunted the Vietcong and trained anti-guerilla units in the south. These elite troops benefited from the support of different units of the US Air Force based at Nha Trang and in the fight against the Vietcong they played, the majority of the time, the envied role of hunter. The guerillas fighting against the power in Saigon having to settle for the less enviable role of hunted. The situation in the south was such that it was a difficult tune to play although not impossible.

It was quite another situation in the north.

Washington had ordered the base at Saigon to redouble its efforts to infiltrate agents into North Vietnam in order to wreak havoc.

Since the partition of the country in 1954, several small teams of North Vietnamese agents were exfiltrated, trained in the south, and then parachuted into the north.

But these 'resistance groups' were rapidly wiped out by the Vietminh. In 1961, the CIA therefore took up the challenge.

Several eight-man teams had been trained to carry out these missions of infiltration and destruction to the north of the demilitarized zone, but the American agency eventually refused to use them. Intelligence specialists had made it known that it was preferable to dedicate their activities to the creation of secret intelligence networks prior to launching destruction operations which would have had the effect of tightening security measures in place in North Vietnam.

The conflict was intensifying in the south and the question of the infiltration of agents came to the forefront again in 1964. Washington was extremely keen to be able to inflict on the North what would amount to a fraction of the turmoil that the Vietcong were inflicting on the government of Saigon.

The American presidency eagerly awaited the results.

Apart from operations from the sea, the CIA organized parachute drops of teams of South Vietnamese or Chinese nationalists (Taiwanese) from the month of April 1964. The agency initially reckoned on one infiltration operation per month, but the pace was in fact much slower.

On the 24th of July in the same year, President Johnson was informed that eight parachuting operations had taken place since the launch of the operation, on average, one every two weeks.

The results were barely acceptable, radio contact was not able to be kept up with more than half of the teams engaged. The CIA rapidly came to find its operations unnecessarily costly in manpower: the majority of teams infiltrated, when they were not eliminated, were probably "returned" by the communists. Without doubt, North Vietnamese society was too hermetic to allow itself to be infiltrated by saboteurs. The memory of the failures in the fifties, in Albania, or North Korea, was still very much alive in Langley. William Colby, chief of the Far East division for secret operations and future head of the CIA, declared to Robert McNamara, the Secretary of State for Defence :

"These operations give very weak results for a very high cost in human lives, they have become too dangerous and useless. It would be better to call a halt!"

"They must not be stopped, on the contrary, they should be increased" replied McNamara.

Secret infiltration operations therefore continued at a steady rhythm. The objective of one infiltration mission per week was reached at the beginning of 1965.

And the result?

Very poor, according to the CIA, which had been convinced for a long time of the futility of these attempts to destabilize North Vietnamese society from within. In the following months the responsibility for these operations passed to the US Army and the CIA was able to wash its hands of the affair, and dedicate itself to other tasks.

With the consent of President Johnson, the CIA unit in South Vietnam increased progressively, until, in 1965, it involved 600 people. The base in Saigon was at that time the biggest in the world, bigger even than the one in Miami which covered Latin America.

The need for personnel in Vietnam had become so urgent that every CIA unit in the world was asked to supply an annual contingent of volunteers for Saigon. The agents, with little motivation, and speaking absolutely no Vietnamese, arrived in the field to set up anti-Vietcong networks. The results obtained naturally turned out to be mediocre. This did not prevent the CIA from giving an enlightened opinion on the conduct of the war in the south. By directly and openly opposing the development of classic military operations, Langley advocated the intensive use of special forces including back-up troops trained in anti-guerilla tactics.

A lot was required for this way of seeing things to be shared by the Pentagon where Robert McNamara reigned. Well known for his exaggerated love of statistics and being familiar with the enemy body count, the US Secretary of State was also informed about the more conventional evolution of the war by the CIA.

"You know, it's difficult to find any meaning in this war", he said one day to Desmond Fitzgerald, number two in the CIA and in charge of secret operations, who had come to present him with a report on the war.

"Mr. Secretary of State, the statistics are very useful, but you cannot judge the progress of a war based on figures alone. You must also have instinct. My instinct tells me that we are heading for a much more difficult time than your statistics indicate..."

"Is that what you really think, Fitzgerald?"

"As I said sir, it's instinct. It's just a feeling I have. It's difficult to explain."

The man from the CIA was right. By going to Vietnam several months after that conversation, McNamara was able to see that the reality of the situation was far more complex than his graphs could ever show. He came back from his tour in Vietnam very doubtful concerning the outcome of the conflict.

On the 8th of March 1965, the first American fighting troops were sent to Vietnam. Initially they were there only to protect the air bases housing US Air Force aircraft, which were regular targets of Vietcong commando operations.

Less than three weeks later, on the 1st of April 1965, the green light was given for these soldiers to be used as attack troops.

From then on, under the terms of Operation Switchback, the US Army was responsible for paramilitary actions in South Vietnam, to the detriment of the CIA. The American intelligence agency could thus concentrate on pacification operations.

For the CIA, pacification was 'the other war', the real war.

"Its importance is such that it must not be the sole responsibility of the military", it was said at Langley. The agency was closely associated with these operations where it was acknowledged that 'the heart and soul' of the Vietnamese would have to be won.

AIR AMERICA IN VIETNAM

As was the case in Laos, the CIA brought its own logistic capacities to Vietnam with Air America. And as in Laos, Air America in Vietnam experienced a marked development due to the war.

But whereas in Laos the role of the airline company was kept secret, in Vietnam everything was out in the open.

The existence of the company in the country was certainly not new. During the time of the French, its ancestor the CAT had put its transport capacities at the disposal of the CIA.

As has been stated earlier, CAT aircraft had participated in supporting secret operations against the newly independent North Vietnam from 1954. Evacuation operations of the Christian population from the north, authorized by the Geneva accords, also had been the opportunity to secretly bring into the north several tons of equipment destined for future anti-communist guerilla networks. However, overall these operations never had the success expected of them.

For approximately twelve years, Air America operations more or less stagnated. A handful of pilots were more or less content with carrying out a few meagre liaison flights for AID, the CIA or military advisers posted in the country.

The situation changed from one day to the next when the Americans established themselves on a grand scale.

In the first ten months of 1965, Air America doubled the number of flights. This figure was again doubled throughout the following eight months. At the beginning of the sixties the company had several light liaison aircraft. In 1965 this fleet was more than fifty strong, including 25 C-46 Commando and C-47 Dakota. Air America had nine different types of aircraft operational. Cargo traffic had grown at an exponential rate : practically at zero in 1964, by the following year it had reached 1,650 tons every month.

In 1967 and 1968, when American engagement was at its strongest, it reached more than 2,500 tons. Air America relied on a pool of 240 pilots for the city of Saigon alone.

Without wanting to encourage the extreme situations that it knew in Laos, Air America nonetheless did credit to its motto : "Anything, anytime, anywhere..."

The company planes transported everything : weapons, ammunition, Vietcong prisoners, CIA agents, animals and the inevitable bags of rice. Not forgetting the VIPs : visiting Vietnam in 1965, Richard Nixon, future President of the United States, was transported by Air America planes, with armed helicopters of the US Army as an escort. The company of the CIA had specially selected three crews to carry out these trusted missions. The chosen pilots questioned each other concerning the possible reasons why they had been selected :

"Maybe because we're better pilots than the others, or perhaps it's because we have nothing to drink...!"

Perhaps it was for both these reasons.

A regular activity of Air America was the transport of CIA liaison agents. The 'couriers' needed their own plane. "The presence of a CIA courier on board stopped us from carrying any other passenger", explains a pilot. "The guys boarded the plane with a briefcase stuffed with secret documents. Like most other passengers he was armed. The plane was at his disposal."

The pilot was a taxi driver, the only difference being that he was immediately requested not to engage in any conversation with his client, Mr. Smith. All CIA agents were called Smith. And Smith could ask his driver to take him anywhere, including North Vietnam.

The pilot complied. The plane used for this type of escapade was the Helio Courier, whose excellent performance at take-off and landing meant it could land in the country, in the fields or on sections of road. Obviously, the pilots were never much at ease with the idea of throwing themselves into, as it were, the lions' den : an unfortunate encounter was always possible either on the ground or in North Vietnamese air space.

It so happened that the plane, having landed, was seen by peasants. By the time they had warned the authorities, the CIA men had already left. Another danger came from North Vietnamese fighters. The planes flew whenever possible at very low altitude, to avoid being detected by radars. One day, however, a plane was intercepted by enemy fighters. The pilot was only able to save himself and his passenger by diving into the clouds. The return journey to the right side of the border was carried out flying with the instruments "sheltered in the clouds..."

As in Laos, Air America also flew on behalf of AID, a good supplier of 'covers' for the men of the CIA, transporting personnel and supplies of all types. Light aircraft and helicopters carried out flights between regional aerodromes and isolated villages. They brought constructiuon materials, sacks of cement and corrugated iron. It was fairly peaceful work without too much danger. For even though the American army had deployed a considerable logistic capacity, Air America planes made their contribution by transporting ammunition.

"I was piloting at that time a Beech Seminole, a small twin-engine normally used for liaison flights", remembers a pilot. "I learnt one day that I had to go and deliver ammunition to an aerodrome near the Cambodian border."

"Your taxi's waiting, loading has already started' the local unit chief told me when I passed him in the briefing room."

"Indeed, the loading was already practically completed by the time I got to the plane. The cabin seats had been removed and replaced by boxes of ammunition and grenades. There was only a narrow passage to reach my seat in the cockpit. The most incredible thing was that after I had sat down they brought yet more cases of grenades and put them in the central corridor. I was stuck in the cockpit surrounded by a mountain of grenades!"

That was not the worst however. Other pilots remember the transport of live animals. CAT was familiar with this, two decades before in China.

AID programmes insisted on the development of agriculture and intensive breeding. Consequently, several chicken breeding centres had been created and it was Air America that had the dubious honour of transporting several tens of thousands of chicks in order to create these centres.

"Transporting several thousand chicks in an unventilated plane was the worst thing about the war", said some of the pilots. "Nothing in the world smells as bad as that!"

Air America was also employed to transfer Vietnamese prisoners to Con Son prison, which proved to be as controversial as the transport of ammunition. A near-regular flight linked the mainland to the island where this penitentiary with a sinister reputation had been built. The flights went off without any problem until the day when a Press agency published a photo of prisoners boarding an aircraft with the colours of Air America on it. The Press was roused by the fact that a civilian company was used for the task. Washington, represented by the American ambassador in Vietnam Graham Matin, declared that Air America had been used to tranport prisoners only for humanitarian reasons. One of the men visible on the photo had an injured leg which was bandaged.

"We did not know that other fit and able-bodied prisoners were also on these flights." Explained the rather pathetic official communiqué...

DRUG TRAFFICKERS

Because of secret operations, the administative authorities were often kept at a respectful distance from company aircraft and the borders were crossed without any checks. Under these conditions nothing could have been easier for the crews than to set up their own little deals, on the fringe of those of their official clients...

For many, the name of Air America was, for this reason, a long time synonymous with the traffic of opium.

It had started in Laos, where the local allies of the CIA found opium to be the source of financement of their operations. The north of Laos, Burma and Thailand formed the 'Golden Triangle' where large areas of poppy production were concentrated. The cultivation of the poppy, which after being treated gives opium, was certainly not a new thing in the area. It was a tradition dating back several decades. Caravans coming from all over Burma and Thailand converged on these provinces in order to buy the produce. The journey was made on piggy back or on horse back, forming long processions snaking into the mountains. It was a slow and often perilous journey.

The drug culture was very much part of the landscape of the local economy, and the arrival of the CIA, who had come to lead its own war in the region, changed nothing. The CIA brought with it a fleet of aircraft which had the effect of revolutionizing the opium trade and giving it wings!

It was reported that Air America helicopters were used to transport men of Vang Pao, the ally of the CIA, who were going to negotiate the purchase of local village production, thus saving them a walk of several days, the helicopters brought these negotiators to the village in question and then left. When the deal was finished, the helicopters were called up by radio and came to pick up the negotiators and their merchandise.

Vang Pao himself received the technical and financial aid necessary to buy and maintain two C-47 Dakotas from the CIA and AID. These two planes obtained from Air America and Continental Air Services allowed him therefore to create his own airline company which operated in Laos. There was no doubt that these two planes also transported opium, between the boxes of ammunition. Maybe it even transported ammunition between the boxes of opium. The CIA was able to wash its hands of the affair, it no longer concerned CIA planes...

The 'politics of opium' was not only a matter of transporting production. The support of crops could equally be indirect and rather nasty: the Americans could, for example, guarantee to supply a village with rice by carrying out parachute drops, thus enabling the inhabitants to fully dedicate themselves to producing non-food, but highly profitable, crops. Very often the heavy losses of able-bodied men due to the war did not allow the villages the possibility to tackle both a subsistence agriculture and another one that would bring in a profit. The Air America planes influenced the choices that were made.

For those that took the time to think about it, there was little doubt the drugs leaving Laos ended up, one way or another, in American territory, or in the bloodstream of G.I.s in Vietnam. But those responsible for the traffic were none other than Laotian Generals who were leading the war alongside the CIA. The agency would find it difficult to fight against this situation without jeopardizing its entire war effort in the region.

These considerations concerned the American Narcotics Bureau who had decided to investigate the drug situation in Laos. A team was sent there by the bureau but its action was rapidly blocked by the Laotians and the CIA. The American Embassy at Vientiane refused to cooperate, reminding them rather hypocritically that Laos was a sovereign country that had no anti-drugs legislation: it was not the business of the Narcotics Bureau to lay down the law within the country. The situation developed slightly at the beginning of the seventies, when the American government, after closing its eyes on its own schemes over a number of years, formally involved itself in an anti-drugs fight on an international scale. But wasn't it already too late?

The work of agents of the narcotics bureau and the DEA (Drugs Enforcement Administration) could at last resume under normal conditions in Laos. Paradoxically, Air America profited from this activity by transporting American agents from the DEA throughout the country. The agents crossed the length and breadth of Laos looking for secret production plants or simply to interrogate US or Laotian personnel present in the field. The DEA had even managed to infiltrate agents in the caravans that were leaving to sell produce beyond the Laotian border. The agents were equipped with miniscule portable radio transmitters, which meant they could report on the progress of the caravan.

Equipped with receivers, Air America aircraft followed the procession from a distance, until an interception operation was decided on, generally at the Thai border.

At the same time, Air America did its utmost to try and correct the image of 'dope airline' which seemed to be sticking like mud. Accusations were thrown in the United States against the airline company and the CIA who both seemed closely linked to the trafficking. Teams were set up in Laos to inspect crew baggage, along with passenger baggage and the cargo loads.

The new regulations were no doubt welcomed by the pilots who had no desire to be associated with this evil trade.

"But we transported all kinds of things", they explained. "It was not possible to look inside every box and crate to find out exactly what was in it..."

This was especially so when refugees, who carried a jumble of possessions with them, were being transported.

"These people didn't understand that the rules had changed from one day to the next, and that the little bundle of poppies that were accepted in the plane yesterday, would today be thrown out."

Everyone agreed however that the heart of the problem lay elsewhere. It was in the industrial scale trafficking which the Laotian superior officers indulged in, with, at the very least, the tacit complicity of the intelligence agency.

Beyond these almost institutionalized practices, some pilots also succumbed to setting up their own little trade. They had the opportunity to make enormous profits transporting little packets, unobtrusively. But this phenomenon was rare : the pilots earned a good enough living without having to resort to breaking the law to have an extra source of income.

The CIA, wanting to avoid legal proceedings, never elaborated on the possible aberrations of several of its pilots. In the CIA, dirty washing was done in private.

Those who returned to the United States millionaires were of course very much the exception.

In the Autumn of 1972, both to silence critics and to try to stop the publication of a book 'The Politics of Heroin in South-East Asia', by Al McCoy, the CIA promptly led an investigation into its own activity in this area. Teams went to south-east Asia to conduct the investigation, and more than a hundred people, CIA agents, AID agents, Pentagon and Air America personnel, were interrogated. The result was made public at the end of the year. The CIA was whitewashed of all accusations which had been brought against it.

"There has never, in the policy of either the agency or its agents, been any trafficking of that nature allowed", it was stated. In the same manner, Air America also had any doubt against it lifted.

"Air America has never permitted such a practice be made possible with its aircraft", wrote the CIA in all seriousness. "The new policy in place using surveillance teams is extra security against any attempt at illegal trafficking", added the report, which recognized the possibility of such a practice…"

It would have seemed rather an exaggeration to say that no-one in Laos touched drugs, when it was generally recognized that the country was known as being one of the largest producers in the world. The intelligence agency let fly a few rumours concerning local Loatians who could be suspected of taking drugs, while at the same time cooperating with the Americans on other operations. "It's a real problem", declared the CIA report with more than a little hypocrisy.

In any case, the aerial activities of the CIA were eventually cleared of any accusations that were levelled against them.

VERY REAL RISKS

Without quite matching the intensity of fighting that the company was familiar with in Laos, Air America operations in Vietnam were nonetheless not without risk.

Less than 150 miles south-east of Saigon, A C-47 was one day shot down by Vietcong fire. The plane was flying very low, less than 1,500 feet above the ground. It was preparing to land in a government-controlled village, when it was badly hit. With one engine out of action and the pilot seriously injured, the co-pilot made an emergency landing in a field. He managed to send out a distress signal while the Vietcong continued firing at the plane on the ground. The distress signal was received by another plane of the company, which relayed it on to a CIA helicopter. In less than fifteen minutes the helicopter was at the crash site but it was welcomed by heavy firing which forced it to turn back. Another aerial attempt several minutes later also ended in failure. It was one hour later when an Air America helicopter managed to land near the wreckage. The Vietcong had left and the men from the CIA were able to approach the plane.

The pilot and co-pilot were still in the cockpit. They had both been killed by a bullet through the head at close range, but their forearms bore the marks of many axe blows which showed the force with which they had been attacked while still prisoners in the wreckage. As for the loadmaster, of Vietnamese descent, witnesses from the village pointed out that he had been led away alive by the Vietcong, but no trace of him was ever found.

While the helicopter was taking off, with the mutilated bodies of the pilots inside, US Air Force fighter-bombers appeared on the scene to desroy the wreck and the ammunition which was still inside.

This episode came at the right time to provoke a violent controversy within the airline company, between the pilots and the hierarchy. It was strictly forbidden for members of a crew to carry a weapon for self-defence. A pilot who had been caught out with an automatic pistol in his flight equipment was dismissed for infringing this regulation. In fact, the majority of flight personnel preferred to take the risk of being found out rather than to fly over the Vietnamese countryside without a weapon...

"It would be tantamount to suicide to leave without a weapon...", they admitted.

The death of the Dakota crew dealt a tragic blow within the company. The pilots blamed the management for not allowing weapons to be carried. "They could have held the Vietcong at bay while help arrived", they said, justifiably.

From that moment, the management chose to close its eyes to those pilots who armed themselves. With the rapid deterioration of the situation in the country, even official policy was in fact totally revised, Air America lent those crews who desired it an M-1 rifle or a Uzi type submachine-gun. The person who borrowed the weapon was simply required to return it after each flight.

What made the crews nervous was not only the possibility of being fired at while flying over the South Vietnamese countryside, but the fact that danger was present even in so called safe zones. There was no clear front-line zone in Vietnam as was also the case in Laos. Government troops controlled urban areas and several other clearly defined regions. But it was never certain whether official government controlled zones were indeed really what they seemed.

Uncertainty seemed to prevail everywhere...

Briefings on the development of the situation took place every morning, and aerial routes, which were more or less certain, were updated. But sometimes the situation developed too quickly and the South Vietnamese were often too optimistic concerning the real extent of their control for the information to be taken seriously. In 1964, a map of areas held by the different factions had the appearance of Swiss cheese, with the holes, representing the Vietcong zones, the smallest areas. Five years later, this scenario had been reversed and there were only a few small islands under government control, lost in a sea of insecurity. Very often, the lack of navigational aids in the first months of American engagement combined with unfavourable weather conditions forcing aircraft to fly under the cloud layer. This near the ground, the planes were therefore easy targets for the Vietcong.

One solution was to fly over the sea, which was practical for planes linking up different coastal towns in the country. Air America maintained different regular lines between principal towns and bases in the country. That was how the plane flying between Saigon and Da Nang, the biggest US Air Force base in Vietnam, came to be nicknamed the 'Da Nang rocket'. An ancient C-46 Commando operated the route, which strongly contrasted with the derisive nickname that it had been given.

So as not to inconvenience passengers who hated being fired at while flying over the Vietnamese countryside, the pilots usually carried out the link by flying along the coastline. During the middle of the monsoon season, one of these flights turned into a catastrophe; the plane got lost in a sea of cloud and the pilot, disoriented, unwittingly flew the plane over dry land and ended up crashing into a mountain.

THE TET OFFENSIVE

On the 29th January 1968, at the same time as the Chinese New Year, the Tet festival, was being celebrated, a ceasefire was announced : it was to last 36 hours. A number of South Vietnamese troops were sent back home for the duration of the festivities. The night of the 30th of January, the Vietcong took everyone by surprise and launched a major offensive.

Almost 70,000 combatants left to attack a hundred or so towns across

A mass container dropping operation for the French Resistance by planes of the US 8th Air Force. At the same period, from January to September 1944, the 801/492 Bomber Group dropped 345 agents in France. (S.H.A.A.)

Cloth insignia of a Carpetbagger veteran.

On the 25th of June 1944, B-17s from the 8th AF carried out a massive drop of containers of weapons and equipment for several French maquis of the Ain, Jura, Haute-Vienne and Vercors areas. (USAF)

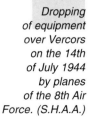

Dropping of equipment over Vercors on the 14th of July 1944 by planes of the 8th Air Force. (S.H.A.A.)

The B-24J serial number 42-50770 from the 856th Bomber Squadron, 492nd Bomb Group after landing in Sweden on the 4th of August 1944. (USAF)

On an American base in the Philippines in 1957, this all-black painted B-17 had a faithful career with the American secret service in Asia behind it. (USAF)

Bearing civilian markings, this B-17G which had belonged to Intermountain Aviation, a company well-known for its relationship with the CIA, was without doubt the first aircraft to experiment with the Fulton system of in-flight recovery. (USAF)

Llegada a Miami del B-26 que bombarde

933
FAR

933

The Bay of Pigs fiasco in Cuba. The press widely covered the arrival of the false Cuban defector in Miami on the 28th of April 1961. The Cuban markings on the plane were the result of meticulous work. (Georges Bencroft)

The remains of Farias' plane after its combat with Cuban fighters and its forced landing close to the invasion beach during the Bay of Pigs operation in 1961. (Embassy of Cuba)

Not far from the Bay of Pigs, Castro came to inspect the CIA B-26 crash site. (Embassy of Cuba)

Preparation for a test flight with the U2 prototype. This plane is carrying USAF markings in order to conceal the real owner. (Lockheed)

The first batch of production U-2s, seen here in 1956, had now received NACA tail markings. The NACA, soon replaced by NASA, was used as cover for the U-2 operations. (Lockheed)

As well as dark blue paint offering good concealment at high altitude against a dark sky, this CIA U-2 received a civilian registration. (Lockheed)

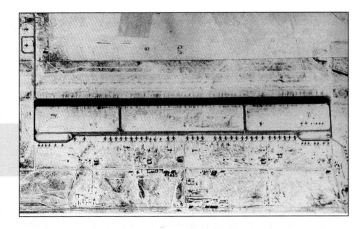

A Soviet air base photographed by a CIA U-2. No less than 32 Soviet bombers are visible on this picture. (CIA)

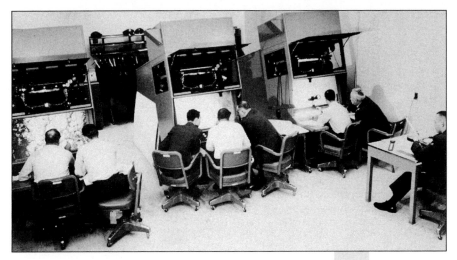

A photo interpretation room for the pictures taken by the U-2. A meticulous and long-drawn out job which represented an important financial investment for the CIA. (CIA)

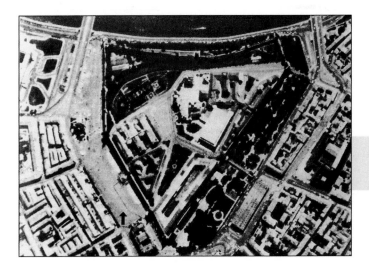

A Kremlin aerial photography taken by a U-2. The black arrow indicates the visitors filing into the Lenin Mausoleum. (CIA)

The instrument panel of a U-2 with,
in the middle, the driftsight which gave the pilot
the possibility to observe the ground below him.
(Lockheed)

The famous American pilot Gary Powers,
captured by the Soviets after his U-2 was shot
down on the 1st of May 1960. (DOD)

Fragments of Powers' U-2 shown
to the public by the Soviets. Following the aerial
victory, they made an important haul of scientific
information. (Embassy of USSR)

The landing of a CIA U-2. This plane, carrying a civilian registration, is equipped with a long fuselage dorsal fairing which houses ECM equipment. (Lockheed)

On this picture taken in flight, the U-2 displays an air-refuelling receptacle installed in the dorsal fairing. (Lockheed)

The first trials of a U-2 on an aircraft carrier. It was by using such a combination that the CIA collected information about the French atomic experiments in the Pacific. (Lockheed).

A group of Taiwanese pilots trained on U-2s by the CIA at the end of the sixties. (CIA)

An impressive victory board for the People's Republic of China who exposed the remains of the first four U-2s they had been able to shoot down in the middle of 1965. (Embassy of China)

Flown by Major Chang of the Nationalist China Air Force, this U-2 was shot down on the night of the 10th of January 1965 while trying to take pictures of a Chinese nuclear site. (Embassy of China)

Photographed between two missions against the Simbas, this B-26K displays its nose with eight .50 cal. machine guns at Leopoldville airport. (Wing Agency)

A superb view of a B-26K flown by CIA Cuban mercenaries over the Congolese jungle. (Wing Agency)

Congo 1964 : the remains of a WIGMO T-28 are checked by European mercenaries near Stanleyville (Boomerang Press)

The B-26s were widely flown in south-east Asia where the CIA used them in clandestine operations over Laos and against the Ho-Chi-Minh trail. (USAF)

*2nd of May 1974 :
on the Moc Hoa
air base, in
South Vietnam,
these vietcong
prisoners are
boarding
an Air American
light aircraft.
(Boomerang
Press)*

The loading of freight for remote areas
of Laos in an S-58 of the famous
Air America company. (DOD)

Right : A C-7 Caribou painted in the characteristic
blue and white colours of the Air America
aircraft in Vietnam. (DOD)

Vietnam 1968. On the US airfield of Vinh Long, in
the Delta, these indigenous troops in black
pyjamas, possibly PRUs, are disembarking from
the back door of an Air America C-7 Caribou,
watched by Americans of the Agency. (DOD)

After probably having been engaged in combat in Laos, this Air America Fairchild Porter received the markings of the ICCS, which did not protect it from Vietcong and North Vietnamese fire. (USAF)

*In April 1975,
an Air America
UH-1B is evacuating
the last American
nationals from
Saigon and
is landing on the
deck of a US Navy
ship off the coast
of Vietnam.
(US Navy)*

It started with helicopters, the Vietnam war also ended with rotary wings. This is the last trip for this Air America UH-1D loaded with fugitives. (USAF)

An Air America C-46 with the markings of the peace agreement International Control Commission, during the last months of the Vietnam War. (USAF)

Nearly 30 years old when it was engaged in the Laos, the B-26 nevertheless showed excellent capability as a strike aircraft. (USAF)

Replacing the Courier and Super Courier, the turbo prop Helio Stallion was much appreciated by the CIA for clandestine operations over Laos in the sixties and seventies. (DOD)

The first A-12, no. 121, during static trials. (Lockheed)

The first camouflage pattern for the A-12 used black paint only around the cockpit, in order to avoid the reflection of light. (Lockheed)

A shape and performance without equal : the A-12, then the SR-71, became exceptional technical successes. (Lockheed)

No A-12 or SR-71 has ever been intercepted during a mission, despite the dozens of attempts... (Lockheed)

For the A-12 as well as the SR-71 later, air refuelling was essential for the success of every mission. (Lockheed)

Despite several years of development, the D-21 drone was never a success. (Lockheed)

Above and below : A D-21 drone fitted on its M-21 launcher. The launching from the M-21 had been abandoned after a failed operation at Mach 2, resulting in the death of one crew and the loss of one aircraft. (Lockheed)

Once the dropping, at Mach 2, had been abandoned, the D-21 powered by powder rocket was launched form a B-52 bomber. (Lockheed)

A first drone was lost by the CIA over China on the 15th of November 1964. (Ryan collection)

A Chinese propaganda picture showing Red Guards near the wreck of a Ryan 147H shot down over China. (Ryan collection)

A Contra Hughes 500 helicopter on a secret airstrip in Honduras, before a deep mission in Nicaragua. (Tony Toffano)

After a search of 24 hours, Eugene Hasenfus is captured by the Sandinist Army. (Embassy of Nicaragua)

*An Air America Convair 440 photographed on a secondary airstrip
in Florida in the middle of the seventies.
The Air America markings had been rubbed out. (Eric Micheletti)*

*An Air America DC-6 transport plane photographed a few years later
on an American airfield. This aircraft is carrying a very discreet registration marking.
(Eric Micheletti)*

*Showing the presence of the company in the third world,
this Southern Air Transport L-100 is carrying out humanitarian
missions in Mozambique, under the colours of the UN. (R. Collins)*

Based in Albania, two GNAT 750 drones were used by the CIA in 1995 to survey ex-Yugoslavia. (General Atomics)

Capable of flying over every point in the globe from an American base, the Global Hawk drone, with the same wingspan as the Airbus A-320, will be a means of investigation into the next century for the CIA. (Teledyne Ryan)

The CIA drones in Yugoslavia were supported by Schweitzer RG-8 like this one, implemented by the CIA as a communication relay. (Laurent Bart)

the country. From the very first minutes of the fighting, the sound of gunfire was mixed with firecrackers which were traditionally used for bringing in the new year.

For the first time in the Vietnam war, fighting initiated by the Vietcong was brought directly to the heart of the towns. The most spectacular aspect of this action was the attack directed against the American Embassy, in the heart of Saigon. Before being moved out by the Marines and the Military Police, a commando of 19 Vietcong managed to hold the premises for almost six hours, creating a shock in American public opinion, a public that was able to follow the fighting practically live on TV.

In the days following the offensive, Air America was put to use transporting officers of the CIA throughout the country to assess the situation. In Hue, the ancient imperial capital, the fighting lasted almost three weeks; some strong troops were entrenched in the ancient citadel and the fighting to get them out was long and bloody. For the pilots of Air America, the most difficult thing was no longer to accomplish the mission itself, but simply to leave their apartment to get to the airport.

The first day of the offensive, some of the pilots, having no doubt drunk too much over the Chinese new year, did not pay attention to the gunfire; they thought it was the usual firecrackers. When they got up the following morning and saw the streets empty of people, with heavily armed patrols at every corner, they realised that something was amiss.

Other pilots were trapped in their apartment buildings, or on the road to the airport. Although no Air America pilot became a direct victim of the fighting, many were believed dead by their friends and colleagues when they were prevented from moving by the fierce fighting.

The situation was no more pleasant for those who managed to get to the airports and airbases where the aprons were subject to Vietcong sniper fire over several hours. To attempt to approach the planes or to refuel them verged on madness. In the first hours of the offensive, another preoccupation of the CIA was to place personnel scattered throughout the whole of Vietnam in a safe area. A helicopter was sent to Dalat, in the centre of the country, where violent fighting had taken place. Eleven CIA personnel were picked up from a football stadium, during an angry exchange of gunfire.

One of the most incredible stories is told by Christopher Robbins in his book 'Air America'; a Helio Courier was one morning called to take urgent supplies of ammunition to South Vietnamese troops cornered in a tiny village. The pilot took off, but he had to stay very low throughout the flight because of bad weather conditions. Surrounded by hills, he rapidly lost radio contact with his base. Arriving at his destination, he spotted the combat zone.

"The situation seemed fairly quiet" he recalled. "I landed without waiting."

Several soldiers were at one end of the terrain but they appeared undecided as to whether to come and unload the plane. Irritated by their passiveness, the pilot shouted at them and the soldiers decided eventually to come over and give him a hand...

"Everything was over in five minutes", the pilot continued, "I thanked them and got back into the Courier, started it up, lined it up on the runway and within a few seconds I was heading back to base..."

Meanwhile weather conditions had improved and the pilot was able to climb high enough to re-establish radio contact with his base.

"That was when the guys on the radio warned me : 'Your mission is cancelled, the village has fallen into enemy hands...Turn round and come back immediately'. In other words the guys that had helped me unload the plane were Vietcongs! I felt ill for the rest of the flight home."

THE UNITED STATES LEAVE VIETNAM

Despite the major operations in Cambodia and Laos, and the tens of millions of dollars swallowed up by pacification programmes, despite also the hundreds of thousands of tons of bombs dropped and the more than 50,000 G.I.s that passed through the country, the United States was not able to prevent the North Vietnamese from launching a wide-ranging offensive in 1972.

President Nixon responded with yet more bombings which eventually brought an end to the communist offensive and the signing of the Paris treaty, on the 28th January 1973.

218

Under the terms of this treaty the United States were to withdraw their last combat units from Vietnam, leaving only military advisers and civilian technicians. Eight thousand American citizens were registered as residents in South Vietnam at that time.

The United States nonetheless continued to supply the Vietnamese with arms and ammunition. Fifty military personnel and 1,200 civilians worked for the DAO (Defence Attache Office, not to be confused with the Military Attache of the Embassy).

General Smith was the last head of the DAO. He took care of the military provisions destined for the South Vietnamese forces and was in charge of inspecting troops from the south. Smith and his department set themselves up in the old HQ of American forces in Vietnam, at Tan Son Nhut airport.

The most surprising thing was that General Smith could practically see the enemy going about its daily business from his office. Tan Son Nhut was in fact sheltering 300 communist military personnel (250 Vietcong soldiers and officers and about 50 North Vietnamese soldiers and officers), responsible for participating in the different committees instituted in Paris to supervise the correct application of the peace treaty.

If the ceasefire was not able to be respected, the important communist delegation had a ringside seat to supervise the deployment of the military potential of the enemy. From its camp, the delegation was in permanent radio contact with Hanoi who it kept regularly infomed of what it was able to learn about the enemy plans, whether carried out by its informers or by direct observation. The North Vietnamese were based in the heart of the airport and were not complaining!

The peculiarities of Tan Son Nhut did not end there; the airport at Saigon housed the HQ of the South Vietnamese army and, opposite, the premises of Air America, with the blue and white aircraft of the CIA stationary on the apron.

Every time the US Air Force aircraft abandoned their transport mission on a theatre of operation, the machines of Air America took over. Vietnam did not break any precedents and within a few weeks aerial activity had more than doubled.

219

I CAN'T CONTROL SHIT...

Air America involved itself with a new speciality: the transport of members of the ICCS, an international commission for control and surveillance, in charge of supervising the implementation of the Paris treaty.

It was an interesting situation; the commission was made up of Canadian, Indonesian, Polish and Hungarian Officer observers. The latter, even though part of the eastern bloc, were nonetheless transported like their colleagues by CIA aircraft.

"If every ICCS delegation had to bring their own aircraft, we would have one accident after another", predicted Thomas Polgar, the head of the CIA in Saigon.

"May as well put the Air America pilots' knowledge of the country to good use" he added.

The Poles and Hungarians did not appreciate the irony of the situation. Better than anyone else, they knew who was really hiding behind Air America. Although the person in charge of the Polish delegation to the commission, who was also the ex Director General of LOT the Polish national airline, had a good idea of the problem :

"To hell with convention" he said to his Hungarian colleagues. "It is also a question of your personal safety." In spite of their initial reticence, the Hungarians were eventually swayed and accepted to fly with Air-CIA. They never had cause for complaint: they trusted the know-how of the American pilots.

To carry the decision, the Canadians had found a system which suited everybody and at the same time could keep up appearances : a subsidiary of Air America, called ICCS Air Services was formed to honour the contract with the international commission. The Air America letters were removed from the planes and helicopters and replaced by yellow stripes with the hope that the neutrality of the aircraft and its occupants would be respected.

"It made a perfect target for the gunmen", said the pilots.

By way of an illustration, an ICCS helicopter was shot down by one of the first anti-aircraft SA-7 portable missiles to be used during the

Vietnam war. All the occupants were killed. The irony was that the helicopter was that day transporting a North Vietnamese Colonel!

Another helicopter, which was also transporting members of the commission, was shot at while it was landing near the crash zone. A Canadian officer got out of the helicopter, pushing a Polish officer in front of him :

"Don't shoot, he's one of yours..."

It's true that the Poles knew how to keep themselves safe. A Polish officer, passenger in an aircraft, on hearing the fears expressed by his pilot before taking off for a zone infested with Vietcong, replied :

"Don't worry, they have been informed of our presence. They won't shoot."

The ICCS had been translated by the Canadians into "I can't control shit."

Bringing their actions into harmony with their thoughts, the Canadians withdrew swiftly from the commission where they felt they were wasting their time. They were replaced by the Iranians who thought they could play an important role on the international stage.

Members of the ICCS were meant to investigate into violations of the Paris treaty which might be noted by each one of the parties present. But every decision taken within the commission had to be taken unanimously, the system was blocked on a regular basis, the Poles and the Hungarians refusing to condemn the Vietcongs. The commission produced reports, reams of paper, but all in vain of course.

The ICCS became an enormous bureaucratic machine which only lived for itself. To advance the peace process, officers of the commission became representatives, assiduously frequenting bars in the grand hotels and diplomatic cocktail parties. For the officers who had come from Eastern Europe, it was very often their first outing in a 'capitalist' country. Their salary, paid in dollars, easily went to their heads.

The Hungarians did not lose the north. Camera in hand, they took the opportunity to hang around South Vietnamese barracks and airports.

When it was not simply a matter of making a little trip in a helicopter, flights on board CIA aircraft also presented a perfect opportunity to take photos, to reconnoitre the terrain. The South Vietnamese were very angry at this and complained bitterly, but in vain: members of the ICCS were untouchable because of their diplomatic status. "We're not going to darken the windows or order aircraft to make detours every time we want to stop them from seeing something interesting!" retorted a rather disenchanted CIA officer.

It was common practice for the Soviets to do this with Western military attaches when they were in the USSR. The Indonesians seemed to be the only ones to take their work seriously. They would venture into combat zones, take notes, search around, assess and evaluate...

"Why are you doing that?" asked the head of the CIA in Saigon, surprised at their over-zealous actions.

"One day we will have to fight against the Vietnamese" replied an Indonesian superior officer. "Perhaps not straight away, but one day soon, definitely..."

In the middle of all that the Air America pilots were playing second fiddle. Every evening the crews would call the Air America headquarters at Tan Son Nhut airport to find out their work schedule for the following day. They could either have a free day, be in reserve or have a flight to carry out.

If there was a flight, it could be either an Air America or an ICCS flight. In the real as well as the figurative sense, the pilots wore two hats. They also had two sets of chest insignia. Depending on what the flight director at Tan Son Nhut told them, they wore one or other of the uniforms.

The most surprising thing was that a plane of the commission linked Saigon and Hanoi every Friday. The principal responsibility of the American officers that took this flight was to discuss the problem of soldiers missing in combat. For the rest, ICCS Air Services was an expensive plaything at the service of a commission which had no great use. The invoices for the flights had to be paid by the signatories of the Paris treaty, in other words the United States, South and North Vietnam and the Provisional Revolutionary Government. In fact, it was of course the United States that picked up almost all of the bills...

CAMBODIA : THE MOST USELESS OF WARS

An old French protectorate and a peaceful Kingdom of 5.5 million inhabitants, Cambodia found itself swept along in the turmoil of events in south east Asia during the second half of the twentieth century. Prince Norodom Sihanouk, who controlled the country, did everything in his power to keep Cambodia out of the conflict that was growing at its borders. But in vain.

The Americans were profoundly irritated by Sihanouk's diplomatic efforts, which they judged to be too adventurous. Notably he wanted to establish diplomatic relations with countries of the communist bloc.

Washington was also appalled to see the Vietcong use the neutrality of Cambodia as a refuge, without Phnom Penh doing anything to get them out, or even letting the US Army do it.

At first friendly, then becoming more threatening, the power of Washington put pressure on the Kingdom over many years for it to abandon its traditional neutrality and for it to put itself at the side of America to fight against the communists. This was all in vain.

Consequently, the overthrow of Sihanouk was the secret diplomatic objective of the United States for almost fifteen years.

The CIA had its protege in General Lon Nol, one of Sihanouk's ministers. Lon Nol made his intentions clear to the American intelligence agency : if he got to power, he would welcome American troops with open arms. Not that the Americans had ever been able to intervene in the affairs of Cambodia; attacks on the territory by planes or raids by special forces had multiplied with the intensification of the Vietnam war. But the Americans wanted to have their hands free to intervene against the Vietnamese present in Cambodia.

On the 18th March 1970, while he was on a visit abroad, Sihanouk was deposed by Lon Nol and one other of his ministers. It is likely that the CIA had knowledge of the coup that was brewing, but did not forewarn Sihanouk. According to some sources, the agency passed information on to Washington and let the conspiraors act. Some even state that it was the CIA behind the military overthrow of Sihanouk.

In the hours following the coup, Cambodian troops launched a very wide-ranging operation against Vietnamese sanctuaries in the east of the country. After several hours of fighting the troops asked for assistance from the US Air Force and the South Vietnamese artillery. The Cambodian war had just begun.

On the 30th May 1970, less than two months after the coup, a first large scale American attack was launched against Cambodia.

Three years and a hundred thousand bombs later, the fighting continued still in Cambodia, even though the Paris peace treaty had put an end to ten years of American presence in its neighbour Vietnam.

A short time before the Paris conference, the American official position was to explain the bombing in Cambodia as a way of saving American lives in Vietnam. The American withdrawal from the country did not however stop the bombing, on the contrary. The aim was at that time to stop the Khmer Rouge gaining power.

When he left his position in September 1973, the American ambassador in Cambodia, Emory Swank, qualified the conflict that was unfolding in the country as "the most useless conflict ever in Indochina."

The Cambodian war had created, within a very short time, an immense need for logistics.

Following a standard scenario, the deterioration of the situation on the roads and in rural areas had created a greatly increased need for aerial transport, whether for civilian commercial activity or for the military.

Many private air companies proliferated in an anarchic way, only the local civil servants had to have their palms oiled to ensure that they would blossom...

Everybody could obtain an adequate commercial license, provided they could pay the minister and his different civil servants. It was enough to then find a plane, its condition mattered little, and a crew more or less aware of the risks, to set up a business. In the cutthroat competition which was getting under way, the only things that mattered were efficiency and that the planes were loaded to their maximum capacity to ensure the maximum revenue. All that added even more uncertainty to an already precarious trade.

Local air transport warmed up a little more when, starting August 1973, the activity of the US Air Force in the country was limited by a decision of the US Congress. Identical to what had happened in Laos a little earlier, private companies were called to the rescue by the CIA to fill the void left by the American military.

Air America occupied a prime place in the scheme of things, which did not always have the scope of its activities in Laos. Of course, the company of the CIA had not finished with its old demons and did not limit its activity to transporting rice to the civilian population.

Every morning one or two helicopters from the company left Saigon for the Cambodian capital Phnom Penh, where they were at the disposal of the embassy and American military personnel present in the country.

"Our missions were 100% paramilitary", explained a pilot who operated flights to Cambodia.

"The guys that flew with us were armed to the teeth, and it was often necessary to take them to areas that were not particularly quiet, in the heart of the fighting." The aircraft were also used for conveying arms and ammunition to government soldiers, things which the US Air Force could no longer do and which were out of reach of the Cambodians themselves.

The helicopters returned at the end of the day to Saigon where they remained overnight. The same system was also applied to cargo planes which transported refugees fleeing from the Khmer Rouge advance. The signing of the Paris peace accords, which were dedicated to an official ceasefire, had given an excuse for the management of Air America to cut salaries by calling off any risk bonuses relating to missions in combat zones. In fact, the confrontation was continuing with the same violence, and was even approaching Phnom Penh with the advance of the Khmer Rouge.

The quibble was worth its weight in gold for Air America: the pilots' salaries went on average from $45,000 to $28,000 per year. This was hard enough to accept, and on top of this, the Paris accords, far from relieving them, deprived them of a possible safety net ; if some misfortune forced them to evacuate from their aircraft over enemy controlled territory, they could no longer count on US Air Force planes coming to get them.

Very bitter at all this, the pilots started to protest. Some threatened legal action against Air America. Others started speaking to the Press anonymously and the echo of these confessions came to the attention of the major American media networks, causing the company much embarrassment.

The situation was very far removed from the flamboyant style that existed in Laos.

The pilots were growing tired of the war in south east Asia and the legal cover of Air America was starting to fray at the edges.

Another facet of Air America activity was to assist the Cambodian Air Force in the upkeep of its planes. A contract, in due form, linked them to the Cambodians up until the 31st December 1974. When the contract expired, a new legal entity was formed to carry on the work of Air America under another name. The company of the CIA had become too famous...but the personnel and the work carried out remained absolutely identical.

THE LAST CHANCE AIRLIFT

The gradual encircling of the Cambodian capital by the Khmer Rouge progressively reduced the field of activity of the air companies. The pilots kept themselves informed of the situation during informal meetings, over a drink or a hasty meal. They spoke about airstrips where fuel was still available, the latest progress of the communists, terrains under enemy fire, friendly positions which were still holding and whose artillery fire was still active; a plane was destroyed in mid-flight when it had flown in the path of 105mm canon fire. It was a real piece of bad luck...

The airport at Phnom Penh, which was soon to be within the reach of Khmer Rouge rocket fire, had become too dangerous a place to work. The communists were expecting the arrival of a heavy aircraft to launch a salvo of rocket fire on to obstructed parkings. The 122mm rocket-launcher tubes were positioned at night only two miles or so from the airport and, supplied with delayed action fuses, were set off in the middle of the day.

The gradual encircling of Phnom Penh by the Khmer Rouge greatly increased the demand of an airlift which would end at the airport of the capital. The support of government troops meant that large quantities of ammunition, supplied secretly by the American government, had to be brought in by air. For political reasons, the US Air Force found itself incapable of ensuring the transport of ammunition. Air America, as well as Continental Air Services, which ensured a regular shuttle between Bangkok and Phnom Penh, were both generally recognized as being linked to the CIA. The American authorities, who were reluctant to entrust them with missions that were too flagrant, preferred to turn towards a man that they knew well from the time of Laos : William Bird.

Bird had sold his air company to Continental a dozen or so years earlier, but he had kept an interest in the business by flying several helicopters in his name. He had significant know-how in the subject of 'special' air transport.

The following proposition was made to him :

"If the Pentagon provides you with 'anonymous' airplanes and is responsible for their maintenance, could you organize an airlift from U Tapao, in Thailand?"

"We can always try..."

Bird Air was recreated to put the five C-130 Hercules, given to it by the US Air Force, into operation. All the military markings of the planes were replaced by a single civilian registration number. Bird supplied the crews while the US Air Force was responsible for the maintenance of the planes and supplementing the training of the pilots if the need arose. The pilots of course were considered to be civilians, even if the majority of them were ex-servicemen, some of them having retired from the US Air Force only a few days earlier!

The C-130 was still at that time a plane used essentially by the armed forces and "it would have been a mistake to look for civilian crews to operate them", recognized William Bird several months later. While he emphasized his contacts with the military, he was accused, once again, of having worked in close relation with the American secret service.

"I signed a contract only with the US Air Force. All the rest is bullshit", he said yet again to anyone who would listen.

The operations over Phnom Penh began in September 1974 with five crews. The pay was very good : $4,500 per month.

Three times a day, each C-130 took 25 tons of ammunition, fuel and food to the Cambodian capital and to different outposts still held by governmental troops.

Two months later, in November 1974, the Khmer Rouge completely blockaded all ground access routes leading to Phnom Penh. Shortly after, river traffic was forbidden on the Mekong. The Khmers had placed underwater mines, which had been supplied by the Chinese, in the river. The plane was therefore the last possible link with the outside world. The Americans decided to intensify the airlift.

In February 1975, the contract with Bird was renewed and amended; the operational crews were more than doubled, from five to twelve. According to the precise terms of the contract, Bird Air had to ensure thirty rotations per day between the logistical base at U Tapao in Thailand and Phnom Penh, which translated into approximately 750tons of supplies every day.

A little rice and a lot of ammunition, these prolonged the agony of the Cambodian capital a little longer...

To avoid being hit by Khmer flak, the C-130 arrived above the airport at high altitude, then engaged in a rapid spiral descent above the zone considered to be the least dangerous. Lying on his front on the rear ramp of the plane, the loadmaster watched out for any possible SA-7 anti-aircraft missiles, which the Khmer Rouge possessed in great number, through the cargo ramp. This infra-red guided missile, fired from the shoulder, used thehot gases emitted by the engines as a target. The answer was to fire a distress flare which could attract the missile by the heat that it gave off.

On the ground the situation was hardly better :

"The rockets fell anywhere on the ground and at anytime" recalls William Bird. "It was getting more and more like a game of Russian roulette."

As soon as they landed, the planes moved towards the unloading terminal where the forklift trucks were waiting. The plane kept its engines turning and, in less than four minutes, the 25 tons were unloaded.

228

Back to the runway, align the plane, full power, release brakes, the plane then took the opposite direction at full speed.

Each one of the C-130 available carried out three return trips per day. One beautiful morning, the Chinese pilots from the Air Cambodia national airline decided that the game was no longer worth it and they left for Singapore with their planes.

"They simply boarded their DC-4 with their families, without saying anything to anybody, and left Phnom Penh. We never saw them again!" said an American pilot.

By mid-April the situation had become intolerable. The pilots landing at Phnom Penh wore bullet-proof vests and combat helmets.

In only a few hours the macabre circus of last minute evacuations would begin.

In Vietnam, the deterioration of the situation had been nothing short of spectacular.

THE END OF AN ERA

The end of the Vietnamese war in april 1975 as also the end of the CIA's 'Airline Companies'.

The conflict drew to an end, the intelligence centre reconsidered its needs concerning air transport and chose to abandon the setting up of full blown airline companies.

The need to have a large fleet of aircraft and their crews on hand 24 hours a day, 365 days a year, had quite simply disappeared with the end of the American commitment in South East Asia.

The CIA had started to tighten the belt as from the signing of the treaties in Paris in January 1973. Air America had started to sell its assets even with its pilots continuing to fly in Vietnam for the ICCS. Selling the aircraft that had belonged to the CIA was sometimes not that easy : it wasn't always easy to identify certain machines, whose past had been carefully camouflaged due to clandestine operations, so as to legally transfer the property to a private operator.

It was a lot easier when it came to selling the aircraft to governments who didn't ask many questions. The Latin America countries that were allied to the United States, were the first to take advantage of these bizarre surplus sales. For example the El Salvador Air Force retrieved three C-123K Providers.

Air America finally put a stop to its operations in June 1976. Air Asia; which regrouped the maintenance installations belonging to the CIA in Taiwan had been sold the year before to private investors. Southern Air Transport or Intermountain, which will be developed upon in the following chapters, followed along the same path.

It seems fairly impossible for the CIA to go back in time and once again allow itself to buy its own airline company so as to have an exclusive service. From this point of view, the Air America example is definitely a thing of the past. The world of commercialized aviation is the object, now more than ever, of tight surveillance by civil authorities and even more so by the companies themselves, who continually spy on their rivals. Any unusual behaviour would quickly be detected, making it extremely difficult to hide tight links with a government service.

But the CIA didn't give up the whole of its air activities. We can be pretty sure that Langley kept up some interest, very carefully dissimulated in small companies that only used a few specialized machines; enough to carry out a few precise operations. The American station also knew that it could count on the US Air Force's aircraft, or on the private companies that collaborated fairly easily with them. The examples of Bird Air or Continental Air Services proved this.

CHAPTER 7

AFRICAN AFFAIRS

A NEW FIELD OF OPPOSITION

In the CIA's list of priorities at the beginning of the fifties, the continent of Africa had last place.

The United States was notably least interested in Black Africa, preferring to leave the colonial powers in charge. As for the Soviet Union, it did not yet have the logistical strength necessary to fully implement the idea, attributed to Lenin, that stated "Europe would be turned by Africa."

A decade of decolonization later, the scenario was hardly recognizable. With the old masters about to leave or having already left, Africa rejoined the rest of the world in the arena of east/west confrontation.

Following the principle which had been its own everywhere else throughout the globe, the American intelligence agency began by taking shares in air companies that were potentially useful to it.

Pan African Airlines (PAA), based in Lagos, Nigeria, was a perfect example of this policy. Like several other companies, Pan African did not really belong to the CIA, but the economic justification of its existence depended essentially on contracts that it received from the American government. The company was founded in 1962 and received, every year, nearly $600,000 worth of contracts.

In his book 'Air America', Christopher Robbins revealed that PAA was the main constituent of Africair, a holding company belonging to a man who had a seat on the board of directors of Southern Capital, an insurance company belonging to the CIA. Other coincidences were able to be revealed, making the existence of links between the air companies and the CIA a mere formality. But that was only the first stage.

The Congo affair was, at the beginning of the sixties, the opportunity for the American intelligence services to add yet more weight to their presence in the area.

CONGOLESE ADVENTURES

Congo was without doubt the only theatre of operation in Black Africa where the CIA organized a combat air force in order to achieve its ends.

The accession to independence by the ex-Belgian colony was an opportunity not to be missed by the United States and the CIA in order to gain a strong foothold in the region. It was certainly done in the name of relentless anti-communism but more often to the detriment of the interests of the old colonial powers in the region, France and Belgium.

Thirty years later this analysis remains true. The Congo affair started at the end of Eisenhower's presidency, when he had his eyes fixed on Cuba and its Leader Maximo.

However, Soviet aspirations in Africa and the post-colonial ambitions of the French and Belgians in the region, facts which were duly pointed out by the CIA in their frenetic warnings from their base in Leopoldville, (now Kinshasa), the capital of the country, led Eisenhower to refer to an atlas. It was above all a matter of locating Congo (renamed Zaire in 1967) on a map of Africa. As big as the whole of Europe, or Alaska and Texas together, Congo could not escape his inquiries for very long.

The communist threat, real or supposed, and the well-confirmed phenomenal wealth hidden underground in the country, were reasons enough for it to become a pawn in the region.

The political history of Congo during the sixties was of a great complexity. From 1960 to 1967, reversals of situations and alliances being overthrown complicated the progress of a civil war which ended in the victory of one man, Joseph Mobutu, or Mobutu Sese Soku, and one organization, the CIA.

To greatly simplify the history of this war, it can be said there were three essential phases of fighting : the Katangaise secession from 1960-1963, the Simba rebellion throughout 1964-1966 and the mercenary revolt of 1967.

The CIA was most active during the second episode of the war. The intervention of the American intelligence agency and the veritable 'CIA Air Force' which was thus formed cannot be explained without putting it into its historical context and retracing the history of the country from its independence.

The independence of Congo was hastily decided by the Belgian parliament in October 1959. Eight months later, on the 30th June 1960, King Baudouin himself travelled to Leopoldville to proclaim the official independence of the country. The Belgians, still in control the day after this memorable occasion, had given Africa an independent state that was certainly able to function, but that was terribly lacking in any kind of 'elite'. A good section of the population were educated, but the country only had thirteen native senior school graduates. Even if they had all passed with honours, the number was remarkably small.

"Teach the Congolese to read and write, but to avoid trouble in the future don't go beyond that, 'Student' rhymes with 'Problem', reasoned the Belgians."

The unified state, represented by Kasavubu, head of state, and Patrice Lumumba, head of government, did not delay in coming under attack from the centrifugal forces of the many and varied peoples that were part of the country. Congo, which had gained independence in complete haste and unpreparedness, was immediately torn apart by civil war.

Only five days after independence, the Congolese National Army rebelled against its Belgian officers and chaos took hold of the country. French and Belgian nationals fled to the neighbouring Congo-Brazzaville Republic. The Prime Minister, Patrice Lumumba, chose to negotiate with the rebels : he dismissed the 1,135 Belgian officers and promoted young Congolese soldiers in their place. Among them was an NCO, who within a few hours reached the grade of colonel and then was made Army Chief of Staff by Lumumba. It was a certain Joseph Mobutu.

The Belgians took advantage of this disorder to intervene militarily, notably by reinforcing their positions in Katanga province, in the south of the country. Characterized by its mining activity, for the most part controlled by Belgian companies, Katanga was easily the richest province in Congo. It was also the furthest away from the central power of Leopoldville. The Belgians had no difficulty in persuading the strong man in Katanga, Moise Tshombe, to secede. This was done on the 11th of July 1960, less than two weeks after Congolese independence.

The situation in the country was growing in its complexity.

At the request of the government of Leopoldville, the UN embarked on a military adventure to silence the secessionists and re-establish a united Congo.

In a crisis of this kind, Washington greatly preferred President Kasavubu. The Prime Minister Lumumba was not highly regarded by Washington. He had the absurd idea of asking the USSR for help to resolve the crisis in Katanga, after the UN and the United States had initially refused their assistance.

From the month of August 1960, the head of the CIA at Leopoldville, who bought and sold Congolese politicians like others bought socks, informed Langley that the Congo would have to face up to a standard attempt by the communists to take power, an attempt orchestrated by Lumumba. The latter became the 'bête noire' of Eisenhower, just as Fidel Castro had.

A meeting took place on the 25th August 1960 at the White House to discuss the Lumumba problem. When plans prepared to act against the Prime Minister of the ex-Belgian colony were presented to him, the American President shared his discontent :

"Lumumba is pro-Soviet : we therefore must not beat around the bush, we must lead a very direct action against him", emphasized Eisenhower. Then he turned to the men of the CIA who were taking part in the meeting :

"I'm afraid that everything you've shown me up to now does not enable us to carry out that objective..."

The President also had CIA reports in front of him depicting Lumumba as a completely mad drug addict. The rest of the discussion was very animated and the meeting ended with the statement : "any action which would enable Lumumba to be got rid of must not be eliminated."

In other words, the American President would not shy away from a 'homo' action if the opportunity were to prevent itself. That is, in secret service jargon, the physical elimination of the troublemaker. The CIA therefore was playing the Mobutu card.

On the 14th of September 1960, the NCO who had become Army

Chief of Staff, launched a military coup d'etat and announced that he was dismissing all politicians until at least the end of the year. Lumumba was put in prison several times, then freed by UN troops. He then left for Stanleyville (now Kisangani) in the east of the country where he formed a new separatist government. On the 1st of December 1960, he was caught by Mobutu troops, without doubt as a result of information supplied by the CIA. Forty-seven days later, Lumumba was put back into the hands of his most bitter enemy, the Katangaise, and the chance encounter with a 9mm bullet put a permanent end to his career.

Meanwhile, conforming to what he had announced, Mobutu had given power to Kasavubu who showed eagerness in naming a Prime Minister more in line with American expectations. Mobutu remained the strong man of the army and the country, the man of the CIA and the United States.

Established with his secessionist government in Elisabethville (now Lubumbashi), Tshombe was still stubbornly opposed to the UN forces which were nearing 20,000 men.

Tshombe benefited from the paid services of a small yet effective troop of white mercenaries, as well as an air force which was rather experimental but nonetheless effective. Three Fouga Magister, a twin-engine jet training plane, equipped with rockets and light machine guns was the spearhead of this unusual collection of aircraft. As Jerry Puren, mercenary pilot, explained, "The Fouga were above all used to show that we had jets that could control the skies above Katanga..."

The small air force worked well, even going as far as to cock a snook at the UN troops in their bases.

In September 1961, the Secretary General of the UN, the Swede Dag Hammarskjold, went to Africa to meet Tshombe and to attempt to bring about an end to the conflict by negotiation. The meeting was to have taken place at Ndola, north of Rhodesia. The DC-6 which he travelled in crashed a short while before landing several miles from its final destination. All the occupants were killed in the accident which happened at night. It remains an unexplained accident even though the presence of a Katangaise plane which could have shot it down was sometimes mentioned.

The new Secretary General of the UN, the Burmese U Thant, therefore asked for more equipment and logistic support from the United States to help the UN troops. Insisting on this request, the State Department recommended to the new American President, John Kennedy, to provide not only the aid requested, but also to send officially a squadron of fighters piloted by Americans to Congo, to make the situation develop more rapidly.

Still scalded from the Bay of Pigs affair which had taken place several months earlier, Kennedy accepted to provide only logistic aid. Eighteen helicopters, ten C-47 Dakota and several C-130 Hercules were put at the disposal of the UN and the Congolese army.

"There is no question of sending combat planes for the time being", explained Kennedy, "except if the Congolese and the UN together expressly ask for them." They did not.

But after Tshombes planes had attacked a UN column which had no aerial protection, the UN decided to send an international contingent of combat aircraft to the area : six Swedish Saad J-29 fighters, five Indian Canberra bombers and four Ethiopian F-86 Sabres were put at the disposal of UN troops present in Congo.

But it was the American aid that played a decisive role in the Katangaise affair. After three years of fighting, his small air force finally crushed, Tshombe finished by throwing in the towel at the beginning of 1963 and left for exile.

The results of this first Congolese crisis were fairly positive for the Americans : Lumumba had been eliminated, Tshombe isolated and Mobutu, their man, had controlling power over the national army. Having neither the economic striking power nor the logistical tools necessary, the Soviets revealed themselves to be totally incapable of intervening directly in the conflict, a conflict too far away from their traditional zone of influence.

The situation seemed to have stabilized at the beginning of 1963.

Nothing could have been further from the truth as the situation started to deteriorate again, this time in the east of the country.

The new rebellion broke out in mid-1963 in Kwilu province. Under the wing of Pierre Mulele, ex education minister in the Congolese government, the rebels experienced an advancement of lightning speed. Despite its superior equipment the Congolese army could not manage to contain the rebellion which was rapidly gaining ground.

Not being able to rely on modern weapons, Mulele had used the services of some very great medicine men. Every one of his fighting men had received a small phial containing a potion, Mulele water, which had the dual advantage of rendering them invulnerable to bullets and making them as strong as a lion. Hence the nickname Simba, which means lion in local dialect.

Terror-stricken by the effects of the potion, whose formula was even more secret than that of a Pastis, the government soldiers fled before the rebel advance or simply joined the rebel ranks. This general confusion coincided with the departure of UN troops from the country, their mission accomplished at Katanga and the government of Leopoldville found itself very much wanting.

During one of these spectacular about-turns which ocurred on several occasions in the country, President Kasavubu chose to bring back Tshombe from exile and name him as Prime Minister. Tshombe had kept a certain popularity in his country, especially in Katanga, even though some had called him 'the least popular African in Africa'.

He was almost openly accused of the murder of Lumumba and of the use of white mercenaries in his secession movement in Katanga.

"I had to engage white officers", he explained, "for they were the only ones my soldiers trusted. Without them, they would not have fought..."

Tshombe returned to Leopoldville in July 1964, whereas the old network that had remained faithful to him in Katanga rapidly re-formed.

In addition to units of Katangaise with mercenary officers, Tshombes luggage contained notably a team of pilots, made up of Europeans and Rhodesians, ex-pilots of the Katangaise air force.

Several T-6s were given over to Congo by Italy at the beginning of the sixties, at the end of training. The aircraft had been brought up to condition and equipped with rocket launchers and light machine guns under the wings to make them light support fire planes.

The first T-6 reconnaissance mission permitted the Tshombe pilots to have a more accurate idea of the famous Simbas who were routing the Congolese army :

"We were flying over the route, twenty or so miles east of Lusambo when we spotted a column of these invincible Simbas..." recalls Jerry Puren, the South African 'Tshombeist' who directed air operations of the Congolese army,

"...a column three hundred yards long, possibly a thousand men. We passed quickly over them and in a flash I saw a jumble of spears and clubs decorated with fur and feathers. Virtually no automatic weapons..."

A firing pass dispersed them, but everywhere else in the east of the country the advance of these invincible warriors was unstoppable. In a few days, they took hold of the regional capital, Stanleyville, and gathered nearly two thousand white hostages.

Five people from the American consulate in Stanleyville were also taken hostage, which amounted to a gross error as this gave the Americans a pretext to intensify their participation in the conflict.

CIA AIR FORCE

From the month of April 1963, more than a year before Tshombes return, two hundred American instructors had been sent to Congo and a number of Congolese officers left for the United States to follow training programmes.

The official side of the intervention was completed by a detachment of four cargo planes of the US Air Force, C-130 Hercules, which ensured logistic missions for the national army.

To withstand the Simba offensive, more and more openly supported by China via Burundi and Tanzania, the United States resolved to intensify aid, this time in the area of secret actions.

Thus in 1964, the CIA was responsible for setting up a small air force capable of shouldering the Congolese army in its offensive actions. The pilots, mercenaries, were recruited without any difficulty; following the abortive operation in Cuba, the American intelligence agency possessed a very full address book with all the Cuban anti-Castro pilots in it. The salary offered was particularly generous, up to $2,000 a month. Gustavo Ponzoa, who had led the attacks on Cuba on board his B-26 several months earlier, was open to persuasion along with twenty or so other veterans.

The plane chosen by the CIA for the Congolese operations was the T-28, an aircraft which allied robustness with firepower. Several Dakota C-47s had also been added to the "secret" air force to carry out liaison and light transport missions. The first aircraft arrived in Congo from April 1964.

As the mercenaries who piloted the genuine Congolese T-6 must have noticed with envy, the T-28 were in very good condition. The Cuban pilots were also judged to be very competent, although overpaid. But that was simply jealousy rearing its head...

The T-6 pilots regarded the intrusion of the CIA Air Force with suspicion. These new planes had come to fight on their territory and if their objectives, the fight against the Simbas, seemed to coincide in the short term, the future remained shrouded in a geopolitical fog which did not bode well.

The predictions were proved correct. In the space of a few days, the T-6s and their pilots were distanced from aerial operations to the advantage of the T-28s of the CIA.

Evidently, Tshombe, who kept a strong hand over the use of the T-6 and derided the idea of having an air force, did not see things in that way. To affirm its control it officially ratified the formation of the 21st squadron of the Congolese National Army (no need to look for the first twenty...) with its meagre force of T-6s, under the command of the South African, Jerry Puren.

The CIA hardly appreciated this show of autonomy and demanded to reclaim the control of the T-6s, openly displaying its iron fist to the Congolese Prime Minister. Washington was playing the Mobutu card and saw with mounting displeasure the South African mercenaries get the key posts, on the ground and in the air, protected by Tshombe.

As a sign of discontent and to pressure the Congolese presidency to disown Tshombe, the CIA stopped its aerial operations for an entire week. Langley even went as far as threatening the Congolese to withdraw its forces completely if Tshombe persisted with his policy. He was therefore obliged to give in, entrusting the direct control of the T-6s to the CIA, which in fact hardly used them.

The more powerful T-28s ensured essential support-fire missions in the very effective hands of the Cubans. Little by little, the T-6 pilots ended up by rejoining CIA operations.

THE B-26K

Because of the desperate flight of the Congolese troops and despite the intervention of the CIA, the Simbas had managed to take hold of Stanleyville, in the east of the country. The capture of the American consulate spread a wind of panic to the Embassy in Leopoldville. The CIA relayed an urgent appeal through the US Ambassador to the White House for new, more powerful planes. The CIA especially asked for the urgent dispatch to Congo of twelve B-26s, the secret operation plane par excellence. The request was heard; an initial batch of three "new" B-26K arrived swiftly in Leopoldville.

The B-26 was an excellent anti-guerilla aircraft which, in 1964, had only one fault : its age. These aircraft, which had been built during the second world war, were assumed to have a life expectancy of several months in the middle of the fighting. To bring them up to active service was a good idea; they were irreplaceable both in the regional conflicts and secret operations. But because of the very pronounced state of fatigue that they more or less all displayed, it could turn out to be foolhardy. The On Mark Engineering Company, in California, was therefore appointed by the US Air Force to study the renovation of the aircraft. To renovate meant not only restoring the potential of the structure but also to incorporate several modifications which would increase the performance.

The result obtained was the B-26 model K, which had its first flight on the 28th January 1963. The plane seemed extremely promising, combining the simplicity of operation of a well-known aircraft of standard technology with excellent war situation capabilities. The K was perfectly adequate for the operational needs of the US Air Force and of the company, within the framework of interventions in the third world. To their great delight, the plane was made quickly available and at a much lower

242

price than that of a new one.

The US Air Force placed a contract of $13,000,000 relating to the transformation of forty B-26 model Ks. The On Mark company selected the majority of planes among those which were drying up under the Californian sun in the immense US Air Force surplus depot. Then it got to work.

The reconstruction of the fuselage and the wings rejuvenated the B-26 and gave it a very clear increase in performance.

New engines were installed, twenty per cent more powerful than the old ones. They developed 2,500 hp, giving a maximum speed of 300mph, almost 30mph more than a 'standard' version. But the increase in power was most appreciable in tropical countries :

"The B-26 can take off with a full load on terrain which would have proved too short for non-modified B-26s" noted the promoters of the plane. "It's offensive capacity in Asian or African theatres of operation will not be curtailed..."

The range of the aircraft was more than doubled because of the installation of extra tanks at the end of the wings, similar to those on T-33 jet planes. Other areas of performance such as climb rate, operational ceiling and so on were in keeping with this.

The cockpit had been modified to permit the installation of two pilots side by side. The position of navigator was done away with, but the plane had modern navigation and radio communications apparatus which more than compensated for this absence.

The B-26K had become a formidable fighting machine: eight hard points had been mounted under the wings, permitting a vast range of weapons to be carried. The load capacity of the plane had passed from 3.5tons to nearly 6tons. The B-26K was equipped with eight .50 machine guns in the nose.

"It's a flying assault tank!" exclaimed the first pilots who were able to test the plane. It was a fair comment for this aircraft which had been conceived more than twenty years previously.

Initially planned to serve in Asia, the first three machines available were rapidly reoriented to Africa.

Scarcely having left On Mark's Californian workshops, the B-26Ks flew to Florida where they were prepared for the long transatlantic crossing.

The planes were escorted by a C-130 Hercules which took control of the navigation and carried several tons of spare parts and a team of mechanics in its hold.

The formation stopped over at Surinam, at Recife in Brazil and the Ascension islands in the middle of the Atlantic. One last hop and the C-130 and the B-26s finished their long journey when they landed at night at N'Djili airport in Leopoldville. Anxious at what might happen to them on their arrival in Congo, the US Air Force crews who had piloted the planes descended from them practically with their weapons in their hands. It was an unecessary precaution which greatly amused the American crews already present on the ground, there in the framework of "official" logistics and already accorded to the Congolese by the American government.

A short while after the arrival of the K models, four non-modernized B-26B also left the United States for Congo. The voyage took the north route, which reduced the flying time over the sea, which the aircraft could not aspire to. Two planes did not finish the voyage however. The first one, incapable of going any further, was left at Okinawa. The other crashed during take off in Aden.

The state of structural fatigue of the two machines that did arrive in Congo was such that the Cuban pilots refused to use them for combat missions.

"Too dangerous. If the plane's handled a little roughly, it will disintegrate in flight." they explained. They were also astounded to learn that the US Air Force itself had forbidden the use of these planes in the United States, yet allowed the Cubans to risk their lives in them in Congo.

One of the two aircraft was transformed into an evacuation plane and left on permanent alert at the airport at Leopoldville. Benches were fitted in the bomb hold and the plane was to be used for evacuating Americans if events turned badly in the country. Subsequently, it was used for carrying out peaceful reconnaissance missions. As for the second aircraft, it was never used in operation and served as a source of spare parts for the B-26Ks.

FIRST MISSIONS

The Cuban pilots mastered their new planes with ease. Almost all had previous experience with B-26s and the apprenticeship with the new model K did not present any particular difficulties. The pilots were, on the contrary, very impressed by the improved capabilities of the plane.

The B-26K first participated in action on the 21st August 1964. One week later, two aircraft were engaged to support the Congolese army attempting to recapture Albertville, on the banks of lake Tanganyika, on the border with Tanzania. Immediately after the combat, the planes landed at Albertville airport which had just passed back to government control.

The B-26 had an effect on the combat which was out of proportion to its real importance. The Simbas were cut to pieces by the devastating fire of the eight 12.7mm machine guns.

"The performance of the B-26 and its firepower so impressed the local commander of the Congolese army that he stopped us from taking off to gain Leopoldville," recalls Ponzoa. "He simply wanted to keep us for his personal use, to have his own little air force. We therefore had to use cunning and after one or two days of waiting, we were able to leave quietly with our planes."

The B-26 and T-28 worked in close collaboration, both planes fulfilled more or less the same missions but with different potential. The T-28 was dispersed around the smallest terrains in the country, providing a local and immediate support-fire capability. The B-26, which had a greater autonomy was used to fire in the heart of Simba held territory.

For political reasons, the planes were never equipped with bombs, allowing the installation of extra tanks in the hold, which gave even more reach to the crews. Practically the whole country was within reach of CIA aircraft. For the veterans of the Bay of Pigs, the K was a remarkable plane, perfectly adapted to its anti-guerilla mission in Congo :

"The existence of two engines made it a very reliable plane, in which we could adventure above the jungle, or Simba held territory, without fear. It was a comfort because we were well aware that in that country the prisoners were used to teach interesting lessons in dissection..."

The only real fault with the plane, born out of the installation of heavier and more powerful engines, was its bad trimming : "The plane was difficult to trim in flight", explained the pilots. "It practically had to be kept constantly in hand. Missions of five or six hours soon became exhausting."

Free fire zones had been well defined in the east of the country. The B-26 crews were authorized to attack all military objectives that they could find there. Obviously, the Congolese army had to inform the CIA of its forays into these zones, so as to prevent any possible 'friendly fire' attacks by the planes. Inevitably, there were several unfortunate mistakes where governmental troops were attacked by the CIA Air Force.

At the close of a swift combat against the Simbas, the regular army took back control of a remote bush station. They were delighted with this, as there were several carriages and a locomotive in perfect condition stationed there!

Not long was needed for the combatants to imagine a very pleasant way of celebrating victory; the soldiers got on to the carriages, the diesel locomotive was started up and the happy troops went for a spin.

But it so happened that, quite unwittingly, the Belgian engineers who had built the line at the beginning of the century had made it pass through an area that had become, fifty years later, a free fire zone. Fateful coincidence, the same day at the same time, two B-26s of the CIA were patrolling in the zone looking for anything interesting.

The combined pleasure of a trip in a train and an airshow, so enjoyable when properly organized, was unfortunately very brief for the poor Congolese soldiers.

The pilot of the first B-26 carefully aligned his sights and fired the eight heavy machine guns on the train he had spotted.

Both planes attacked the train meticuloulsy for many minutes, inflicting heavy losses to its occupants. It was only a few hours after their return to base that the pilots learnt the tragic truth.

"Don't worry", a Congolese officer told them. "It is not your fault : the troops should not have been there. And also you've taught them a good lesson : the next time they won't mess about with trains."

The Congolese officer could indeed be magnanimous; the most important thing was not harmed during the attack on the train. It mattered little that there were several dozens killed and injured. The important thing was that, conforming to instructions, the diesel locomotive had been spared from the accurate fire of the Cubans. A locomotive was such a rare and precious commodity in Congo that even those in the hands of the Simbas were not to be attacked : they could be needed by the government of Leopoldville one day or another.

In the absence of any aerial opposition and anti-aircraft fire, the effectiveness of the B-26 was practically without limit. In September 1964 the planes were used to stop a Simba attack against the town of Boende.

The Belgian officer in charge of the ground troops informed the group of B-26s that the Congolese army still held the town's airport, but that it would certainly not be enough to effectively counter the advance of the Simbas.

"I will be present at the airport where I'll be easily able to guide your attack", he added over the radio to the crews who were preparing themselves.

When the B-26s arrived on the scene, they discovered that the enemy was approaching the town in light vehicles, which formed a long line. According to pilot estimates, there were approximately 250 men.

"When we flew over them, the soldiers were getting out of the vehicles", recalls Rene Garcia, the Cuban who directed the group of CIA 'volunteers'.

"Our arrival didn't change anything. They continued to disembark as if nothing was happening. They did not try to seek cover or disperse. The worrying thing was that they were in uniform and therefore resembled a unit of the national army. I asked for confirmation from the officer on the ground."

"I confirm that they are Simbas" replied the Belgian. "They opened fire when you flew over them."

The two B-26s therefore went to attack, in the first instance destroying the cars and lorries that had been used to transport the troops. Then they concentrated their fire on the soldiers themselves."

Garcia could not believe his eyes. "It was astounding! Those guys stayed put in the middle of the road so we could fire at them. It was a duel between 250 immobile men armed with peashooters and sixteen heavy machine guns firing at more than 250mph."

Quite obviously, the Simbas totally believed in the power of the Mule-le water which was meant to make them invincible. None of them sought cover. They fell like flies under the B-26 fire, but still they stayed in the middle of the road, emptying their magazines every time the plane flew over.

"I almost felt sorry for them", said Garcia. "I felt like shouting 'Go and hide, Get out of the way'! but all they did was to pile up their dead on the side of the road...!"

Short of ammunition, or simply tired of this type of massacre, the B-26s finally stopped the attack and pardonned the last Simbas who remained standing.

BIRTH OF THE WIGMO

Other rebel columns arrived later and the town of Boende finally fell into their hands. It must be acknowledged that the Simbas were victorious because they were not alone in believing in the magic power of Mulele water : terrified at the idea of confronting invincible Simbas, the government soldiers fled from the fighting the majority of the time.

Back on the ground at Leopoldville after the intervention at Boende, the B-26s were carefully examined; only the trace of a few small calibre bullets were found on the fuselage and wings. It was the only punishment which was able to threaten the planes. The most serious damage was often as a result of the pilots flying too low. The planes sometimes came back dented because of hitting branches of trees, or even perforated by rocket fragments that they had fired themselves. The mechanics plugged the holes with pieces of sheet metal and the planes were ready to leave again within a few minutes.

No aircraft was destroyed, in spite of three years of intensive use and several thousand flying hours. The most serious accident that happened to a B-26 was a collapsed landing gear on touch-down. After several weeks work, the plane was put back on its feet and was able to continue its career.

The enlargement of the unit, following the arrival of the B-26s, brought about a profound re-organization of operations. A slightly less empirical administrative structure was set up to welcome the many technical personnel that were joining the CIA operation. A company registered in Liechtenstein, the WIGMO (Western International Ground Maintenance Organization), was officially created on the 21st of September 1964, to manage the entire staff, about a hundred men in total. There were some Cubans of course, but also British, Polish in exile in London, Swedish, Germans, Spanish and Danes... pracitically the whole of Europe was represented around the planes of the CIA.

When it reached cruising speed, it was estimated that WIGMO operations cost the American taxpayer a million dollars a day.

Officially, WIGMO was under contract with the Congolese army to maintain the planes, while all aircraft operated by the CIA in Congo were (officially) part of that same army. It in fact controlled very little indeed, missions were defined by officers of the CIA or directly by the American Embassy.

RED DRAGON, BLACK DRAGON

At the end of 1964, the Simba offensive was stopped definitively and the surge began, notably under the pressure of the many white mercenaries who arrived along with Tshombe.

The takeover of Stanleyville and the rescue of the many hostages who had been held there over many weeks was therefore launched. Two motorized groups were formed, Lima I and Lima II, to go straight into the town and the heart of Simba territory.

The two columns led by heavily armed jeeps left simultaneously on the 1st of November to attack the small town of Kindu which was swiftly recaptured.

After a brief regrouping, the tactical vehicles carried on their way. Direction Stanleyville 250 miles to the north.

The B-26s and the T-28s, guardian angels of the two groups on the ground, followed the progress, ready to support if necessary.

The planes were in permanent radio contact with the columns and were both scouts and guard dogs. Every morning, one B-26 covered the route to Stanleyville, while the other B-26 stayed on alert, in case an important target was spotted. But while Lima I and Lima II progressed towards the town, the American and Belgian authorities worried more about the fate of the hostages held by the Simbas with every passing day.

An airborne operation was therefore swiftly set up by the Belgian army with logistic assistance from the Americans.

On the 24th of November 1964 at six in the morning a battalion of Belgian airborne-commandos was dropped over the town from a dozen C-130 Hercules of the US Air Force. Leaving from the French base at Evreux, (France was still a full member of NATO at that time and as such welcomed American units on its soil), the transport planes had gone to Belgium where the parachutists embarked. They then went south and stopped off in Spain and then the Ascension islands in the south Atlantic.

Because of the great number of countries involved in one stage or other of the operation, the United States and Belgium could only count on the poor information networks in the heart of Congo to keep the operation, code name Red Dragon, a secret.

By sheer luck, that is exactly what happened. In the Ascension islands, the commander of the raid had a choice; he could train his men at an aerodrome several dozens of miles to the south of Stanleyville, or he could take the risk of jumping directly on the town, without knowing what was waiting for him on the ground. For fear of seeing the white population massacred before being able to intervene, he chose the second option.

The planes flew over the Atlantic, a part of Gabon, crossed over Congo-Brazzaville before penetrating ex Belgian Congo and heading directly to Stanleyville. The two B-26 of the CIA which had carried out a weather reconnaissance mission stayed in the zone to provide support fire if necessary.

When the five C-130s of the first wave appeared above the airport, the situation seemed calm. The parachutists were dropped and came under inconsequential enemy fire and were able to regroup without any losses. Being ignorant of the magic powers imparted by Mulele water, the paras eliminated the few Simbas present on the ground swiftly and simply. A dozen or so minutes later, the runway was in their hands and

250

the other Hercules were able to land.

Everything was going as planned, except for a small hitch which had unfortunate consequences.

A C-130 was more than an hour late taking off from the Ascension islands. Unfortunately, it concerned the aircraft transporting armoured vehicles which were to support the progress of the parachutists. They waited for the arrival of this last plane therefore before moving towards the town.

This delay proved fatal for forty or so Westerners, shot by automatic weapons in the centre of Stanleyville where all the hostages had been gathered.

Shaking up the Simba defences, the Belgian parachutists nonetheless arrived in time to save more than 1,500 people who had experienced an unspeakable fear.

Less than five hours after the parachute drop, having carried out that morning a lightning advance of almost 125 miles under the protection of some B-26s, the Lima I and Lima II columns went in turn to clear the town of the presence of any Simbas.

The presence of numerous white mercenaries in the operation had given rise to many protests, not always without self interest, on the international scene. The combined American and Belgian airborne operation was also in their sights and in the hope of silencing those who were condemning neo-colonialism, the Belgian parachutists were rapidly withdrawn from the combat zone.

But in the east of the country, many Europeans had remained at the mercy of the rebels. At the announcement of their defeat at Stanleyville, the Simbas multiplied their massacres.

Two days after their first intervention, the parachutists were once again hard at it, playing their part in Paulis, approximately 220 miles to the north-east of Stanleyville. This was operation Black Dragon.

The jumps went off perfectly, the C-130 were on the receiving end of several small calibre bullets only. One parachutist was injured during the descent. Like in Stanleyville, the B-26s of the CIA were used as scouts.

This time the Belgians did not wait for their armoured vehicles and went straight to the town where several whites had already been murdered. This rapid intervention saved the lives of 400 people. When they were assembled, the survivors were led under protection to the runway where the Hercules had been able to land.

This was the last airborne operation of the Westerners. The last remaining whites staying in 'zone Simba' were too scattered to justify other operations of such a scale. International pressure was making itself felt very strongly and from the 29th of November, five days only after the beginning of the operation, the Belgian parachutists climbed back into the American planes and swiftly left for Europe.

The success of the Operations Dragon operations had dealt a bitter blow to the Simbas. But they still held large sections of the country, forcing the CIA to pursue its air operations. Without this support, the Congolese army seemed incapable of being able to lead offensive operations, let alone obtain a total victory.

THE END OF THE SIMBAS

The combat did not only take place in the bush. In Leopoldville there was a mild struggle between partisans of Mobutu and those of Tshombe. The latter, even though Prime Minister in name, could practically consider himself under house arrest in the Congolese capital.

The efforts made by the CIA to put the old Katangaise Air Force out of action ended in success. WIGMO regained full control of the planes, the missions and some of the pilots.

In the spring of 1965, the American special forces were also deployed in Congo over several weeks. The White House had got wind of the presence of Che Guevara in the country. Attempts to locate his whereabouts having all ended in failure, the special forces went back across the Atlantic.

The CIA station chief in Leopoldville took advantage of the situation to make a proposal to Mobutu to the effect that the recruitment of mercenaries should be entirely the responsibility of the CIA. Mobutu refused outright; there were certain limits not to be stepped over. The strong man of the Congolese army, who was to be successful with a new coup d'etat several weeks later making himself the undisputed master of Congo, did not wish to put the whole of the armed forces, from

252

which he drew his 'legitimacy', back into American hands.

1965 and 1966 were years dedicated to the complete crushing of the Simba rebellion, a job done by the ex-Katangaise mercenaries.

Three units were formed; Commando 5 under the command of the South African Mike Hoare, number 6 under the command of the Frenchman Robert Denard and number 10 under the command of the Belgian Jean Schramme.

The operations of these commando units, particularly those of number 5 which was engaged in an offensive in the north-east of the country, were supported by the CIA Air Force. After having been retaken from the Simbas, Stanleyville had become a major base for air operations. The CIA had received two extra B-26Ks and several other T-28s. A dozen C-47 Dakotas ensured transport missions and several light aircraft were appointed for liaison flights.

This increase in power posed several problems concerning labour at WIGMO. There were fewer pilots, which meant sometimes the Cubans had to fly alone, without a co-pilot, on board their B-26.

The rebels were losing ground at a faster pace. Several months earlier, in June 1965, operation Imperial Violets launched by the mercenaries in the north east of the country had permitted the last two towns of any importance still in the hands of the Simbas in that area to be recaptured. The CIA Air Force was constantly on the heels of the runaways, not hesitating to pursue them beyond Congolese borders. The Sudan protested on several occasions against the intrusions by planes which did not hesitate to attack Sudanese villages where Simbas had sought refuge.

The affair was not however totally finished. The Simbas had received considerable quantities of arms from the Chinese, via Burundi and Tanzania, which would enable them to lead isolated operations all throughout 1966.

But from the beginning of that year, a decision was taken by Langley to progressively reduce the scope of operations in Congo until they were stopped completely. This was carried out over a period of eighteen months.

The first B-26K returned to the United States in October 1966, followed closely by the four other machines. Another career was waiting for them in the hands of the pilots of the US Air Force in south east Asia. The pilots left Congo at the same pace. At the end of 1966, there were only a dozen or so Cubans left in the country responsible for operating the T-28s which had been officially given up to the Congolese Air Force in 1967. The CIA nonetheless kept a permanent eye on air operations which it continued to finance. As for WIGMO, it was to keep a controlling hand on all logistic operations in the country for some time to come.

The history of the B-26 of the CIA in Congo would not be complete without mentioning a comical episode that Dan Hagedorn and Leif Hellstrom reported in their book 'Foreign Invaders'.

Doubtless very impressed by the firepower of the B-26, and with the CIA aircraft having just returned to the United States, the Congolese decided to buy several planes for their own needs.

The Hamilton Aircraft Company, based in Tucson, Arizona received the visit of an emissary from Mobutu one day in 1967. The man carried a small suitcase with him and was accompanied by a Greek interpreter.

"What can I do for you?" enquired the boss of the company, rather surprised by the duo in front of him.

"My client would like to buy ten B-26 planes", announced the Greek.

The Congolese nodded his head very seriously and opened the case : he was carrying 500,000 dollars in large notes in order to pay cash immediately. It was obvious he very much wanted to conclude the deal as quickly as possible. Was he responding to a desire of his government or was he trying to get rid of his treasure, a treasure that stopped him from sleeping, as quickly as possible?

Hamilton used to have several B-26s, but in 1967 all the planes had already been re-sold and therefore the deal did not go through. The potential buyer left, extremely vexed.

Rumour has it that the case stuffed with dollars was stolen from him while he was trying to buy planes from another company on the west coast of the United States. On his return to Congo, he was hanged.

THE REBELLION OF THE MERCENARIES

Throughout the months, the mercenaries had established their authority in the regions under their control to such an extent that the new leader of Congo, who suffered no competition, started to worry. With the Simba threat quashed, Mobutu was able to separate himself without risk from the mercenaries close to Moise Tshombe who had left for exile, his task accomplished. The number 5 Commando of the South African Hoare was demobilized without any setbacks.

The next on the list was Schramme's 10 Commando. A manager of a plantation before becoming a war leader, Schramme had almost succeeded in creating in the Yumbi area in the south of the country, a state within a state. The zone under his control, which formed a considerable part of the country, benefited from a remarkable stability and a certain prosperity, which contrasted greatly with the rest of the country. Mobutu wanted to take back control and instructed his best troops and Denard's 6 Commando to demobilize Schramme's men.

There was no doubt for Denard that as soon as the job was finished, his unit would also be dissolved. The seeds of a rebellion were starting to grow.

The interpretation of events which followed on the strategic front is even more interesting.

Whereas Mobutu was without question the man of the Americans, it seemed that the return of Moise Tshombe, supported by the mercenaries of Denard and Schramme, would not have displeased France or Belgium, the respective countries of the commando chiefs.

But even before the mercenaries had started to move in Congo, Tshombe was captured and led to Algeria. His plane was hijacked by one of his bodyguards off Spain, between Majorca and Ibiza. Coincidentally, the pilot of the plane, who was also in collusion with the hijacking, was an ex member of WIGMO.

Evidently, the CIA who was protecting its protege Mobutu, had just scored a goal. Tshombe died in prison in Algeria two years later.

The mercenaries who relied on Tshombe to give them a political dimension to their rebellion were dumbfounded. Were they going to continue with the coup?

In fact they would, because they had no choice. Mobutu sent his best soldiers, a parachute regiment (which had never made any parachute jumps), trained by the Israelis, to rejoin Denard's men and then disarm Schramme's commando.

The coup began on the 5th of July when Denard attacked Stanleyville by the north and Schramme from the south. The affair got off to a bad start for the mercenaries and, from the first day, Mobutu declared a state of emergency and general mobilization.

Injured by a bullet in the leg, Denard was evacuated with a dozen other wounded mercenaries to Rhodesia on board a 'requisitioned' Dakota.

The Americans provided three C-130 Hercules to transport Congolese troops to Stanleyville, the town that Schramme had abandoned after a week's occupation. Deprived of any effect of surprise and confronted by many more troops than he had, Schramme's only option was for him and his troops to pack their bags. A possible escape to Rwanda was mentioned. Still with logistic aid from Washington, Mobutu therefore sent his troops to the Bukavu region, on the border with Rwanda, with orders to cut them to pieces when they arrived.

But far from throwing themselves into a frantic escape, the five hundred mercenaries, supported by approximately eight hundred Katangaise soldiers, arrived in Bukavu in good condition. They drove the Congolese troops from the area, and set themselves up in their place. Schramme allowed himself the luxury of announcing the formation of a provisional government in front of the world's television cameras.

Mobutu wanted to wash away this insult and declared the siege of Bukavu. Half of his army, 15,000 men, took position around the town. Quiet Bukavu, the 'pearl of Africa', built by the Europeans, was transformed into a solid, entrenched camp under the intelligent Schramme's iron rule.

The Congolese Air Force supported by the CIA was launched into battle. The B-26s had been sent back to the United States, but there remained still a dozen fully-operational T-28s in the country, as well as several Congolese pilots who were doubtless rather less operational.

The T-28s started their attack using rockets on the town, with fairly average accuracy of fire. Three T-28 were fairly swiftly shot down, which put Mobutu into a fearsome rage. The Congolese pilots were consequently replaced by Cubans who were officially employed by WIGMO.

But the Cubans put little enthusiasm into their attacks. Was this the usual thing between mercenaries, or was it a way of making the fighting last longer, so as not to become unemployed?

Mobutu grew impatient and put his pilots back in the line of fire. This time they chose to attack from a great height and because of the resulting lack of accuracy in the bombing, eight weeks after the capture of Bukavu, Schramme and his men seemed well on the way to holding the town indefinitely.

In the morning of the 28th of October 1967, the Congolese launched a general attack against Bukavu. The offensive began with a rocket attack by four T-28s. After two days of fighting, Schramme managed to ward off all attacks from a force fifteen times stronger than his own. But he was running out of ammunition.

His last hope therefore was Denard opening a second front in the south of Congo, in Katanga. After having treated his injury, Denard assembled a force of a hundred or so white and Katangaise soldiers in Angola, then a Portuguese colony. The Portuguese had shown cooperation but not to the extent of supplying vehicles. Denard and his men therefore crossed the border between Angola and Congo on bicycles.

Leaving the bicycles behind, Denard and his troops "borrowed" some lorries. But after having come up against a Congolese garrison and enduring an attack by WIGMO T-28s, Denard abandoned his lightning offensive and withdrew to Angola. Cleverly advised by the Israelis and the CIA, Mobutu was then able to launch his entire force against Bukavu which fell the following day, the 4th of November.

The Cuban pilots of the CIA were in the air again on the last day of the battle. Schramme's men knew this by listening in to the aircraft's radio frequency. A dialogue was consequently struck up between the mercenaries of the two camps.

There are two versions of the attitude of the Cubans that day. According to some, the pilots, in a spirit of brotherliness, informed their 'colleagues' of the places where they were going to fire, so they could seek shelter. According to other witnesses it was the opposite, the besieged pointed out to the pilots which buildings (empty) to destroy. In fact, the result was the same, the planes flitted about in a spectacular, but not at all dangerous, way...

At the close of the last day of combat, all ammunition supplies exhausted, Jean Schramme and his men left Congo on foot, taking the bridge joining Bukavu with Rwanda, where they were interned for several months. Some Red Cross planes came and took them to Europe to be repatriated.

With that, 'CIA Air Force' offensive operations in the country were finished definitively.

ANGOLA, NEW THEATRE OF OPERATIONS

The sixties was the decade of decolonization in Africa and the Portuguese could not escape the trend. Lisbon was in fourth colonial position in Africa, behind the French, British and the Belgians.

Angola was incontrovertibly the richest of these possessions and the war of decolonization began there in 1961. Even though they were not surprised by the birth of an armed rebellion, the Portuguese were nonetheless surprised by the extent of the events.

Two movements were opposed to the power in Lisbon: the MPLA of Agostino Neto and Roberto Holden's FNLA. Later, the UNITA movement led by Jonas Savimbi appeared on the scene, created as a result of a split within the FNLA. Two or three years later, hostilities began in the other Portuguese possessions, Guinea-Bissau and Mozambique.

The entry of Portugal in NATO had certainly considerably widened its military potential, but it still remained undeniably too weak to endure several simultaneous 'wars of liberation' in the four corners of Africa.

Eight Sabre F-86F jet fighters were based in Guinea from 1962. But the American recriminations concerning the deployment in Africa of aircraft intended for the defence of NATO put an end to this after several months.

The mainstay of Portuguese air power was in fact the tireless T-6.

From the end of 1963, Lisbon hoped to acquire some B-26s to complete the numbers. But the international protests against Portugal and the colonial wars it was conducting in Africa ended in the setting up of an embargo on military supplies which were to have been used in African theatres of operation.

In this way an official offer to purchase thirty B-26s was officially rejected by the American State Department.

In order to obtain their planes, the Portuguese engaged themselves in a slightly less official deal by going, in the Autumn of 1964, to the Luber SA company in Geneva. The Swiss accepted the role of intermediary and organized the purchase and delivery of the aircraft, using the services of a Frenchman, Henri de Montmarin. Old pilot of the Free French forces, de Montmarin began his search for available B-26s. His agreement with the Swiss stated that he would earn 15% of any transaction. After several fruitless searches in Europe, de Montmarin, in collusion with different American intermediaries, eventually found what he wanted in California with the Hamilton Aircraft company.

This company benefited from a certain reputation with anything to do with the B-26, (this fact meant that several years later it would receive a visit from an emissary of Mobutu mentioned earlier). Cleverly situated close to the huge spare parts depot of Davis Monthan, Hamilton Aircraft had already the repair of more than 200 B-26s for different civilian clients to its credit.

De Montmarin's American correspondent passed a contract for the purchase of twenty B-26s to be delivered from May 1965. Hamilton Aircraft started working on repairing them. Not everything however was quite clear concerning the final destination of the planes and the American company shared its doubts with the customs service, but without provoking any reaction.

The first planes to be made as good as new left the workshops in dribs and drabs. An ex Royal Air Force pilot, John Hawke, had been engaged to carry out the escorts. Hawke was paid $3,000 per convoy, this was a godsend for the pilot who had been reduced to selling encyclopaedias to earn his living.

Seven aircraft had already fraudulently reached Portugal, where their official owner was meant to be a Canadian citizen, when during the summer of 1965, things turned sour.

The Hamilton Aircraft Company, which was having more and more difficulties in getting its bills paid, refused to deliver the eighth aircraft while the customs men awoke from their state of lethargy.

Hawke and de Montmarin were arrested in Florida while they were preparing to send spare parts to Portugal on board a C-46. The American intermediary, a certain Gregory Board, just managed to escape the law by fleeing to the Caribbean.

The Frenchman and the Englishman were brought before a federal court and the affair began to get remarkably complicated. Participation by the CIA was mentioned during the hearing:

"Yes, I did escort planes to Portugal", recognized Hawke. "But I was only carrying out instructions, the whole operation has been set up by the CIA and the State Department."

De Montmarin adopted the same tone. He and the pilot were nothing but scapegoats, he explained.

Soviets and Hungarians took hold of the affair and attacked the transaction in the tribune of the United Nations. The United States fiercely denied any implication of government services. The CIA also denied all the accusations thrown against it. But it nonetheless acknowledged having caught wind of the affair well before the customs...

De Montmarin and Hawke were eventually acquitted. The charges that were levelled against Board, the intermediary who had fled to the Caribbean, were finally lifted in 1973.

The worrying thing was that in the meantime this man was working for Air America in Vietnam!

INTERMOUNTAIN AVIATION

Another company was also mentioned several times during the trial of Hawke and de Montmarin; Intermountain Aviation Inc.

Intermountain was established on an old US Air Force base in Marana, Arizona. The company had been created by the CIA in 1961, the day after the Bay of Pigs fiasco. During the course of the operation, political contingencies had prevented the US Air Force from bringing tactical support which the CIA needed so much in the field.

Very bitter at this, the CIA therefore decided to rely on its own forces in the future. This meant the constitution of an aerial support-fire for-ce available for secret operations. Intermountain had to carry out this task : to keep a batch of machines adapted to combat missions perma-nently handy, while maintaining a perfectly commendable facade of maintenance and aeronautical equipment.

Intermountain offered to the public the image of a company that was very active in the area of maintenance and storing planes, notably for different federal services.

The company also developed a real know-how for adapting planes to particular missions for its 'normal' clients. It goes without saying that the CIA knew how to extract a part of this know-how by making Inter-mountain carry out improvements to its own aircraft.

The implication of the official services in the trafficking of the B-26 went even further : according to certain sources, the White House, whi-ch had been informed of what was in preparation, had decided to turn a blind eye to the circumvention of the embargo against Portugal, indeed to make it easier. Several Cubans, ex pilots in Congo and the Bay of Pigs, had already offered their services to the Portuguese.

The media campaign which surrounded the Montmarin Hawke trial eventually dissuaded the Portuguese from using immediately the seven B-26s which had reached them in Angola.

The Hamilton Aircraft Company, in whose workshops three planes were found in an advanced stage of overhaul, was left high and dry.

In order to recoup their costs, the company was authorized by the State Department to sell these planes to the Portuguese government, quite legally. The Portuguese simply had to undertake not to use the planes outside Portugal. Lisbon declined the offer, the B-26s were of no use to it in the European theatre.

In December 1971, in the absence of any other available plane, six of the seven aircraft present in Portugal were finally sent to Luanda to repla-ce some worn out F-84Gs. The planes were operated by Portuguese crews who carried out an average of three missions per day. Connecting reconnaissance flights and ground attacks, the B-26s were mainly used against the Independent movement of the Cabinda enclave.

The carnation revolution which began in Lisbon in the spring of 1974 put a brutal end to the period of Portuguese colonialism. The time of indecision due to the revolution led the military present in Africa to suspend their operations. The guerillas meanwhile were free to enlarge the areas under their control.

The situation in Angola rapidly became agitated.

Some cease-fire agreements had been signed at the beginning of 1975 between the Portuguese and the guerilla movements, united in a national union government. The accession of independence was planned for the following 11th of November, but, after several weeks, the fragile entente between the different guerilla factions broke up and the race for power began to the sound of automatic weapon fire.

While in Washington, the Church commission, made up of senators, was investigating into the actions of the CIA over the past years, preparations were being made at Langley for the next great adventure of the CIA : Angola.

Washington had certainly helped its Portuguese ally to lead a war against the rebels in Angola. But the provident CIA had also thought of the future, knowing for a fact that the Portuguese would have to give up their power sooner or later.

The American secret service even paid for an independent movement, in this case Roberto Holden's FNLA (Angolan National Liberation Front). At the same time Moscow was backing Agostino Neto's MPLA (Popular Movement for the Liberation of Angola) and, to be with the big guns, China supported Jonas Savimbi's UNITA (National Union for the Total Independence of Angola). Savimbi went to China in 1965 accompanied by several of his lieutenants, to follow guerilla training at the military academy in Nankin. The following year he left Holden's FNLA to found his own movement.

"He's a phenomenal, charismatic character, with enormous courage," wrote Alexandres de Marenches, ex head of the French Secret Service. For Ronald Reagan, the man who had been trained in China and wanted to promote his 'African socialism' became within the space of a few months, the 'champion of the fight against communism in Africa'.

But prior to 1975, the Angolans were still looking for backers when the superpowers only wanted to back the right horse. The three independent parties were more or less Marxist-socialist, the roles of each one being almost interchangeable.

To tone things down a little, Roberto Holden, the leader of the FNLA, was from the same ethnic group as Mobutu, and in fact they were brothers-in-law. The CIA, which was already supporting the leader of Congo could not then reasonably go against Holden. Zaire, which was a rear base for the FNLA, was also the bridgehead of the CIA in Black Africa. By a strange coincidence, the central intelligence agency's HQ in Kinshasa was scarcely a few hundred yards from that of the FNLA.

THE GOOD AND THE BAD

At the beginning of 1975, a senator had asked the head of the CIA, William Colby, the question that had been on everybody's lips :

"Why are the Chinese supporting UNITA?"

"The simple answer to that is because the Russians are behind the MPLA."

"And that's why we are supporting the FNLA?"

"Absolutely."

John Stockwell directed the CIA operation in Angola. In his memoirs he gave a precise description of the first briefing given by the Director of the CIA to the Security Council which surrounded President Gerald Ford :

"Gentlemen, here is a map of Africa, and here is Angola. There are two liberation movements in Angola ; the FNLA of Roberto Holden, the good guys ; and the MPLA of Agostino Neto who is a pscychopathic drunkard poet, with a hint of Marxism to him. They are the bad guys."

With that, the members of the Security Council were agreed on the forces present and were clear in their analysis of the situation.

If UNITA was not explicitly mentioned, it is because very little was known about the smallest of the three movements. Its leader, Jonas Savimbi had spent more time with his men in the field than in diplomatic receptions in Luanda.

Each group in fact represented a specific ethnic group and, under the Portuguese, they had spent a lot of time fighting each other rather than the colonial power. The support of the super powers remained rather symbolic just enough to be present in the race for power when it began in earnest.

This happened abruptly in 1975.

Eliminating the National Union government which was to conduct the organization of free elections, the parties threw themselves into capturing Luanda, their weapons in their hand.

Fighting for the control of the capital ended in July 1975 with the victory of the MPLA which had been very effectively supported by Cuban advisers from the end of May. The MPLA grew in strength even more in the following weeks : the Soviets sent them rocket-launcher vehicles, T-54 and PT-76 tanks, while several hundred extra Cuban instructors flooded into the country.

Meanwhile, the CIA was conveying, in great haste, emergency aid to the FNLA. The Soviet aid arrived by boat, American aid by cargo plane. One was bringing heavy tanks and helicopters, the other assault rifles and portable anti-aircraft missiles.

Stimulated by the presence of several thousand Cuban combatants, the American administration, with Kissinger at its head, committed itself to a total fight against the new power in Luanda, in order to "prevent a complete and easy victory of the communists" in the country.

A financial support of $300,000 was granted by the CIA, at the beginning of 1975, to the FNLA, a sum thirty times greater than in previous years.

On the 18th of July in the same year, the FNLA operation aid budget, code name 'IA Feature' was boosted to $6,000,000.

President Ford said simply "Go ahead", to William Colby, the Director of the CIA at the time. The existence of the operation 'IA Feature' was never admitted, even to the parliamentary commission which had the task of overseeing the activities of the intelligence agency.

There was never a question of mentioning Angola directly. President Ford evoked simply "the material support of the moderate nationalist movements so as to promote self-determination in the new African states." After the humiliation in Vietnam and Cambodia, the White House simply wanted to show proof of its determination to stop the communist steamroller. Angola had been chosen as a battleground.

The operation took on such an importance that John Stockwell believed it was necessary to inform Langley :

"The secret support operation IA Feature is too limited to ensure an FNLA victory, but it is also too important to remain secret for long."

During the weeks that followed, the budget for the operation was progressively boosted to $25,000,000. The CIA ensured reconnaissance flights and cargo plane rotations would multiply between Zaire and Angola. A team of American technical advisers, CIA and special forces combined, penetrated Angola. This did not stop Roberto Holden and the FNLA from complaining bitterly about the irregularity and the small size of the CIA supplies, which did not include heavy armaments. Fortunately for Holden, the South Africans were more consistent and more generous.

SOUTHERN AIR TRANSPORT

The DC-6s of the Rhodesian company Air Trans Africa, with veteran pilots of Congo and Biafra at the controls, participated in the evacuation of hundreds of Portuguese nationals when Angola fell. The company subsequently received several contracts from the CIA to carry out deliveries of arms and ammunition destined for the FNLA.

However the favoured transporter of the American secret service in the region was Southern Air Transport (SAT).

Less well known than Air America, the contribution of SAT to CIA secret operations was nonetheless of the first order in Latin America and Africa.

SAT was a small transport company, operating flights on demand, which was heading towards voluntary liquidation when it was bought by the CIA, or rather by its financial intermediaries, in 1959. The company had started its operations in July 1947, with a single C-46, which was a war surplus craft. When it was integrated into the empire of the CIA twelve years later, its situation had scarcely changed : it still possessed only one rather tired C-46, sometimes joined by two other aircraft on lease.

It cost the US intelligence agency $300,000 to acquire the dying company, whose activity was mostly in the direction of the Caribbean.

Through this purchase, which was a miracle for the two founder-owners of SAT, the CIA sought above all to anticipate its future logistic needs in the direction of Latin America. Langley was expecting to have to intervene more and more in this region where a certain geopolitical instability was gaining ground. The financial situation of SAT changed from the minute its repurchase was signed. The company acquired two four-engine DC-6s from Air America and following the example of other air companies of the CIA it started to receive some good contracts form the US government. The company accounts were perking up.

Subsequently, SAT recuperated a part of Air America activity and therefore its range was now far wider than Latin America. Southern Air Transport spread its wings as far as the far east where a 3.7 million dollar contract signed with the US Air Force permitted it to transport passengers and freight, in a direct link with the Vietnam war. In 1968, SAT sounded the alarm : faced with the explosive growth of air traffic worldwide it was vital to modernize its fleet if it wanted to keep up with the opposition. This time it was definitely not a question of buying cheap army surplus planes. Investments had to be made in jet planes and with millions of dollars.

The CIA were unpleasantly surprised when they heard of the cost.

The project was submitted to EXCOMAIR, a working group which had been created several years previously within the agency, to coordinate the activities of air companies linked to the American secret service.

EXCOMAIR (Establishment of Executive Committee for Aid Proprietary Operations) set up an in-depth study of the situation. It was only after several stormy meetings, CIA financial experts begrudged the necessary effort, that the SAT development project was accepted.

The Pacific branch of the company, based in Taipei, bought three Boeing 727s which permitted it to open semi-regular lines for the American government, still because of the Vietnam war.

In 1968 SAT also received its first Lockheed L-100. A civil version of the C-130 Hercules, the Lockheed L-100 had the capabilities of a military cargo plane under an impeccable civil appearance. The plane was a perfect resume of the activity of SAT throughout the world over the following years.

SAT was re-sold in 1973 for a little more than $2,000,000. It has since continued its development and is today one of the largest cargo companies in the world. But, in spite of everything, the company's links with the American government remained close after its return to the private sector: the investor who bought the company (at a reduced price) was Stanley Williams, the man of straw who had been part of the facade of the CIA for over thirteen years.

SAT therefore continued to serve American interests loyally. In 1978, it made almost half of its turnover in working for the air force of the Shah of Iran. A contract which was of course blessed by Washington.

When Williams re-sold his shares in the company in 1979, it was entirely in the hands of a certain James Bastian. Bastian had been the lawyer for SAT during the CIA years...

AFRICAN DOMINOES

Better organized and equipped than rival movements, the MPLA succeeded in becoming master of the Angolan capital in the summer of 1975.

As they had announced, the Portuguese lowered their flag on the 10th of November 1975 and left Luanda definitively, leaving it in the hands of the MPLA and its Cuban allies.

The FNLA threw itself head first into an attack of the capital which turned into a catastrophe, in one stroke eliminating it from the Angolan political game.

The South Africans, intervening in a decisive manner alongside the CIA to support UNITA, found themselves alone and dangerously vulnerable against the heavy armaments used by the MPLA.

"If the Russians and the Cubans take Angola, then other African states will fall like dominoes", predicted Kissinger before the Intelligence Commission of congress. The CIA increased its participation in the conflict with another $7,000,000.

Several weeks later, the press revelations of the CIA action in the area led to a vote in Congress (the Clark amendment) which forced the White House to interrupt operation IA Feature from the 9th of February 1978. The CIA therefore stopped its re-supply flights, officially at least.

In actual fact, the flights continued at a regular rhythm throughout the following days. Twenty two flights were counted in the direction of a secret, rebel-held airfield. A fraction more than 70 tons of armaments could be delivered at the last minute, before the CIA was really forced to interrupt its operations. A last present from the agency, a special credit of $2,000,000 was released to support the last FNLA soldiers in their combat. The money was given to Mobutu, it was his responsibility to distribute it. Twenty years later, the last survivors of the FNLA are still waiting for their money...

The election of Jimmy Carter in November 1976 sealed, for a long time, the activities of the CIA in Angola. The accession of the Governor of Georgia to power, who made himself famous as a UFO witness, was also the occasion to review a reduction in the CIA budget. Priority was given to electro-magnetic intelligence gathering and secret actions were soon to represent only the smallest share of 'the company' budget : less than 5%.

That being the case, the South Africans carried out the work of supporting UNITA alone and very well.

In the name of the fight against communism and the 'evil empire', the Reagan administration cancelled the Clark Amendment in 1986. As the Secretary of State Alexander Haig, ex head of NATO explained : "the time of adventure for the Soviets in the Third World was over."

The work of lobbying by UNITA and the CIA to the White House and Congress had been in a way made easier by the extreme nature of the aid coming from communist countries. More than thirty thousand Cubans and hundreds of other military advisers from the Eastern bloc were deployed in Angola. Material and ammunition arrived in entire ship loads in the port of Luanda.

An American press correspondent admitted into the Angolan capital compared the air traffic to that which was seen at the same period in Kabul: the rotations of Antonov and Iliouchine were incessant.

The cause seemed to be understood.

But in deciding to back UNITA and his 'freedom fighters', President Reagan clashed head on with the interests of the American oil companies present in the country since 1977 to exploit the natural resources.

Hand in hand with the government of Luanda, the American capitalists (and several other Europeans) had invested more than $800,000,000 in Angola, making the country the second oil producer in Black Africa, after Nigeria. They had thus made the United States the first economic partner of Marxist power. The business was making good progress and the status quo suited both partners perfectly.

To make the situation understood, a concert bringing together various American stars, including Bruce Springsteen, Stevie Wonder and Miles Davis, was organized in Luanda in December 1985.

Another interesting paradox, Southern Air Transport, which had worked for the CIA and against Luanda several years earlier, carried out several hundreds of flights in Angola from 1984, this time for the communist government. A hundred or so flights at least took place between the United States and the port of Benguela in Angola.

It can easily be imagined that SAT was chartered by oil and mining companies, but the State Department judged it preferable to warn the company against any transport of Cuban troops inside Angola.

Following this warning, SAT stopped its activity in the country.

BIG MONEY, SMALL MISSILES

A visit by Savimbi to the United States during which he was officially received at the White House and at the Pentagon sealed the renewed cooperation between the American executive and UNITA.

The promised armaments, worth about $15,000,000, started to arrive in Angola in the first weeks of 1986.

UNITA inherited a highly coveted prize of fifty Stinger anti-aircraft missiles. Savimbi's combatants were therefore the first "rebels" in the world, several months before the Afghans, to receive this extremely effective portable missile for use against low-altitude aircraft. The South Africans had mixed feelings. They feared the missiles could escape the control of UNITA and one day be used against them. But, on the other hand, they were themselves eager to lay their hands on a missile of that type to be able to examine it closely...

The press mentioned the special role played by Santa Lucia Airways, which operated four flights between January and April 1986, from an American military base to Kamina, the CIA logistic base in Zaire. The airline company used two Boeing 707 cargo planes and a Lockheed L-100.

The company denied "any flight in the direction of Angola." The words had been carefully chosen, because in fact the planes of Santa Lucia Airways stopped in Zaire without crossing into Angolan territory.

From Kamina, supplies then left for Mavinga and Jamba, the principal towns in the hands of UNITA in the south east of Angola.

If the tonnages quoted at the end of operation IA Feature were to be believed, 70 tons transported over twenty rotations, we can imagine that the craft used to distribute the material arriving in Zaire were medium tonnage twin-engines. It would hardly have been surprising to come across the eternal Dakota in this war. UNITA itself had several light aircraft, including a twin-engine Fokker 27, the Savimbi's personal aircraft.

In his war effort, Savimbi continued to count principally on South African aid. American aid could stop as quickly as it had started and only really involved very specific arms. The South Africans, interested above all in the protection of the northern border with Namibia, wanted to see a Cuban defeat for their own security.

The C-130 Hercules of the South African Air Force came regularly to deliver arms and ammunition to UNITA, penetrating Angola as low as possible so as to avoid detection by Cuban held radars.

On the 7th of April 1986, the Angolan minister of Defence announced that his jets had shot down a C-130 in a surprise attack while dropping supplies to UNITA.

The South Africans refuted this. It was subsequently shown that the Angolans had shot down one of their own civilian C-130s, most likely belonging to a mining company.

In 1988, with the idea of distancing UNITA from South Africa, the latter being very burdensome on the international stage, the Americans made it known to Jonas Savimbi that they were ready to multiply their military aid. With the same impulse, they made it publicly known that their aid would stop only when Moscow and Havana pulled out of the conflict. This is what finally happened after the disintegration of communist power in the USSR.

Cuba withdrew its troops from Angola in 1991 and, during the same year, Savimbi and de Santos, Angolan head of state, came to an agreement which put an end to the combat. For the time being at least.

For Savimbi, who believed victory was within his reach, the elections organized in September 1992 were an immense disappointment. Accusing the MPLA of fraud, Savimbi made tension grow in the towns still under his troops' control. The following 30th and 31st of October, the Police in Luanda therefore launched a vast campaign of assassinations against UNITA members and sympathisers present in Luanda.

This was a new departure in a civil war which could so easily be set off again.

But in the meantime the deal had changed.

The Cubans had left the country, the cold war had finished and the way was clear for economic interests to dictate the rules.

The American choice was made immediately. The CIA completely withdrew its aid to Savimbi, while the White House offered its guarantee to the government of Luanda, even lifting its seventeen year old embargo on the export of arms. The South Africans who had also known a revolution with the arrival of Nelson Mandela to power, followed closely behind. Once a victim, Savimbi was now the guilty one. The Freedom Fighters had become new world order hooligans, stopping things from running smoothly...

From the month of October 1994, new and lengthy peace negotiations started up again. Angola remains stuck between war and peace to this day.

CHAPTER 8

FREEDOM FIGHTERS

DESTINATION ISLAMABAD

Just as usual, the plane arrived in the middle of the night on the Chaklala air base, on the outskirts of Islamabad.

As soon as it had landed, the imposing dark grey C-141 taxied towards the military terminal and stopped a short distance away from the dark building. The aircraft was swiftly surrounded by armed guards who positioned themselves at a respectful distance and then did not move. An observant eye would have noticed the plane was equipped with the most recent detection systems, for jamming and luring anti-aircraft missiles.

If he could have then glanced inside the plane, the observer would have been extremely surprised. The austere cargo bay had been replaced by two vast soundproofed units, giving this military plane all the comforts of a presidential one.

The first unit, taking on the exact dimensions of the bay, was fitted out like a VIP lounge, with large armchairs and sofas as well as sleeping and washing areas. The second unit, joined to the first, contained an ultra-modern communication system allowing coded communications from any point in the world.

With the jet engines turned off, the passengers got out of the plane. Surprisingly they were all wearing civilian clothes, even though the plane bore the colours of the US Air Force. At their head was a tall, elderly man.

William Casey, Director of the CIA, was back in Pakistan.

From his arrival at the head of the CIA in 1981, Casey, in his role of emissary, had the habit of spending two days a year in Pakistan. He came to discuss with the local leaders and the Pakistani secret service about aid to the Agfhan Mujaheddin.

Invariably, his plane landed in the middle of the night and took off again in the middle of the night. The Americans took care of their own baggage. One or two CIA men remained permanently on board the C-141, while the Pakistani soldiers, who were responsible for the external security of the plane, were not authorized to approach.

The invasion of Afghanistan, just before Christmas 1979, came after a succession of communist attacks on Kabul and a preparation which

275

had lasted several months. The satellites had seen and heard almost everything and the attack, which was announced as such, was not a real surprise for the Americans. One country which was greatly concerned by the turn that these events was taking, south of the Amou river, was neighbouring Pakistan. Its president, General Zia-Ul-Haq, rapidly chose to back militarily the Afghan rebels. He did this by taking care not to openly provoke the very powerful Soviet Union and to avoid any direct confrontation. In reacting this way, Zia gained enormous prestige throughout the Arab world as a champion of Islam, but also in the West as a champion of anti-communism.

Conversely, from the very first months of the Soviet presence, the Americans adopted a very reserved attitude. The opinion that predominated in the State Department as well as the CIA was that Afghanistan was already a lost cause.

The fierce resistance of the Afghans pushed the Americans into revising their judgement. They were beginning to have an idea of the wonderful opportunity to be able to avenge the defeat suffered in Vietnam.

Afghanistan would be the Soviet Vietnam.

Doubtless there were also good geostrategic reasons to support the Mujaheddin, but it can be stated without fear of contradiction that the main reason in the eyes of the Americans was to make the Red Army bleed through a third party, and without endangering American lives. With, in addition, the stirring causes of liberty and democracy thrown in. The task of the CIA was to find arms and ammunition of communist origin throughout the first years, then from anywhere in the world after 1985 when any inhibitions had disappeared, then to prepare their transport to Pakistan.

The American intelligence agency organized deliveries in entire boatloads to the port of Karachi and, of particular interest to us, by cargo plane to Islamabad. The division of these loads between the different Mujaheddin movements was the responsibility of the Pakistani secret service. From 10,000 tons in 1983, the arms deliveries reached the record figure of 65,000 tons in 1988, the period of the most intense fighting.

As the hub of CIA transport operations, the Saudi base at Darhran served both as a store and a place of transfer for the planes delivering from Great Britain, the United States, even Israel, and those leaving for Pakistan. Up until 1986, Saudi Arabian or Pakistani military aircraft ensured rotation flights between their two countries. This system, a cause of much friction, was finally abandoned : the Pakistani aircraft were sometimes forced to make about turns without being able to land in Saudi Arabia. As for the Saudis, they sometimes lacked punctuality, or reached Pakistani air space without warning. From 1986, US Air Force planes therefore took charge of the essential air deliveries for the CIA.

The aircraft did not always come just from the west, but also from the east: for the Chinese also this was a wonderful opportunity to fight against the Soviets.

The most well known deliveries were those of Stinger portable ground to air missiles. The first consignments were sent in the summer of 1986 and a thousand missiles made their way to Afghanistan, via Pakistan, over the course of a few months. According to CIA reports, around 340 were fired against the Soviets. Taking into account the various losses and malfunctions, the CIA estimated that more than 400 missiles in working order remained in the hands of Afghan fighters after the Soviet withdrawal, thirty months later. In 1994, the agency threw itself into a vast campaign to repurchase these missiles. From 50 to a 100,000 dollars was offered to the Afghan chiefs (even though they only cost the US Army 35,000 dollars) to recover the missiles which had been given to them free of charge. These repurchase operations were failures.

Less dangerous in the long term (although perhaps not...), the CIA had thousands of copies of the Koran delivered to the Mujaheddin, to increase their spirit of resistance against the Soviet invader. When the Soviets completed their withdrawal on the 15th of February 1989, the champagne was cracked open in Washington and Langley.

But from that day, and by a strange irony, American and Soviet interests coincided : it suited them both to put a stop to the fervour of the Islamists, who had been the most zealous Mujaheddins, in their fight against the residual communist power which remained in Kabul. Washington had played the Islamists against the Soviets, but now that the latter had withdrawn from the game, the Americans preferred to see the Islamists held in check by the Afghan communists.

Neither the White House nor the Kremlin wanted to see a new Islamic republic in the region.

The CIA consignments stopped abruptly and the Afghan resistants, who had victory within their grasp, sank into a war of brother fighting against brother which neutralized their efforts and at the same time fully satisfied the two superpowers.

ALL BUT MARINES

Arriving on the case during the first days of 1981, the William Casey-Ronald Reagan duo brought with them the wind of change to the White House as well as Langley. In the space of four years, between 1981 and 1984, the budget for intelligence increased by 25%.

Rarely had such a close working relationship been seen between an American president and the head of the secret service. Casey was both a highly valued adviser and a very effective communicator with the president. An old chief of the OSS in the European theatre of operation during the second world war, Casey had then become an accomplished businessman before directing, in 1980, Ronald Reagan's (victorious) electoral campaign.

Casey was an old hand in secret operations.

He was in Angola, Afghanistan, then in central America, another hotspot in the cold war that was ending.

Ronald Reagan took the oath of office in January 1981, only eighteen months after the Sandinista revolution in Nicaragua had overthrown Somoza. Central America very rapidly became the focal point of foreign policy for the Reagan administration.

Between 1850 and 1945, no less than twelve Marine landings had taken place in Nicaragua to protect North American economic interests. The arrival of the Sandinista government, which in 1979 landed the dictator Anastasio Somoza by force, could have provided a reason for a thirteenth landing. But times had changed and, in the presence of another great world power, the policy of gunfire was much more delicate to put into practice than at the beginning of the century. Traumatized by the experience of Vietnam, the Pentagon had no wish to get embroiled in a central American adventure with a rather doubtful legitimacy. Casey, with the approval of President Reagan who feared the appearance of a new 'continental Cuba', embarked on a campaign to engage the United States in a policy of aid to the Nicaraguan counter-revolutionaries, the 'Contras'. During a meeting which was held in November 1981, the National Security Council, dependent on the White House, approved the setting up of secret aid to the anti-Marxist guerillas in Nicaragua.

Consciously or not, the Contras were the Spanish speaking Marines of a thirteenth potential landing.

A UNIT NAMED SEASPRAY

The failure of the attempt to rescue the American hostages in Iran, in April 1980, had led to a profound reorganization of US Army special forces. A 'Special Operations Division' had been newly created to enable the army to undertake special secret operations. In order to lead these operations properly, it was however necessary that the US Army had the aerial equipment needed to ensure the transport of men and material both rapidly and secretly.

But, theoretically, only the CIA were legally in a position to lead secret operations, the existence of a secret air force within the US Army would have been quite illegal.

The Army therefore suggested that the CIA become associated with its project on order to get round this legal difficulty. The CIA accepted willingly : without paying a single dollar, they found themselves the co-owner of a secret aviation unit named Seaspray.

The project was started, officially but secretly, on the 2nd March 1981. Seaspray was amalgamated to a prosperous and highly respected commercial company, even though it belonged to the CIA, Aviation Tech Services.

"The Pentagon could not allow itself to control any umbrella companies, and that's where the close collaboration with the intelligence agency that was used to this type of situation became important" explained an old member of Seaspray. "Aviation Tech could supply any sort of machine secretly and very rapidly anywhere in the world."

Consequently, one day, an anti-terrorist group looking for a Boeing 737 to carry out a particular type of training operation went to see the US Air Force.

"Allow a wait of three months", they were told. "All our planes are being used." The group then went to see Seaspray which found them a 737 in three days, and the manoeuvre in question, a simulation of an attack on this type of aircraft, took place in the alloted time.

Seaspray had up to fifteen aircraft, including fixed wing, Cessna and Beechcraft King Air, but the best were the Hugues-500MD helicopters.

The army paid for these helicopters which were bought in the name of an umbrella company of the CIA, in such a way that the machines totally escaped the official accounts of the Pentagon.

The Hugues were equipped with the absolute best special equipment. They had an instrument panel that could be used with night vision goggles, which meant they could fly in total darkness and at low altitude without exterior aid. The helicopters also had an infra-red vision system, the image was relayed to a screen positioned in front of the pilot. The system was not new in itself, but its installation in a light helicopter was a first. The Hugues had been equipped with folding steps which meant commandos could be transported outside the cabin. Flexible reserve tanks could also be fitted, increasing the range.

A dozen or so pilots were selected from the immense pool of the US Army, the first helicopter user in the United States, well before the Air Force.

Seaspray proved its effectiveness very soon after its creation. In August 1981, the Lebanese Christian leader Beshir Gemayel went briefly to Washington at the invitation of the CIA. Gemayel wanted to request political, financial and military secret support from the Americans, which was duly granted.

The return trip from Lebanon , which had to be kept secret, was dealt with by the CIA. It was not an easy task because of the civil war which was tearing the country apart. Gemayel left Beirut on a small patrol boat. He then joined a US Navy ship off the coast. From there, a helicopter then a plane took him to Washington.

The return journey was going to be more problematic. For reasons which remain unknown, the CIA announced that it would not be able to follow the same procedure. It was therefore necessary to find another method and Seaspray made its contribution : Gemayel would return by helicopter. It was decided that the machines would leave from Egypt, fly along the Israeli coast, the Israelis had been informed and would close their eyes to the affair, to arrive at Jounieh in Lebanon, a port under Christian control. The biggest difficulty would be to escape the vigilance of the Syrians who kept a close watch on all the approaches to Lebanon. The Hugues 500, repainted in false commercial colours, could be set up in Egypt without arousing suspicion. They were also easily transportable by air, and their positioning in Egypt was carried out with the help of a C-141 US Air Force cargo plane without any problem.

Gemayel took his place in a first H-500, his wife and bodyguard in a second. The aircraft took off from Cairo, then headed towards the area of Al Arish, near the border with Sinai, where they refuelled before the long Mediterranean crossing.

To avoid Syrian radars, the two machines flew as low as possible for almost two hours. This exercise demanded great concentration from the pilots who sincerely hoped that the Israelis, whose coast they were flying along, had not forgotten their agreement that they had given a little while before!

After two hours spent just above the waves, foam from the sea formed a crust of salt on the windscreen, but Jounieh was in sight and the two helicopters landed without being spotted by the Syrians.

The mission, which had been set up in four days, had been a complete success and delighted the CIA.

ELECTRONIC EAVESDROPPING

In the central American theatre of operation Seaspray once again played its part. In March 1982, the CIA turned to the Pentagon and the 'special Operations division' to obtain planes with electronic eavesdropping equipment enabling communications to be intercepted. Both the guerillas and the death squads threatened to disrupt the progress of the elections which were being prepared in El Salvador. The CIA certainly intended to neutralize any aggressive desires before they manifested themselves.

A Beech Queen Air U-21 usually reserved for Army VIP flights was more or less legally diverted from its primary role by the special forces in order to be rapidly transformed into a plane equipped for electronic eavesdropping.

A company in Pennsylvania took charge of the plane and started by emptying it of all its VIP equipment to install the electronic devices. It was at that moment that the hierarchy of the US Army, who was responsible for the plane, noticed its disappearance and demanded that the machine be returned immediately to its base and restored to normal.

The men of the division did not get discouraged and looked towards the civilian market. A Beechcraft King Air 100, twin-engine, propellor driven aircraft, as robust as it was versatile, was loaned from a civilian operator.

The plane was sent to Nashua, in New Hampshire, where the Sanders Associate took care of its internal fittings. There was several hundreds of thousands of dollars worth of electronic material and, to speed up the process and to remain discreet, the purchases were made by carefully avoiding the normal method of invitations to tender. The CIA and the special forces would settle for the most sophisticated material.

The plane was then sent to Middletown, in Delaware, to undergo the final adjustments from the Summit Aviation company. Summit was used to working for US Ministry of Defence or secret service confidential projects. The company held the closest possible links with the CIA, indeed it was said that the CIA was the real owner.

In 1978, several weeks before the fall of the Somoza regime, Summit Aviation hurriedly trained half a dozen pilots for the benefit of the Nicaraguan dictator. It was not enough.

Afterwards, it worked on aircraft destined for the Contras, notably fitting out the Cessna O-2 with rocket pods. Summit worked well, quickly and with great discretion. It was a good address that the CIA did not hesitate to recommend to its close associates...

Summit finished the work on the Beechcraft which was then painted in false commercial colours and took flight for Honduras. Less than a month had passed since the launch of the operation, and to work so quickly was in itself a considerable feat.

The plane and its mixed crew, pilots and electronics engineers, were based at San Pedro Sula, industrial capital of Honduras, in the north west of the country. The Beechcraft supposedly belonged to an American company, Shenandoah Aerolease, whose controlling company, Amairco, had agreed a contract with the government of Honduras to carry out geophysical and cartographic studies.

Amairco and Shenandoah were evidently umbrella companies belonging to the CIA. When the cover of Amairco grew thin from 1983, another facade was used, that of XMCO Inc. based in Virginia.

The aircraft took off each day to carry out eavesdropping and intelligence gathering missions. Eighteen thousand feet above the bay of Fonseca, on the border between the three countries in the area, Honduras, Nicaragua and El Salvador, the Seaspray plane kept its big ears open and picked up a large quantity of radio traffic.

What was captured seemed phenomenal. The communications intercepted between Nicaragua and El Salvador, or even between the different guerilla groups inside El Salvador, meant above all that the position of the rebels could be checked and their operations more clearly understood. The paths of infiltration from Nicaragua to El Salvador were updated. Numerous ambushes against Salvadoran government forces, almost a dozen according to some sources, were even able to be thwarted.

Planned to last ten days, simply over the period of the elections, the operation, code named Queens Hunter, was extended to three months, then three years!

Meanwhile the team as well as its missions, were expanding.

Launched with a single plane and a dozen men to keep watch on El Salvador, operation Queens Hunter subsequently received other Beechcraft, with high-performance equipment. Once the elections were finished, the missions were resolutely turned towards watching over Sandinist Nicaragua. The aircraft did not hesitate to lose themselves a little over Nicaraguan territory.

The plan was completed at sea by ships with electronic gathering equipment which were circling in the water, off Managua.

"Our intelligence work on Nicaragua is so good that we can hear the toilets flush in Managua", they joked at the CIA.

From San Pedro Sula, the men and planes were able to move to La

Ceiba, a tourist resort on the Atlantic coast. Still with their false commercial colours, the King Air were stationed on the civilian section of the airport, equipped with anti-sabotage devices.

The Queens Hunter crews decided to live in a vast villa in the residential quarter of La Ceiba. The house, discreetly watched over by plain clothed special forces men, was equipped to withstand a siege. To stop the men, who had had enough of videos, from getting too bored and talking too much in the town, something which in fact had already started to happen, someone from the special operations division had the idea of having a satellite dish installed.

This was done at the beginning of 1983. The impressive object, which had cost 7,500 dollars, was more than 15 feet high. It was certainly not discreet.

The agents of the CIA at the base in Managua were one day examining photos of the region taken by satellite when they noticed, in the heart of La Ceiba, a strange white mark, which was highly visible. If it was able to be seen from space, then it could also probably be seen from the pavement opposite...so the impressive object was taken down.

In spite of this blunder, Queens Hunter had supplied, according to the CIA, some 70% of all the intelligence gathered electronically in central America from 1982 to 1984. Seaspray had not yet had that success, and it had drawn a blank on a very specific point : a Hugues 500 equipped with an infra-red vision system had been used to try and prove that planes were secretly in transit at night between Nicaragua and El Salvador. Despite their infra-red vision instruments, no interception was able to be made and the programme was stopped.

In 1984, the US Army took over complete control of these electronic eavesdropping missions and Seaspray was obliterated. In the framework of operation royal Duke, several Beech King Air 200 alias RC-12D were set up on the military base at Palmerola from where they were operated without hiding their real nature...

The surveillance of Nicaragua was a task which involved the whole panoply of US Air Force planes. Lockheed U-2R, SR-71, RC-135 and even AC-130 Gunship, the latter were used because of the night vision equipment, all these craft were used one after the other or simultaneously along the Nicaraguan border or in the heart of its air space. Even the AWACS were, it seemed, used to observe aerial movements between Nicaragua and El Salvador. Without a convincing result...

AID TO THE CONTRAS

The first groups of Contras appeared from mid-February 1979.

Based in Honduras, the FDN (Nicarguan Democratic Force) controlled by Enrique Bermudez, ex-colonel of Somoza's National Guard and ex-miliary attache to Washington, launched his attacks against the northern border with Nicaragua. Subsequently Eden Pastora's ARDE (Democratic Revolutionary Alliance) appeared on the scene.

Pastora, alias Commandant Zero, had participated in the Sandinista revolution. He had even become vice minister of Defence and head of the Sandinista popular militia, before stepping back when faced with the new leaders of Managua. Disagreeing with the radicalization of the Sandinistas, in 1982 he announced his intention to fight against his old comrades. He had therefore established his underground network in Costa Rica, on the southern border of Nicaragua. Pastora was as allergic to contact with the old Somozists of the FDN as he was with the CIA.

On the 1st of December 1981, a budget of 19 million dollars was released by the American administration to enable a first contingent of 500 Contras to be trained by Argentinian officers. The CIA wanted to make the Contra movement, which was still in its early stages, an effective military tool directed against Managua. The programme was presented to the intelligence commission of the Congress as an effort aimed at protecting El Salvador from infiltrations of weapons from neighbouring Nicaragua. The ultimate objective of the CIA, the overthrow by force of the Sandinista regime, was carefully evaded.

In return for several minor financial arrangements, Honduras, in the north and Costa Rica, in the south, followed the United States in their policy and made their presence official on their territory which provided a sanctuary for the Contras.

The first deliveries of weapons from the CIA arrived at the beginning of 1982 while the necessary infrastructure to conduct these operations was being put into place progressively.

The hub of these operations was the airfield of Aguacate, in the east of Honduras. An airstrip had been specially built by US Army engineers during the course of joint manoeuvres with the Honduran army. When the manoeuvres were finished, the airfield had been left at the disposal of the Contras. The pretext of US-Honduran manoeuvres was used several times by the CIA to send a quantity of equipment to the Contras : the material arrived with the US Marine or Army logistic then, at the end of the manoeuvres, was declared 'surplus' and left there. Hondurans and Contras shared the spoils.

The US Air Force also profited from the good will of the Hondurans to install an air surveillance radar on Isopo mountain. The site, occupied by fifty or so technicians and known by the code name Carrot Top, overlooked neighbouring Nicaragua just perfectly and enabled the air traffic to be observed permanently; it was also certainly used as a guide for Contra planes thus multiplying their forays into Nicaraguan territory. The whole thing was reminiscent of Lima Site 85 in Laos.

BIRTH OF A CONTRA AIR FORCE

It was Lieutenant-Colonel Juan Gomez, ex Chief of the fighter units of the Somozist Air Force who had the privilege of creating the Fuerza Aerea del Ejercito de la Resistencia Nicaraguense, in 1982.

Taking the facts into account, the title of air force of the Nicaraguan Resistance army was a little grandiloquent. But if the Contra air force was poor in material, it was rich in human potential which matched its ambitions. Neither courage and manpower, two-thirds of it was composed of ex-Somozist pilots and mechanics, were lacking. Without waiting for the aid of the CIA, Gomez started his air operations alone and with a certain panache. On the 19th of July 1980, even before the Contras were organized militarily, he insisted on celebrating the anniversary of the Sandinistan seizure of power :

"I had a little surprise prepared for them", he explained several years later on the airfield at Aguacate. "I had just taken off at the controls of a little Cessna lent by some friends and, armed with a few grenades, I launched an attack on the Sandinista barracks at Leon, half-way between Managua and the Honduran border."

Gomez subsequently kept up the tradition. The targets changed from one year to the next and in 1983 the Contra Air Force, which had gained in fire power, attacked the Salvadoran guerilla radio which transmitted from Nicaraguan territory. Following this attack, Radio Venceremos (We will win), which was set up in the crater of a volcano, remained silent for three good months.

In 1980 also, Gomez had planned to eliminate Castro and nine other Sandinista commanders : the ten men were attending a secret meeting in the Nicaraguan town of Montelimar. Gomez took off in the night, once again at the controls of a light aircraft. Compared with the previous operation of the 19th of July, the 'weapons system' had developed considerably : the plane carried under its fuselage a home-made bomb made from a carboy of gas fitted up with a grenade detonator.

Gomez was very lucky: the flight went off smoothly, the carboy remained attached to the plane, without exploding at an untimely moment. The 'bomb' was then dropped perfectly, exploding in the middle of the courtyard of the targetted building. The damage caused was minuscule, but the panic caused among the Nicaraguans and the Cubans was equal to the risks taken by the pilot. After a few days, Gomez learnt with pleasure that the raid had nonetheless taken one victim : the head of Nicaraguan security, who had been shot for his incompetence, and more especially because of the leaks of information which had enabled the operation to take place.

The aid of the CIA to the Contra air force was first of all in the form of two C-47 Dakotas; Perhaps the Contras were expecting to receive better material and in a greater quantity, which led to ironic comments from some:

"If you go to Washington, you will see the same plane suspended from the ceiling of the National Air and Space Museum."

The choice of the CIA was not however entirely without foundation. The C-47, more than a thousand of which continue to fly throughout the world, was an aircraft suffciently robust and easy to maintain which suited a secret operation perfectly.

On the ground as in the air, the aid from the CIA intensified consi-

derably throughout 1982. The American pilots of the CIA were directly involved in flights over Nicaragua, whether it concerned parachute
missions in aid of the Contras, or more rarely, real combat missions
against the Sandinistas.

But at the same time, the official cover of CIA operations, which was
to fight against the smuggling of arms in the direction of El Salvador,
began to wear very thin.

In April 1982, the revelation by the Washington Post on the existence of an aid budget to the Contras and its direct use against Managua
pushed the US Congress for once to take a tougher stand: the CIA was
firmly reminded that the only secret activities that would be tolerated
should concern the prevention of the traffic of arms between Nicaragua and El Salvador. But several months later, revelations by Newsweek
magazine which forced the American administration to admit officially its aid to the Contras, put the cat among the pigeons once again.

Congress reacted in no uncertain terms by prohibiting the CIA and
the armed forces, in the last days of 1982, from providing material and
training capable of overthrowing the Sandinista regime. This was the
Boland amendment, which took the name of the democratic senator
who then presided over the intelligence commission of the House of
Representatives.

"To want to prevent Nicaragua from exporting its revolution is one
thing. To help the Contras to overthrow the Sandinistas is another",
explained Boland without respite.

Reagan made amends and repeated to Congress that support to the
Contras was only justified to stop Managua from exporting revolution
in the region, not for bringing down the Sandinista regime.

This was a white lie : in the field, the deception continued and the
defeat of the Sandinistas was still the number one objective of the Contras,
who were making very little progress with their efforts.

Their number was increasing, but it still remained divided between
different factions and they proved themselves incapable of mastering a
significant part of Nicaraguan territory, from which they could have
proclaimed a provisional government.

The CIA therefore wished to move things up a gear.

In September 1983, the CIA sent a list of material to the US Army and Air Force that they wished to obtain without delay. There was in total 28 million dollars worth of equipment, everything from jungle boots to light attack aircraft. The initiated started to refer to it as the 'Christmas present list'. This material was officially destined for the Salvadoran army, to help it fight against the FMLN guerillas. Nobody was fooled: it was in fact going to equip the Contras.

This first list, having been the cause of a little friction within the administration, prompted a new, less ambitious 'order' to be placed. This time it involved only 12 million dollars worth of equipment and the list was honoured.

The biggest 'Christmas present' was three twin-engine, propellor driven Cessna O-2A belonging to the New York ANG. These planes were suddenly declared 'military surplus' in December 1983 and officially sold for a nominal sum to El Salvador. The planes were then given back to Summit Aviation who equipped them with rocket pods under the wings. From innocent service or liaison planes, the O-2As of the US National Guard were transformed into light support fire aircraft. The CIA then took responsibility for sending them to the Contras during mid-1984.

Stimulated by the aid received from the CIA, the Contras had started to intensify their air operations from the Autumn of 1983. The C-47 were used intensively for resupplying base camps set up along the border or columns which had infiltrated Nicaragua. The missions above Nicaragua were brief but intense. Shortly before his accidental death, a Contra pilot described a resupply mission for the French magazine RAIDS :

"After an uneventful take off from Aguacate, we headed for Nicaragua. Tension was high in the cockpit. We were all well aware that the Sandinistan army had a number of SA-7 anti-aircraft missiles, so we chose to fly near the ground to avoid making our plane an easy target.

After a half an hour of flying engine power was reduced as we were approaching the drop zone. At the rear, the three dispatchers leaned through the gaping hole in the fuselage (the doors had been removed for the mission) to try and locate the DZ.

Walkie-talkie at his ear, the chief air dispatcher received the orders that I gave him from the cockpit: the straps which held the pallets in place were removed. While we were making the first run over the drop zone, the first pallet was moved close to the door.

On the ground, everything seemed OK. During our first run, several dozen Contras appeared in the clearing and started waving their arms. Radio contact was established.

You can send everything. The zone is safe... we have been waiting for this...

We made a large 360° turn and came right back above the small clearing. The flaps were down, the plane had slowed down as much as possible, the ground was only 300 feet below.

Go! The chief air dispatcher shouted the order in the cabin which was vibrating under the power of the two 1,200hp Pratt and Whitney engines.

The air dispatchers leaned hard against the pallets to push them into the void. The small parachutes opened when they left the plane. We thought the loads were going to miss the clearing and land in the trees. But no, the packages, too heavy for the parachutes, descended vertically towards the ground and the accuracy of the drop was very good.

There was a final run over the DZ to see if the 'aim' had been good.

On the ground, the Contras rushed towards the packages. Jungle boots, ammunition, automatic weapons, everything was picked up and loaded onto the mens' backs. The parachutes and the wooden crates were also taken away by the combatants who then headed for their base camps, on the other side of the border.

We went back to Aguacate in a very happy frame of mind, with the feeling of a job well done."

AMERICAN INVOLVEMENT

With their weak aerial capabilities, the Contras also launched offensive operations. On the 8th of September 1983, Eden Pastora, Chief of the southern front, sent two Cessna equipped with light bombs under the wings, to bomb the airport at Managua. An aircraft was destroyed during the attack and crashed near the civilian terminal of the airport. According to reports from the crew of the other plane which returned and landed in Costa Rica, the aircraft was flying too low and was hit by the explosion of its own bombs. The ARDE crew, pilot and co-pilot were all killed. According to Managua the plane had been shot down by AAA. The anti-aircraft defence at the airport, in the normal course of events just two heavy machine guns, had been increased by fifteen other automatic weapons the day before the attack. Without doubt the Sandinistas had been forewarned of the operation. But that was not the end of the affair.

When the attack was taking place, two American senators, the Democrat Gary Hart and the Republican William Cohen, were on their way towards the Nicaraguan capital.

"Go and see for yourselves what is happening in Nicaragua", Casey, the Director of the CIA had told them, so they could respond to criticism of the CIA operations. Hart and Cohen took his advice.

While they were still one hours flying time away from Managua, they were informed that the Augusto Sandino airport had just been closed, following an air attack. Their plane was re-routed to Tegucigalpa, the Honduran capital. After a wait of several minutes Managua informed them that the airport was to open especially for them. The two senators got back in the plane and set off for Managua. When they landed in the middle of the afternoon, the wreck of the attacking plane was still there, near the fire-ravaged terminal. The official waiting area, where they were to have given a press conference, had also been hit. The two men realised that if they had been on time, they could have been killed in the attack.

The Nicaraguan press who welcomed the two senators immediately focused on the attack which had just taken place :

"The bomb raid was organized by the Contras who are supported by the CIA", challenged a journalist.

"The CIA is not that stupid", replied the senators.

The Nicaraguans found some very interesting things in the wreck of the plane : a driving licence issued in Florida along with American social security and credit cards. Also found were other documents with coded inscriptions. Confronted with these documents the senators were forced to admit that it was evidence : they were authentic CIA documents.

A little later in the day, they let their anger show when they met the CIA station chief in Managua.

"It's the most stupid operation imaginable! To attack a civilian airport with CIA documents on board the plane..."

The CIA man defended himself as best he could :

"It was Pastora's operation. He does what he wants, he chooses his own targets..."

The man from the CIA was very careful not to tell them that the planes (and no doubt the pilots aswell) had been supplied by the agency. The operation itself ensued as a result of a decision by the CIA, at its highest level, to have something 'new', and to show that the Contras could do more than start simple skirmishes on the border...

The next day, a North American T-28 attacked, unsuccessfully, fuel tanks at the port of Corinto, on the Pacific coast. A dozen planes of this type were at that time serving in the Honduran Air Force... In spite of that unfortunate circumstance, Congress eventually acceded to the requests of President Reagan and authorized, for the following year, an aid budget of 24 million dollars to the Contras. Reagan had once again explained to the appropriate commissions that the secret operations programme was conceived to put pressure on the Sandinistas, to make them give up helping the Salvadoran guerillas...

On the 3rd of October 1983, an FDN transport plane was shot down by Sandinistas in the north of Nicaragua. One crew member was killed, the other two, ex-Somoza national guard members, were taken prisoner.

The new year of 1984 was lucky for the Sandinistas : on the 11th of January they shot down a US Army helicopter. The pilot, an American officer, was killed when the aircraft crashed. The helicopter, which was no doubt heading for Aguacate, had lost its way and had penetrated into Nicaraguan air space.

Several weeks later, in March, a C-47 flown on behalf of ARDE, crashed in the north of Costa Rica. An American pilot was on board. Throughout the following weeks, one, possibly two O-2 were lost by the Contras, in circumstances that were unclear. The circumstances surrounding the loss of a helicopter the following September however were better known.

The Contras decided to carry out a sizeable air raid on the Nicaraguan town of Santa Clara, where the presence of Cuban advisers was suspected. The Contra Air Force attacked using all its offensive capabilities, three Cessna O-2 (those very planes which had been equipped with rocket pods by Summit Aviation), and a Hugues 500 D helicopter. The Hugues, which was also equipped with rocket pods had been loaned to the Contras by the CIA which had itself 'borrowed' it from the US Army.

The Army never saw its machine again, it was shot down during the attack. The pilots, both American, as well as the door gunner, a Contra, were all killed.

Contrary to assertions from Managua, the two Americans, Dana Parker and James Powell, were not part of the CIA. They belonged in fact to a private organization with an elegant, yet rather confusing title, the Civilian Military Assistance. The organization had been active in Honduras, from Autumn 1983, in organizing dispatches of clothes and medicines to the Contras. Powell was a helicopter pilot in Vietnam, where he was shot down three times. Parker was a member of the Hunstville police in Alabama. According to the Contras, both men had taken several days leave to come and help them and had agreed to pilot the Hugues in the attack. Officially, they had been shot down during a rescue mission.

The Contras announced that they had killed four Cubans during the attack on Santa Clara.

"A cook and three children", added the Sandinist spokesman in Managua soberly.

Several days later in October 1984, a Cessna O-2 crashed after taking off from the Salvadoran base of Ilopango. The four occupants, agents of the CIA, were killed in the accident. The plane was leaving for an electronic eavesdropping mission against Nicaragua.

This accident came at a moment when the CIA was preparing to stop completely the operations supporting the Contras, because of the new Boland amendment, itself a consequence of the mining operations.

It had all begun a year previously in October 1983. Some teams of Contras trained by the CIA had managed to destroy a great number of oil tanks in the port of Corinto, in an attack from the sea using gunboats.

It was a matter of bringing to an end a very ambitious programme which had been launched several months earlier in cooperation with the special operation division of the US Army. The CIA wanted to operate a boat from which secret operations could be launched against Nicaragua. The CIA had skillfully managed to manipulate the special forces of the US Army by painting them an enticing picture of the advantages they would have in sharing the cost and operation of such a vessel. A boat for the US Army!

"It will be extremely useful in the event of hostage taking on the other side of the world, you will no longer be dependent on the Navy..."explained the CIA to the representatives of the special forces. But the latter had been duped.

After some enquiries, a large grain ship was bought in Norway by a CIA cover company, Pacific Gulf Maritime Inc. It was decided that the ship would be used in standard commercial operations, when it was not taking part in CIA and special forces secret operations.

The grain ship had powerful communication systems installed and was fitted up so as to be able to put a fleet of small, heavily armed gunships into operation. The cargo ship of the CIA would play the role of a mother ship, remaining in international waters to resupply the gunships which would then go to attack objectives on land. On the foredeck there was an area from which helicopters could be operated.

The first raid took place on the 10th of October 1983, against the port of Corinto. When he showed Ronald Reagan photos of the damage taken by satellite, Casey was exultant. Another equally spectacular raid was carried out several days later. But the CIA wanted to go even deeper into this military and economic war that it was keeping up against Nicaragua.

It was proposed to mine the ports of Nicaragua. This would have been a discreet and inexpensive way to make the blockade against the Sandinistas last longer.

The operation, accepted by Langley and the White House, was launched immediately. There had to be enough mines to frighten off the shipowners, but not be powerful enough to sink a ship. Many Soviet or

Eastern bloc ships used Nicaraguan ports and, showing proof of self-restraint, the White House only wanted to bring down the local economy, not to start a third world war.

Seventy-five mines, specially built for the operation, were laid in the three main ports in Nicaragua in January 1984. Conceived by the CIA, these 330 pound contraptions had been made in Honduras where they had been given a false home-made appearance to give credibility to the idea that the mine-laying exercise had been carried out by the Contras. The mines were, however, fairly sophisticated, combining acoustic and magnetic detection systems, and functioned very well. The ships which were not damaged made an about turn and the produce, coffee, cane sugar, accumulated in the ports. In Managua, there was talk of an economic catastrophe. As in every secret operation, the truth was eventually revealed, and in this particular case it was rather swift. The false idea of a Contra operation was hardly convincing and, in April 1984, after ships of six different nationalities had been damaged, Congress requested some serious explanations from the CIA, whose director was forced to recognize his agency's involvement. The CIA seemed to have exceeded any permitted limits. The US Congress, furious about this affair, cut off all credit to the Contras for six months.

Another disastrous consequence for the Contras, on the 24th of May 1984 a new Boland amendment was voted in, forbidding all military or paramilitary support to the Contras, from the CIA, the Ministry of Defence or any other intelligence agency. The law had to take effect from October 1984 until the end of 1985. As a direct consequence of the Boland amendment, the last contingent of 73 CIA advisers left the camps of the Contras in Honduras on the 10th of October 1984.

This was bad timing for the FDN who lost, at the same time, one of its two C-47s. The plane crashed shortly after taking off from Aguacate. The aircraft had been sabotaged by a Sandinistan mechanic who had infiltrated the Contra ranks. Gomez could only use a four-engine DC-6 (10 tons of payload) and a C-47 for his resupply operations.

The two aircraft lacked a supply of spare parts and the Contras were more or less rendered immobile in Honduras.

But at the White House, Reagan had not yet had his last word...

PROJECT DEMOCRACY

While the CIA had been put out of action by the Boland amendment, the NSC or National Security Council, set up a second secret service under the direct orders of the White House and took responsibility for the cost, totally illegally, of aid to the Contras.

This was Project Democracy.

But contact remained very close between Langley and the Lieutenant-Colonel of the Marines Oliver North, key figure in the NSC and king-pin concerning aid to the Contras.

The first thing to be certain of was a regular financement of the Contras and North immediately set about finding foreign backers.

Israel, a large supplier of arms in the region, refused. It had already supplied several dozen military advisers to Honduras and Guatamala for anti-guerilla training. South Africa appeared interested, but the White House rejected (initially) its involvement because of political considerations. At the beginning of the 80's more than ever, the 'country of apartheid' did not have a good press.

In the month of May 1984, Saudi Arabia made it known that it was ready to give 12 million dollars to the Contras. The operation was to be carried out in the utmost secrecy, at the level of heads of state. To avoid communications of the American official services being intercepted, and so that no record of the operation was left, exchanges were made by messages, using the Saudi Arabian ambassador in Washington as an intermediary.

The reward for this aid, for there is always a reward in these cases, was that the White House gave authorization for the discreet sale of 400 Stinger anti-aircraft missiles to the Kingdom of Saudi Arabia. From the month of July, a million dollars was transferred regularly every month for the Contras, to a numbered bank account in Switzerland.

The Americans were very grateful. In 1985 this Saudi participation was considerably increased, reaching more than 20 million dollars.

North also took responsibility for finding weapons, a task which presented hardly any difficulties, potential dealers were rife. The purchases were made in Europe, with Guatamala or Honduras as the official destination.

Other large deliveries were made from Israel, China or indeed South Africa. Pretoria had use of several dozens of tons of weapons originating from the communist bloc after its successful operations against the Cubans in Angola. In January 1985, 200 tons of arms were sent from South Africa to Costa Rica, in aid of Eden Pastora's ARDE.

But ARDE did not have the means to send these weapons to its troops, so the loads were eventually directed to Contra movements based in Honduras. In February and March 1985, several flights of Southern Air Transport, also contracted out to the Arrow Air company, were organized to deliver several thousand Kalashnikovs, AKMs, G-3 weapons and RPG rocket launchers to the Contras.

During the course of that same year, 1985, China supplied more than 500 tons of weapons paid for by Saudi funds, including SA-7 ground to air missiles of Soviet design. But in spite of the quantity of money and the material which was starting to arrive in the field, the Contras were not performing particularly well. In July 1985, a veritable war council gathered in a hotel room in Miami; Oliver North, the Contra Chiefs Calero and Bermudez and General Secord.

Secord had become a key figure in Contra support operations. A General of the US Air Force, he took sudden early retirement in May 1983, to enter the world of business. Secord kept up his close links with the CIA, the NSC and the special forces of the Ministry of Defence. Even though he had no official function, Secord set up a whole web of companies capable of replacing the actions of government departments when it would have been illegal for them to act. In brief this was the secondary secret service, supported by private funding. Secord had the ambition, if he were to return to public service one day, to direct secret operations for the CIA.

North had recruited Secord and the mission that he had entrusted him with was simple enough in theory; it involved offering the Contras an air logistic capability sufficient for them to be able to lead large scale operations inside Nicaragua. Up until then, the Contras were only just able to carry out very limited action in lauching small raids from their bases in Honduras.

North also wanted to reactivate the southern front which had been practically abandoned since the ARDE leader, Eden Pastora, was seriously injured in an assassination attempt. But in order to supply this front in a regular way, it was vital to have use of a secret airstrip in Costa Rican territory.

Despite its claimed neutrality, Costa Rica tolerated the presence of ARDE Contras in its territory. All the influential power of the US Ambassador, intervening at the request of North, was required for them to accept an airstrip for Contra use aswell.

"It's in your own interest", explained the Ambassador. "The quicker you help the Contras to reconquer a part of Nicaraguan territory, the quicker they will leave Costa Rica..."

The Costa Ricans accepted this explanation, on the express condition that the airstrip be used only by empty aircraft that were permitted to land only to take on fuel. There were to be no stocks of weapons involved.

The United States in return undertook to intervene on its behalf to the International Monetary Fund so that Costa Rica could obtain the rescheduling of its external debt. Honduras was also involved in helping the Contras. Their support was through the sale, by the Americans, of F-5 fighter-bombers at very reasonable prices...

Fifty miles from the border with Nicaragua, North found a perfectly suitable site in Costa Rica for Contra operations. It was a large farm, whose owner, a certain John Hull, was a fervent supporter of giving aid to the Contras. Hull had dual nationality, American and Costa Rican, and there were no difficulties in encouraging him to sell a part of his farm.

For five million dollars, Secord offered North secret installations, with the code name Plantation, comprising a 6,000 feet long airstrip with a hard-packed surface, an open hangar and a building capable of accommodating thirty people.

The only disadvantage was that the terrain was highly visible from planes beginning their descent to San Jose international airport, in the capital of Costa Rica.

When the installations of Plantation were put into place, North and Secord started looking for tactical cargo planes. Both men first of all considered buying planes from the Venezuelan army. This option was swiftly abandoned.

Two DHC Caribou and one C-123K were finally bought in the United States, in the name of Corporate Air Services, an umbrella company managed by Secord. Several other small light aircraft completed the fleet, including a Maule M-5 bought for 65,000 dollars by an American businessman and given directly to North.

Nine pilots, three loadmasters and seven engineers were then recruited by the same company, based in Pennsylvania. The salary, 3,000 dollars per month all expenses paid, was adequate, but not astronomical. It was nonetheless six times the amount that Gomez's men received, the 'authentic' Contras, which would create a little jealousy...

Secord's choice of pilots had always been very good, and they all had experience.

The chief pilot, William Cooper, had 25,000 flying hours under his belt and had been the chief pilot of the Air America C-123s which were based at Udorn in Thailand at the end of the sixties. His assistant John McRainey had 19,000 flying hours behind him. Like all the other navigators, with the exception of the Englishmen in the crew, he was also an Air America veteran.

When he was contacted by Secord to participate in the programme, McRainey called one of his friends in the CIA to learn a little more: "We are aware of this operation", replied his contact "but it's not really one of ours. Be careful John..."

The CIA was totally aware of what North and Secord were preparing and little wonder : William Casey, the director of the CIA, had received Secord shortly before Christmas 1985. Casey had asked to be given an assessment of the situation in Nicaragua : "The Contras have no possible chance unless they have logistical aid, from an airlift which will support them in the field and enable them to launch long term operations of some depth" replied Secord.

To bring ammunition and food to the troops that were fighting on the northern border was a start, but it was not enough. Secord doubted in fact the capability of the Contras to bring about a military victory over the Sandinistas without opening up a second front, in the south, from Costa Rica. Despite Congress prohibiting this, the CIA had to be able to help in one way or another, why not by supplying intelligence? Casey took note of this.

FIRST MISSIONS

The planes were based in El Salvador, on the base of Ilopango, the old international airport converted into a military base. The negotiation with the Salvadoran authorities had been carried out speedily thanks to a surprising character, veteran of the Bay of Pigs, American citizen of Cuban descent, also Lieutenant Colonel in the Salvadoran Air Force! The crews were housed in three villas in the Colonia Escalon, in the desirable part of San Salvador.

A first aircraft, a DHC Caribou, was to arrive at Ilopango in February 1986. But the plane had a problem with one of its engines en route. To try and lighten the plane which was rapidly losing altitude, the crew decided to jettison all its load which was situated in the bay. This included a new spare engine which would have been better positioned under the wing rather than in the bay...

These desperate efforts were not enough and the plane had to crash, causing a good deal of unwanted press coverage.

In March 1986, the Sandinistas launched a general offensive, operation Dante, against Contra camps in Honduran territory.

At the instigation of the United States itself, Honduras requested military support from the Americans, support which materialized without delay. Thirteen thousand Marines landed on the Honduran base of Palmerola and remained there for two weeks, ready to intervene if the situation at the border deteriorated. During this time, the US Army transported a Honduran infantry battalion to the main routes of Nicaraguan penetration.

The CIA observed with interest the development of fighting on the border. A pilot from the Agency was seriously injured in an accident in his helicopter.

In the forty-eight hours following the beginning of the offensive, the planes of Project Democracy were used to attend to the most urgent things first and resupply the Contras who were attempting to stop the

Sandinistas. In the space of three days, between the 24th and 27th of March, more than a dozen flights were carried out to Aguacate.

The planes of Southern Air Transport (SAT) were also used on several occasions to parachute provisions and medicines while the Hondurans, benefiting in other respects from the US Army, lent four of their helicopters to the Contras.

In 1986, SAT worked on a regular basis with the Pentagon to transport soldiers and materials on US soil. It worked also on behalf of the State Department, carrying out a flight to Havana every month. Ironically, the same contract was used as a legal cover to carry out deliveries to Honduras, this time for the Contras. SAT was at that time a prosperous company with 600 employees, operating eight Boeing 707 and seventeen Lockheed L-100s. The SAT planes were sent to Aguacate, in Honduras to bring humanitarian aid. The official part of their mission having been executed, it was planned that the L-100s would make the most of their presence in Aguacate and load up with arms and ammunition and bring them back to Ilopango, in El Salvador. The material would have been repacked in Ilopango to be in a condition to be parachuted to the Contras on the southern front.

The airstrip of Plantation was not yet ready, and would not be before Spring and the planes had to be capable of making a return trip to El Salvador without a stopover. Because of their range, the SAT L-100 were the only planes capable of carrying out this work.

In the last days of May, the first mission, with little or no preparation behind it, was a failure before it had even begun.

One SAT L-100 from Washington was bringing humanitarian aid to the base at Aguacate. This was the official mission of the aircraft and up to that point everything had gone well. But when the time came to load the weapons on to the aircraft for them to be taken back to Ilopango, it did not go as planned:

"On our arrival at Aguacate, we realised that there was nobody waiting for us", recalls a member of the SAT crew. "No load was ready, the CIA men present were not aware of anything." The plane took off for Ilopango empty. The Contras in the field inside Nicaragua were forewarned of the cancellation of the drop at the very last minute.

A second attempt took place on the 9th of April with another L-100 from SAT. The material to be parachuted had this time been brought directly from New Orleans. The plane took off from Ilopango and headed for the south of Nicaragua. But when it arrived at the DZ, the crew could not establish radio contact with the Contras on the ground. The plane returned to Ilopango.

The third attempt, on the following day, was successful. The load was dropped and picked up by the Contras. Five or six of these parachute missions were carried out in total.

But generally speaking, the air transport operations for the Contras did not work well : numerous missions were unproductive mainly because of poor coordination between the various participants.

SMALL PROBLEMS AND BIG SNAGS

On the following 20th of April, Secord and North went to El Salvador to meet with the pilots of Project Democracy and the Contra leaders.

The leaders, who had been able to witness the L-100s of SAT in operation, complained bitterly of the age of the cargo planes which had been put at their disposal.

"If we had more money we would have bought some L-100s" North explained to them. "But there wasn't enough cash for that..."

"The planes were given to you and you have to make the best of them", he added.

It was a strange slip of the tongue. If the planes were indeed at the service of the Contras, they did not belong to them in any way : they were the property of Secord and his web of commercial companies. The meeting ended with North promising

to expend even more effort to activate the southern front.

It took a while before the operation started.

The airstrip of the Plantation posed a great many problems for its designers : its realization was slapdash, it had insufficient drainage and when the first C-123K landed in the month of June, during the rainy season, it got bogged down in the mud. One week later, the drainage problems seemed to have been resolved somewhat and a first mission to the south of Nicaragua was planned. Unfortunately the Contras in the field could not be contacted in time and the parachute drop was cancelled.

Several days later, the only available C-123 deviated from its course during a resupply mission, apparently because of faulty navigation equipment. Flying in the mist, the plane got stuck in some trees at the top of a mountain and, by some miracle,escaped crashing. With one engine out of action, it was only just able to reach the secret airstrip.

Secord therefore decided to buy a second C-123 and two new engines for the first aircraft.

This did not stop the pilots, among them the two who had only just escaped death, from complaining in the strongest terms about the poor maintenance of the aircraft. The damaged C-123K was sent to SAT installations in Florida to be completely overhauled, while a second plane was rapidly found in Tucson, Arizona. At the end of June, the second C-123 had been brought back to Ilopango, ready for action.

June was also the month when Secord's men brought off the first resupply mission of the southern front. A Caribou took off from Ilopango with four pallets of arms and ammunition in the bay. The drop was successful, but the range of the aircraft, which had lost several vital minutes situating the DZ, proved to be barely enough. Short of fuel, the Caribou did not have the opportunity to land as planned on the Plantation terrain. Instead of that, it went to land at San Jose international airport, which had the result of angering the Costa Ricans greatly.

The Ambassador of the United States was used to try and calm them down. The incident was repeated several weeks later when, once again, a Caribou was forced to land at San Jose, short of fuel.

The missions continued also on the northern front but at a fairly slow pace. The idea of resupplying the Contras by air was not compatible with local conditions, a fact which neither Secord nor North had anticipated.

The drop zones were particularly difficult to find in the jungle. When, in spite of all the difficulties, the plane showed up at the right place at the right time, it turned out that the Contras did not always have the ground signals and the radio codes ready at the right time. The Contras also had a terrible lack of training for guiding the planes.

It should be added that the ground troops did not speak English and the pilots had not mastered Spanish. There was also much confusion between miles and kilometres. Several drops went totally wrong because of these futile reasons.

Therefore a new arrangement was conceived to avoid aircraft having to return to their base without being able to drop their loads : the material would be dropped in well-defined zones, the map reference of which would be given to the Contras in the field. The idea was not put into practice : going into the jungle to pick up parachute drops that could be seen arriving was a difficult enough pastime, it did not need complicating any further!

For reasons of security, principally to avoid a sudden meeting with a Sandinista missile, the crews preferred to fly over Nicaragua at night. But the inadequacies of their navigation system did not allow it. They had to be able to identify drop zones by sight. One solution would have been to fly at dawn or dusk: but apart from the fact that these periods of the day were so brief in this region, the existence of the rainy season conflicted with this idea. There were thick morning mists which hid the ground. As for the end of the day, it was mostly a time of great storm activity.

Despite these difficulties, Project Democracy had reached an honourable pace. Secord was supervising a fairly large aerial fleet, including a C-123K, two Caribou, one DC-3, two DC-6 and several light single engine planes.

The change of government which took place in May 1986 in Costa Rica changed slightly the deal for the Contras. The new government, very determined to make the neutrality of the country respected, was particularly exasperated by the accident of a DC-6 loaded with weapons which crashed in the south of Nicaragua, only a few minutes after having taken off from a secret terrain. Faced with the general outcry that the accident provoked, Secord was forced to stop activities from Costa Rica and evacuate Plantation.

On the following 3rd of September, the Costa Rican authorities officially occupied the terrain, neutralizing the airstrip and prohibiting access to installations. They would also have made the existence of a secret base public, if it were not for the last minute intervention of the American ambassador at San Jose which made them reverse their decision.

In 1986 the Contras were in top form and their boldness was becoming a cause for concern for Managua. The Contra Air Force was also at a very high point. It employed a hundred or so people, including twenty pilots. These planes were able to support logistically the columns that were infiltrating deep into Sandinista territory.

On the 19th of July 1986, Contra planes launched an attack (once more) on the town of Santa Clara which housed the Sandinista cadet school. The Contras shouted victory : under the rubble a Cuban general, four Algerian colonels and forty or so Sandinista cadets and troops were found. To continue the efforts embarked upon with the Contras, North estimated his immediate financial needs to be in the region of 10 million dollars For the planes, Secord needed high-performance and costly navigation systems, as well as weather radars.

The aid from Saudi Arabia was used up by the end of March. The country had been very generous in 1985, but there was little chance that it would be repeated in 1986. It became imperative to find another generous donor to finish the year. This benefactor was the Sultan of Brunei whose country was a minuscule yet wealthy state, very rich in oil, situated in the China sea.

Brunei agreed to donate 10 million dollars to the Contras, settling for the sincere and secret thanks of Ronald Reagan, the American people and the Contra fighters in return.

But history shows that sometimes events can take unusual turns, which are not mapped out in the minds of men. The Sultan of Brunei was an example of this : his transfer of 10 million dollars was to have been into a Swiss bank account, the number of which had been written, by hand, on a visiting card given to an emissary. The transfer was carried out in mid-August 1986.

Several weeks went by without the Americans receiving any money. Little wonder!

Oliver North's secretary, who had copied the account number onto the visiting card, had unfortunately reversed two figures. The mountain of dollars from Brunei had landed in the account of an honest Swiss doctor!

The mystery was solved only after several weeks of uncertainty on both sides. A mystery which could have soured relations between Washington and Brunei somewhat!

A change of opinion meanwhile had showed itself to be against the Sandinistas and Congress had approved an aid package of 100 million dollars to the Contras, 27 million dollars of which was allotted to humanitarian actions. Immediately afterwards, the CIA was officially authorized to resume its assistance to the Contras.

By coincidence, this aid arrived shortly after Southern Air Transport doubled its fleet of Lockheed L-100, by buying back twelve aircraft from the Transamerican Airlines company which had ceased commercial activity in the Autumn of 1986. It was pointed out that this doubling of its capacity came at the right time to ensure the distribution of 100 million dollars of aid. The SAT advertisement in the yellow pages of the Miami telephone directory specified very aptly "deliveries to isolated areas."

The vote of Congress re-established the CIA in its prerogative of 'conspirator' and North and Secord looked into the possibility of integrating their operation into those of the CIA.

The assets of Project Democracy comprised not only six cargo planes, maintenance workshops, several tons of diverse supplies, but also the gunboats which had attacked Nicaraguan ports, transmission equipment and an airstrip in Costa Rica. For the latter, it is true that the arrival of the new Costa Rican government had rather complicated things...

The only aerial equipment was estimated at 4.5 million dollars. North planned to sell this material to the CIA, or possibly even loan it for a little more than 300,000 dollars a month. Circumstances prevented either one of these possibilities from happening.

EUGENE GOES PARACHUTING

On Sunday the 5th of October 1986 a C-123K, bearing a Panamanian registration number, took off from the air base at Ilopango at early dawn. Its mission was to take it to the south of Nicaragua, where it was to supply a contra Maquis. The code name of the ground reception team was Sophia. The markers identifying the drop zone were to be five smoke bombs arranged in an 'L' shape.

At the controls of the plane was William "Bill" Cooper, the man with 25,000 flying hours behind him, the chief pilot of Project Democracy. Sitting on his right in the cockpit was his co-pilot, Wallace "Buz" Sawyer. Buz was at the controls of the Caribou which had carried out the first drop on the southern front, several months earlier. Behind the cockpit, two men had made themselves as comfortable as they could in the cold, noisy cabin. One was a Nicaraguan Contra, the other Eugene "Gus" Hasenfus, an American.

Soon after take off, the plane began a wide turn to the left to head south. Fifteen minutes later, having reached the Atlantic ocean, it again turned to the left to head for Nicaragua. On the distant horizon, slightly to the left of the plane, the sun was just beginning to rise. Their sun glasses attached firmly to their nose, the two men in the cockpit talked about this and that. Fifteen thousand feet below on their left was the coast of Nicaragua. In less than three hours they would be back in San Salvador. Sawyer said he would go for a dip in the pool at the Hotel Presidente. Cooper would head for the bar. Hasenfus came to have a look in the cockpit.

"Where are we?"

"We'll reach the border of Nicaragua and Costa Rica in eight minutes. We'll begin our descent and you can start to unstrap the pallets."

Hasenfus went back to let the other dispatcher know. A meticulous character, he put on his parachute and attached it carefully.

At the appointed hour the plane arrived above the southern border of Nicaragua. "Let's go!" said Cooper.

The plane left the relative protection of the altitude and the sea, came tumbling down several hundred feet above the waves and took the direction of the shore. In a few more seconds it would penetrate Nicaraguan territory, several miles from the northern border of Costa Rica.

On board the plane, the men were a little tense, but confident. It was not their first time and they knew that they had nothing to fear from enemy fighters which were non-existent. Their only worry came from portable SA-7 anti-aircraft missiles. The Sandinistas had several hundred of these in their possession, and an attack was always a possibility.

The plane had already flown sixty miles or so in Sandinista territory, and it was nearing the drop zone. The pilot made one last turn to the north-east, towards the town of San Carlos. A horn sounded to warn the two dispatchers to get ready to push out the first pallets. Through the wide open rear ramp, the two dispatchers saw the forest pass beneath them, several hundred feet below.

The tension of the first few minutes had disappeared, and Cooper concentrated on flying, not thinking about the potential danger of missiles. He was flying in a straight line, without fear, and without taking any preventive, evasive manoeuvres.

The Sandinista patrol had been advancing for a little more than an hour when the plane was spotted. It was coming from the south and was heading towards San Carlos. Its flight-path was going to take it almost directly above the men on the ground.

A young soldier of 19 put the SA-7 missile, that he had been carrying on his back for several days, on his shoulder. Up until then he had never fired a real missile, but in Managua, on the range simulator, he had been told that he was a good shot. In a few seconds the heavy, twin-engine plane was above him. The marksman waited calmly for it to pass over, counted to three, aimed at the target which was slowly getting further away and fired his missile. Guided by its infra-red sensor, the SA-7 had no difficulty in finding the heat of one of the two engines of the C-123.

After a flight of less than two seconds, the missile exploded against the right engine, tearing the right wing of the C-123 which toppled over to the left as a result. A fraction of a second later, the right wing was torn from the fuselage because of structural stress and the plane fell to the ground, spiralling as it did so like some grotesque toy.

Eugene Hasenfus, 45, dispatcher, ex-Marine, was holding on near the ramp when the explosion happened. He had always taken care, since Laos, not to take any unnecessary risks. He wore a parachute systematically during the drop phases, a habit which saved his life this day.

Without hesitating a single second, Hasenfus had plunged into the void the moment he felt the plane roll over on its wing. By the time he had felt the smack of the wind against his face, pulled the handle and found himself stunned - but alive - under the canopy of the parachute, the C-123 that a few seconds earlier had been transporting him had already disintegrated on Nicaraguan soil.

When the plane hit the ground several miles away from them, the soldiers cried out for joy. But when they saw the parachute float down a little further away, they stopped congratulating themselves and headed off to find the Gringo who had survived.

Hasenfus was found 24 hours later, hiding in an abandoned hut. Even though he had an automatic pistol, he offered no resistance and was rapidly taken to San Carlos. The next day, he was transported by helicopter to Managua where, looking rather haggard, he made a brief statement to the press :

"My name is Eugene Hasenfus. I come from Marinette in Wisconsin. I was captured yesterday in the south of Nicaragua. Thank you."

A short while before, he had told the Sandinistas what he sincerely believed to be the truth, not knowing the real nature of the instigators of the flights :

"The plane which was shot down was part of a CIA operation. There were four men on board and I am the only survivor."

The reality of the situation was more complex. But this statement came at an opportune moment for some troubling questions to be asked concerning the exact role of the United States and the CIA, since Congress had forbidden all aid to the Contras in 1984.

If it was not an official CIA operation, then the agency was certainly aware of its existence as it had approved, indeed supported it. Project Democracy had been a perfect temporary campaign, while the CIA waited for a legal return to the Nicaraguan theatre of operation.

The Hasenfus affair caused an earthquake in Washington. The White House denied any official participation by the United States. The CIA also denied any involvement. These denials were repeated before Congress.

North, meanwhile, was trying to deal with the most urgent things first : the second C-123 was being repaired in a Southern Air Transport workshop in Miami. It had to be hastily finished and flown to El Salvador before the law started to get too interested in the activities of SAT.

SAT was also the old owner of the shot down plane, but also the ex employer of the two pilots that were killed. The link, indirect as it was, of the plane with the CIA, was not just limited to this coincidence : the DEA (Drug Enforcement Administration) confirmed that the destroyed plane was the one that in 1984 the CIA had used to show that the Sandinistas were involved in international drug trafficking. Hidden cameras, installed by the CIA in the bay of the plane, had filmed an official from the Nicaraguan Ministry of the Interior loading sacks of cocaine into the plane.

During his second presentation to the press, Hasenfus, who the Nicaraguans called proudly 'the first American prisoner of war', made a ten-minute statement :

The organization that he was responsible to, Corporate Air Services, employed about twenty-five people in San Salvador. It was managed by two Americans of Cuban descent working for the CIA and known by their pseudonyms, Max Gomez and Ramon Medina. These two men prepared the flight plans of the resupply missions.

"I was recruited by William Cooper, an old friend from Air America in Laos. Cooper pointed out that he was working for Corporate Air Services and he invited me to join him..."

Another 'coincidence', which this affair had plenty of, Corporate Air Services shared the same address as SAT at Miami airport...Hasenfus acknowledged having been paid 3,000 dollars, plus expenses, like all the other crew members. He also acknowledged having carried out ten flights over Nicaragua :

"Four from Aguacate in Honduras and six from Ilopango in El Salvador."

The Salvadoran President, Napoleon Duarte, pathetically denied the evidence which implicated his country. The thorough search of the wreck of the plane was very fruitful for the Sandinistas. They found dozens of Kalashnikovs, more than a hundred thousand cartridges,combat uniforms, jungle boots, but also the bodies of the crew, including the two Americans. Managua had plenty of clues to suggest the direct involvement of the United States.

The flight log book found in one of the pockets of the co-pilots, Buz Sawyer, 41, showed that he had previously flown for SAT, on behalf of the American DOD. Sawyer was in fact an 'independent' who had worked for SAT, Seaspray and the CIA. His notebook contained the other flights carried out for the Contras, detailing the names of the crew members, mostly ex SAT also. A flight log book, useful during the normal course of events, was not meant for use in secret operations.

At the time of his death, Cooper was also carrying two small red notebooks which confirmed Hasenfus's statements. These notebooks showed that Cooper, apart from the ten missions with Hasenfus, had also carried out 18 other flights from Honduras or El Salvador.

Other elements enabled the threads of operation Project Democracy to be untangled a little more.

The bodies also had Salvadoran Air Force identity documents showing them as military technical advisers. An examination of telephone calls made from the villas at Colonia Escalon, where the crews were lodged, enabled the ends of the threads to be followed...to the office of North and the White House.

Americans and Salvadorans denied any official participation in these missions. But the proof in the hands of the Sandinistas was really damning. Hasenfus had also revealed to his captors that the Corporate Air Services had a warehouse filled with several dozen tons of arms and ammunition at Ilopango. There was little chance that a 'purely private enterprise' according to references made by the White House and the CIA, would have use of such facilities in El Salvador. The smallest country in central America was a victim of a civil war and thus received an annual aid of 500 million dollars from the United States. For this price, Washington as well as Langley were perfectly aware of everything that was going on in the country...

The trial of Hasenfus, which started on the 20th of October 1986, ended a few days later with him being sentenced to thirty years in prison for terrorism and violation of public order. This was the maximum penalty under the Nicaraguan legal system.

While all eyes were on central America another, equally confusing, game was being played in the Middle East.

At the end of 1984 and throughout the following months, a dozen Americans had been taken hostage by the pro-Iranian Hezbollah in Lebanon. Among these hostages was William Buckley, head of the CIA base in Beirut.

The freeing of these hostages rapidly became a major preoccupation, not to say obsession, of the White House. An obsession which eighteen months later gave birth to one of the greatest scandals of the Reagan presidency, Irangate.

Desperate at not being able to free their hostages, the Americans appealed directly to Teheran, going as far as offering the sale of missiles to the Islamic state, as a sign of good will. At the same time on the international stage, the United States was the standard-bearer of the embargo against Iran, who was accused of spreading international terrorism.

In this affair, Israel was used as a buffer state and a circuit breaker. President Reagan authorized the sale by Israel of spare parts for combat aircraft and TOW anti-tank missiles to Iran. At the same time, the Pentagon undertook to complete Israeli stocks, and added without doubt a good percentage. The system was simple and effective, and everyone was happy with it.

The Israelis had already dipped into a good number of doubtful affairs with the United States. They had widely intervened in the Contra affair, not only by sending instructors to the area, but also in supplying weapons of Soviet, Chinese or North Korean origin recuperated from the PLO during the invasion of Lebanon in 1982. These weapons had been paid for by the Americans in the form of discounts on the sale of combat aircraft.

Once again, the National Security Council, in liaison with the CIA, played a pivotal role in the affair. And again, Lieutenant-Colonel Oliver North, responsible for setting up the logistics, was the kingpin within the NSC.

In August 1985, the Israelis sought the agreement of the United States before sending the consignments to Iran. They received the green light.

Two deliveries were organized in September 1985, rapidly followed by a third flight in early October. A DC-8 cargo plane unloaded several dozen TOW anti-tank and Hawk anti-aircraft missiles onto the terrain at Tabriz. Another consignment arrived by plane in November, before the deliveries by sea took over.

At the same time, the charter company Santa Lucia airways, which was also to be active between the United States and Zaire delivering arms to UNITA, was used to 'complete' Israeli stocks.

The transaction was completely secret and could only be done with the collaboration of a private company, which was very attached to the American secret service.

Two Boeing 707 were chartered for the transport of several dozen missiles to Israel. Subsequent revelations in the press concerning the links between the airline company and the CIA led Santa Lucia airways to break off its activity several months later, after an existence of twelve years.

But the day when this happened, a new company appeared, Caribbean Air Transport. Was it quite by chance that the latter took both the crews and the planes, three Boeing 707 and on Lockheed L-100, from Santa Lucia under its wings?

From the month of December 1985, North worked to use the results from the sale of the missiles for the use of the Contras. The mechanism which was to lead to the Irangate scandal was thus put methodically in place. But finally, the sale to the Iranians brought back scarcely twelve million dollars to the Contras, a third of which, at the very most, was earmarked for air operations. The rest, estimated at several tens of millions of dollars, found itself lining the pockets of intermediaries, evaporating in Swiss bank accounts...

The traffic continued throughout 1986 : a first direct consignment of missiles took place in February. The Pentagon transferred five hundred TOW missiles to the CIA who in turn undertook to transport them to Israel. There the missiles changed planes and continued their voyage to Iran. The manoeuvre was repeated twice throughout May.

In the summer of 1986, going totally against the decision of Congress, the first weapons bought with Iranian money were parachuted to the Contras of the FDN.

During this time the deliveries continued : 23 tons of missiles and spare parts arrived in Iran on the 4th of July 1986, American Independence day. It was the penultimate consignment, the last one taking place in November, meanwhile news of the scandal was beginning to filter through to the public.

The CIA learnt furthermore that three businessmen, who claimed to have lost 10 million dollars serving as intermediaries in the sale of arms to the Iranians, threatened to bring legal action against the American government. The affair was starting to smell and Casey warned North who destroyed the most compromising documents he had in his possession.

It was at this point that the Iranians started to let everything out to the press, with a certain pleasure. The same operation had allowed them to skirt round the arms embargo and put the American government, the great Satan, in serious difficulty.

Ronald Reagan denied having sold arms to the Iranians in exchange for the release of the hostages. The great communicator got in a muddle with his statements, multiplying the semantic contortions.

His press conference on the 19th of November 1986 has gone down in the annals of history. He started with this declaration, astounding from a man who had been at the instigation of an embargo against Iran:

"...To eliminate this widespread yet false idea that claims we exchanged arms for hostages, I have requested that no other sale of arms, of any nature, be made to Iran."

The sale of arms to Iran was therefore admitted, but secret within a secret, the fact that the money from these sales was given to the Contras still remained hidden. Not for much longer however.

The truth broke out at the end of the month of November. The United States had therefore infringed the embargo by selling arms to Iran, they had trampled the sacred principle of non-negotiation with the terrorists underfoot, by trying to exchange arms for hostages. But in addition they had flouted the decisions of Congress by secretly financing the Contras with the money obtained.

And all that for what result apart from lining the pockets of a few intermediaries?

More than 2,000 TOW missiles, 2,008 to be precise, were delivered to the Iranians, as well as 235 Hawk anti-aircraft missiles and several tons of spare parts. In Beirut, three hostages had been released, but at the same time others had been captured!

Buckley, the CIA station head was without doubt dead by the summer of 1986, after several months of torture. The CIA learnt from a reliable source that his debriefing had provided the Hezbollah with a report more than four hundred pages long on its pursuits in Lebanon. The activities of the CIA in the region were seriously destabilized.

The hundred million dollars worth of aid voted in the summer of 1986, or at the very least the seventy million for military purposes, was immediately postponed by the scandal of Irangate. The allocation of the remaining budget was influenced by the application of a new clause: any new aid could not be used less than 20 miles from the Nicaraguan border. This meant particularly that CIA air operations from Aguacate had to be moved to Swan island, a minuscule American islet off Honduras in the Caribbean.

Even though the Sandinistas were holding their own from a military point of view, the discontentment among the population, tired of ten years of fighting and deprivation, was growing. This situation forced the Sandinistas to show proof of their open-mindedness. At the same time, the Soviet Union was clearly multiplying the signs of military disengagement. Pragmatic as ever, the Sandinistas therefore engaged in negotiations with the Contras from which a ceasefire emerged then, in August 1989, a political agreement. The Contras for their part undertook to carry out a precise plan of demobilization.

The last air operations of the Contras were made under the watchful eye of AID officials, to whom Congress had given the responsibility of supervising non-military aid. In the last months of the war, the Contras lost a DC-6 (which ran out of fuel), a Dakota and a twin-engine light Beechcraft.

The elections which took place in February 1990 established the victory of the anti-Sandinista coalition backed by the United States and pushed the Sandinistas to the opposition. On the following 27th of June, noticing the democratic evolution of the country, the Contra chiefs of staff wound down and officially laid down their arms. From then on, the CIA as well as the White House, at that time occupied by George

Bush, seemed to be disinterested in the country. The spasmodic rebirth of new Contra movements, disappointed by the slowness of reforms, met with no real response in Washington, only a condamnation.

For its part the American intelligence agency seemed to have turned another page in its history, the last one in the chapter of the Cold War.

CHAPTER 9

THE U-2, CREATURE OF THE CIA

AN UNAPPEASED NEED

Apart from the multiplication of increasingly heavy clandestine operations, the all powerful CIA had found, during the Cold War, an opening in the development of highly sophisticated sensors. This was not referring to cameras or spy microphones that are so precious in the classic secret agents paraphernalia. The Intelligence Agency launched itself into different, extraordinarily ambitious, aeronautical programmes.

The incredible thing was that they were nearly all successful.

Faced with the mitigated successes of the clandestine operations that were undertaken world-wide, the success of these programmes made the agency and the people in charge particularly happy!

The first programme was that of the U-2 aeroplane.

In March 1953 the head of the CIA, Allen Dulles, plainly admitted the serious weak points of the CIA opposite the USSR. The Central, without a doubt, had no important network in the country and, from the following year, the parachuting of agents into Soviet territory was stopped, due to the lack of results obtained.

"We mustn't stop trying" Allen Dulles noted. A sentiment that was shared by Dwight Eisenhower, the president of the United States at that time.

A CIA station was set up at Moscow, which had not been done before because of the State Departments opposition. The result was poor. Carrying out intelligence work in the USSR was not an easy job.

During these years, when observation satellites were still only in engineers dreams, Eisenhower bitterly complained about the lack of information available concerning the number one enemy, the Soviet Union.

The only thing possible was to 'probe' the length of the USSR borders, this was carried out as from 1949. Hundreds of flights were sent, with special electronics sensors aboard. The planes sometimes crossed over the border and then 'lost' their way directly over Soviet territory. But these aircraft, which most of the time were only US Air Force bombers converted for this use, were extremely vulnerable to the Russian fighters. The development of a tightly linked radar network, coupled to efficient interceptor units, allowed the Soviets to quickly put a stop to this practice.

A few bitter failures punctuated these operations on the American side : in 1950 and 1951, two electronic eavesdropping aircraft, with a dozen men on board, were shot down while trying to gather a few bits of information along the Baltic coast. In 1956, the toll was a dozen US Air Force and US Navy aircraft damaged or destroyed by the Russian fighters. Eighty crew members were reported missing, presumed dead. According to certain sources, a few dozen had been captured alive and more than twenty of them were still in the hands of the Soviets at the end of the 1980's.

The situation was not a very pleasant one for the Americans in charge, who soon had to severely reduce these missions, the aircraft that were used had become too vulnerable.

Eisenhower, who had been the Supreme Allied Commander during the Second World War, frequently made references to the importance of strategic reconnaissance above the European and Pacific theatres of operation at the end of the war.

The explosion of the first Soviet Hydrogen Bomb in August 1953, nine months after the American one, added to their frustration : no information had been given to the Americans about the progress of the work being carried out.

The next year, the presentation of new strategic bombers during the traditional Ist of May parade at Red Square, sent a wind of panic through the Pentagon : not only did the Russians have the H-bomb, but they had the means to transport it to American territory...

The US Air Force also had H-bombs and strategic bombers to deliver them. But the problem was to find and make a list of enough objectives on Soviet ground to justify the construction of a thousand B-47 strategic bombers.

The knowledge of the USSR was so bad that the Air Force embarked onto desperate programmes to try and erase its ignorance.

An attempt was made using balloons. The idea was to let go of balloons, equipped with automatic cameras, at high altitude, then to let them float over the USSR, pushed along by the strong air currents that usually went from the West to the East. Five launch sites were selected from Norway to Turkey, whilst the balloons were to be picked up in the

320

Far East after having crossed the width of the workers Paradise.

More than 500 balloons were launched, but only about forty were able to be picked up by the Americans. About 14,000 photos of the Soviet Union were taken, but they were of poor quality and not of much interest. The CIA found this programme idiotic and asked, with insistence, for it to be stopped, which it finally was.

The Air Force went back to more practical considerations and launched a programme of high performance reconnaissance planes. The aircraft had to be capable of crossing Soviet territory in all immunity, so as to bring back potential industrial objectives. To be able to do this it had to be able to fly as high as 70,000 feet, while carrying 350kg of cameras and film. No defence armament was asked for, the high altitude was to be the aircraft's greatest protection. At 70,000 feet the US Air Force counted upon the fact that its aircraft would be out of reach of the opposing air defence and, anyway, practically undetectable by the radars.

Three constructors were in for the competition, but finally it was a fourth one, Lockheed, that won the contract.

Lockheed had gained the information about the needs of the US Air Force quite by chance, at any rate in a very informal way, from rumours. In fact the Californian constructor already had such a project in the pipe line.

This project was thus presented to the US Air Force, in the meantime the latter had already pronounced that it favoured the firm Martin who proposed a modified version of the B-57 bomber. The Lockheed project also presented some crippling inconveniences in the eyes of the military, for example, the idea of having the plane take off on a wagon and then to land on its belly.

The Lockheed engineers did not give up and modified the study. Then, instead of knocking once again at the US Air Force's door, they had the intuition to propose the aeroplane directly to the CIA who, they thought, could have some need for this kind of material.

The idea paid off.

THE CIA GRABS THE OPPORTUNITY

Extremely frustrated about not being able to obtain information about the Soviet Nuclear programme via the US Air Force, the intelligence agency tried to find ways of developing its own system of reconnaissance.

The Lockheed proposition came just at the right time.

It offered the CIA the possibility to propel itself to the head of the race in collecting information. For Allen Dulles it was an opportunity not to let slip past.

The project was submitted to Eisenhower. The thought of possessing an aircraft capable of shamelessly flying over the USSR to bring back pictures filled the American President with enthusiasm, who immediately gave the go ahead to launch the programme. In the absence of information on the Soviet military programmes the United States were haunted by the idea that an atomic Pearl Harbour was possible. At Eisenhower's request a commission, made up of well known scientists, had been set up not long before hand, with the objective of studying the different ways possible of having some kind of warning against a surprise attack by the USSR.

But, in an amazing foresight of what was to happen a few years later, Eisenhower warned against being too enthusiastic :

"I think that our country needs this kind of information and I approve this project of reconnaissance flights. But I am warning you, one of these days one of these planes is going to be caught. When that happens we're going to have a hell of a problem on our hands..."

Always with the thought that one day things could go wrong, Eisenhower categorically refused the possibility of letting someone from the US Air Force fly one of the aircraft.

"If such an aircraft was to be shot down whilst it was flying over the Soviet Union, I'd prefer it to be a civilian aircraft with a civilian pilot, the provocation would then be slightly less in the eyes of the Communists..."

Another consideration weighed heavily in the decision to take away the responsibility of the flights over the Soviet Union from the US Air Force : Eisenhower, like other intelligence analysts, was worried that if the US Air Force had the monopoly of military information it would

322

change the analyses and exaggerate the Soviet menace, so as to justify an increase in its budget.

The CIA was therefore given the control of the undertaking of the project, christened Aquatone, as well as putting into action the planes that were needed in the future. On the terms of sharing the responsibilities, the US Air Force had to be content with assuring technical support and it abandoned its own project of reconnaissance planes.

This situation did not help to ease the relationship between these two government agencies.

EIGHT MONTHS TO CREATE THE U-2

The aeroplane, that the CIA called 'The Article', was thought up by the Skunk Work, the Lockheed research department that specialised in dirty tricks. Under the direction of a certain Clarence "Kelly" Johnson, engineer of genius and the author of numerous extraordinary projects, the Skunk Work also had to its credit the first American prototype of the jet engine fighter, that had been conceived in 1943 in less than five months. The Skunk Work is also famous today for having conceived the F-117, the first stealth aeroplane to have known a large operational use, notably during the Gulf War.

The Skunk Work had promised to construct the aeroplane in less than eight months and the promise was kept. The chronometer was started on the 9th of December 1954, when the CIA signed the contract to buy the first batch of twenty planes. The financing, 54 million dollars to start off with, came from the CIA's secret funds, whilst the US Air Force took care of the perfecting and fabrication of the jet engines.

The project was placed under the responsibility of Richard Bissel of the CIA.

Bissel led the operations with a masters hand.

To mislead the Communist Intelligence Services the aeroplane was baptised the U-2, the letter U signifying 'Utility' in the US Air Force designation code. The U-2 was initially presented as a study aircraft to be used to collect certain data for another Lockheed prototype, the F-104 Starfighter. After that the services of NACA, NASA's ancestor, were called upon to accredit the idea that the U-2 was only a meteorological research plane, used to study the upper layers of the atmosphere.

Because of the low power given out by the jet engines at very high altitude, due to the short supply of air, the aeroplane had to be as light as possible. All the defining work of the prototype was based around this major constraint.

It was calculated that the chosen jet engine, an adaptation of the Pratt and Whitney J-57, when at the maximum altitude of 70,000 ft, would provide only 7% of the available power at sea level. This was considered as satisfactory, enough anyway to keep the plane in a horizontal flight without it breaking away.

But the margin for manoeuvre was very narrow : the maximum speed of the aeroplane at its highest altitude would not exceed 12 mph, the break away speed. The pilots nicknamed this narrow speed slot as "coffin corner".

Everything was tried to minimise the weight and better the planes performance : the opening of the canopy was manual, the flight commands were not assisted and the first U-2 models were not equipped with an ejectable pilot seat. A few fatal accidents later made Lockheed change their mind over this point.

The pay load was placed behind the cock pit. The apparatus, mainly cameras and electronic recorders, were mounted on interchangeable supports which allowed the aircraft to be rapidly adapted to the needs of the mission to be carried out.

When devising the U-2, the Skunk Work engineers had taken technical choices that were to give the U-2 specific flight characteristics and shape. This consisted notably of a wing of great aspect ratio and single track undercarriage. To ensure its stability on ground, the U-2 was equipped with ballast weights fixed to the end of the wings. Nicknamed 'Pogos', the ballast weights were dropped by the pilot when the aeroplane took off. They were then put back into place at the end of the flight by the ground personnel, when the aeroplane had finished its landing manoeuvre. Although slightly strange, this technique was perfectly feasible and easy to control with a minimum of training.

The U-2s long wings had got the aircraft the usurped reputation of a motorized glider. Nothing was further from the truth : because of its lightness and its powerful motorization, the U-2 was capable of surprising performances at take off and in ascent!

A quick glance in the cockpit, as cluttered as it was ordinary, gave no clues away as to the strategic importance of the plane and of the sophistication of the sensors on board. However two over sized instruments immediately caught the eye : firstly the enormous fly wheel that seemed to have come straight from an airliner cockpit. Its generous dimensions allowed the pilot to continue to manoeuvre it if his suit happened to inflate in the case of depressurization.

Then, standing out on the instrument board, there was the large circular screen of the Driftsight, the "pilots third eye."

Coupled to a sort of periscope looking downwards, the Driftsight allowed the pilot to see everything that was going on underneath his aeroplane. He could use it as a navigation instrument or to identify his objectives as it was possible to enlarge the image four fold. But the mobility of 360° on the objective positioned under the nose of the aeroplane allowed for even more : the pilot could, during the flight, inspect the lower surface of the plane, make sure that he left no condensation trails behind and even, as it actually happened a few times during the career of the aeroplane, observe the interceptors that flew towards the plane vainly flying around a few thousand feet lower.

Even with all its intrinsic qualities the U-2 would never have had the success that it did without the quality of the equipment that it carried on board.

Edwin Land, inventor of the Polaroid film and future Nobel prize winner, joined the scientific commission that Eisenhower set up to guarantee some kind of vigilance opposite the USSR. Land quickly realised the advantage that could be gained from the association of the latest developments in air photography with a very high altitude flying aircraft.

The cameras that were allotted to high altitude reconnaissance were exceptionally cumbersome (the most powerful models were more than thirteen feet high) they could only be installed into the converted bombers. The U-2 was the complete opposite. The space that was available was no more than one cubic metre and the whole of the equipment had to weigh no more than 550 pounds.

In March 1959 Lockheed went as far as modifying the U-2 so as to allow it to drop its 'load' that was placed in the hold that was reserved for the apparatus.

On the subject of loads, it had been thought of using the U-2 to parachute clandestine agents into the heart of the enemy territory, in keeping with the best Carpetbagger traditions. The CIA even tested at high altitude, for the back seat passenger, an ejectable seat that fired down. The idea was soon abandoned.

The progress in the domain of mirror optics and emulsions allowed the apparatus that was conceived for the U-2 to match perfectly with the schedule of conditions, whilst offering a standard detail that was staggering for the era. On the stereoscopic photographs brought back by the first U-2's, details could be identified of less than twenty inches from photos taken from an altitude of nearly 16 miles.

It goes without saying that all this progress was possible because of the enormous amount of funds that the CIA had at its disposition.

GROOM LAKE UNEARTHED

Tony LeVier, Lockheed's head pilot, was naturally called upon to carry out the first trial flights. But the first mission that his boss gave him was of a completely different nature : it consisted of finding a site that was away from inquisitive eyes so as to be able to start the test flights, the existing US Air Force bases did not offer enough guarantees for the CIA.

With a Lockheed technician, LeVier got into the company's Beech Bonanza and set out in search of an adequate site in the Nevada desert.

The matter was so secret that the two men had to explain that they were going for a few days to nearby Mexico to hunt. The height of paranoia (or precaution) was such that they had to dress themselves accordingly before getting into the little aeroplane!

After two weeks comparing the studies, during which they did not kill a single rabbit, LeVier and his associate decided upon Groom Lake, an isolated site practically only accessible by aeroplane.

Groom Lake was then only the dried up bed of a huge lake lost in the middle of the Nevada Desert. In the space of a few weeks a secret base was put together. Forty years on it is still the most secretive of the United States and the cradle of the most weird and wonderful prototypes conceived the other side of the Atlantic.

Only seven months after the signing of the Lockheed contract the first prototype was ready in the Skunk Work workshops in Burbank. The aeroplane was dismantled, put into an US Air Force cargo carrier and taken to the Groom Lake base. After a few weeks work the plane was once again in one piece, the last controls were carried out, ready for the first running tests. Tony LeVier was at the controls.

From then on all the U-2's built at Burbank followed the route. But to preserve the confidentiality of Groom Lake, the flights of the cargo aircraft that took the precious planes in their holds were only carried out at night. A bit nervous because of the strange procedures, the pilots of the big C-124's were guided by radar towards a site that was unknown to everyone. The markings of the secret runway were only lit at the last minute and the amazed pilots saw emerging from the darkness a full scale air field where on their maps only a section of desert was shown.

The crews, who were slightly distressed by the experience, were then asked never to speak of what they had seen......

From the very first running tests the U-2 proved itself to be a very special aeroplane indeed. Tony LeVier thought that he had finished his third high speed running test, he had already pulled the throttle back, when the plane decided to take off after all and left the runway after no more than 1,300 feet! The big aerodynamic lift wing already showed its effectiveness...

Obviously the aeroplane had its own characteristics and this was confirmed during the first real flight on the 4th of August 1955. For Tony LeVier, who was once again at the controls, everything had gone perfectly. The problems arose on landing : the plane simply refused to land.

Each time it was the same scenario : LeVier reduced the fuel, brought the aeroplane above the runway and put down the undercarriage. The plane then took over, choosing to bounce at a few feet above ground forcing the pilot to go round the runway again. The sixth time round the pilot decided to change tactics. The aeroplane was nosed up to the limit of disengagement, brought down to the runway... and stayed there!

During this maiden flight, Tony LeVier had discovered everything that was later to become the 'joy' of several generations of U-2 pilots.

"The U-2 is the most difficult aeroplane to pilot in the world" pilots still like to say. "It's slenderness, that often means it's compared with a glider, makes it an ideal plane in the stratosphere. The aircraft is very smooth and pleasant to pilot. The U-2 is an aeroplane that can fly effortlessly for a long time at an altitude of more than 75,000 feet. All that changes when you get back on the ground. The U-2 is very bad-tempered, it refuses the ground like a glider and the landings, complicated because of the narrowness of the undercarriage, are always an act of bravery."

As well as that, imagine the pilot cramped in his stratospheric flying suit, only average visibility straight ahead, with his legs coping with eight or nine hours of flying. Then you can get a small idea of the stress he had to face when dealing with the most delicate part of the whole flight.

To help the pilot, the landings nowadays systematically take place under the close surveillance of a following car where another pilot is seated.

As soon as the U-2 crosses over the runway the car drives behind it and its driver informs the pilot of the exact behaviour of the plane.

The first flight tests in American air space confirmed all the hopes that had been placed in the aeroplane. The altitude world record (64,000ft) held by an English aircraft was regularly broken by more than 9,000 feet. The men from Groom Lake were however modest about their triumph : the very nature of their mission didn't allow them to announce these extraordinary accomplishments to the outside world. The U-2 set off on a fabulous career in utmost discretion.

In the meantime the US Air Force, and in particular the Strategic Air Command, lead by the fiery-natured General Curtiss LeMay, engaged into a rear-guard battle to try and regain the control of the programme. Even the President Eisenhower was called to witness in the quarrel with the CIA.

In vain. Central Intelligence kept the upper hand of the programme and serenely prepared the first operational deployment. The Strategic Air Command (SAC) was however given the responsibility of training the pilots, when the Air Force on the whole were confirmed in their role of logistical support.

The initial selection of the first pilots was carried out by the SAC. Certain fighter outfits were being disbanded to move them over into another commandment of the US Air Force, this meant that the SAC had several young pilots at hand waiting for new posting. Some of them could therefore slip away to join the CIA and the U-2 programme without arousing the curiosity of their colleagues.

Keeping in mind the piloting difficulties of the U-2, the Air Force tried to pick the best pilots for the secret programme.

Most of all the pilots had to be volunteers. But volunteers for what?

"It's a secret! All that we can tell you is that it will be very special and well paid. So do you accept..."

Those that answered positively to the recruiting officer were then taken care of by the CIA. An array of tests, a very close investigation into their past, interviews in anonymous hotels, trips to Washington, even more interviews, medical examinations that were so strict that some of them thought that they were on the point of becoming astronauts, not forgetting the traditional encounters with the lie detector, the CIA brought all of its elaborate tests to filter the candidates out of the cupboard.

Extremely impressed by the turn of events, the young pilots started to wonder what kind of mission they had signed themselves up for!

Twenty five were selected. The task that lay ahead of them was far from easy, the risks were high, the CIA took great care to free them from any material problems.

Being civilians again, they earned a salary that was nearly four times as much as their pay in the Air Force. As well as that they were assured that, at the end of their contract, they would be able to rejoin the Air Force with the rank that they would have had if they had followed a normal career. The first group of pilots arrived at Groom Lake at the beginning of 1956.

"The urgency was such that the first training flights started even before the final adjustment flights had been completed", Richard Bissel noted in his diary.

Four months later the pilots were ready for Operation Overflight

OPERATION OVERFLIGHT

The dream that had been for so long in the minds of the American leaders was finally to become reality. Reconnaissance planes were going to be able to fly over the USSR with complete impunity, all the time taking pictures of the most secret sites. Great Britain had given its agreement to be used as a departure base for the CIA aeroplanes, two U-2s were dismantled and transferred by plane to the British base of Lakenheath.

It was a logical choice : the United States and Great Britain had cooperated for a long time in the intelligence field as well as in reconnaissance planes and gladly exchanged their little secrets.

At the beginning of the 1950's Royal Air Force pilots had even carried out flights over the USSR (and even Moscow) for the US Air Force. The Americans had lent the planes and indicated the objectives, the British had provided the crews. The over flights, that were carried out at night with the objective of bringing back radar pictures, had quickly stopped. Apparently it hadn't needed much for the Soviets to shoot down the intruders who could only count on the darkness to slip through the net.

Less than ten years later, the allies did not hold back from laying it on again.

One squadron officially christened, First Weather Reconnaissance Squadron, was created from scratch. For the initiated, it was in fact A Detachment where Air Force, CIA agents and pilots and Lockheed technicians were brought together. The pilots were of course paid by the CIA, but their official 'cover' was that of Lockheed employees working for the NACA on studies of the atmosphere. Fate would have it that the first deployment coincided with an official visit of Nikita Khrushchev to Great Britain. The latter had arrived there aboard a Soviet Marine cruiser and, contary to the instructions that their goverment had given them, MI-6, the British secret service, could not stop themselves from sending a famous combat diver, non other than Crabb who distinguished himself during the Second World War fighting against the Italian frogmen, to inspect the propulsion elements of the ship. The British recovered only the barely recognisable body of the diver, washed up on a beach in the proximity of the ship. The Soviets shouted about a diplomatic incident and the head of the MI-6 was promptly given the handshake by the head of the government.

To avoid any more embarrasment to the British government, the CIA moved its two U-2 before any mission had been able to be launched.

The new deployment airport was to be found in West Germany, near the town of Wiesbaden. It was from there on the 19th of June 1956 that the first mission of Operation Overflight left.

FIRST ATTEMPT, MASTER STROKE

The U-2 took off at dawn, heading towards the East, it flew over Warsaw, then turned around, flew back towards the West and flew over Berlin where the East German tanks were occupied with quelling the riots, then went back to land, without any problem what so ever, at Wiesbaden. The CIA had its first pictures and, on examining them, the analysts jumped for joy : their quality was better than any that been taken before, without taking into account that the U-2 seemed to be able to fly over the communist bloc as easy as if it was flying over the Nevada Desert.

The second mission was launched three weeks afterwards. Impatient to take full advantage of the progress they had made the CIA chose to take the step : the U-2 was going to the USSR.

Either by coincidence or deliberately thought of by the Americans, the U-2 took off from Wiesbaden on the 4th of July 1956 and once again crossed over into Eastern Europe. East Berlin was quickly reached, then over Northern Poland and the aeroplane entered into Byelorussia. It went to Minsk, then headed North in the direction of Leningrad. Flying over the most westerly part of the USSR on its way home, it flew over a few long distance bomber bases that had so often made the officers of the SAC fantisize, before going back to land at Weisbaden. The flight had lasted 8 hours 45 minutes and they had encountered no problems.

Contrary to the American's hopes, the Soviets had managed to detect the first flight over Poland. They also detected the flight on the 4th of July and you can imagine the agitation when the unidentified aircraft entered their territory at an altitude that made it invulnerable.

Scanning the ground through the Driftsight, the U-2 pilot had been able to watch several interception attempts made by the Soviet fighter planes in the Leningrad region. There had also been encounters with the Soviet air defence Radar Fire Control picked up by the electronic monitoring equipment on board the U-2.

The CIA gave Eisenhower several copies of the photos and the American President didn't try to hide his satisfaction when looking at them. When examining the copies with a powerful magnifier, Eisenhower could distinguish the nuclear arms loading bays on strategic Bomber bases, as well as several other details of installations never seen before by the Western services.

He was, in all evidence, enthralled with the results, for quite a while Eisenhower studied the photos, amazed by the precision of the details that were visible.

"Did the Soviets try to intercept the plane?" he finally asked.

To answer the question the man from the CIA pulled out more photos from his file. On them could be seen the silhouettes of the Soviet interceptors a few thousand feet below the U-2, trying in vain to get near.

But in the rarefied air of such high altitude the Russian fighter planes jet engines suffocated and died. One after the other, the MIG and Sukhoi all came up against the limit of their operational ceiling.

Eisenhower listened with delight to the explanations.

The third mission took place less than 24 hours after the second one. The objective this time was Moscow. When the project of the mission had been presented to Richard Bissel, it gave him a start.

"Moscow! Are you sure that it's sensible?"

"Let's try for the jackpot straight away! The longer we wait, the longer the Russians will have time to get a special welcoming party ready..."

The plane took off from Wiesbaden and gained altitude flying towards the north-east. Cracow, in Poland, was flown over once again. Kiev and Minsk followed. An important cloud cover hid the ground but soon, as predicted by the weather men (who listened to the Radio Moscow bulletins...), the cloud cover dispersed on approaching Moscow.

Sixty nine thousand feet further down, the Russians were going crazy watching the progression of the aeroplane on their radar screens. The whole of the air traffic was interrupted so as to leave the field free for the interceptors who took off wave after wave.

The American pilot, who could see them coming towards him, hoped only one thing: that the men from Lockheed had not lied to him when they had assured him that no plane in the world could fly as high as his.

In truth the pilot also hoped for something else as well : that the jet engine did not pack in in those crucial moments. The U-2's main weak point was the possibility of its jet engines dying out like the others. Of course the engine that it was fitted with had been especially modified to function at very high altitude, but from time to time it also had suffocated. The pilot then had to glide the plane to the thicker atmosphere, re-start the engine, and return to the stratosphere. But to go down to 32 or 49,000 feet in altitude put the U-2 in easy reach of the enemy interceptors.

During the third mission the engine held out.

The U-2 flew twice over the anti-aircraft defence belt that protected the Soviet capital then headed back to the West.

Like the previous missions it had gone without a hitch.

Only one thing deeply worried the Americans : the apparent ease with which the Russians had been able to locate the aeroplane on radar. During the following weeks and months Lockheed tried very hard to make the U-2 'stealthy'. But the insufficient techniques of that time meant that nothing came of the efforts made. The only thing that had been done was to paint the aeroplanes dark blue and then black, to merge it into the colours of the sky at that altitude.

The Soviets were a lot less enthusiastic about the over flights, even if it did give them the motivation to develop new surface to air guided missiles and interceptors. But they must have been appalled with which ease the Americans, as it could only be them, violated their airspace. It can be imagined without too much trouble the animated discussions that took place at all levels at the Soviet Air Defence...

Not having come up with any other solution, the Soviet Ambassador in Washington was given the task of delivering, on the 10th of July 1956, a formal protest to the American government. It was requested that the over flights "of these US Air Force aeroplanes based in West Germany (...) stop immediately."

The Americans had the pleasure of answering that no military aeroplane had ever flown over the USSR. The idea of confiding the missions to the CIA, civil governmental agency, at least gave Eisenhower the rare pleasure of denying the obvious whilst still telling the truth.

Thoroughly aware of the diplomatic consequences that these flights, in the long term, could create, Eisenhower insisted that his agreement was needed before the launching of each mission. However the protocol stayed the same at the end of each flight : a CIA officer went to the White House to show the results obtained.

The enthusiasm and the faith that Eisenhower had for the information brought back by the U-2's was such that, during the meetings with intelligence men, the president asked :

"What do the U-2s have to say about that?"

At the height of U-2 activity, nearly one thousand people were involved in the chain of the treatment of the pictures and their interpretation. The activities of the CIA spy planes became such that more than 90% of the information about the Soviet Union came from them.

In May 1956 a second crew of CIA pilots started their training with the planes. When they were declared operational, a second detachment, B Detachment, was put into place at the Incirlik base in Turkey. The detachment, which consisted of half a dozen pilots and five planes, had as principle zone of activity southern USSR. But very quickly the CIA had to expand its fields of investigation to cover the whole of the Mediterranean Basin.

Only a few weeks after arriving, B Detachment's services were often called upon during what was to become the Suez Crisis. This crisis was only the first in a long list of regional conflicts during which the U-2 was greatly made use of to provide the American government with the best information on the evolution of the situations.

THE SUEZ CRISIS

On the 26th of July 1956, openly defying the British Crown, the Egyptian leader Gamal Abdel Nasser, decided to nationalize the Suez Canal.

Seizing the opportunity the Israelis, the French and the British chose to carry out joint military action to regain the control of the Canal and, whilst they were at it, removing the embarrassing Egyptian leader.

The Israelis were to launch an attack against the Egyptians across the Sinai Desert, to arrive on the eastern side of the Canal. The British and French would then have had the pretext to officially ask for the retreat of the two belligerents each side of the canal. Nasser's refusal however was predictable and the British and French would then be prepared for a military intervention, officially to separate the belligerents, but in fact to take back the control of the Canal.

The United States were kept in the dark about the plans, the British thought wrongly that they could count on the tacit good will of Eisenhower in this affair.

The CIA got wind of the fact that a secret agreement was being prepared between the Israelis, French and British, without knowing what it was exactly about. At the same time, the marked increase in the amount of radio exchanges between the three countries confirmed that something was brewing. But what?

The CIA therefore decided, with Eisenhowers agreement, to use its U-2 to follow more closely the three countries preparations. Based in the heart of the Mediterranean Basin, the Aircraft at Incirlik were there just at the right time to carry out the work. For more than two months the aircraft flew practically every day over the Mediterranean and the surrounding countries, from Southern France, where the Port of Marseilles was under heavy surveillance, right to Israel.

"I don't like doing this to my friends, but if I need to spy on them, I'll do it without any hesitation" Eisenhower was supposed to have said to justify the flights.

The first tangible result of the reconnaissance flights was to make a precise assessment of the Israeli military power. That was how the CIA noticed that Israel had received 60 Dassault Mystère fighters from France, not 24 machines as the official transaction stated.

The CIA aeroplanes regularly followed the logistical supplies and the dispatching of aeroplanes and soldiers from Great Britain to the island of Cyprus.

At the end of October, the U-2 over flights revealed that the number of British bombers present on Cyprus had doubled in the space of only a few days.

The Israeli attack, launched on the 30th of October, still managed to surprise the Americans, because of its strength and also because of the direction taken : Egypt. Up until the last minute the Americans had thought that the attack would be carried out against Jordan.

During the first hours of the 31st of October, the Franco-British forces launched their first air raids on the Egyptian airfields. Coincidentally a U-2 was on a surveillance mission above Cairo when the bombardment started. The aircraft stayed in the area for the duration of the attack. When the bombers had done their job they took photos to try and estimate the damage.

The next day the photos were given to Eisenhower who was once again enraptured with the quality of the information gathered and the rapidity of its availability. At dawn on the 5th of November French and British parachutists launched the assault of the Suez Canal. By intercepting Egyptian communications the Americans learned that the Soviets were about "to do something" to help Nasser. Eisenhower immediately ordered U-2 over flights above Syria.

"If the Soviets use the Syrian bases to deploy fighter planes, the French and the British could try to destroy them" he said to the head of the CIA. "Could all that start off a Third World War...?"

No Soviet aircraft was identified on the Syrian bases, but the Americans chose to exercise considerable pressure on their allies to immediately stop the combats.

On the night of the 6th of November, the parachutists, who had nothing to stop them from taking hold of the Canal, were called back by their respective governments. Nasser stayed put, the asset of the Canal for the French and British was lost for ever and the detachment at Incirlik received congratulations from the White House for the quality of its work.

A consequence of the Suez crisis was that Eisenhower, on the 18th of

December 1956, ordered the CIA to interrupt flights over the USSR for an undetermined period of time.

Eisenhower feared that it would be too much of a provocation towards the Kremlin, who were already extremely annoyed over the Suez episode and the Hungarian revolution that had needed to be quashed with 200,000 soldiers....

But only a few days were needed for him to go back on his decision.

As, following the example of the whole of the American Intelligence community, Eisenhower became very worried with the idea that unexpected developments in the Soviet Intercontinental Ballistic Missile (ICBM) programme could escape all surveillance. A report made by the American Intelligence services, that had made a lot of fuss in the community, stated that there was a possibility that the USSR could launch an artificial satellite before 1958.

In the first few days of 1957, after less than fifteen days interruption, the over flight missions above Soviet territory started up again.

When the Suez affair got under way the Incirlik aircraft didn't just fly over the USSR. Missions were launched practically over the whole of the Middle East and Near East countries, according to local and regional crises. Syria, Iraq, Saudi-Arabia, Libya, Yemen... the list is still a current affair.

In the meantime, C Detachment was set up in Japan, with, in line of sight, Communist China. In February 1957, the last lot of CIA pilots finished their training and the newly qualified pilots were split up and sent to the different detachments that existed.

THE U-2 AND THE SOVIET SPACE PROGRAMME

Still as fascinated by the photos brought back by the U-2s, to the point of some people talking of dependency as if it was like a drug, Eisenhower took an ever increasing part in the preparation of the missions over the USSR.

He even selected certain objectives himself and sometimes decided on the flight routes which, from an operational point of view, was perhaps not of the utmost rigour.....

Richard Bissel went to the Oval Office in the White House to meet with the President, he showed him the planned route of the next flight, on a huge map of the Soviet Union.

Bent over the document Eisenhower commented :

"Don't bother going that way, go directly from there to there..."

He traced; with his finger, the route that the aeroplane was to take a few hours later at very high altitude. The zones that were heavily defended sometimes made him hesitate. It could be sensed that he was weighing up the for and against, the risk of losing a plane against the pleasure of bringing back exclusive pictures. Then he would decide :

"Too dangerous. Forget about that corner..."

A good part of the American effort was put into the supervision of the Soviet space programme. Two parallel and complementary races had been started between the Americans and the Soviets : one leading to space, the other perfecting the ICBM.

At the beginning of 1957, a pilot flying over Turkistan spotted, slightly off his route, the Tyuratam test centre, whose very existence was unknown to the Americans. The reconnaissance flights were multiplied. Eighty two thousand feet over the icy steppes, the Americans had an unrestricted view of the Soviet space programme. What they saw did nothing to reassure them.

Where as they had estimated, a few weeks before, that the Soviets would not have an operational missile before 1960 or 1961, they were forced to review their estimations to a much nearer date.

The 4th of October 1957, the Soviets launched Sputnik, the Earth's first artificial satellite. The strategic missiles, that used the same technique, were not far behind, warned the CIA.

From then on all the over flight missions were geared towards the same goal : find and keep an eye on the fabrication and launch sites of the future ICBM, as well as the nuclear warhead production sites.

The obtained results slightly reassured Washington : according to the scientific analysts, and the faith put into the pictures brought back by the U-2s, the Americans estimated that they were one year behind on the subject of propulsion and one year ahead in the development of nuclear warheads.

338

Paradoxically Eisenhower could not give an account of these figures, reassuring on the whole, nor show the proof that he had at his disposition, as the U-2 programme was still a tightly held secret. After Sputnik was put into orbit the hysteria over the Soviet atomic menace and the supposed American scientific delay therefore developed at a leisurely pace amongst the general public.

But at least the information brought back allowed the American government to resist, to a certain point, the pressure of the complex military arms industry, always ready to use the Soviet pseudo- advantage to ask for regular increases in military equipment credit.

BRITAIN THE FAITHFUL ALLY

Despite the excellent results that were obtained, and against Richard Bissel's advice, Eisenhower still wanted to limit the number of USSR over flights so as not to irritate the Kremlin more than could be helped.

Frustrated with this resistance, Bissel proposed to ask the British to join the programme, so as to increase the number of missions. The idea was quite simple : on one hand carrying out the missions authorized by the American president and on the other hand the missions authorized by the British government, it was possible to double the number of USSR over flights in one go.

In spite of the unfortunate episode of the Suez Canal, where the British had voluntarily deceived the United States about its real intentions, the links between the Intelligence services were still very strong between the two countries.

The U-2 had been presented to the British by the CIA as early as November 1956.

Remembering reconnaissance missions carried out over occupied Europe during the Second World War, Eisenhower agreed to the project.

As from May 1958, five Royal Air Force pilots were sent to train in America. Three months later the British Prime Minister, Harold Macmillan, was able to authorize the first over flights in the name of Her Majesty The Queen!

Squadron Leader Robinson was the second pilot to follow the programme. Unlike the other officers that had been selected, he was an experienced pilot of the high altitude reconnaissance version of the Canberra bomber.

"We were used to flying at altitudes of more than 49,000 feet, which made us ideal candidates..."

Robinson was sent to replace another RAF pilot who had been killed during a U-2 training mission.

In January 1959 Robinson was affected to B Detachment at Incirlik where three other British pilots were already present. At that time the number of USSR over flights had already been greatly reduced, most of them having taken place between 1956 and 1958. Most of the missions therefore took place over the Mediterranean Basin and along the USSR borders to carry out electronic eavesdroping. From certain sources it seems that at least two USSR over flights were carried out by the British pilots between January 1959 and May 1960. "No comment" answered the witnesses of that period.

The British pilots, unlike the Americans who were officially civilian pilots, flew over the USSR as RAF officers, their only 'cover' was that of the supposed meteorological research. Whereas the Americans spent most of their time collecting information about the ICBM, the British orientated their activities to the surveillance of the manufacturing sites and strategic bomber bases. The list of British objectives was defined by London and then sent to Washington to be integrated into the plane's programme.

The British participation in the U-2 programme lasted right through the sixties. After the training of the first five pilots, six others followed between 1961 and 1967. But in the absence of any requests from London to accomplish operational missions, these pilots only activity was to transfer the U-2 between the United States and the foreign deployment bases.

A MENACE COMES TO LIGHT

The CIA operations with the U-2 carried on in a regular fashion all through 1957, 1958 and 1959. Thirty USSR over flights were undertaken during the three years, that is to say just under one per month.

When the Aquatone programme had been launched, the CIA and Lockheed had estimated that two years would be the amount of time the U-2 would be able to fly over the USSR with relative freedom.

"After this time limit" estimated the specialists, "the Russians will have found a way of catching us." This suggested time limit however passed by and the Soviets still did not seem any nearer to being able to attack the U-2. All the interception attempts, by the MiG-19 and-21 fighters or SA-1 missiles, had ended in failure.

Mid 1958 the Soviets brought into service a new missile, the SA-2, which seemed capable of reaching the altitude at which the U-2 operated. Even if the CIA estimated that there was less than a 2% chance that the missile would hit its target, this probability was not zero and forced the Americans to take a few precautions.

The SA-2 sites were duly listed and carefully avoided during the flights. Unfortunately for the CIA, the SA-2 was a mobile missile that could be moved around depending on the air defence needs. Keeping track of every launcher was impossible.

These imposed detours did not however alter the quality of the information that was obtained too much. The equipment that had been developed for the U-2 allowed extremely valuable photographs to be taken more than 93 miles away from the objective. As for the electronic reconnaissance, that grew more and more important as the years went by, the direct over flight of the objective was not really necessary.

In September 1959, Khrushchev went on an official visit to the United States. Eisenhower should have visited him the following year, but it had been agreed that the two men were to meet in between time at a summit in Paris.

Khrushchevs visit was accompanied by a calm on the over flight front. Probably the Americans didn't want to overdo it, afraid that the jovial Secretary General would make a scene. The Paris summit, set up for the 14th of May 1960, was not the object of as many precautions.

USSR over flights should have been carried out during the first trimester of the year and, in accordance to instructions, a list of the over flight missions was submitted to the American President for his agreement. Eisenhower gave the go ahead with no hesitation. He did however point out the closeness of the last flights on the list to the summit in Paris and it was agreed that the ones in question would be launched no later than two weeks before the summit. The last possible date was therefore the 1st of May.

On the 9th of April 1960 an over flight of different test sites in Kazakhstan by an aircraft from Peshawar in Pakistan, revealed that the Soviet ICBM programme was going quicker that had been thought. This report made the CIA plan another mission over the same area as quickly as possible.

Even with the approaching Paris summit, Eisenhower let himself be convinced that it was absolutely necessary that there was a second mission. As he was accustomed to do, he personally studied the mission with the help of a large map on his desk. First planned for the 28th of April the mission was postponed to the 29th and then the 30th and then finally the 1st of May because of bad weather conditions over the objective. The Americans thought they had a good opportunity : the first of May, Labour Day, a very important day in the USSR, would probably make the Soviet air defence less vigilant they thought.

They were disillusioned.

Gary Powers was the pilot that was supposed to do the flight, one of the first on the programme. Since his arrival at Incirlick in 1956, Powers had already carried out several USSR over flights and a good number of electronic eavesdropping flights along the Southern borders of the Empire. Powers was one of the most experienced pilots of the CIA with some 500 flying hours on that type of aircraft and 27 operational missions.

As with the last USSR over flights, Peshawar had been chosen as the departure base, the reason being that it was geographically close to the objective in the south of the USSR.

This zone was also known to be the USSR's soft spot in air defence matters. The CIA were also wary of a possible KGB infiltration at the Turkish Incirlik base, where the American Agency could not always organize the security conditions that it deemed necessary.

Through the years nearly twenty advance bases, similar to the one at Peshawar, were used around the world. In that way most of the planets hot points were near at hand for the CIA aircraft.

The deployment technique was well worn and put the accent on discretion. The CIA wanted to avoid these deployments being quickly known by the Soviets. The latter would then have been tempted to pressurise the welcoming country to cease its hospitality.

The U-2s logistics fitted into two C-130 Hercules. The first aeroplane carried a team of technicians and all the up keep material, the second one was filled with the special fuel for the reconnaissance plane. The U-2 itself was flown to the base the day before the mission by a convoy pilot.

THE UNREAL FIRST OF MAY

Power's U-2 was therefore to take off from Peshawar, fly over the missile trial centre at Tyuratam (better known today as Baikonour), in the Sverdlovsk area of the Oural mountains, known for hiding numerous secret industrial sites linked to the nuclear industry, an ICBM base in the process of being built at Yurya and finally at the end of the flight the Plesetsk site, thought to hold a new ICBM base. Finally the red cherry on the top of the proletarian cake, the mission was to end with the over flight of the Naval Construction site at Severodvinsk, the Naval base at Mourmansk. The U-2 was to land in Bodo, Norway.

The mission, that was to last nine hours, was to be the longest ever carried out by a U-2. The pilot and aeroplane alike were pushing themselves to their limits, they were to fly more than 4,350 miles, 3,100 being over forbidden territory.

When Powers left Peshawar, the CIA had thought about sending off another U-2 from Incirlik, for an electronic eavesdropping mission along the southern borders of the Republics of Tadjikistan and Turkmenistan. The coincidence was, if possible, to create a small diversion.

Less sure as time went by of the impunity of their aeroplanes against the Russian air defences, the CIA tried to think of every possible solution to reduce risks.

The point of entry into the Soviet Union was different from the precedent flights and the planes flight had been equally planned out with great care to avoid the more recent SA-2 missile sites. The mobility of the new anti-aircraft system made these efforts quite uncertain. Electronic recordings had shown that missiles had been fired at the U-2 during the preceding few months, even if the pilots had not seen anything themselves.

The CIA, as well as President Eisenhower, realised the danger that the new weapon could hold, but neither one or the other could have realised how dramatic the earlier missions could have been if the incompetence of the Soviet administration hadn't been there to save them!

If we are to believe the general who commanded the anti-aircraft defence at that time, an earlier U-2 nearly received a volley of SA-2. The missiles were ready. The only problem was that they hadn't been fuelled up. So they stayed on the ground. Another time everything was ready but the Battery Commander was absent and nobody knew what to do without him...

It was said that Khrushchevs anger made the Kremlin walls shake. All had not been in vain.

Nikita Khrushchev was presiding over the ceremonies of the First of May 1960 in Red Square at Moscow, when the head of the army headquarters whispered to him one magical sentence :

"Comrade Secretary General, an Imperialist aeroplane has just been shot down in the Oural area!"

Showing two rows of shiny white teeth, that would have liked nothing better than to bite into capitalism, Khrushchev smiled broadly at the red clothed crowds who paraded by at the foot of the stand. Never had a delegation from the heavy tractors and fertiliser factory, who were going past at that very moment, seemed so exquisite.

CHRONOLOGY OF A DISASTER

So after three successive cancellations due to bad weather, Powers was woken up on the first of May at two thirty in the morning.

After a protein-rich breakfast he started the dressing ceremony and the physiological preparation. The replacement pilot carried out the pre-flight visit of the aeroplane. Along with the navigator who had prepared the mission, Powers went through, for the last time, the details of the different flight phases.

Once again cursing Washington for having ordered a mission that would push the plane to its extreme limits, the navigator insisted upon the range problems :

"If you're short of fuel at the end of the flight, forget Mourmansk and head directly for Norway. There is even an airfield in northern Sweden where you could land if you're in trouble."

Powers approved. He knew the Bodo airfield in Norway where he was to land. An airfield that was difficult to access and on which it was better to avoid glider landing, as would be the case if he ran out of fuel. He assured the navigator that he wouldn't take any unneccesary risks.

He then got up and went slowly towards the plane. An assistant held a small air conditioned case that would assure the ventilation of his flying suit, as long as it wasn't wired to the system on the aeroplane.

Powers seated himself in postion and equipped himself with the help of the technicians. The starting up of the engine was normal. Giving the thumbs up the ground technician signalled that everything was OK. The chocks were taken away from underneath the wheels and Powers started to manoeuvre towards the runway. It was then just after five in the morning and the sun had already started its rapid climb in the East.

The procedure stated that take off only went ahead after the final green light from Washington. That day Washington kept them waiting for more than a hour. Strapped into his aeroplane at the end of the runway Powers waited.

At 6h 20 the signal finally arrived, the road was clear. Six minutes later the U-2 climbed into the sky in the direction of Afganistan and then the Soviet border. The mission ran according to plan up until the U-2 flew over the nuclear complex at Maiak, in the Sverdlovsk region. Powers had been in the air for 3 hours 27 minutes and he was 1,500 miles into Soviet territory.

Everything happened very quickly.

Powers heard and felt a muffled explosion at the back of the plane. In the same instant the sky turned a brilliant orange colour. A second later the right wing gave way. The pilot restabalized the plane but that wasn't enough : the fin had been touched by the explosion and the aeroplane started to dive. That time Powers did not have time to correct the movement : the dive suddenly got steeper and the aeroplane flipped onto its back.

A fraction of a second later the mechanical constraints, caused by the sudden over turn, caused the wings to separate abruptly. Less than five seconds had gone by since the explosion and, at present, Powers fell, a prisoner of a fuselage in perdition. Powers said later on that as the plane was disintegrating around him he had tried to reach the auto-destruction buttons of the different systems that were aboard. But he couldn't remember if he had managed to reach them or not.

Positioned to the left of the control panel, and difficult to reach in normal circumstances, the auto-destruction commands left the pilot 70 seconds delay before the instrumentation bay, that was positioned behind his back, exploded.

Powers life was saved thanks to his flying suit that had immediately took over from the cabin pressurisation, when the jet engine had stopped working. Cramped into his Bibendum suit, the visor frozen with the cold that entered the cockpit, he struggled to survive. What was left of the aeroplane was engaged in a spiral dive and fell to earth like a dead leaf that weighed several tons.

One consolation, the altitude at which the drama took place meant that Powers had several minutes to get out of the doomed aircraft before it hit the Earth.

The centrifugal force pushed him into the control panel and put him in a atrocious position for an ejection.

He therefore tried to get out of the plane by himself.

At an altitude of over six miles, he had already fallen more than 36,000 feet, he managed to get rid of the canopy and left the cabin. But in his haste he forgot to disconnect the tube that supplied his oxygen mask. After a few seconds effort he finally managed to free himself from the fuselage.

Just in time : a few seconds later, at 11,800 feet in the parachute that was controlled by a barometer opened automatically.

In the eye of the cyclone Powers drifted for a few minutes under the silk dome before landing in the middle of a agricultural field. Country folk rushed from neighbouring Kolkoze. Involuntary explorer on modern unknown ground, the CIA pilot Gary Powers had landed on the planet Khrushchev in the socialist constellation.

BOOBY TRAPPED SEAT AND POISONED NEEDLE

Since the aeroplane had been brought into service, thirteen U-2s had been destroyed and eleven pilots killed, mainly during training over American territory. But on at least two occasions aircraft had been lost during USSR spying missions. Luckily for the Americans they hadn't been over flight missions that went deep into Russian territory, the aircraft had only flown to the steps of the empire. One plane had crashed into the Caspian Sea and another in the Black Sea, out of reach of the Soviets. Each time the pilot had been able to be retrieved by an American sea plane.

After four years of fruitless attempts, Gary Powers was the first pilot to be captured by the Soviets.

Eisenhower heard the news a few hours after Khrushchev. When he learnt that a U-2 was reported missing he was immediately convinced that the aircraft had fallen onto Soviet ground. But, like the CIA men, the American President was convinced that the pilot could not have survived.

When the American President had given the go ahead for the over flight missions he had been assured that in the case of a successful Soviet interception the structure of the aircraft was so fragile that the U-2 would nearly entirely disintegrate before reaching the ground. It had been said that because of this the Communists would never be able to lay their hands on intact equipment, even less so on a pilot that was in a fit state to talk.

"It was a cruel presumption" wrote Eisenhower in his memoirs. "But I was assured that the young pilots who participated in these flights did so with full knowledge of the facts, with patriotism as a motivation, their braggart spirits and also the materialistic considerations that were not negligible."

The pilots did not say exactly the same thing. The more recent models of the U-2 were fitted with an ejectable seat and the pilots still had a parachute at their disposition, of course.

Rumours circulated about the ejectable seats. Numerous pilots were convinced that the seats had been booby trapped so that the aeroplane would be destroyed and the pilot killed if they had to eject. When the CIA found out about this mistrust it offered the pilots the opportunity to thoroughly inspect the material. But the rumour still went round, carried along by a certain distrust that the pilots had towards the Intelligence Agency...

Maybe that was the reason that had made Powers get out of the plane 'manually', rather than attempt an ejection.

The existence of the poisoned needle hadn't helped matters. The CIA had thought to provide the pilots with a needle coated in cyanide, hidden in a piece of false money, with which they could chose to die rather than be taken prisoner. Contrary to the wildest rumours that went round after the Powers episode, suicide rather than capture was definitely not a CIA instruction.

So why provide the needle?

The agency had also thought of the possibility of escape and had equipped the pilots with a survival kit that contained 7,500 roubles, 24 gold coins as well as a written message in 14 languages explaining that anyone that helped the pilot would have a reward. But Powers had above all things a parachute, and that is what saved his life.

CAUGHT RED HANDED

Persuaded that the U-2 was lost, somewhere between Pakistan and Norway, Eisenhower approved the NASA press release. The American space agency, who had had this lie imposed upon them by the CIA and the White House, explained that a U-2 aeroplane, that was on a joint meteorological study mission for NASA and the US Air Force, had been reported missing over Turkey.

On the 5th of May Khrushchev officially announced the destruction of the American Reconnaissance plane above Soviet territory but he did not mention anything about the pilot. The Russians knew exactly what the U-2 did. If they had had the slightest doubt, then simply reading the specialised Western press of that period, where allusions supporting the ridiculous story of weather research had been made, would have been enough to enlighten them.

Through the years, the Soviet Union had used the diplomatic channels to complain a few times, whether to the United States or the UN, about the reconnaissance plane over flights of their territory. But they had never insisted about them, afraid that it would accentuate their incapacity of intercepting the U-2 and make them look ridiculous in the eyes of international opinion.

At present Khrushchev celebrated.

Apart from the American pilot he also had in his hands practically all the scientific equipment from the plane, which left no doubt about the real nature of the mission. Contrary to the Americans hopes, numerous pieces of equipment were still perfectly identifiable, and the Soviet scientists gathered a good deal of technical information. They even managed to reconstruct, in detail, Powers accomplished mission, bringing forth a bloody refutation of the Americans denials.

Not knowing about these latest developments, Eisenhower and his advisers continued with the official version, choosing to multiply the details so as to prove their good faith :

"It is absolutely possible that after having an oxygen supply problem, that would have lead to the pilots loss of consciousness, the aeroplane would have continued its flight for quite a while thanks to the automatic pilot, eventually penetrating Soviet air space." Stated the official press release.

Khrushchev let the Americans sink deeper into their lies before finally letting it be known, on the 7th of May 1960, that the equipment that had been salvaged from the plane could only have been of slight use for weather studies and that the pilot was in their hands, in good health...

"We have caught the thief red handed" declared Khrushchev before the Supreme Soviet "(...) We have given the Pentagon time to demonstrate its bad faith and its methods of intoxication..."

Khrushchev continued along this line for a few minutes, baptising along the way Allen Dulles, the CIA director, as great meteorological specialist. Delighted with the trick that they had played on the Americans and the ease with which they had been duped, the Supreme Soviet auditory exulted, laughing like a class of school children.

"Incredible, absolutely incredible!" repeated Eisenhower. No other word could suit the situation and the embarrassment in which they found themselves.

The alternatives that the Americans were presented with were very clear : they had to officially admit that they were responsible for carrying out spying activities during peace time or continue with the lies, in spite of the blatant proof that the Soviets had provided.

Eisenhower didn't have any other choice but to admit that it was in fact espionage and take responsibility for it. He did however add that the flights were "detestable but vital (...) given the taste that the Russians had for secrecy and concealment."

"Intelligence work is practised in every country" Washington also added. This comment made some sarcastic minded people say that the White House had managed to transform a high lie into an imprescriptable right, in the space of a few days.

Gary Powers was judged and sentenced to ten years in prison. Less than two years later he was exchanged with the master spy Rudolf Abel, the man that had lead the KGB's affairs in the United States for nearly 25 years before getting caught in the FBI's nets.

The CIA's reaction was, of course, to totally stop the USSR over flights. The enormous publicity that the Soviet had given the affair and the menaces that Khrushchev was sending to the countries that hosted the U-2 detachments, obliged the company to considerably reduce their activities outside American borders. In the space of only a few weeks, the B and C Detachments in Turkey and Japan were deactivated.

The consequences were difficult to overcome for the intelligence centre, they had become quickly used to the ease with which photographic and electronic information could be obtained. Around forty USSR over flights had been carried out since the beginning of Operation Overflight.

The CIA pleaded their cause to keep a 'U-2 potential'. There were still quite a few countries around the world to spy on who didn't have as good anti-aircraft facilities as the Soviet Union. Also the satellites and the U-2's successor an aeroplane which was even more extraordinary that Lockheed was working on, were not ready to take over ...

350

The CIA won and were allowed to continue operations with the U-2. The Intelligence Agency's fleet was however reduced to ten aeroplanes and seven pilots, a lot less than what the US Air Force could come up with and who therefore became the main users of the plane.

After Khrushchev revealed that the spy plane pilot had been captured alive, the British that were present at Incirlik quickly packed their bags. Their activities in Turkey, if they were found out, could lead to severe complications in the crisis that had started between the two superpowers. Luckily Powers did not reveal any information to the Russians about the participation of the British pilots in Operation Overflight.

"The Russians asked me for the names of other American pilots involved in the operation", he explained on his return to the United States. "It never entered their heads to ask me about the presence of pilots of other nationalities. So I never had to tell them or hide anything from them..."

After the Powers affair, there were never anymore USSR over flights by the U-2, officially anyway. But the British collaboration continued at least until the end of the sixties. There are still rumours around to this day that talk about a collaboration that is still going on....

BARRAGE FIRE

Forty years on questions are still being asked about the destruction of Powers' aeroplane.

The U-2 in question, Item 360 on the CIA's list, was known to have had a series of small problems during its operational life. It was what the Americans called a 'Hanger Queen', a regular in the maintenance hangers.

Six months before the fatal mission it had landed on its belly in a field, short of fuel. It was then part of C Detachment based at Atsugi in Japan. The aeroplane had been taken back to Lockheed and repaired. But from then on it had a bad reputation. All that hadn't seemed to be incriminating enough to allocate Powers with a different aircraft for his mission on the 1st of May.

The official version of the drama was that Gary Powers had been shot down by a missile. Then, based upon the information given by different Soviet renegades, it was admitted that it wasn't an isolated missile that had done the damage (the pilot would certainly not have survived a direct hit), but more likely turbulence created by a barrage of fire of several missiles that had destabilized the plane.

Fourteen missiles had been fired at Powers, the plane never having been directly hit as the minute examinations of the wreck, that the Soviets carried out, showed. But the shock wave was such that the U-2 was momentarily driven into Coffin Corner, broke off and finally went into a back dive. One of the Russian Sukhoi 9 fighters that had taken off to intercept the aeroplane was shot down on the way by one of the missiles fired by his own side.

The incredible thing is that the Americans seemed to have been aware of the presence of SA-2 missiles in that area. Whilst on a journey in the USSR a few months before hand, when the official aeroplane on which he was travelling had flown over the area, the American vice-president Richard Nixon had himself recognised the 'star of David' lay out of the missile installations. But a few weeks later the first over flight of Sverdlovsk by a U-2 had not encountered any shots being fired and the danger had not been considered as enough to justify a deviation.

The bases of the controversy that developed afterwards was to find out whether Powers had been shot down whilst he was still at his cruising altitude or whether he had been forced to descend (because of a jet engine failing) to a lower altitude that had therefore put him in the firing range of the anti- aircraft defences.

On his return to the United States Powers explained to the CIA that he had managed to convince the Russians that he been flying at only 67,000 feet when he was shot down and that this was the maximum altitude that the U-2 could fly at. But on the other side the story was that through listening into Soviet communications they learnt that the plane had been off its trajectory for about thirty minutes, all the time losing height. The rumour, that soon took the form of the unofficial truth, that spread around the American officials was that the aeroplane had had a jet engine failure and had been forced to descend into the vulnerable zone.

This version was confirmed by the public affirmation given by the American government, which stated that Powers had signalled by radio a jet engine failure, just before being shot down. A very important piece of information that proved to be totally wrong.

Powers only had a UHF radio that carried for only 250 miles, on which he would have had a lot of trouble being heard on when he was more than 1,500 miles into Soviet territory. Powers who maintained that he had never left the cruising altitude that was more than 68,000 feet, and who also had no reason to hide an eventual jet engine failure, greatly contested this version of events. Powers had experienced several jet engine failures during his career unlike all the other U-2 pilots, so he would definitely have known if one had happened.

According to him this theory had been thought up by some of the superior officers of the US Air Force who were anxious to hide the effectiveness of the new Soviet surface to air guided missiles at such a high altitude.

The US Air Force was then involved in the extraordinarily ambitious project of the XB-70 Valkyrie, a bomber capable of flying at Mach 3 at very high altitude. The funding of the project, which was opposed by the holders of intercontinental missiles, was discussed in Congress. To admit to the Soviets that is was easy to shoot down a U-2 above 68,000 feet meant that the Valkyrie project was immediately condemned. Anyway the plane was never mass produced, the Air Force finally admitted that penetration at very high altitude was sentenced to failure.

Powers also accused the CIA of going along with engine failure theory so as to be rid of any responsibility in the fiasco.

Powers, who died in a helicopter accident in 1977, is buried in the Arlington cemetery in Washington and his secret is buried with him. His version of events seems to be the most coherent and it was confirmed over the years and in other theatres of operations by the proven destruction of U-2's by SA-2 missiles. It is also to be noted that this version, that he upheld throughout his debriefing on return to the United States, was also the one that he had given to the KGB immediately after his capture.

Powers knew that the Soviet radar's permanently followed him and that they estimate, with a fair amount of precision, his altitude. He therefore gave the figure of 68,000 feet to keep the extra few hundred feet of the U-2's performance secret, but he couldn't have given a figure too much lower in his statement without having raised the suspicions of his interrogators.

According to a more recent theory, Power's aircraft was not shot down by a SA-2 missile but was destabilized by one of the Sukhoi 9 that was in chase. At least that is what Igor Mentioukov, who had been the pilot of the Sukhoi, stated in the Russian daily paper 'Troud' in 1986.

"When the alert had been given on the Ist of May, I took off in my aircraft and I climbed up towards the spy plane as quickly as possible. Guided by our radars on the ground I joined the American aeroplane and I went slightly above him. Caught in the slipstream of the jet engine the plane started to twirl and its wings broke..." tells Mentioukov.

This version supposes that the U-2 had experienced a jet engine failure that had meant it was within the interceptors reach, which Powers always denied. It also doesn't take into account Powers having reported hearing an explosion at the back of the plane and the sky becoming orange in colour. Difficult to believe, as the Russian pilot tries to make out, that Powers had mistaken the explosion of a missile with the flame of a jet engine that had got close!

This version of events was supposedly kept secret from everybody, including Khrushchev, so as not to underestimate the value of the anti-aircraft missiles. A rather thin argument...

Finally, the Gary Powers affair would not be a real spy story if the theory of sabotage was not mentioned.

This theory was advanced by Colonel Prouty, who at the era in question served as liaison officer between the CIA and the Pentagon for the special missions. In his memoirs 'The Secret Team', Prouty makes it understood that the CIA itself had sabotaged Powers aircraft, simply because the flight was to take place shortly before the Paris Summit. A successful outcome of the summit could have brought on the warming up of Soviet-American relations therefore entailing a considerable fall in the role of the CIA.

"It would have been very easy to discreetly sabotage the U-2" explained Prouty to back up his hypothesis.

According to him the J-57 jet engine of the U-2 needed injections of liquid hydrogen to function correctly at very high altitude. It therefore was only necessary to only partially fill the liquid hydrogen reservoir before the take off from Peshawar to force the plane, sooner or later, to come down from its height. It was then that the Soviets took advantage.

"In making them believe that they were capable of shooting down Powers at his maximum height, the Soviets would have looked to take revenge for the four other fruitless attempts" Prouty summed up in his book.

THE CUBA MISSILE CRISIS : K VERSUS K.

As soon as Castro was in power the CIA focused their attention on Cuba. It was predictable that they would use the U-2 in this theatre of operation.

The spy planes were of course used in the preparation of Operation Pluto. The U-2 systematically photographed all the possible sites for the debarkation of the anti-Castrists. After the Bay of Pigs fiasco the surveillance operations of the island were increased, sometimes offering fine examples of the American paranoia.

It was in this way that the U-2 brought back photos that showed strange structures that looked like satellite reception aerials. The analysts racked their brains over the bizarre constructions until one day a photo published in a Cuban newspaper cleared up the mystery : they were the buildings for a revolution museum, the roofs had been given the shape of inside out umbrellas so that they could hold rain water...

Less anecdotal, on the 28th of August 1962 one of the CIA's U-2's brought back information of the installation on the island of SA-2 anti-aircraft missile sites, the same as the ones that had shot down Powers.

Some thought that it was only Castro installing a new anti-aircraft defence system. But for John McCone, the CIA's new boss, it perfectly matched up to other information received from his agents who were present in Cuba : the Soviets were getting ready to install medium range surface to surface guided missiles on the island, fitted with a nuclear charge and pointed towards the United States.

Within an hour President Kennedy had been informed. Very worried he asked for an intensification of U-2 over flights.

But the weather decided to meddle and the Americans were only able to launch three reconnaissance flights before the end of September. The results obtained were quite poor, the photos taken during the second mission were judged unusable because of the cloud cover that hid most of the objectives.

The CIA on its side were scrupulous about risking their planes in the zones where the anti-aircraft missiles sites were multiplying.

After numerous debates the Americans soon had the certitude that offensive missiles pointed towards them were on the island, less than 125 miles from the Florida coast. All that was left to do was to find them and take photos of them.

The old quarrel between the Air Force and the CIA stirred up again. With the possibility of a war rearing its head the Air Force insisted that the reconnaissance flights should be carried out by their own U-2 unit. The CIA defended its territory and finally a compromise was found : the CIA's machines, better equipped with electronic counter-measure equipment would be used over Cuba. But Air Force pilots would be behind the commands.

On the 14th of October 1962, one and a half months after the first warning signal had been given, a U-2 finally managed to photograph the work that was going on to install surface to surface guided missiles near Havana. Later missions confirmed the nature of the contraptions : they were SS-4 medium range missiles with nuclear warheads, easily capable of reaching the heart of the United States.

The news was kept secret for a week. That allowed Kennedy, surrounded by his advisers, to multiply crisis reunions without the pressure of the media playing on the decisions made. Several options were considered : from direct negotiations with the Russians to quite simply the invasion of the island considering blockades or the bombing of the sighted installations along the way.

It was even considered Cuban opponents bombing the missiles from 'anonymous' planes. This solution had quite a bit of 'déjà vu' about it and reminded the White House of some unpleasant memories. The idea was soon put aside.

Engaged in another sabotage operation against Cuba the CIA proposed to land a dozen commando groups each made up of six men, so as to guide eventual invasion forces. This hypothesis was also abandoned.

Whilst waiting for a decision to be made the U-2 flights increased. There were sometimes six or eight per day and the proof accumulated on Kennedy's desk.

On the 18th of October the CIA analysts had localized sixteen medium range missile launching pads (about 1,120 miles) and six for intermediate range (2,500 miles). A few days later these figures rose respectively to twenty-four and twelve launch pads spread over nine sites. The over flights of the Cuban air bases also showed the notable reinforcement of the Cuban aviation : Iliouchine 28 bombers and MiG-21 fighters that had arrived from the USSR in boxes were starting to line up on the aprons.

According to the CIA all the goings on were not simply a demonstration of force by Khrushchev : the Soviet Union was turning Cuba into a major deployment base for its atomic weapons.

THE TENSION MOUNTS

On the 20th of October another crisis reunion took place at the White House. The latest photos that had been brought back by the U-2s were given to the American president and his closest advisers :

"At present we have photographed 95% of the island" announced the CIA representative to his audience. "The nature of the 5% of ground left makes it unnecessary to do photo coverage of it..."

The representative then gave the details of the different sites that had been observed. When he had finished his presentation Kennedy got up and shook his hand :

"I want you to pass on to your organization my gratitude for the remarkable work that you have supplied" he said.

Since the 14th of October, when the first photos had been brought back, over twenty missions had been accomplished by the U-2s. But at the same time the Cubans had multiplied the air defence sites. At that time 24 were registered in locations all over the island, opposite the United States.

On the 22nd of October Kennedy announced to the American public

357

the presence of the missiles and made it public that a blockade to the island was being put into place. Just beforehand he had taken the precaution and had enough tact to inform, though their special emissaries, the principal leaders of the Western world about what was going on in Cuba. He had also informed them through the same channels, the decisions he had taken and that he was about to make them public. The State Department emissaries had been accompanied by CIA agents who carried in their briefcases the photographs that had been taken by the U-2s and that were classified 'ultra-secret'.

The Canadian and British Prime Ministers, the German Chancellor Konrad Adenauer and the French President Charles de Gaulle were also met with :

"Have you come to consult me or to inform me?" de Gaulle asked the American emissary.

"I am here to inform you Mr. President."

In spite of this cold opening onto the subject the American was obviously pleased with the interest that the French president seemed to show in the photos that he was being shown. De Gaulle obviously had no trouble at all in identifying the MiG 19 and 21 on the photos. When it was explained to him that the photos had been taken at an altitude of 75,000 feet he exclaimed "That's fantastic, that's fantastic!"

He then asked the American emissary to assure President Kennedy that he had his support.

"I would have acted like him" he said.

The reactions of the other Western heads of state or governments were identical.

After the Americans public announcement more reconnaissance flights of a standard nature at low altitude and great speed were undertaken by the US Air Force. Nevertheless U-2 over flights carried on.

It was during one of these flights that a CIA aircraft, flown by Commandant Rudolph Anderson, was targeted by a volley of SA-2 when he was flying over the eastern extremity of the island.

One of the missiles exploded behind the aeroplane, riddling the fuselage with white-hot fragments of metal. One of these pieces penetrated into the cockpit and tore the pilots pressurised flying suit, the pilots suit could not take over and he died within a few seconds.

From then on the situation seemed to be too tense and the air defence too dense to be able to risk sending new aeroplanes. The standard reconnaissance aircraft of the US Air Force then completely took over. The pictures that were soon being brought back showed the progressive dismantling of the missile launching sites, to the great relief of the Americans.

The need to confirm the retreat of the missiles did however mean that pictures needed to be taken from a wide angle so as to have a view of the whole island.

On the 4th of November 1962 an ambitious mission was launched using five U-2's. The aeroplanes, who flew practically in a straight line, were to fly over the whole of the island from east to west, sweeping the whole of Cuba in one go. But the menace from the SA-2 sites was such that special precautions were taken by the US Air Force. The pilots had instructions to immediately stop the mission if the anti-aircraft missile sites were a threat to them. The U-2's were equipped with their own danger detectors and, to be even safer, several electronic eavesdropping planes circled in the distance.

Just as the U-2's crossed the Cuban coast several radar controls started to lock in on the American planes. The five aircraft immediately stopped their mission and turned back.

After a period of reflection the US Air Force finally decided that the precautions had probably been excessive. Isolated U-2 missions were started up again allowing them to leisurely detail the packing up of the missiles onto Soviet cargo ships.

The Cuban episode, which however wasn't quite over, still gave U-2 pilots a few frights. When flying over an air base in the Havana area one day, a pilot saw two MiG-21 take off to try and intercept him. He wouldn't have needed to worry if at that exact moment he hadn't had a jet engine failure. Slowly the U-2 started to lose height whilst its interceptors climbed towards him.

The pilot could follow the Cuban planes progression by watching their condensation trails through the Driftsight. After having considered for a moment escaping towards Mexico, he decided to try to reach

Florida all the time radioing the American fighters for help. This SOS calls were relayed by another U-2 in high altitude.

When he passed below the bar of 39,000 feet the pilot managed at the last minute to restart his engine and regain a more peaceful altitude before the MiG managed to catch him.

At the beginning of December 1962 the US Air Force accomplished the one hundredth reconnaissance mission with a U-2.

The crisis was then practically over.

It is to be noted however that the wrestling match between Kennedy and Khrushchev during this crisis was partly won thanks to the information which had been brought back by the CIA's U-2's during the previous months and years. During the USSR over flights these aeroplanes had notably permitted the facts to be gathered that showed the poorness of the Soviets ICBM fleets, which proved that Khrushchev was bluffing when he brandished the sceptre of an atomic war.

THE CIA'S NAVAL AVIATION

In 1963, faced with the difficulty of finding deployment terrains abroad, due to the pressure that the Soviet Union put onto the host countries, the idea to base U-2's on aircraft carriers rapidly made its way.

A first aircraft had structural modifications made and several external changes, the most visible being the addition of an aircraft arresting hook. The tests at sea started in August 1963 and proved to be totally satisfactory.

The apparent contradiction between the flight qualities of the U-2, that made it a very difficult machine to land, and the operations on the aircraft carriers, which needed great precision on landing, was resolved by putting destruction devices on the wings. As for the take off, it was helped along by the aide of a catapult, the bridge length available on the vessels was more than large enough for the U-2.

During the first few weeks of 1964, five CIA pilots were totally qualified for this type of operation. With forethought the CIA had already made up a list of objectives that could only be reached with the use of aircraft carriers and they did not wait until the end of the trials to launch the first operation.

First on the list figured a study of the French atomic experiments that were being actively prepared on the atoll of Mururoa, as the site of Reggane, in Algeria, had been closed down. Mururoa, in French Polynesia, was isolated in the middle of the Pacific Ocean, several thousand miles from any inhabited land. This was as much as to say that is was definitely out of reach of a U-2 which was based on land.

All the Americans had to do was to send an aircraft carrier into the zone, which was carried out during the month of May 1964 : it was the Operation Seeker.

When the first French atomic explosion took place at the site in 1964 the Ranger aircraft carrier was stationed a few hundred miles away from the French atoll. The U-2 that had been taken aboard was used to carry out several collections of radioactive particles in high altitude. From the study of these particles gathered during the flight, the scientists could deduct quite a bit of information about the quality of the bomb, and more precisely, about the material that had been used. This, in the eyes of Washington, was information of great value about the advanced state of the French research that progressed alone but with success.

It was also certain that the U-2 took advantage of the situation to take photographs from every direction of the French experimental sites.

THE U-2 AND CHINA

After the US Air Force had taken over the responsibility for most of the U-2 flights, the CIA did however keep the control of the U-2 operations over a specific theatre of operation : Communist China.

The misadventure of Gary Powers had definitely put an end to the over flights of the USSR but nobody (at the White House) had forbidden the CIA to fly over the other Communist countries. For more than ten years China was a choice objective.

The Chinese venture started at the end of the fifties with the training of a first contingent of Taiwanese pilots on American ground.

"OK for China but make sure that no other American pilot is captured" Eisenhower had basically said.

The CIA had resolved the problem in a very orthodox way, by having the planes flown by Chinese nationalist pilots. This had already happened, Taiwan was a faithful ally on whom the Americans could count to carry out their most dirty tricks.

When their training finished the nationalist pilots returned to Taiwan; to the Taoyuan airport, thirty miles south of the capital Taipei. Taoyuan was an American air base more specifically orientated towards air reconnaissance and was already regularly used by the US Air Force for launching its missions over continental China.

Two CIA U-2's were based there to begin with. To legally cover the American government collusion, contracts were signed in July 1960 between Lockheed and the Taiwanese government, formalizing the sale of U-2 aeroplanes. In reality the U-2's remained the property of the CIA who also provided the logistic back up necessary for their use.

Taiwan continued to provide the pilots of this strange unit where US Air Force aircraft artificers, dressed as civilians, CIA agents, Lockheed technicians and different companies all took part in the work load. From time to time even the CIA's own pilots were present to carry out special missions that the Americans wanted to keep to themselves.

The operations from Taiwan gave Washington the very first small information about Peking's military and nuclear programmes. The missions were prepared together by the Americans and the Taiwanese and the results were shared between the intelligence services of the two countries.

As was also the case for the USSR, it obviously involved the blatant over flights of Chinese territory. The only 'big' difference being the distances to be covered were even greater over China. The nuclear experimental sites, that the Americans were especially interested in, were nearly 2,300 miles away from Taiwan.

The flights were carried out to the limit of endurance, for the pilot as well as the plane, permanently over hostile territory and with no alternate airfield in case of mechanical problems.

Some centres were totally out of the U-2's reach and the CIA considered using advance bases in the Indian sub-continent. It goes without saying that the consequences, that were still very sensitive, of the Powers affair made negotiations extremely difficult with the governments concerned.

From 1961 the Taiwanese made up to three over flights per month of the continent. Some over flights went no further than the Chinese coast just opposite Taiwan, while others went deeply into Communist territory. During an over flight of continental China a pilot experienced a jet engine failure, but he managed to get back to Taiwan, nearly 125 miles away, by gliding!

PEKING FIRST VICTORIES

The room for manoeuvre in endurance was so small that the pilots often had to be content with flying in a straight line in the direction of their objective, without even attempting evasive measures to escape the ground radars. It was therefore easy for the Communists to guess the nature of the missions and even to lay in wait for the nationalist aeroplane on its way back, which was also a straight line, with the hope of shooting it down.

In July 1962, probably fed up of seeing aeroplanes circling over their heads without being able to do anything about it, the Communists made it known that they were offering 280,000 dollars to the nationalist pilot that defected with his plane.

Less than three months later, on the 9th of September 1962, Peking announced that they had shot down the first U-2. This victory, no doubt carried off with a SA-2, did not receive all the publicity that the Chinese could have hoped for. The difference from the Powers episode being that the pilot had been killed during the interception and, more importantly, the pilot wasn't American.

The White House could therefore give the press, quite dubiously, the official version of events, that is to say the sale of two aeroplanes by Lockheed to the Taiwanese Air Force.

"It's an affair strictly between the Chinese" said Washington. What the CIA retained from all that was that even with the rupture of relations with Moscow two years earlier the Chinese seemed to have kept an efficient network of anti-aircraft defence made up of Soviet missiles.

The Nationalists were to have the confirmation in the following months.

On the first of November 1963 another U-2 was shot down over Shanghai. The pilot, a Taiwanese, was captured this time.

Apparently confident about their SA-2 network that was in place, Peking could announce triumphantly that its air defence was "capable of shooting down U-2s at any altitude, day or night." A few months later another pilot was lost, this time during a training mission in the Formosa Strait that separated Taiwan and continental China. The man had lost control of his plane during a curve at high altitude.

This accident was a tragic reminder about the qualities of flight and the difficulties of piloting the U-2 at very high altitude.

In July 1964, a third U-2 was lost to the Chinese, in quite particular circumstances. Wing Commander Lee, who was at the controls of the aircraft, had already made an over flight of China. This second flight was to take him over the southern provinces of China, where the essential of the Chinese military aide passed on its way to North Vietnam. Washington lived in the fear that Peking would one day throw their forces into the conflict, the same as what had happened during the Korean War.

The surveillance missions using the U-2 had therefore been started up over the south of China, so as to avoid another strategically unpleasant surprise which would have been the second in less than fifteen years...

Lee had nearly finished his flight and was getting ready to head for his departure base, Cubi Point in the Philippines, when his threat detector manifested itself. His plane was 'engaged' by the Fan Song radar of a SA-2 missile site. A few seconds later another control button lit up on the instrument panel : indicating that the radar had been put into firing mode. A volley of SA-2 missiles was probably about to be fired!

Frantically Lee announced over the radio that a radar had spotted him. That was all.

A few seconds later a radar that was situated at the southern point of Taiwan noticed a unidentified object, without a doubt Lee's U-2, falling towards the Chinese town of Swatow near the coast.

The next morning Peking announced another victory against the 'capitalist hooligans'.

MISSILE COUNTER-MEASURES

After this new loss the CIA equipped its aircraft with extra counter-measures that allowed them to deceive the missiles as to the real position of the plane. Very soon the new system proved its usefulness.

During an over flight of the continent a pilot experienced a memorable fright when he was momentarily blinded by a SA-2 that passed only a few feet away from his plane. Misled by the U-2's counter measures the missile brushed its objective without exploding and got lost a bit further away in the sky. A thorough analysis of the electronic recordings revealed that not one but three missiles had been launched that day against the U-2. All had been deceived with the same amount of efficiency.

The absolute necessity to possess counter-measures was shown on several other occasions. Whether with their optic or electronic sensors, Taiwanese U-2 brought back the proof of numerous interception attempts that had failed.

At 68,000 feet a pilot, having detected a missile having been fired, had about 40 seconds before the latter reached his flight level. It was only just enough time to start off the evasive manoeuvres, if the counter-measures themselves were not enough to protect the aeroplane. At very high altitudes the explosion of a missile with a proximity fuse, could prove to be fatal in a radius of nearly 980 feet.

When the Taiwanese could not directly follow the progress of one of their aeroplanes that was going deep into the continent with their radars, they listened to the Communists channels to follow the sequence of events.

Frantic calls from air defence units paradoxically signified that all was going well : the U-2 was carrying out its mission and annoyed those that followed it on the ground. One night in January 1965 the Taiwanese operators witnessed such a scenario when, suddenly, the tension dropped on the Communist side of things. The Chinese anti aircraft defence commander signalled the end of the alert.

The next morning Peking announced the destruction of a fourth U-2.

The race between the sword and shield, between the missile guidance systems and the counter-measures thought up by the technicians was permanent. Each progress that one made was followed with the reaction of the other, so the advantage passed regularly from one side to the other. But each time the American side lost the round a plane fell.

Another problem was becoming clear to the CIA : the result of forever adding self-protection systems started to noticeably hinder the aeroplanes performances.

The U-2s range was less and the list of Chinese objectives that were out of the planes reach when based at Taiwan was getting longer each time the U-2s got heavier. The nuclear trial centre at Lop Nor, in the Western part of China, was one of these sites that were out of reach and it had always aroused the curiosity of the CIA. One solution was to have an aircraft take off from Peshawar, in Pakistan, but this base had been abandoned after the Powers affair. Another possibility was to have planes leave from Indian territory : border disagreement went on between China and India, who looked at each other but didn't speak, during the calmer moments at least.

In 1962 a quick rise in temperature had led to hard fighting between the two armies of the two countries in the Kashmir area. India had then looked for support from the Western side.

The United States proposed New Delhi to host a detachment of U-2 on its territory, in return they would share the information obtained. After long negotiations, during which the Indians tried to up the bids, an agreement was found in the spring of 1964. Only two or three missions were accomplished, the Americans gathered the much wanted information about Lop Nor, as for the Indians, they were delighted with the information gathered about the Chinese military deployments on their doorstep.

When the Vietnamese War intensified the U-2's were quite naturally put into use. Whilst the US Air Forces U-2s were used to keep watch over the battle fields and the Ho Chi Minh trail, the ones from the CIA concentrated their activity on the supply routes that relayed North Vietnam and Chinese territory.

Flights of this kind had already been carried out leaving from Taiwan, but wanting to be efficient, the CIA decided to set up a semi-permanent detachment on the Thai base of Takhli. Over the years the latter had become the centre of the Americans war effort in the area. As well as the U-2's, Takhli also hosted a complete squadron of F-105 fighter bombers of the US Air Force and a good part of Air Americas activities in the country.

The presence of Air America gave the CIA the idea to pass its Taiwanese pilots as Americans from Hawaii who were employed by Air America. Like that they stayed with the people they knew....

THE U-2 GROWS

After a dozen years in operation about fifteen of the fifty or so U-2's initially built were still available. The other aircraft had been destroyed during training or during operations.

Along with this worrying record was added the regular fall of the surviving planes performances, increasingly heavy with the addition of new equipment.

The study of the fabrication of a new model was quickly decided. As usual the Skunk Work worked quickly and effectively and, in 1967, the first U-2R took off for the first time. The U-2R, of which the first examples were operational the following year, were bigger, higher performing and easier to pilot than its predecessor. It offered an endurance record of fifteen hours, if the pilot could last that long. The first six aeroplanes were delivered to the CIA, who didn't waste time in putting two into service over the Chinese theatre of operation.

The geopolitical circumstances helped, the U-2R was also used to keep watch over other hot points in the world, top of the list the incessant skirmishes between the Egyptians and the Israelis.

The last over flight in the area went back to 1967 :

After the start of the Six Days War, aircraft and crew from the intelligence agency had been urgently deployed to the British base of Upper Heyford. From there they had waited for the go ahead of the political authorities to go and fly over the battle fields. But the go ahead was never given. The Spanish and then the French had refused the CIA's planes the right to fly over their territories, and the British hesitated as to whether they should authorize them to land at their Cypriot base of Akrotiri.

It was thought to use the few aircraft they had that could both be air refuelled and could also land on aircraft carriers. But even for the CIA it presented too many complications for a need that they were not really required for.

The matter was quickly dropped, for the time being anyway. As in 1970 a new deterioration in Israeli-Egyptian relations put the U-2 back into the foreground. The Egyptian efforts to regain possession of Sinai which was occupied by the Hebrew State had started a war of attrition in which the two countries engaged over the Suez Canal. They were an inch away from an open war.

On the 7th of August 1970 a cease fire was signed under the aegis of the UN and the United States.

Two of the CIA's new U-2R were quickly sent into the zone to check that the cease fire was respected on each side. After a stop over at Upper Heyford they finally established themselves at Akrotiri. The surveillance of the Suez Canal, with the two armies entrenched on each bank, was not exactly a leisurely position for the crews engaged in the photographic missions.

The Egyptians didn't immediately consent to the over flights whereas the Israelis only agreed after dragging their feet, they suspected the Americans of being more interested in their manoeuvre than they liked to make out.

The pilots threaded their aircraft through the two sides, under close surveillance of the missile batteries of the two belligerents. With two flights per week the CIA's aircraft carried out around thirty missions during the three months that the operation lasted.

END OF AN ERA

For the American Intelligence Agency there was only one deployment zone left that permanently received aeroplanes : it was of course Taiwan.

Quite surprisingly the over flights of China carried on in a more or less regular fashion up until 1972, even with the protests made by Peking. It wasn't until the official visit of President Nixon to the Chinese capital that, to show his goodwill, he announced a definite stop to the spy flights. The sacrifice wasn't a big one to make : the over flights were becoming more risky, the crop of information was already a good one and mainly, giving proof of fine duplicity, the Americans had only promised to stop the "piloted flights" above Chinese territory.

In other words the door was wide open to over flights made by planes without pilots. In fact, what luck, the CIA and the US Air Force had started to work on this kind of machine especially designed for reconnaissance missions!

With the end of the Chinese period the CIA turned an important page in the history of its air operations and it completely abandoned the running of the U-2 to the US Air Force.

It was without regret, as with help, once again, from Lockheed, the intelligence agency was getting ready to start working with aircraft that were even more spectacular than the U-2.

CHAPTER 10

ESPIONAGE OF THE HIGHEST DEGREE

A WISH FULFILLED

At the end of the sixties, the CIA left the 'U-2 business' without any difficulties. The US Air Force rapidly took over the planes, pilots, ground installations and U-2 missions completely. All that was done without any hysterics or open warfare between the two administrations...how come?

It was the fact that the CIA, having obtained yet more beautiful playthings from the taxpayer, was in a position to give up its old ones without regret.

The U-2 was capable of flying high but not very fast.

The CIA knew that its plane would one day be vulnerable to anti-aircraft defences. They could not accept this as the surveillance of Soviet activities was a fundamental reason for its existence. From 1955, Richard Bissel asked the Skunk Works (code name for Lockheed's research unit in charge of the 'black' projects) a question : what could be done to exceed the performance of the U-2?

The CIA wanted a plane which would fly very high and very fast. A plane which, if possible, would be difficult to observe by radar. The U-2 had been fairly disappointing in this respect.

A great deal of freedom was accorded to Skunk Works to design a plane which would fulfil a number of specifications summarized as follows: high, fast and far, very discreet.

This miracle plane was called the A-12, code name Oxcart. The A-12 would later give rise to the famous SR-71 Blackbird. The creator of both the U-2 and the Blackbird was Kelly Johnson. And for both these planes, Johnson and Skunk Works applied their motto : "Be quick, be quiet and be on time."

Once again, Skunk Works created a success which seemed on first sight to be an impossibility. The success of the A-12/SR-71 programme can be better understood if it is remembered that this plane, which made its first flight in 1962, is still the fastest plane in the world today!

To answer the demands of the CIA, Kelly Johnson tried initially to see if the U-2 could be improved. Three areas were subject to particular scrutiny : speed, altitude and stealthiness against radars. It was quickly realized that only the factor of altitude had some chance of being scaled up. The very specific construction of the U-2 prevented the machine from being thought of as a supersonic or even a stealth aircraft.

It remained for Johnson therefore to wipe the slate clean of the past and start from a completely new beginning. The objective that Skunk Works decided on was simple enough in theory : the CIA plane had to be able to cruise at Mach 3 at an altitude of more than 80,000ft. To shelter it from possible interceptions by missiles, it had to have the weakest possible radar signature, and possess effective electronic counter measure (ECM) equipment.

Put together, these characteristics merged into an awesome industrial challenge.

A thick volume would be required to detail all the technical constraints raised by the A-12 programme and the answers that were found. In particular, it was necessary to open up new territory in the science of metallurgy in order to give the plane a structure capable of resisting a cruising speed greater than Mach 3. At this speed, in spite of an exterior temperature of minus 50°C, the nose of the plane would heat up to more than 200°C and the windscreen to more than 150°C. The only adjustment of this and of the lenses of the on board cameras, which had to conserve excellent optical qualities in spite of the temperature restrictions, lasted three years and cost more than two million dollars!

The response found by Skunk Works was the generalization of the use of titanium, a metal capable of resisting very high temperatures. Titanium had, up until then, only been used in very small quantities in the aeronautical industry because of its cost and also because it was difficult to work with. In the case of the A-12, more than 85% of the structure of the plane was in titanium and the engineers at Lockheed had to take the plunge and learn how to work this metal on a large scale.

The heating of the structure at great speed also caused the plane to stretch by a few inches. A consequence of this was that the sheets of metal as they expanded sealed the tanks very tightly and rendered them absolutely leakproof. When the plane returned to the ground, the metal started to cool, returned to its normal dimensions and the A-12 started to leak. It was a characteristic of the plane...

Another first for the A-12 was that it was a large user of composite materials capable of 'absorbing' electromagnetic waves from radars. The idea of creating a 'stealth' plane was certainly not new as it began at the same time as the radar. What was for many only an engineer's dream had, with the A-12, found its first successful application.

The unusual technical solutions chosen were reflected in the futuristic appearance of the plane. The A-12 was a beast which displayed its unique capabilities in its shape. The plane was 102 feet long, with a wingspan of 55 feet. The long, flat fuselage was flanked by two enormous engines, which fitted flush in a wide delta wing which extended by two apexes right up to the point of the nose. The plane had something of a Manta Ray and an arrow about it.

This menacing appearance was reinforced by the black paint which covered the entire aircraft.

Not content with piloting alone the most complex machine of his epoch, the pilot of the A-12 had also to be sure of faultless navigational skills (even though his aircraft was flying at more than a mile every two seconds)! and be able to utilize the on board cameras. He had an enormous workload and this was reflected in the cockpit layout with its instruments and indicators of all sorts.

"Even though it was a little narrow at head height, because of the pointed shape of the canopy, the cockpit was fairly comfortable", noted the pilots. "Even wearing a pressurised suit, the controls were very accessible."

Borrowed from the U-2, the driftsight figured prominently on the instrument panel of the A-12. The pilot also had use of a small retractable periscope which enabled him to see behind. When the periscope was up, it rose only a few inches above the fuselage and gave the pilot the possibility of checking, before entering a sensitive zone, that he was not leaving any trail of condensation behind as this could have betrayed his presence.

"We could also cast an eye over the engines, the stabilizer and fins and the rear of the fuselage. A quick look through the periscope gave us more information than a hundred warning lights!" said the pilots.

The payload was set out in a vast bay just behind the pilot. Very large cameras could be carried, allowing very high quality pictures to be taken. The logic which prevailed later with the SR-71 was a little different : a second member of the crew, the reconnaissance systems operator (RSO), was installed behind the pilot, resulting in less space for the payload. The decreased quality of the documents was a direct result of this situation, before miniaturization did away with this handicap.

THE CIA PLACES AN ORDER

The CIA financed the Lockheed Skunk Works through special accounts; and even though the Air Force also participated in the A-12 programme, the project never appeared in Pentagon records.

The CIA had nonetheless not put all its eggs in one basket. Several other aircraft manufacturers had been asked to come up with proposals for supersonic reconnaissance aircraft. But, unsurprisingly, the Lockheed Oxcart project prevailed in this secret and informal competition. On the 29th of August 1959, the CIA officially entrusted Kelly Johnson's Skunk Works with the development of a reconnaissance aircraft capable of flying at Mach 3. Four months later, a second contract was placed for the construction of twelve aircraft.

The CIA insisted that the top-secret project should benefit from a level of confidentiality similar to that which had prevailed with the U-2 programme. Some even drew parallels with the Manhattan Project, which gave the United States the atomic bomb during the second world war.

In November 1961 the CIA selected a first group of pilots. To the men of the US Air Force who volunteered it was simply a matter of "piloting a very technically advanced plane." Even though it was rather terse, the proposition was sufficiently appetising to attract enough volunteers. The CIA established extremely rigorous selection procedures, similar to those carried out for the NASA space programme, and a first group of eleven pilots was selected. As for the U-2, they had to undergo the close scrutiny of the CIA before being fully accepted in the programme.

The manufacture of the first prototype progressed rapidly, but following the problems encountered working with titanium and the difficulty encountered with the engines, the programme was soon a year behind. When the plane was finally ready, it followed the way of the U-

2 seven years earlier : The prototype was taken apart and taken to the secret base of Groom Lake, where it was put back together and prepared for the first flight. The installations which had been used to conduct the U-2 tests were renewed and enlarged.

This first flight took place on the 26th of April 1962. Because of their insufficient motorization, the first prototypes barely passed Mach 1 during the first months of adjustment.

The situation improved greatly when the A-12 started to receive J-58 jet engines at the beginning of 1963. The J-58 however, continued to give the Pratt and Whitney engineers nightmares and its adjustment was very difficult. The A-12 reached at that time a speed of Mach 3; but several more months of work and many more dollars were necessary for the plane to be considered fully operational at that speed.

On the 27th of October 1962 the loss of a U-2 above Cuba during the missile crisis highlighted the need for the CIA to have a fast moving successor to operate in 'sensitive' zones. The pursuit and success of the Oxcart programme became a priority for the American intelligence community.

When he arrived at the White House after the assassination of Kennedy, President Johnson was informed of the existence of the Oxcart programme. He chose to make the existence of the A-12 public, but in a roundabout way which would not reveal the role of the CIA. On the 29th of February 1964, Lyndon Johnson spoke to the American nation of an interceptor with staggering capabilities, able to reach 2,000 miles an hour. The secret had been so well kept that it was a big surprise even within the US Air Force. As for the real role of a spy plane operating for the CIA, it was passed over in silence.

In August 1965, the CIA asked Lockheed to rapidly make all the final adjustments to the plane, so as to have at least four operational machines capable of flying over Cuba from the following November. Following the missile crisis, the U-2 continued to fly over the island at a sustained rhythm, which exasperated the Soviets as much as the Cubans. The Soviets had announced their intention to shoot down all American planes which persisted in violating Cuban air space. Even though it was initially limited to Mach 2.9 at cruising speed, the A-12 displayed far better possibilities for survival than the U-2 in this context.

However, no CIA pilot had yet fully qualified on the plane, which demanded a long apprenticeship. Lockheed therefore offered to contribute its own test pilots. According to Kelly Johnson, an A-12 piloted by a man form Lockheed flew over Cuba on the 10th of November 1965 as part of operation Skylark.

The CIA version of events differed on this point :

According to the Agency, it had indeed been decided to use the A-12s even though they had not yet reached the performance level expected and did not have their electronic counter measure equipment. Nonetheless, as it was able to flirt with Mach 3 at 75,000ft, the A-12 was judged sufficiently effective to be used in the field. The simulations of reconnaissance missions, conducted in American territory, had been conclusive. A detachment of five pilots and five planes, able to be mobilized at short notice, was set up. According to the CIA, this detachment was however never used above Cuba, the U-2s succeeded in playing the game well.

Paradoxically, the performance of the A-12 was so exceptional that it demanded an equally exceptional theatre of operation, in order to be used at maximum potential. This critical situation, long awaited by the CIA to be able to engage its planes, finally arrived in Asia. As we have seen earlier, the flights over China by the U-2s became more and more uncertain. From the month of March 1965 the CIA therefore started to prepare its A-12s in view of a deployment on the Kadena base in Japan.

The A-12 was then in its final form. Its teething troubles had been corrected and the plane fulfilled perfectly its specifications. It flew four times faster than the U-2 and 15,000ft higher. Lighter than the SR-71 which was to be its successor, the A-12 displayed capabilities which were never exceeded. It reached Mach 3.56 and a record altitude of 96,200ft.

Meanwhile, anti-aircraft defences were certainly improved with the increase of SA-2 sites, but the engineers of Skunk Works remained absolutely confident in the virtual invulnerability of the A-12.

The planes and pilots were ready : a unit had been created, the 1129th Special Activities Squadron. Even though the CIA was technically in charge of the programme, the unit, made up of CIA and Air Force personnel along with civilian technicians, was integrated into the Air Force.

In addition to the A-12, the unit put several other jets into operation (F-101, Voodoo, F-104 Starfighter) for training and technical support.

The CIA was waiting for the green light from the political authorities to use the plane. All throughout 1966, the requests to fly over China and North Vietnam were refused. There was a great fear, based on the political consequences rather than the highly secret nature of the plane itself, that an A-12 would be shot down. It was out of the question to have the A-12 piloted by Taiwanese as the U-2 had been.

The CIA, which had every confidence in the plane, was fully in favour of these flights. Conversely, certain high-ranking individuals in the Pentagon and the State Department, as well as the President himself, were strongly opposed to them, considering the technical and political risks to be too great. As we will see further on, the drones (pilotless planes) and satellites took over and presented less of a risk...

Such was the situation at the end of 1966 : if it was impossible to justify the operational use of its planes, even though they were the most high performance aircraft in the world. The CIA was ready to stop their use and to keep the remaining planes in storage (two A-12 had been lost during training missions).

FIRST OPERATIONS

At the very last moment, the A-12 was saved by the Vietnam War.

At the beginning of 1967, the Americans noticed with concern the increase in the number of SA-2 ground to air missile sites around the North Vietnamese capital, Hanoi. Their fear was that this deployment would preclude the installation of ground to ground missiles, more dangerous and loaded with significance, because they were capable of carrying a tactical nuclear load. Once again, the experience in Cuba was never far from the minds of the CIA...

The Agency took the opportunity to return to the attack with its A-12s and President Johnson conceded to their use in mid-May 1967. Operation Black Shield, which was one of the best kept secrets of the Vietnam war, was therefore launched.

In the space of a few days, a detachment of three aircraft was set up in Kadena in Japan and, on the 29th of May 1967, the unit was declared operational. The first mission, officially the very first in the career of the A-12, took place two days later.

The flight preparation procedure began thirty or so hours before take off, with an initial study of the weather over the objectives to be covered and a basic preparation of the route to be followed. At H-12, a second weather study was carried out. If the results were favourable, the sequence continued with a detailed preparation of the navigation, the setting up of the support planes, preparation of the payload etc. Two hours before take off, there was a general review of the means of action, particularly for those who were connected with the refuelling planes along the flight path of the A-12. The weather was also analyzed a last time, not only above the target, but also over the planned refuelling areas and the departure and arrival fields, and any diversion areas.

In parallel to this, the pilot was briefed twice : a first time the day before the mission and a second time on the day itself. The plane was obviously the object of much care and attention from the technicians of Lockheed, Pratt and Whitney and other companies participating in the programme. In case of last minute unavailability, a second plane was ready to take over from the first in an hour.

It was Major Mel Vojvodich who had the honour of leading the first mission over Vietnam on the 31st of May 1967 :

"Immediately after taking off from Kadena, I joined up with a Boeing refuelling plane to fill my tanks. Heading south west, I then flew over the island of Hainan, before flying above North Vietnamese territory directly over the port of Haiphong."

The plane was flying at Mach 3.1 and at 80,000ft. It crossed North Vietnam in about twelve minutes, before reaching Laos, near Dien Bien Phu.

Of the 170 to 190 anti-aircraft missile sites in North Vietnam, 70 were photographed during this single, lightning fast run. Nine other important sites were also flown over. According to Lockheed, the plane was not at any time 'engaged' by communist radar, which meant that the passage of the plane had been completely unnoticed from the ground.

Major Vojvodich continues his account : "After this first crossing, I went down to 30,000ft to refuel a second time. After refuelling, which took place in Thai air space, I climbed to fly over Vietnam again, passing this time near the demilitarized zone. Reaching the China sea, I headed directly back to Kadena where I landed after a flight of 3 hours and 39 minutes."

The success of the mission was total.

As soon as possible after landing, the films were taken out of the A-12 and sent by special plane to the United States, to the Kodak laboratories in Rochester, on Lake Ontario. Several hours after the launch of the mission, President Johnson was given the assurance that no ground to ground missiles had been deployed in North Vietnam. Subsequently the films were developed in Japan which permitted the American High Command present in the Vietnam theatre to have the information in a little less than 24 hours.

Throughout the following ten weeks, seven other Black Shield missions were carried out. Then between the 16th of August and the 31st of December 1967, fifteen others followed.

The North Vietnamese started to become agitated when the A-12 passed over : the planes were sometimes followed by radar and several SA-2 missiles were fired. The A-12s brought back to Kadena photographs showing the ascent of the missiles to the plane and their explosion at a great distance away. The ECM equipment on board offered effective protection to the CIA planes. Several years earlier, the U-2 had obtained the same surprising pictures involving interception attempts by fighters.

On the 30th of October 1967, the pilot Dennis Sullivan, at the controls of his A-12, detected the activity of two North Vietnamese anti-aircraft sites during a first run over the country.

"The radars were following me but no missile was fired", he explained. "Things changed during the second run. This time, at least eight missiles were launched against me. Perhaps even more that I didn't see..."

Once again the films brought proof of missile launches and detonations quite far from the plane. On his return to Kadena, a single, small fragment was found in the wing of Sullivan's A-12.

Throughout 1967, the A-12s were placed on alert 41 times and 22 missions were actually launched.

Operation Black Shield continued into 1968 : four missions were launched over North Vietnam and two over North Korea during the first four months of that year. American policy was still not keen on the idea of increasing flights over enemy territory. It was acceptable in Vietnam, where American pilots were taken prisoner every week, in the context of 'standard' combat. But North Korea was quite another scenario and the obsessive fear of losing a pilot here was very strong.

The CIA and the US Air Force eventually won the decision be explaining that the speed at which the A-12 flew, to fly over Korea would only take seven minutes. It was highly unlikely that the aircraft would be shot down in such a short lapse of time. In the event of mechanical failure, the plane would have easily enough altitude and speed to leave the zone and land elsewhere other than in enemy territory...

The missions over Korea came after the capture of the USS Pueblo, an electronic surveillance ship cruising in international waters, by the North Koreans on the 23rd of January 1968. An A-12 was sent to try and locate the ship that had been taken to a Korean port. At the controls of the plane, Jack Weeks described how easily he succeeded in his mission:

"After take off from Kadena, I immediately had the tanks filled by the refuelling plane, then I got into position to begin my first reconnaissance run : with the camera on, I left Vladivostok and I went down the entire eastern coast of North Korea, where we thought the ship would be found. When I approached the port of Wonsan, I was able to see the Pueblo on the screen of my driftsight. The port was icebound, apart from the entrance, and that is where the ship was found. I continued my flight up to the border with South Korea then I turned back and headed north to fly over the area again."

Weeks made four photographic reconnaissance runs over North Korea in total. The length and breadth of the country was covered, from the demilitarized zone separating North and South Korea up to the border with China. If his flight passed off completely undetected by the Koreans, it was detected by the Chinese, who passed the information to their North Korean allies, who did not react. What would they have been able to do against the A-12, which was so completely out of their reach?

A third mission over Korea took place on the 8th of May 1968. Then the A-12 ended its operational career unobtrusively. Its successor and cousin, the SR-71 Blackbird, learnt to take over from it.

This decision was not a surprise. In the first weeks of 1961, Kelly Johnson had proposed a slightly larger version of the A-12 to the Air Force and more particularly to the Strategic Air Command. The plane in question, which was to be christened SR-71 Blackbird, was therefore developed practically in parallel with the A-12.

THE SR-71 ENTERS THE STAGE

From the end of 1966, five months before the A-12 finished its first missions over Vietnam, the finalizing of the SR-71 was well under way. For this reason, it had already been decided to put an end to the civilian A-12 programme, that of the CIA, at the end of 1967, so as to put the maximum effort into the purely military SR-71 programme.

Even though its exterior was very similar to the A-12, the SR-71 was 1.5 metres longer and 50% heavier. The plane benefited from several new aerodynamic refinements, and a second crew member, a Reconnaissance Systems Officer (RSO), responsible for operating the on board systems, was placed behind the pilot. Slightly slower than the A-12, the SR-71 embarked a much greater variety of payload allowing it to carry out electronic information gathering, and optical or radar photography. The latest versions of cameras on board gave a resolution of around 1 to 1.5 inches on the ground. Enough to make out the pawn in a game of chess!

According to initial plans, all the A-12s of the CIA had to be gradually put into storage between July 1967 and January 1968. But the highly successful deployment at Kadena, which gave rise to a wealth of information, turned the calendar upside down. The withdrawal of the A-12s and their replacement by SR-71 of the Air Force was put back several weeks, without the idea being abandoned however. It was not before March 1968 that the first SR-71s arrived in Kadena from Beale in California. Meanwhile, the CIA planes returned definitively to the United States where they were mothballed. Only eleven years had elapsed from the drawing board in 1957 to the withdrawal of the plane in 1968. Out of fifteen A-12 built, five were lost during training or development flights. Of course no machine had ever been lost in operation.

As in the case of the U-2, the Air Force greatly assisted the CIA during the finalizing of the A-12. It participated financially but also offered logistic support and provided specially modified refuelling planes, essential to the A-12 missions. But certainly there was a certain amount of frustration, as was the case for the U-2, in seeing the A-12, the fastest plane in the world, escape its control.

Fairly swiftly, the Air Force took its revenge and got an interesting return on investment by obtaining the SR-71. As the A-12 and the SR-71 were fairly similar planes, it was soon decided that the CIA would stop its operations with the A-12, the SR-71 taking over with a more diversified payload. All was not lost for the agency insofar as the SR-71 of the Air Force was classified as being a means of strategic reconnaissance put at the disposal of the National Reconnaissance Office (NRO).

The NRO was an organization so secret within the American intelligence community that its existence was not admitted or made public before 1992, some thirty-two years after its creation. It had been set up to arbitrate and administer the different means of strategic reconnaissance between the CIA and the Air Force : reconnaissance planes, satellites, both administrations engaged in a continuous trench warfare to obtain control of new systems. These quarrels over territory were only resolved by creating a third organization, a neutral ground in the middle of the other two. The NRO, which had an astronomical budget of 6 billion dollars, had the upper hand concerning reconnaissance satellites and, under the heading of piloted planes, the SR-71.

In order to keep a certain balance between the CIA and the Air Force, the NRO was placed directly under the control of the Ministry of Defence, but at its head was the Director of Central Intelligence, also the head of the CIA.

Taking the place of the A-12 at Kadena, the SR-71 carried out some 600 reconnaissance missions over Vietnam throughout the duration of the war.

THE BLACKBIRD ON ALL FRONTS

During and after the Vietnam War the Blackbird flew over practically every hotspot in the world, as much for military intelligence services as for the CIA. In spite of its extraordinary performance, the SR-71 made do with a quite simple logistic, which facilitated its deployment in forward operating locations, as had also been practiced with the U-2. Apart from Kadena, a semi-permanent detachment was also set up at Mildenhall in Great Britain.

In 1973, during and after the Yom Kippur war which had put Israel against its Arab neighbours, two SR-71s carried out nine reconnaissance missions over the battlefield. So as not to bring down the wrath of the Arab countries on them, the British had refused the use of the Mildenhall base. The planes left directly from the east coast of the United States. The flights lasted more than eleven hours and there were six in-flight refuelling operations.

From the Suez canal to Lebanon, the passage over combat zones lasted no more than 25 minutes at Mach 3. The intelligence gathered (with complete impunity) was transmitted to the Israelis by the CIA.

The speed of the Blackbird was not always an advantage : there was barely enough time to carry out the gathering of electronic intelligence with a plane that was flying too fast. The Blackbird therefore played the role of stimulating anti-aircraft defence, leaving other specialized and slower aircraft (Boeing RC-135 or EC-135) the task of gathering the electronic intelligence after its passage.

The SR-71 did not fly over the Soviet Union, being content to follow its borders to cast an inquisitive eye or ear inside the empire. The USSR had however some justification in complaining about the activity of the Blackbirds along its borders as by flying at more than 60,000 ft, the American planes could easily see several hundred miles inside their territory. Positioned at the rear of the SR-71, the RSO took great care to control the path of the plane correctly by putting the different sensors into operation : optical photographs or radar, the latter being used in the event of bad weather over the target. With the progress of electronics, radar imagery left its secondary role and became a fully fledged primary system, with notably in 1986, the arrival of the first synthetic aperture radars.

The event of a Blackbird approaching the Soviet border always led to several Soviet fighters taking off to try and catch up with the American plane, to no avail.

Lieutenant Belenko, who defected to the west in September 1976 with his MiG 25, the most powerful Soviet interceptor of the time, tells here of an encounter between a Soviet interceptor and a Blackbird :

"The American SR-71s flew along the Soviet coast, staying just on the edge of our national airspace. (...) They scoffed at the interceptors that had been sent to meet them, climbing to altitudes well beyond our reach, or fleeing at speeds that we could not equal."

To intercept an SR-71 with a missile posed certain problems that the Soviets did not seem to be up to overcoming at that time: at Mach 3, the SR-71 was too fast to be caught up by a missile fired from behind it. As for a missile fired from head on, it would quite simply mean a complete defeat for the calculators of the period, not powerful enough to handle aircraft-missile closing speeds of more than Mach 6!

Above countries such as Cuba or Nicaragua, the SR-71 could quite happily give its all. Totally invulnerable, they flew over 'sensitive zones' in a few seconds or minutes at the most. On his arrival at the White House, President Carter banned all flights over Cuba as a sign of good will. But in 1978, satellite photos showed the presence of a Soviet cargo ship unloading large boxes in the port of Havana : fifteen MiG 23s had just been delivered to Castro. This caused some emotion in Washington, for a very specific version of the MiG 23 was known to be able to deliver nuclear weapons. Two flights over Cuba by SR-71s were ordered in November 1978. They brought confirmation that the MiG 23s delivered to Castro were the 'air defence' and not the nuclear attack model. The difference between these two versions is summed up by the presence of several antennae on the plane, which incidentally reveals the extraordinary precision of the images brought back by Blackbird. Another lesson from these missions, later very soon forgotten, was the perfect complementarity existing between the SR-71 and the satellites.

In 1981, fearing a Soviet military intervention against Poland, the SR-71 based in Mildenhall led several surveillance missions from the Baltic sea for the CIA and other American intelligence agencies.

For every plane leaving on a mission, there was always a spare one capable of being put into operation very rapidly. If it was only a 'routine' flight, the reserve plane simply remained in the hangar, available if the need arose. At the next level of priority, the replacement aircraft was ready to take off with the crew in position in the cockpit. In the event of the initial plane failing, take off was immediate. As far as the most important missions were concerned, the reserve plane flew thirty minutes behind the first SR-71!

Such a case ocurred in July 1987, during a reconnaissance mission over the Persian Gulf. Iran had threatened to block the strait of Hormuz and an SR-71 was sent from the base at Kadena to fly over the zone and spot possible coastal batteries of Iranian Silkworm anti-shipping missiles. A first Blackbird took off followed thirty minutes later by the reserve plane.

On nearing the strait of Hormuz, the SR-71 slowed down to Mach 2.5. Above this speed, the turning range was too large and the crew would not be able to correctly negotiate its navigation between the different national air spaces. Forty thousand feet lower down, an American AWACS was keeping an eye out for any trouble. But the passage of the Blackbird was so fast that the Iranians did not have the time to try anything against it.

After a total flight of eleven hours and three refuelling operations, the SR-71 came back to land at Kadena in Japan. It was therefore the longest mission ever undertaken with an SR-71.

On the morning of the 15th of April 1986, the SR-71s from Mildenhall flew over Libya, to evaluate the damage inflicted by the US Air Force bomb raids which had taken place earlier in the night.

Several weeks later, on the 26th of August 1986, a Blackbird was finishing a flight along the demilitarized zone separating North and South Korea when two SA-2 missiles were launched against it by the North Koreans. The plane's ECM system functioned perfectly and the missiles flew by at a good distance without troubling the plane, which was flying in South Korean air space. The crew took note of the firing and the affair degenerated into a diplomatic incident between the United States and North Korea.

Since they were put into operation, the SR-71s recorded more than 1,000 attacks against them, the majority being at the end of the sixties and during the seventies. A significant number of these attacks occured during missions directed against North Korea and Vietnam.

The plane, which had never been taken by any anti-aircraft defence, 'fell' however in January 1990, a victim of the end of the cold war. With 3551 operational missions and more than 11,000 hours of flying at Mach 3 to their credit, the SR-71s were restricted to a forced retirement (out of 31 aircraft built, twenty were still available at that date and a reserve of eight planes was kept permanently operational). It was said that the plane was expensive to operate. Taking into account the fleet of refuelling planes and the highly specialized ground personnel needed to keep the last SR-71s operational, the cost to the Air Force was from 300 to 350 million dollars a year.

The Pentagon thought it would be able to do without these services by relying only on a single production of satellites and U-2s. Outside the small community of Blackbird users, very few people realized the complimentary nature of the three different systems.

The SR-71 had only just been withdrawn from service when the Gulf war began and, very quickly it was asked whether the plane would be brought back into service. But it was not before 1995, at the height of the crisis between the United States and North Korea, that the step was taken : a small detachment comprising only three planes was reactivated. The aircraft received yet more sophisticated equipment, notably a transmission capability in near real time, which doubled their value as an intelligence system.

But the experience was short-lived. At the end of 1997, Blackbird fell again, this time a victim of Congress, an assembly far more fearsome than all the anti-aircraft missiles in the world together. Rumours concerning the existence of a secret successor to the Blackbird, capable of yet more stunning feats, were re-launched. A logical mind would have noticed that the withdrawal of such an exceptional plane was perfectly justified only with the possibility that there was another one to replace it.

The existence of this other plane remains a matter for speculation, even though it has already been given a name : Aurora. Many hypotheses have been put forward concerning the propulsion, architecture and the performance of this aircraft. Indeed on whether there is a pilot on board. Is the successor to the Blackbird, if it exists, an unmanned aeroplane?

LIKE MOTHER, LIKE DAUGHTER

The humiliating capture of Gary Powers in 1960 gave the concept of a reconnaissance drone an impetus which was to be decisive.

A pilotless version of the A-12 had first been discussed between the CIA and Lockheed. But faced with the technical difficulties that such a project would have raised, the idea was abandoned in aid of an autonomous vehicle of smaller dimensions, and complimentary to the A-12. This was the drone D-21.

From the initial outline, the D-21 was conceived as an extension of the reconnaissance capabilities of the A-12. The drone was carried on the back of the A-12, which had the double mission of transporting it near its target and giving it the speed required for the light up of its ram jet engine. This aircraft, whose existence was only made public well after it had stopped being used, was even more secret than the A-12 or the SR-71.

The project was launched at the end of 1962, after the CIA had given the go ahead for an initial feasibility study.

The objective was to obtain an aircraft with a range of 3,000 miles at Mach 3 and with a payload permitting very high quality photographs to be brought back (a resolution of 6 inches was required). The plane would be sent to fly over zones considered too 'sensitive', either for military or diplomatic reasons, for the A-12.

Launched form an A-12, the D-21 was not recoverable at the end of its flight: it was programmed to jettison its payload (camera and film) and its brain, its inertial navigation system, at a very precise point, before self destructing.

Two A-12 were specially modified to carry the drone on their backs. These planes were therefore christened M-12, M for Mother, and the

D in D-12 was for Daughter. The first flight of the M-12/D-12 unit took place on the 29th of December.

In May of the following year, the two aircraft combination reached Mach 2.6. The major difficulty in the programme was to make a success of the delicate separation phase between the drone and its mother plane, at Mach 3. This crucial test was carried out with much delay on the 5th of March 1966. If the first three tests went off correctly, the fourth one turned into a drama, suddenly bringing to light the foolhardiness of the concept of a launch at Mach 3 : the D-21 knocked into the mother plane at the moment it was released form its pylon. The M-12 nosed up under the impact of this, which at Mach 3 led to the immediate breaking of its structure. The two crew members managed to eject, but as the plane was flying over the sea, one of them drowned when his pressurised flying suit filled with water.

The idea of launching from an M-12 was swiftly abandoned, in favour of launching from a B-52 heavy bomber. The D-21 was carried under its wing and, after its drop, it was accelerated by a powder booster to Mach 3, the speed at which its ram jet engine could ignite itself and take over.

Propulsion, autonomous navigation system, recuperation of the payload sequence, the pitfalls concerning the perfecting of the aircraft were as numerous as they were difficult to overcome. It was not before June 1969, seven years after the launch of the programme that Lockheed could at last inform the CIA that the D-21 was finalized : conforming to its specifications, the drone forty feet long and weighing 5 tons when fully laden, happily exceeded Mach 3.3. It flew at more than 95,000ft and had a range of 3,000 miles. A minuscule and ultra-fast target, the D-21 was going to prove difficult to intercept.

It remained, however, to convince the President of the time, Richard Nixon, to use it in a real situation. This was done on the 9th of November 1969, when the first D-21 was launched from a B-52. The objective was China.

To preserve the secrecy of the operation, the B-52 took off at night from the Beale base in California, and landed on the island of Guam in the middle of the Pacific. The plane took off again the next day for the second stage which led it to the doors of China where the drone was launched. The B-52 immediately headed back to Guam.

This first mission was a failure: quite simply the drone disappeared! The Lockheed engineers thought it was due to an error in the navigational software which had been the cause of some concern during the adjustment phase, they then got back to work.

Just over a year later, on the 16th of December 1970, a second mission was launched. The flight took place normally, the drone followed its programmed flight path perfectly, but the payload could not be recovered and so this was another failure.

The third attempt took place a little less than three months later. The flight was once again a success, but the payload was once again lost : it had however been correctly ejected from the drone at the end of the mission, but the recovery phase, which involved a C-130 meant to hook up the load attached under a parachute, went badly wrong. The parachute was damaged and the payload, enclosed in its watertight box, fell into the water. It floated for a moment, but then the box was subsequently damaged by a ship during the recovery operation and it sank.

A fourth mission, also with China as its objective, was attempted. The D-21 this time did not complete its flight and was reported missing in action while it was flying over a highly sensitive zone. This was the last operational flight of the machine.

Four missions, four failures, and a total of 21 development flights which had not all been successful, not by a long way...

Despite the technical feats which had marked the development of the D-21, the programme still lacked maturity. The CIA, whose interest in the programme had decreased due to the fact that the tests were taking too much time, put a final end to the experience after the failure of the fourth flight above China.

The programme was officially ended in mid-1971 and the surviving machines, 38 D-21s had been built, were put into storage.

However, the idea of reconnaissance drones was not buried. Even though the D-21 had a long and difficult development, these machines without pilots were beginning a spectacular career owing to the Vietnam war.

THE RYAN FAMILY

At the end of the fifties, the American firm Ryan was at the forefront of production of aerial combat training drones. During the course of a presentation of its different models to superior officers of the Air Force, the directors of Ryan mentioned the idea of models that were specifically adapted to reconnaissance missions.

The existence and use of the U-2 started to be known in "well-informed circles" and it was easy to foresee the embarrassing consequences that would arise from the capture of a pilot in the middle of the Soviet Union.

Extrapolated from existing machines, the development of a reconnaissance drone posed few problems for Ryan. The machine would be content with a standard performance, subsonic speed, reasonable altitude. For want of claiming invulnerability, such a machine could be rapidly operational and at a modest price.

This idea of course was given a tremendous boost after the capture of Gary Powers on the 1st of May 1960. Several weeks later, it was the turn of an RB-47 electronic surveillance plane of the US Air Force to be shot down by the Soviets, off Scandinavia. The need for planes without pilots was therefore very pressing, but the Air Force, which had committed considerable sums in the development of the SR-71, could not really keep two pots on the boil.

It was therefore the turn of the CIA to become interested in the secret reconnaissance programme which originated at Ryan's, under the code name Red Wagon. But this programme was still born : after the victory of John Kennedy in the presidential elections in 1960, the change of administration meant it was abandoned.

Once again the ball was in the court of the US Air Force: the loss of a U-2 during the missile crisis was yet another impetus. The Air Force had at that time two prototypes of a new reconnaissance drone in phase of development in its possession. Plans were made to use them without delay above Cuba, but a last-minute counter order cancelled the operation and the drones remained in the United States, to follow their test programme.

Not long was needed before they found their real operational use.

Following the example of the U-2, the pilotless planes were sent in great number to China. The Taiwanese, who had lost several pilots during flights over continental China, showed themselves to be very favourable to the use of these machines. For once, there was no jealousy on the part of the pilots who saw themselves supplanted by machines in the high-risk missions. The U-2s were showing an ever increasing vulnerability againast the SA-2 missiles and the arrival of a new reconnaissance system was welcomed with relief.

The US Air Force was responsible for the programme but of course the CIA, through the NRO, received its share of information picked up by the drones. After what had happened with the U-2s, the idea of a purely Taiwanese operation was maintained: national markings were applied to the drones before each mission; and were removed after the flight.

After several weeks of operation, a first machine was shot down above communist China on the 16th of November 1964. Peking directly accused the United States who shrugged their shoulders and responded with a "no comment". The loss of a single machine was decidedly easier to manage for the State Department than the capture of a pilot...

The drones used above China belonged to the AQM 147 family from the aircraft manufacturer Ryan. Extrapolated from target-drones, the AQM 147 had given an extraordinarily prolific and successful family of reconnaissance machines. China had been the site of their first deployment in Asia, but very quickly the 147 became known by its participation in the Vietnam war under the colours of the US Air Force. This participation alone was a real saga, going outside the framework of this book. The Ryan drones were at the source of several of the greatest intelligence victories during the Vietnam war, notably for anything which was connected with the use of SA-2 missiles by the North Vietnamese. It was an AQM 147 which brought back the first information on the operating frequencies of the SA-2s, subsequently enabling the Americans to develop effective electronic counter measures.

Between 1964 and 1975, 1,016 drones carried out a total of 3,445 combat missions, almost one every day for ten years!

Extremely impressed by the work that was accomplished on a daily basis in Vietnam, in 1968 the CIA again ventured in the development of a drone responding to its own needs : this was the Ryan 154. In accordance with an arrangement concluded with the Air Force, the CIA was only to become directly involved in the processing of information brought back, while the Air Force would be in charge of the operational control of the machines.

Model 154 was a machine designed specially for high altitude strategic reconnaissance, in a hostile environment. The machine had to be able to fly at 78,000ft over more than 2,000 miles. The accent was put on its weak radar signature, the construction of the 154 required a great use of composite materials transparent to electromagnetic waves. The drones ability to survive also depended on very complete electronic counter-measure equipment.

The payload was made up of cameras and lenses of different focal lengths, giving a resolution of 12inches directly below the drone, while authorizing the scanning of a 27 mile wide area at maximum altitude. Weighing two tons when empty and measuring a little more than 30feet long with a wingspan of 43feet, the Ryan 154 was, like the 147 models, released in mid-flight by a specially equipped C-130 Hercules. At the end of the mission, it was able to be recovered by a helicopter, by descending to the ground hooked under a parachute, or simply to land, the contact with the ground being softened by inflatable cushions.

The first flights took place in September 1968 and, less than two years later, the Ryan 154 was operational. But circumstances dictated that the need for such a machine became less clear at precisely that moment. The reconciliation with communist China was on the right track and the drone, which had been conceived particularly for this theatre of operation, was kept in the background : flying over Chinese territory, never mind an unexpected landing, was the last thing the diplomats in the State Department wanted.

As for the Vietnam war, the fight was led there by tactical machines, almost 'consumable'. In the Middle East, the U-2 or the SR-71 were sufficient for the task.

The "154" never found the geopolitical circumstances that it needed to prove its capabilities and through lack of use, the machines were eventually scrapped!

THE YUGOSLAVIAN CRISIS

Even if certain countries, such as Israel or South Africa, confronted with urgent crisis situations, continued to manifest a certain interest for the pilotless planes, the drone had an interval of use after the Vietnam war which lasted twenty years.

Paradoxically, the East-West confrontation was breathing its last when, in the field, there was a renewal of interest from American strategists and tacticians for these machines. The Gulf war, in 1990, and particularly the conflicts in ex-Yugoslavia several months later, marked a strong return of the drones in the field of intelligence.

In the case of Yugoslavia, the direct use of surveillance drones by the CIA was a known fact and recognized officially.

Two GNAT 750, a machine developed and built by the Californian firm General Atomics, were used above ex-Yugoslavia by the Intelligence Agency.

The GNAT 750 was a standard tactical surveillance machine in its conception : taking off and landing like a plane, it was propelled by a Rotax internal combustion engine, similar to those equipping the ULM. According to the constructor, the plane could reach an endurance of 20 hours at 25,000ft. At the time when the CIA was familiarizing itself with its use, General Atomics was exporting a complete system (three or four planes and a ground control cabin to receive the images) to Turkey, officially to take part in anti-drug operations. Bearing in mind the facilities granted to the activities of the CIA by the Turkish authorities for several decades, this sale was hardly surprising.

In February 1994, the drones were sent to Europe. Faced with the refusal of Italy to welcome the machines of the CIA on its soil, the intelligence agency finally chose to deploy its planes on Albanian soil. Albania, which had remained the cradle of Marxist orthodoxy in Europe while the rest of the continent was throwing off the fetters, was sucked into the sphere of influence of Uncle Sam as soon as the fall of the communist system was accomplished. NATO, in other words Washington, offered Albania joint manoeuvres in the Adriatic, sent instructors, modernized equipment, while the CIA advanced its pawns...by propeller.

What better symbol could have existed of the cards dealt again in the particularly confused game that the 'big' and little ones were playing in the region...?!

The field of operation chosen was that of Gjader, thirty miles north of Tirana. The CIA demanded that the drones be operational before the 4th of February 1994, this was indeed carried out.

The day after this deadline a mortar shell of doubtful origin exploded in Markale market, in the heart of Sarajevo, killing 66 people and injuring 200 others. Was it nothing more than a simple coincidence that gave the Americans the excuse they needed to launch fresh attacks against the Bosnian Serbs?

The GNAT 750, whose instrumentation consisted of one daylight camera and one infra-red camera, only remained in Albania a short time. After a few weeks of activity, the flights were stopped because of bad weather and problems in the transmission of data to the ground reception station. The operations started up again in July 1994 from the Croatian island of Brac. If the CIA never responded favourably to the demands of the United Nations forces present in ex-Yugoslavia to share the information obtained, there is nothing to stop us from thinking that this information was given to the Croats who welcomed the detachment on its territory.

Another coincidence (there were many in this conflict...), the fact that Croatia put into operation at the same period a surveillance drone allows us to suppose that foreign technical assistance was involved. But, to render unto Caesar the things which are Caesar's, it was a possible participation of the Israelis, very knowledgeable concerning pilotless planes, that was most often put forward. Note that the GNAT were accompanied in their flights over the Balkans by another aircraft of the CIA, with the responsibilty of relaying information exchanged between the drones and the ground control station. This plane, a Schweitzer Condor, is worthy of mention.

The Condor, a type of very light motorized glider devised for aerial surveillance at minimum cost and with great discretion, had been conceived at the beginning of the 80s for the US Army. The stress had been put on the silence of operation of the engine and the propeller. Very light, it nonetheless had remarkable qualities of endurance, in the order of eight hours at a speed of 150 mph. The American coastguard was interested in the Condor, for use in the fight against drug traffickers. They were rapidly joined by the CIA, who saw in this rather ordinary and frail looking plane a discreet and effective tool for surveillance missions and, as was the case in the Balkans, for transmission relays.

The good performance of the Condor and the interest of the American official services led to the development of a twin-engine version, the Twin Condor. It is apparently this version that was found once again in the hands of the CIA, this time in the skies above Peru, in the first weeks of 1997.

The beginning of the year was marked by a particularly spectacular seizure of hostages in Lima : the Japanese embassy, with several hundred VIPs attending a diplomatic reception inside, was attacked by a very daring terrorist commando unit Four months later the situation was still continuing. The confrontation ended on the 22nd of April 1997, after 127 days of suspense, after a brilliant intervention by the police. The success of the attack is explained principally by excellent preparation : after several weeks the Peruvian secret service was reached to 'sound out' the entire embassy, following the actions and gestures of the fifteen or so hostage takers. The embassy was also closely observed from the surrounding rooftops. It is however less well known that this surveillance was extended several miles up. Orbiting in silence directly over the diplomatic buildings, a Twin Condor operated by the CIA could provide precious information to the Peruvian authorities. Its sensors, infra-red and daylight video cameras with high magnifying power, enabled a very indiscreet look in the innermost recesses of the complex of buildings which were not visible from the outside.

RETURN TO THE BALKANS

In June 1995, the Predator took over from the GNAT 750, again from the Gjader terrain in Albania. Certain sources mentioned however the passage of these machines via the Croatian island of Brac and incidentally, the questioning of the German military attaché, posted to

Zagreb, 'straying' near the base where the Predators were launched from.

The Predator belonged to a programme run by DARO (Defense Airborne Reconnaissance Office), an organization created in 1993 to harmonize and administer American needs concerning aerial surveillance. DARO had the responsibility of assuring a certain coherence between the needs expressed by the different governmental agencies, particularly between the US Army, Navy, Air Force and Marines.

In the summer of 1995, the Predator was not yet totally operational and the three machines that were sent to the Balkans were prototypes. The Predator was a larger and more powerful version of the GNAT 750 and had wider operational capabilities but the two planes kept a certain similarity. With a wingspan of almost thirty feet and carrying more than 300kg of fuel, the Predator flew higher (25,000ft) and longer (an endurance of 40 hours) than the GNAT. Even though it was powered by a wooden propeller, the ten million dollar drone had a very professional appearance. A dish aerial positioned under a voluminous fairing, which gave it its characteristic silhouette, permitted the transmission in real time of video or fixed images, via a satellite relay.

A surveillance drone, the Predator was also capable of carrying out electronic eavesdropping and intercepting hostile radio communications. The system was of a high enough quality to intercept transmitter-receiver and cellular telephone communications. Put into operation by the US Air Force, the Predator was expressly placed under American command but also left however at the disposal of the UN Forces command at Zagreb. There is no doubt that the CIA was also very well placed in this situation to receive its share of information brought back by these machines. And beyond the CIA, the Croats themselves had used drones during the great offensive of August 1995 to recapture Krajina. The experts were surprised by the very accurate information that Zagreb had at its disposal during the combats.

To return to the Predator of the Air Force, two of them were lost in operation in the Autumn of 1995, indirect victims of the difficult weather conditions over the area : in order to free themselves from the bad weather which hampered surveillance missions, the US Air Force programmed its machines to fly at low altitude, under the cloud layer. They became at the same time vulnerable to ground fire and subject to encounters with high ground.

In October 1995, the Predator detachment, or what remained of it, was withdrawn from the theatre of operation in order to be reorganized. The drones received a new payload and six months later, three machines were once again deployed in the region, this time from the Hungarian base of Taszar. The Predators had been modified to fly without risk in icy conditions and the optical surveillance systems had been replaced by a synthetic aperture radar allowing radar imaging through the clouds. The resolution of the system was given for around thirty centimetres to a distance of ten kilometres.

But while the operation, highly popularized through the media, followed its course in Bosnia-Herzeginia and in the old republics of ex-Federal Yugoslavia, a far more discreet operation was turning into a disaster for the CIA in the mountains of Kurdistan.

FAILURE IN IRAQ

Kurdistan, 30th of August 1996. The sun had not yet risen over Erbil, site of one of the largest conglomerations of Iraqi Kurds. In an outlying part of the town , a small group of Westerners swept out of an anonymous building like a whirlwind. Bags were hastily thrown in the back of some four wheel drives which were waiting for them in the street, engines running. The men got in the vehicles, the doors slammed shut.

"Let's go!"

The Toyotas drove at great speed along the avenues of Erbil, deserted at that hour. Inside were men of the CIA and US Army special forces. These men who were fleeing hurriedly towards the north and the Turkish border were leaving several hundreds of thousands of dollars of computer and radio equipment behind : powerful transmitters for broadcasting to the rest of Iraq and radio-satellites. And above all, it could be said as usual, they had abandoned compromising dossiers and put collaborateurs in jeopardy.

Columns of Saddam Hussein's army, the reason for their haste, were only a few miles from the town. In launching a brusque offensive in the north of Iraq, Saddam Hussein had just put an end, which was as unforeseen as it was humiliating, to an ambitious CIA operation in the region.

In May 1991, the day after the beginning of the Gulf war, George Bush had launched the secret operation to support the Kurds. It was initially only a low intensity operation, designed to keep the flames of opposition to Saddam Hussein burning in the mountains of Kurdistan. Budget : a mere 20 million dollars per year!

Everything was tried to weaken the 'Master of Baghdad': economic warfare, propaganda, support to Kurdish movements, everything under the umbrella of UN resolutions forbidding aircraft from Baghdad to clean out the north of the country, declared an 'exclusion zone'.

After his accession to the Presidency, Bill Clinton authorized the CIA to intensify its efforts. The agency had made the support for the Kurds its principal operation since the period of Afghanistan. The CIA used some good old tricks which had worked so well thirty years earlier in Laos: under the cover of humanitarian operations providing support to Kurdish refugees (notably the air supply operation Provide Comfort), the American agency set up a team of 25 people in Kurdistan Iraq, near the Turkish border, and sent arms and ammunition to its accomplices.

The CIA also made use of pilotless planes to drop leaflets over the towns and villages of Kurdistan still under the control of Baghdad. The concept was not new : leaflets had been dropped from drones fitted with external containers in Vietnam with machines from the Ryan company. The planes which carried out this work were nicknamed 'Bullshit Bombers'.

In promising also to provide aerial support, the CIA managed to convince the movements opposed to Saddam Hussein to launch an offensive against the Iraqi army.

Once the offensive was launched however, the aerial support did not arrive and the rebels, whose ranks had been infiltrated for a long time by the Iraqi secret service, failed.

The plotters began to be arrested at the end of the month of June and nine weeks later, the lightning offensive launched by the Iraqi army and the Kurds allied to Saddam Hussein swept away the rather mediocre CIA set up in the region.

On the 30th of August at dawn, after several hours on the road, the

Americans reached the safety of the other side of the Turkish border. Their back-up troops did not have this good fortune.

If the operation in Kurdistan was the most recent use of the drones by the CIA, it will definitely not be the final one.

The DARO projects, which the CIA will certainly take advantage of, are preparing to give a new dimension to the utilisation of drones before the end of the century. Two very spectacular machines commenced their test flights at the beginning of 1998. Both should be fully operational in 1999 or 2000.

The Darkstar is a stealth drone, supposedly indetectable by radar. Seen from the front it resembles a frisbee with wings of 68 feet across grafted on to it. It will be able to carry out surveillance missions of eight hours up to 625 miles from its base. The Global Hawk is a yet more ambitious project. This observation plane conceived by the Ryan company has a wingspan of 100feet, equal to that of an Airbus A-320. Designed to fly for 41 hours in succession at 60,000ft, it will be able to rejoin any point on the globe leaving from its base in the United States. By communicating via a network of satellites, it will be able to transmit its observations in real time from the other side of the world.

HIGHER STILL

Let's finish this general survey by briefly mentioning the surveillance satellites and the extraordinary achievements that they put at the service of the CIA.

Since1958, the United States and the USSR have launched some 3,000 military satellites, including about a thousand surveillance and observation satellites which also have application in the world of intelligence.

Today, satellites give intelligence services about 95% of all their classified information. And without risk : satellites don't lie, don't misrepresent the truth; they are tough and don't risk being caught. Qualities which are sometimes lacking in human sources...

When Gary Powers was shot down at the controls of his U-2, the window that the Americans had opened with force onto the Soviet world was abruptly closed. From one day to the next, the CIA was plunged into darkness.

This reign of darkness lasted only a short while however, barely three months. While Khrushchev was polishing his missiles, the CIA was already preparing the post-U-2 period with the SR-71 in the left hand and, in the right hand, observation satellites.

The idea of making satellites into instruments of observation (or espionnage, depending on your point of view) returned to the Rand Corporation. For the most part financed by the US Air Force, the Rand Corporation is a non-profit making private institution, operating as a Think Tank on behalf of American public organizations, such as the armed forces or intelligence services. Gathering together specialists from all areas, the Rand Corporation devoted itself to the delicate game of futurology, with sometimes some good fortune.

By analyzing, just after the war, the brilliant German achievements, notably the V-2 rockets, the Rand Corporation had put forward the idea of manufacturing surveillance satellites capable of flying over countries with total impunity, setting itself free from problems of national sovereignty.

Throughout the fifties, the Pentagon worked on spy satellite projects. Problems associated with their development were as numerous as they were complex, but the Americans rapidly had an effective catalyst from the Soviet Union available to them : by launching their Sputnik 1 on the 4th of October 1957, the Russians had in fact given a powerful boost to American research. From that moment, Eisenhower gave absolute priority to the space race with, in the background, the idea of using spy satellites.

On the 3rd of November 1957, less than a month after the launch of Sputnik 1, the Americans received a second shock : the USSR had just placed a second satellite, Sputnik 2, in orbit. This new satellite weighed 500kg whereas the first American satellite, which was not going to be ready before the 30th of January 1958, weighed only five! The Soviets had an overwhelming superiority. The general public had their attention held by the presence of a dog, Laïka, on board. More importantly, the Soviet satellite was also carrying photographic equipment. The era of espionnage by satellite had begun.

The Americans put on a spurt to catch up on their delay and launched the Corona programme, giving rise to the Discoverer family of observation satellites. While the Air Force was responsible for the launch of the devices, the CIA assured the technical side of the programme and the future treatment of the information.

From its simple name through to the development of the different phases, its technical objectives and not forgetting the industrialists involved, everything in the Corona programme was more than top secret (before 1955 and the declassification of the programme, a single photograph taken by a spy satellite was published by a British magazine. The journalist in charge of the publication went to prison! The best of American industry was mobilized in this affair : Lockheed constructed the launcher, Fairchild the photographic equipment, Kodak the special emulsions...

Eisenhower gave the green light to the programme in February 1958, only a few hours after the launch of the first American satellite.

THE CORONA PROJECT

Discoverer 1, the first satellite of the series, was launched on the 28th of February 1959 from the Vandenburg site in California. Barely one year had passed since the programme had been started. As in the case of the U-2, a scientific 'cover', the study of the 'climate in space', had been given to the project.

In the following three years, between February 1959 and February 1962, Discoverer was launched 38 times, to perfect the adjustment.

The principle of the functioning of the Discoverer was simple enough in theory : once it had been placed in orbit, the satellite photographed its objectives until the supply of film was exhausted. The exposed film was then ejected towards the Earth in order to be analysed. It was simply a matter of making a satellite out of a very expensive disposable camera. To recover the film which was ejected in space in a special capsule was not easy and the first thirteen Discoverers served to finalize the launch and recovery techniques. The technical domain to be opened up was vast indeed. Everything had to be invented and failures were legion : between Discoverer 1 and Discoverer 13 one launcher exploded on the launch site, three did not manage to place their load in orbit, two satellites were positioned in the wrong orbit, three cameras did not function... and so on until the 18th of August 1960, three months after the Powers episode.

On that day, Discoverer 14 was launched. The photographic equipment carried enabled views with a resolution of around sixteen feet to be taken. The satellite had to be positioned authorizing the overflight of the secret site of Plesetsk, the very one that Gary Powers would have been able to photograph had he finished his flight.

Discoverer 14 was a success, the first of the Corona project.

After seventeen revolutions round the Earth and less than 24 hours in space, the 10kg capsule, with more than half a mile of film on board was ejected. The recuperation sequence passed off perfectly: after entering the atmosphere, the capsule emitted its radio signal enabling it to be located while it descended towards the sea suspended from a parachute. A C-119 from the US Air Force, specially equipped for the mission, hooked up the parachute in mid-flight and recovered the precious load.

Ironically, the announcement of this successful recovery shared the front page of the American newspapers along with Gary Powers receiving a ten-year prison sentence in Moscow, after a trial of twelve weeks.

The analysis of the images from Discoverer 14 in specialized CIA laboratories (which a few months later became the National Photographic Interpretaion Center) created rather a shock. The quality of the photos was definitely not as good as those brought back by the U-2s. Less precise and a little dark, they were all of fairly average quality. But during a single mission, in less than 24 hours, the satellite had photographed a surface area of the Soviet Union greater than that of the U-2s after 24 flights and four years of operation!

Incidentally, the CIA could congratulate itself for having taken up the surveillance of the Soviet Union once again, interrupted since the U-2 overflight missions were stopped.

The following mission, Discoverer 15 was a failure: the capsule landed in the ocean some 940 miles from the planned zone. Planes and boats headed for the zone, without being able to recover it because of bad weather.

If the U-2 programme had been managed rather roughly by the CIA, outside all usual procedures and by getting the better of the US Air Force, it was not going to be able to do the same with the Discoverer programme which was taking on phenomenal proportions.

The satellite programme gave rise to a close cooperation between the two administrations, which however did not prevent any friction. The objectives assigned to the satellites were the object of bitter discussions : the Air Force, which above all was seeking precise information concerning Soviet weapons systems, wanted a high resolution. The CIA was more interested in strategic analyses not requiring such a high level of detail.

To arbitrate the differences which arose between the two users, Eisenhower authorized, on the 25th of August 1960 (only five days after the return of the first images to Earth) the creation of the NRO, the National Reconnaissance Office. The NRO, traditionally directed by a superior officer of the US Air Force, was responsible for the control of the satellites in orbit, the scheduling and the management of their operations, which translated into the choice of objectives.

The existence of the NRO was not officially admitted until 1992, even though in 1973, an error from Congress meant the name of the agency had appeared in an official document. Its budget in 1996 was 8 billion dollars, in other words two and a half times that of the CIA.

THE SURVEILLANCE SATELLITE, DIPLOMATIC WEAPON

The multiplication of observation satellites meant that, by the beginning of the sixties, the USSR could be rapidly covered with a fine tooth-comb. Several rare intercontinental missle sites were found, bringing the CIA to review its estimations of an overwhelming Soviet power: the USSR in fact possessed only twenty or so operational missiles, that is ten times less the figure that Khrushchev boasted of!

This important development arrived at the right time to outwit the bluff of the communist leaders throughout the different east/west crises: the building of the Berlin wall, missiles in Cuba and so on. Khrushchev may well have showed his force by exploding several tens of megatons of atomic bombs on experimentation areas, Kennedy, aware of the true extent of Soviet power, was not giving in. The American President would have shown Khrushchev some satellite images from 1961, to show him he knew Khrushchev was bluffing when he spoke of his lead in the area of bombers and missiles. Incidentally, the information obtained by the satellites also permitted the CIA to bring down the claims of the Air Force, always ready to put forward the quantitive superiority of the Soviets in order to justify its own expenditure.

The Soviets knew for a fact however that the Americans were observing them from space. At the time when the satellites passed, they would write insulting messages in the snow. When there was no snow, the Chinese wrote messages with stones! This idea also spread to other camps : the activities of the SR-71 detachments were observed very closely by the Soviets and, on the roof of one of the hangars at Beale AFB they wrote "You watch us while we watch you."

Based on the images brought back by the satellite Discoverer in the summer of 1964, the CIA was in a position to foresee that China would become an atomic power within the following weeks. This became a fact on the 16th of October 1964.

In July 1966 the KH-8 series of satellites was launched (KH for Key Hole). The KH-8 were particularly successful and fortunate, as 51 of these satellites were launched over 18 years, with a 100% success rate.

The KH-8 were placed in an orbit with a very low perigee, in the order of 97 miles. (When a satellite's orbit around the Earth is not circular but elliptical, the point of the orbit which is closest to the Earth is called perigee, the furthest away is called apogee). The lower the altitude of the satellite, the more detailed the photographs, but the shorter the life expectancy of the satellite, which succumbs rapidly to the gravitational pull of the Earth. The operator had to find a balance between the resolution that he hoped to obtain and the life expectancy he wanted his satellite to have.

The KH-8 was the last model of the generation of satellites expelling film cartridges. Each satellite carried several cartridges capable of being expelled at regular intervals or to order, depending on the specified circumstances. As for the method of recovery, it had not on principle changed since the first Discoverers. The C-119 had simply been replaced by the more modern C-130 Hercules.

As well as a satellite life expectancy limited by the number of cartridges able to be expelled, the fault in the system was the time necessary before the images were obtained. The expulsion of the cartridge, its recovery usually from the middle of the ocean, its transport to the laboratory, the treatment of the images, took many hours, even days.

In 1967, photographs of the six-day war did not arrive on the CIA analysts desk until after the lightning war had finished. Six years later, on the same battlefield, the satellites showed the disadvantages originating from their fixed trajectories : two passages of Key Hole took place during the Kippur war above the Middle East, the first on the 13th and the second on the 25th of October 1973. The first was too early, the second came too late. The most critical phase of the war unfolded between these two dates. Fortunately for the intelligence services, the SR-71 had been able to effectively complement the satellites, because of their flexibility of use. The first to benefit were the Israelis, who, on the basis of intelligence provided by the Americans, were able to intercept and destroy an Egyptian armoured brigade thereby opening up the route to the Suez canal.

In parallel to the KH-8, which continued to be launched with regularity, the first KH-9 was launched in June 1971. The KH-9 is a veritable beast, which swiftly earned the nickname of "Big Bird". Five times heavier than the KH-8 that it complemented, Big Bird is forty nine feet long, ten feet in diameter and carries into space a collection of cameras equipped with lenses of different focal distances, for both daylight and infra-red photography. The innovation of the KH-9 is to be able to transmit images by radio. Even though it still has ejectable capsules (around half a dozen), the Big Bird carries a processing unit on board. The films are thus developed automatically in space before being 'scanned' by a camera and transmitted by radio. The quality of images obtained suffers a little from the procedure, but the technical breakthrough is appreciable. The delays are shortened and, for the first time, the satellite is no longer dependent on the number of cartridges remaining to be ejected. The principle of return to Earth is nonetheless kept, for it is the guarantee of a very great accuracy in the images, impossible to reach with the transmissions by radio. The last of the KH-9 series was launched in 1986, the launch itself was a failure.

THE MODERN EPIC OF THE KH -11S

The following generation of observation satellites, the KH-11 family, brought a new revolution along : the KH-11 were the first satellites to function without any film on board. The images were collected only by electronic sensors (CCDs comparable to those in video cameras today). There was obviously no further need to eject the capsules and all the images obtained were transmitted by radio. When the satellite was not in a position to directly transmit its images to the American listening stations, there was also the possibilty of using satellite relays. From wherever it was, a KH-11 was able to send images to the American intelligence services in less than 90 minutes.

In the first instance the result of this revolution was a slight reduction in the quality of documents obtained, the electronic imagery initially revealed itself to be very inferior to standard negative images. For this reason, the Americans continued to resort to the 'classic' services of the Big Bird with its unrivalled accuracy. The handicaps of electronic imagery were subsequently overcome, the electronic images allowed any sort of handling and enhancing in order to improve their quality. Today it is reckoned that a resolution of between two and a half to five inches is reached by these systems.

The first KH-11, launched in 1976, was also an enormous observation instrument 62feet long which naturally aroused a great deal of interest on the part of the Soviets.

Seeing that the new satellite did not eject any cartridge as its predecessors had done and that it transmitted a great amount of radio traffic, they believed it was an electronic eavesdropping satellite. Ignorant of the fact that the KH-11 took photographs, they therefore neglected to take certain protective measures every time the KH-11 passed over their heads.

This state of ignorance proved to be a godsend for the CIA, who was able to observe for instance the inside of the intercontinental missile silos, the Soviets having neglected to close them, at their leisure.

But the secret was only kept for one year.

While the Soviet experts were still pondering over the exact nature of the satellite, which had been placed in a high orbit and seemed to be very talkative, a CIA employee took it upon himself to dispel their questions.

Disappointed with his pen-pushing life at the service of the intelligence agency, William Kampiles decided one day to create for himself a new life of adventure which he had always dreamed of. Shortly before leaving the CIA for good in October 1977, he went home one evening with the KH-11 technical manual in his pocket. Several weeks later he sold it to the Soviets for 3,000 dollars.

At last the Soviets understood the real capabilities of the KH-11 and immediately took the necessary precautionary measures, which immediately aroused the suspicions of the CIA: the Agency understood that one way or another the Soviets had become aware of the real nature of the satellite. The arrest of Kampiles by the FBI confirmed their suspicions. The pathetic apprentice spy had thought it was clever to boast of his contacts with the Russian embassy to his friends...

In the morning of the 4th of November 1979, a crowd of several hundred Iranian 'students' scaled the walls of the American embassy compound in Teheran and took the personnel within hostage. The militants had initially planned to remain only a few hours in the building, in order to protest against the Shah of Iran arriving in the United States to receive medical treatment.

But having become national heroes and being openly supported by the Ayatollah Khomeni, they chose to stay in the embassy and the affair took quite another turn.

Two days after the capture of the hostages, President Carter gave his agreement for a rescue operation, while playing the negotiating game as best he could. Weeks went by without any tangible result, and Carter finally gave his consent for the launch of a military operation.

The satellites played a major role in the preparation of this attempt. The phenomenal capabilities of Big Bird and the KH-11s permitted President Carter and the officers of the special forces to examine what was happening inside the American embassy compound almost in real time.

That is how the Americans saw that stakes had been placed in the embassy gardens, to prevent any possible landings by helicopter.

There being no informers on the spot, the preparation of the rescue raid required a quantity of precise information that could only be provided by satellite. American plans anticipated the launch of a rescue force by helicopter from the ships cruising the Persian Gulf. CIA analysts carefully studied the photos which had come from space in order to find different sites which the helicopters would have to use during their progress towards Teheran. Around 220 miles south of the Iranian capital, a potential site for the refuelling of the helicopters was held. The satellite photos showed a vast flat and clear area, sufficiently large to receive ten aircraft and for a C-130 to land. It was nonetheless necessary to send a team to the area to check that the ground was firm enough for the C-130s to land.

On the 22nd of March 1980, President Carter gave his agreement for this reconnaissance operation to be carried out, under the responsibilty of the CIA. A Twin Otter, a small twin-engine propeller plane, left the United States for Iran. On board were a crew of two CIA pilots as well as an officer of the US Air Force, responsible for collecting sand samples and placing beacons in the ground. Extra tanks and a small mountain motorbike took up the space of the cabin and the officer had to travel lying down on the flexible containers of extra fuel.

In the first hours of April 1980, in the dead of night, the Twin Otter landed without difficulty on the terrain which had been named Desert One. A desert road passed nearby. As soon as the plane was immobilized, the Air Force officer, John Carney, got out his small motorbike and got to work. He loaded a small spade and five light beacons on to his motorbike. He then adjusted his night vision glasses and left to explore the zone. Firstly he stopped at regular intervals to collect soil samples.

Then he dug five holes into which he placed the beacons. The first four were laid out in a square shape 100 feet wide : The planes had to make contact with the ground aiming for the inside of the square. Carney positioned the fifth beacon several hundred yards from there, at the edge of the terrain : this last one would indicate to the planes the direction of the landing area and its extremity. The beacons operated in infrared and would therefore be totally invisible to the naked eye. It was also anticipated that the lighting of the beacons would be operated from the

410

planes themselves, when they arrived within sight of the zone.

Discreet, simple and effective, the system functioned perfectly on the day of the raid.

His work finished, Carey covered Desert One a last time in every direction, to make sure that there was no obstacle to obstruct the planes and helicopters when they came to land. Totally reassured concerning the condition of the terrain, he rejoined the Twin Otter. The pilots helped him to load his motorbike onto the plane and, a few minutes later, the three men left Iranian soil, their mission accomplished. Less than an hour had passed since they had landed.

The tragic results of this operation are well known.

The very complex plan concocted by the American special forces did not have the opportunity to reach its end. Only six helicopters out of the eight engaged arrived at Desert One to be refuelled by the C-130s. A third helicopter rapidly succumbed to a mechanical problem which put it out of action. With only five machines available for the second phase, the operation had to be cancelled. It was the moment when the aircraft were starting to leave Iran that disaster struck : caught up in a cloud of sand which disoriented the pilots, a helicopter crashed into a C-130 and the operation ended in explosions of kerosene. Quite apart from the burnt out carcasses of three aircraft, the Americans left eight of their own on the cursed terrain of Desert One.

SATELLITES ON EVERY FRONT

William Casey, very familiar with advanced techniques, never hesitated to put them forward, even if the cost sometimes seemed prohibitive. Every morning, a summary of the documents obtained during the night was presented to the director of the CIA. Other summaries were also prepared for the White House and, among these, there was a large red file labelled "TOP SECRET TALENT KEYHOLE". Inside the thick cardboard cover the most recent information caught by the observation and electronic eavesdropping satellites was contained.

Throughout the previous six years at the head of the CIA and of the American intelligence community, Casey found himself induced to take a decision between the pursuit or the cancellation of a new and very ambitious observation satellite programme : the Lacrosse system.

Using radar imagery, Lacrosse was therefore capable of being entirely free from meteorological conditions, even piercing through the thinner layers of vegetation, during the day or at night... Because of different computer enhancing procedures, the image obtained by the radar promised to be as precise as that of a photograph.

By perfecting this system even more, its designers were heading towards the possibility of 'seeing' through the walls of buildings.

The Soviets also knew the possibilities of radar imagery, but the insufficient power of their computer systems meant that the quality of the images obtained were not of such good quality.

The CIA anticipated that each Lacrosse satellite would cost at least a thousand million dollars, a fact which did not discourage Casey. He gave the green light for the starting up of research and authorized a first line of credit of 200 million dollars to be released.

This was the equivalent of the budget consecrated by the CIA to clandestine operations, of which it was said that Casey was also very fond.

The first Lacrosse was eventually built and launched in 1988. A second followed at the beginning of the nineties, then a third in the middle of 1997.

Conceived initially to follow the progression of communist tanks in the event of a confrontation in Europe, the Lacrosse adapted their mission to the collapse of the communist bloc and the 'new world disorder' that ensued. There is no doubt that these powerful means of observation were used firstly against Iraq, and more recently against the Serbs in Bosnia.

Once again, the arrival of this new system does not mean the abandonment of the old techniques. Radar imagery has come to complete 'standard' photographs, and will never replace them. The KH-11 remains a very useful tool which Casey uses with consommate skill.

The traditional allies of the United States know they can count on the fantastic images of Key Hole in case of any problem. Great Britain during the Falklands War, possibly even France during its operations in Chad from 1980, there is no lack of potential applications.

But Israel is certainly the greatest beneficiary. The Israelis had asked for complete time slots during which the satellite would be at their disposal alone. The Americans refused, but showed themselves to be generous in other areas and allowed them to benefit from a number of documents. This was reciprocated, and the Israelis proved themselves to be cooperative in the Irangate affair as on other occasions...

With the intention of harming the Soviets as much as possible, Casey did not hesitate to put his ultra-secret satellites at the service of the Afghan resistance. The satellite images were in fact transmitted to the Pakistani secret service who coordinated support to the Afghans.

"I could ask the CIA for photos of a particular zone and, shortly after, I would receive them on my desk and study them" recalls general Mohammad Yousaf, on whose shoulders all the unofficial help to the Mujaheddins rested.

The photos were not however left in the hands of the Pakistanis, for fear that they would finish in the hands of the Soviets : all the details were transferred onto maps which were left at the disposal of the secret sevice in Karachi. Each map had a list of possible objectives attached, their precise description, approach and withdrawal routes, enemy positions and so on.

"Nothing on the ground could escape the all-seeing satellite. The images (...)showed the tanks, vehicles, bridges, means of access and the damage caused by bombs or rockets with a clarity that astounded me", explains Yousaf in his book 'The Trapped Bear.' "(...) Combined with the local knowledge of the Mujaheddin, this information considerably increased our ability to lead effective operations."

This aid nonetheless had a limit: while the Pakistanis wanted to bring the fight directly on the portion of Soviet territory adjoining Afghanistan, through which all the supplies destined for the Red Army transited, the CIA refused to give its backing to that idea, for fear of overstepping the tacitly accepted limits. The photos or maps provided by the CIA invariably stopped at the border marked by the Amou river. On the documents provided, the area to the north of the river was left entirely blank. It was up to the Afghans and the Pakistanis to manage on their own...

Some satellite photos of Afghanistan showed Soviet troops in the process of decontaminating their own bases. This confirmed on the one hand the use of chemical weapons on the terrain, and on the other hand the information which stated that, on different occasions, Soviet soldiers had been victims of their own manoeuvres.

In Lebanon, the Key Holes were used to situate the American hostages. In November 1985, their utilization, combined with other means of reconnaissance, had accurately found the location of five of the six American hostages. The preparation of a rescue raid began, with models of the detention sites being made on the basis of information from satellite photos. This information was never used and the White House opted to negotiate with Syria and Iran.

In mid-1990, the attention of the CIA was brought to the Middle East. In July of the same year, several KH-11 and a radar imagery Lacrosse observed the border between Iraq and Kuwait. Never had such a narrow geographical area received such attention.

On the 17th of July, the CIA informed President Bush that more than thirty thousand Iraqi soldiers were moving towards Kuwait. Ten days later, some infra-red images showed the CIA analysts that hundreds of trucks were transporting water, petrol and ammunition in the direction of the troops amassed along the Kuwaiti border. Despite all the extremely precise information that had been given to him, President Bush, an old director of the CIA, let Saddam Hussein continue until the invasion was finally confirmed, on the 1st of August 1990 at 9 in the evening, Washington time. Feigning surprise, George Bush then became the head of a world-wide anti-Iraqi coaltion, a league of virtue smelling of oil.

BIG EARS

In September 1997, the American magazine Aviation Week & Space Technology announced the launch of two new observation satellites by the NRO : a KH-12 and a Trumpet.

If the first, a successor to the KH-11, represented the absolute best in the subject of optical reconnaissance, the other marked the success of a family which is interesting to mention in a few words, electronic eaves-dropping satellites.

The gathering of electromagnetic intelligence was always done, and will continue to be done, with a vast range of planes. The manufacture of specialized satellites in this mission was a logical consequence of the space race of the fifties.

On the 24th of October 1952, President Truman authorized the creation of a National Security Agency (NSA) for the obtaining and exploitation of all this 'electronic' intelligence. Functioning according to the objectives and needs expressed by the Director of Central Intelligence and the CIA, the NSA swiftly took a dominant role in the race for intelligence while remaining one of the most secret cogs in the American intelligence machinery.

Some of the most incredible machines put at its disposal were satellites from the Rhyolite family, equipped with extraordinary capabilities of intercepting communications, and the first example of which was put into orbit in 1973. Because of its antenna measuring 69 feet across, the Rhyolite permitted the Americans to follow very closely the Soviet ballistic missile tests by intercepting the transmissions telemetry, but also to record radio communications over a vast range of frequencies. That was how over several months, radio-telephones of Soviet generals and dignitaries were systematically spied on without their knowledge. Once again, the secret of this operation was sold for next to nothing by an American citizen disappointed with the consumer society. From one day to the next, the exceptional crop of information stopped...

The Trumpet satellite launched at the end of 1997 multiplied the capabilities offered by the Rhyolites even more. Its antenna, approximately 300 feet wide, which folds up automatically in space after satellisation, is a real technical challenge in itself. Its surface larger than two tennis courts, traps the electromagnetic waves like an immense trawl net. It is said that the Trumpet is capable of listening to several thousand sources of radio on the ground, in the air or even space, simultaneously.

These extraordinary performances must not however delude us : in the world of intelligence, and particularly for the CIA whose ambition is to let nothing get past, satellites are not a panacea. Their outstanding performance must be paid for with a certain rigidity of use. Their presence is known, their trajectory is able to be predicted : the effect of surprise is often lacking.

Drones, U-2 and SR-71 make an effective complement. By choosing recently to do without the services of the SR-71, the only machines capable of rivalling the satellites in the overflight of forbidden areas, with in addition the element of surprise distinctive to aircraft, the United States have taken the risk of removing a pillar from their edifice of intelligence. The future will say if it is too fragile. Unless of course an aircraft with even more extraordinary capabilities is ready to take over.

EPILOGUE

EPILOGUE

Zagreb, December 1995. A handful of men leaning at the bar of the hotel Intercontinental in the Croatian capital, having a chat.

Some are dressed in civilian clothes, others in black flying suits with a matching base-ball cap. Is it deliberate, unintentional or just the result of a certain indifference? The men of Southern Air Transport are easily identifiable, even here right in the heart of the Balkans.

What changes in less than three years!

While maintaining a close interest, the Americans nonetheless kept out of the fighting that put the Croats against the Serbs, during the dismembering of Tito's Yugoslavia.

When, in 1992, the conflict flared up in Bosnia-Herzegovinia, their wait-and-see policy faded. The international community made Bosnia a nation by right. By taking more or less overtly the side of the Bosnian Muslims, the USA once more showed proof of its good will in relation to the oil-based monarchies of the Middle East and perhaps to set themselves up, at little cost, as the 'guardian of liberty'.

Well before the first fighting, the CIA gave information concerning Yugoslavia to the American government, particularly on the events that took place in Kosovo after the death of Tito. Keyhole satellites were therefore in the front line to follow the development of the troubles within the Yugoslavian federation. When, in mid-1990, Croatia and Slovenia were ready to start a race for independence, the images from space became the object of rather more sustained attention. The importance of these images was subsequently reinforced, the Pentagon and NATO using them widely for planning armed interventions, by land or air, against the Serbs.

That was simply traditional surveillance activity. The subsequent uprising in Bosnia however made the CIA return to its "usual activities of a smuggler", and it would have been wrong to think these activities had been abandoned since the end of the cold war.

So, from 1993, numerous cargo planes left the Croatian island of Krk, with its unpronounceable name, for central Bosnia. Parachute drops of arms and ammunition on central Bosnia under Muslim control were therefore noticed. In January 1994, the international authorities decided to re-open the airport at Tuzla, an old MiG base, to be able to send humanitarian aid to the north of Bosnia, an area under Muslim control. Fearing that this re-opening would also benefit the Muslim fighters, the Serbs went against it. In vain. The runway at Tuzla was to be largely used several weeks later for the secret resupplying of the Bosnian troops with arms. Moreover, 1994 was to be marked by a flood of arms in the direction of the Croats and the Muslims, made easier by the strange blindness of the NATO AWACS patrolling high in the sky enforcing a theoretical embargo.

"The most common procedure", explained an ex Croatian general in a French newspaper in January 1995, "is for the CIA to buy Argentinian, Chinese, Indian or even Cuban arms on the Hungarian or Rumanian black market."

In the months that followed, American provisions took over, Washington was no longer in hiding. The Bosnians as a result wore US combat uniforms and were armed with M-16s.

A French reconnaissance plane was hit by a Stinger ground-to-air missile. These missiles would have been bought from the Iranians, and come directly from Afghanistan...

Furthermore, members of the German press had noted air supplies coming in from Iran throughout 1995 : Iranian planes embarked the weapons in Sudan or in certain eastern European countries and then delivered them to the island of Krk. The Croats took their share before allowing the cargo to leave for its final destination, Tuzla more often than not.

An Italian newspaper explained in 1995 that an air lift had been organized by the CIA between Pula in Croatia and Tuzla. The CIA itself delivered the arms the article stated. But as the Serbs had shot down three planes, the CIA entrusted the mission to the Turkish air force.

From December 1995 until February 1996, the men of Southern Air Transport were to be found in Zagreb.

The situation had therefore developed a great deal. The American support to the Croats and the Muslims was common knowledge and the bygone days of secrecy.

The L-100 of SAT carried out numerous flights between Israel and Zagreb and Israel and Tuzla. SAT had also hired out two Boeing 747 cargo planes and an Antonov 124, the largest cargo plane in the world with a capacity of several tens of tons. But what were the planes transporting?

"Definitely not grapefruit", said one of the pilots leaning on the bar, before downing his Bourbon.

From Yugoslavia to the great lakes of Africa constituted a short hop of 3,000 miles that the CIA crossed happily.

A very unseemly air lift started from the months of July and August 1996, to Uganda and, to a lesser extent, Rwanda. Local observers were able to note many dozens of rotations of large American heavy lift aircraft, belonging to the Air Force as well as civil airline planes chartered by an administration wishing to conserve its anonymity. These aircraft brought dozens of tons of military material, combat uniforms, light weapons, ammunition and communication equipment to African soil.

But before reaching the Ugandan army, its official destination, the unloaded material often vanished into thin air. Where to? In fact very few western embassies asked themselves that question.

In the weeks following these massive deliveries however, a rebellion broke out in the east of Zaïre. By African standards, this 'spontaneous movement' seemed to be incredibly well-equipped and disciplined. Despite denials from Washington, persistent rumours, backed by solid information, were evidence enough of general American support.

This support lasted until the 17th of May 1997, the day the rebels led Laurent-Desiré Kabila to Kinshasa, the capital of Zaïre. When the scale of the invasion became too strong to be resisted, American aircraft then resupplied the rebels in Zaïrean territory, on the airport at Goma.

The Bosnian and Zaïrean operations, occuring recently and in a short lapse of time, show to those who doubted it that the period of small and large secret trafficking of the CIA did not end with the collapse of the Berlin wall and the end of east-west confrontation.

This is a fact that always angers those who would like to see the CIA, as a good intelligence agency, limit itself to information gathering and analyzing and avoid embarking on adventures as explosive as they are extraordinary.

In truth, a pious hope...

BIBLIOGRAPHY

Afghanistan, l'Ours Piégé,
Mohammad Youssaf & Mark
Adkin.
Alerion, 1995.

L'Aigle et le Dragon,
Vietnam 1954 -1973,
Claude de Groulart.
Rossel Edition, 1973.

Air America,
Christopher Robbins.
Avon Books, 1979.

Air War Over Korea,
Larry Davis.
Squadron Signal
Publications, 1982.

L'Armée de l'Air en Indochine,
Volume 1,
Alain Crosnier
& Jean-Michel Guhl.
Sup Air, 1981.

La Bataille de Dien Bien Phu,
Jules Roy.
Julliard, 1963.

Bay of Pigs,
The Untold Story,
Peter Wyden.
Simon & Schuster, 1979

Boeing Aircraft,
Peter M. Bowers.
Putman, 1989.

The CIA,
A Forgotten History,
William Blum.
Zed Books Ltd.

CIA, Les Guerriers
de l'Ombre,
Steven Emerson.
Economica, 1991.

Cruel Avril,
Olivier Todd.
Robert Laffont, 1987.

Dragon Lady,
Chris Pocock.
Motorbooks International, 1989.

Encyclopédie du Renseignement
et des Services Secrets,
Jacques Baud.
Lavauzelle, 1997.

Espionnage, l'Histoire
du Renseignement,
Les Cahiers de l'Express.

Foreign Invaders,
Dan Hagedorn & Leif
Hellström.
Midland Publishing, 1994.

For The President's Eyes Only,
Christopher Andrew.
Harper Collins, 1995.

From A Dark Sky,
Orr Kelly.
Presidio, 1996.

**Guardians. Strategic
Reconnaissance Satellites,**
Curtiss Peebles.
Ian Allan Ltd, 1987.

Guerres d'Indochine,
Bernard Fall.
J'ai Lu, 1970.

**Histoire du Transport
Aérien Militaire Français,**
General Raymond Barthélémy.
Editions France-Empire, 1981.

Inside CIA's Private World,
H. Bradford Westerfield.
Yale University, 1995.

Instruments of Darkness,
Alfred Price.
Granada Publishing, 1977.

**Land Based Air Power
in the Third World Crises,**
David R. Mets.
Air University Press, 1986.

Lightning Bugs,
William Wagner.
Armed Forces Journal
International, 1981.

Lockheed,
René Francillon.
Naval Institute Press, 1988.

Lockheed's Skunk Works,
Jay Miller.
Midland Publishing Ltd, 1995.

Military Space,
Brassey's Air Power Vol. 10,
1990.

Mondes Rebelles,
Jean-Marc Balencie
& Arnaud de la Grange.
Michalon, 1996.

The New Mercenaries,
Anthony Mockler.
Sidgwick & Jackson, 1985.

The Perfect Failure,
Trumbull Higgins.
Norton, 1987.

President's Secret Wars,
John Prados.
Elephant Paperbacks, 1996.

The Ravens,
Christopher Robbins.
Pocket Books, 1987.

Savage Peace,
Daniel P. Bolger.
Presidio, 1995.

Soldiers of Fortune,
Sterling Seagrave.
Time Life Books, 1981.

South Africa's Border War,
Willem Steenkamp.
Ashanti Publishing, 1989.

Spy Book,
The Encyclopedia of Espionage,
Norman Polmar & Thomas
Allen. Greenhill Books, 1997.

SR-71 Revealed,
Richard H. Graham.
Motorbooks International, 1996.

Suez 1956,
Paul Gaujac.
Lavauzelle, 1986.

MAGAZINES

Air & Space,
RAIDS,
Le Fana,
Wings of Fame,
Aviation Week,
Air et Cosmos

MAGAZINES

Air & Space, RAIDS, Le Fana, Wings of Fame,
Aviation Week, Air et Cosmos

──────────────

ACKNOWLEDGEMENTS

The author would like to thank Eric Micheletti, intrepid head of collection and willing archivist, for his help and advice given throughout the writing of this book. Bob Collins, for his authoritative views on American history. Carol Geismar for her pursuit of spelling mistakes. Jean-Pierre Husson and Gil Bourdeaux for their assistance, along with all those men of the art of spying who were willing to tell a little of their history through these pages.

CONTENTS

CHAPTER 10 : ESPIONAGE OF THE HIGHEST DEGREE

Printed in France in August 1998
by Aubin Imprimeur - L 56595
Poitiers - F-86240 Ligugé